Praise for the series:

It was only a matter of time before a clever publisher realized that there is an audience for whom *Exile on Main Street* or *Electric Ladyland* are as significant and worthy of study as *The Catcher in the Rye* or *Middlemarch*.... The series, which now comprises 29 titles with more in the works, is free-wheeling and eclectic, ranging from minute rock-geek analysis to idiosyncratic personal celebration—*The New York Times Book Review*

Ideal for the rock geek who thinks liner notes just aren't enough—*Rolling Stone*

One of the coolest publishing imprints on the planet—*Bookslut*

These are for the insane collectors out there who appreciate fantastic design, well-executed thinking, and things that make your house look cool. Each volume in this series takes a seminal album and breaks it down in startling minutiae. We love these. We are huge nerds—*Vice*

A brilliant series…each one a work of real love—*NME* (UK)

Passionate, obsessive, and smart—*Nylon*

Religious tracts for the rock 'n' roll faithful—*Boldtype*

Each volume has a distinct, almost militantly personal take on a beloved long-player… The books that have resulted are like the albums themselves—filled with moments of shimmering beauty, forgivable flaws, and stubborn eccentricity—*Tracks Magazine*

[A] consistently excellent series—*Uncut* (UK)

The nobility—and fun—of the project has never been questioned…a winning mix of tastes and writing styles—*Philadelphia Weekly*

Reading about rock isn't quite the same as listening to it, but this series comes pretty damn close—*Neon NYC*

The sort of great idea you can't believe hasn't been done before—*Boston Phoenix*

We…aren't naive enough to think that we're your only source for reading about music (but if we had our way…watch out). For those of you who really like to know everything there is to know about an album, you'd do well to check out Continuum's "33 1/3" series of books.—*Pitchfork*

For reviews of individual titles in the series, please visit our website at www.continuumbooks.com and 33third.blogspot.com

Titles available in this series:

Forthcoming in this series:

and many more . . .

Greatest Hits, Volume 1

edited by David Barker

continuum

NEW YORK • LONDON

2006

The Continuum International Publishing Group Inc
80 Maiden Lane, New York, NY 10038

The Continuum International Publishing Group Ltd
The Tower Building, 11 York Road, London SE1 7NX

www.continuumbooks.com

Library of Congress Cataloging-in-Publication Data for each
individual title in the 33 1/3 series is available from the Library of Congress.

ISBN 0-8264-1903-8

Contents

Introduction

To most people, the idea of reading one book devoted to one album is crazy. (Even when that book is small, cute, and readable in one sitting.) Most people, although they enjoy pop music, would rather listen to it or see it performed live than read about it. Why take something so visceral, so immediate, so downright entertaining, and squeeze all the fun out of it by converting the experience into words on a page? A 200-word review in *Mojo*, or *Pitchfork*—sure, that can be useful. But a whole book?

The 33 1/3 series, as you may have guessed, is not for most people. And that's not a claim to any kind of cool exclusivity—it's a simple fact. It's why if we sell more than 5,000 copies of one of these books we're pretty happy. This series is based on the idea that, when we fall in love (with a person, a city, a film, a writer, cloud formations, or an album), we want to immerse ourselves in the object of our love. We want to know the history, the back story—and often, we want to know what other people think. Surely we can't be the only ones to feel this way about "Veronica Mars," about Jonathan Coe, about the islands of the Aegean, or about *Led Zeppelin IV*?

The impetus behind this series was to find a selection of interesting writers who might be able to convey and share their own love for a chosen album. My hope was that these writers might describe their love in many different ways—not always by chronicling what the band did in the studio on January 5th and which bass guitars were used that day (although that can be a perfectly valid approach), but sometimes by getting more personal, more intimate, more creative.

I put together a list of around 50 albums and emailed it to some writers, musicians, broadcasters, professors, and a few folk who remain uncategorizable. (That list is now lost to the mists of time—or, more prosaically, to my inability to save documents properly. I do remember it definitely included both *Thriller* and *Bat Out of Hell*.) Those who replied to my initial approach seemed very excited by the idea of writing one of these books and most of them, quite rightly, ignored my list of suggested albums and nominated one of their own. The project snowballed from there.

When the first finished manuscripts arrived in my inbox a few months later, it dawned on me that I really hadn't given these writers any guidelines whatsoever. Andy Miller's book about the Kinks was a wonderfully researched, concise, evocative tribute to an amazing album that was recorded under very difficult circumstances. Warren Zanes' book about *Dusty in Memphis*, on the other hand, was full of rambling anecdotes about Stanley Booth, tips on how to eliminate the smell of cat urine, and a whole chapter on youthful voyeurism in New England. The problem was, I loved them both. From that moment on, the series has been unpredictable, and I hope it remains that way. Not so handy perhaps for you, the reader, but maybe this book will highlight the approaches in the series that you enjoy the most, and you can proceed from there.

Anyhow, what you hold in your hands is a book that contains extracts from the first 20 titles that we published in the series, starting in September 2003. Many of them are first books by young writers, and it's my real hope that plenty of the writers in this series will go on to bigger and better things. In this spirit, at the end of the book you'll find an essay on *I Ain't Marching Any More*, an album by Phil Ochs. It's written by 20-year-old Dan Connelly, and was the winning entry in our inaugural Under-21 Writing Contest. A large number of the entries we received were of a very high quality, and it's strangely touching to see so many kids (that's a term of affection!), in this fragmented MP3 world, still falling in love with albums.

David Barker, New York, July 2006
www.33third.blogspot.com

Dusty in Memphis

by Warren Zanes

Chapter Two
Breakfast Was My Idea

When I first met Stanley Booth, and every time thereafter, he mentioned his friend, the pioneering producer and record man, Jerry Wexler, the guiding conscience of *Dusty in Memphis*. But for some reason, the lasting image Stanley left me with as regards Jerry Wexler is of a boat, Jerry's, in which Sam the Sham and Stanley are mixing cocktails in the stern. The drinks in question, as I remember being told, are called life preservers. (Of course, I have yet to meet a bartender who can make such a drink or, for that matter, has heard of such a concoction—it has become clear enough that the name served the sole purpose of affording the seabound participants the opportunity to shout, "Help! Throw me a life preserver!") And perhaps because Stanley seems to regard Jerry as one of the true masters of anecdote—which is saying something, because Stanley's mind is itself an archive of situations—in this image I also see Jerry Wexler standing at the helm of the boat, in midtale, gesticulating, and wearing a deep blue cravat, which, perhaps not arbitrarily, matches the ocean that surrounds him. His audience is a little narrow in the eyes but nonetheless all ears.

Of course, I seriously doubt the validity of this memory fragment. I suspect it's a Frankenstein of my own making, comprising available parts and not all of them reliable. But the fact is, many of Stanley's stories are peopled by giants, and the minute a name like that of Sam the Sham enters the scene, I am fully capable of losing my sense of order and scale. Which is to say, I can embellish and construct, add and subtract without realizing just what I'm up to. And if I can do this with Sam the Sham, there's little doubt that I can arrive at still more flamboyant distortions in relation to any anecdotes housing not just a name like Sam the Sham but, more profound and far-reaching, that of Jerry Wexler. The latter is a name—I can instantly see it in my mind, in that black typeface of early Atlantic albums—that appears on albums by Wilson Pickett, Aretha Franklin, Bob

Dylan, Solomon Burke, Willie Nelson, Ray Charles, and many, many others.

It was no surprise to me that several people, Stanley included, responded to news of my little book about *Dusty in Memphis* by saying, "It would be great if you could talk to Jerry Wexler." I agreed entirely, of course. Of all the parties involved in that album's creation, if anyone stood "at the helm" with Dusty it was Jerry. But a few significant issues stood in my way. First, I wasn't entirely sure that Jerry Wexler was still alive. And for one writing a book about *Dusty in Memphis*, it was shameful to come right out and say that I didn't know this rather crucial piece of information. Any sense of authority that I might be hoping to project would diminish significantly if I was caught speaking of Jerry as someone I planned to call with a few questions when, in truth, "It would be great if you could talk to Jerry" meant that it would be great but not possible.[1] My lack of assurance regarding Jerry's status was based on the simple fact that I couldn't believe someone with his deep history could still be around to comment on it. Jerry Wexler is, after all, the man who changed the *Billboard* category of "Race" records to the new heading of "Rhythm and Blues."

In relation to handling my conundrum, Andy Paley came to mind. Andy is a fine resource for information of all kinds. When my wife and I couldn't get rid of the smell of cat urine in the back hallway of our house, Andy introduced us to Nature's Miracle, an effective, natural product that has served us well since that time. My wife, often quicker to move toward solutions than I am myself, suggested I call Andy to find out if Jerry Wexler was available for interview. Having seen, from a number of angles, the massive cogs of the music business turn, Andy was indeed the man for the job. And as it turned out, and to no one's surprise, Andy had information. He knew Jerry from the Rock and Roll Hall of Fame nominating committee on which both men sit. Immediately launching into story, Andy described one committee meeting at which he and Jerry Wexler had shared the view that Bruce Springsteen's E Street Band was perhaps a premature candidate for induction in the band category when New Orleans' Meters had not yet been discussed as a possibility. Which is to say, I quickly found

---

[1] The question regarding my authority in writing this book is a significant question, of course, appropriately handled in a lengthy preface but here relegated to a footnote. And I'll be frank: my authority rests on the fact that *Dusty in Memphis* is an album that spoke to me, even through the thick gauze of cool and cynicism in which I was wrapped when I first heard it in 1985. The editor at Continuum told me that, regarding authority, this was enough: write the book. His name is David Barker. If you have any questions or a fundamental argument with this issue, please direct such matters directly to Dr. Barker.

out that Jerry Wexler was indeed alive and well and, gloriously so, had a few opinions on it all.

Through a gentleman in the UK, responsible for the reissue of some great Eddie Hinton recordings, I got Jerry's two addresses, one on Long Island and the other in Florida. Perhaps my mind is that of the fan, but I'd seen Jerry Wexler's name on too many great records to think he lived in a world resembling my own. Where could a Jerry Wexler live? Whoever made up the name Ahmet Ertegun likely contrived Wexler's, too. I imagined wonderful places for them both, nothing along the lines of Long Island. But the two addresses were promptly emailed to me. So I sent letters, obsequious letters of the kind that young PhDs facing a grim job market write on a fairly regular basis. And was I wrong, or did I actually get a call back from Jerry Wexler three hours after I put those letters in the mailbox? This is a man whose books are in order. If I had thought Jerry Wexler would be the most difficult person to contact, because he was such a looming figure in my mind, I was wrong.

When he called I was in the midst of what was, at least for me, an unnervingly adult phone call. It was the Bank of New York on the other end. I was refinancing. Call waiting. A gravel voice, thick New York accent: "This is Jerry Wexler calling for Warren Zanes." I'm not even sure they can make voices like that any more. I simply left the Bank of New York on the other line—I could call them anytime—and my relationship with Jerry Wexler was underway.

* * *

"Who else do you want?" It was fifteen minutes into our conversation and he'd already given me Chips Moman's home phone number, Tom Dowd's cell phone number, Arif Mardin's Manhattan apartment number, Donnie Fritts' number in Florence, Alabama, Vicki Wickham's number in New York. "I'm a famous Judas. I'll give you any number you want." I took them all. And he said it was fine if I told them Jerry sent me.

Of the people who answered their phones or called me back, exactly one hundred percent of them said, "I love Jerry." Chips Moman, himself the man behind a hundred hits, twice referred to Jerry as his "hero." Perhaps Jerry wouldn't have given me the phone numbers of people with unfavorable commentaries, perhaps he would have, but, still, this was a very good batting average in the friendship game. Part of this, I assume, stems from the fact that Jerry is a conversationalist of the old school. He has an informed take on just about everything and the grace to listen when others offer their own views. In my handful of phone calls with Jerry, we discussed fiction as much as we did music. He knows his cinema. He can traverse the world of fine art better than most of the young art historians

I have taught. And he understands that literature does not live in the library alone, that literature knows many forms. Our first phone call ended thus: "I want to tell you a joke. Do you have a minute?"

> A postman is retiring. It's his last time on his old route. At one of the houses, a woman invites him in for a special breakfast, a real gourmand affair: poached eggs florentine, the cheeses of France, fresh-squeezed juice, you know. He's overwhelmed—a fantastic meal. Then, when he's done eating, she tells him to follow her upstairs, and—he can't believe it—she balls his ass off. When it's over, he puts on his postman's uniform and, just as he's leaving, the woman stops him and gives him a five dollar bill. This he just doesn't understand, so he asks her why she's giving him the money. "Well," she says, "I told my husband you were retiring, and when I asked him what he thought we should get you, he said, 'Fuck him—give him five bucks.' Breakfast was my idea!"

I got more comfortable talking with Jerry Wexler. The gap between my first, certainly formal letter to him and the second was considerable, and I include it below because it suggests just that. The occasion of this second correspondence, however, was that I'd just heard of Tom Dowd's death. Of course, Tom Dowd, along with Arif Mardin and Jerry, formed the three-man production team responsible for *Dusty in Memphis*. Though Jerry had given me Tom Dowd's cell phone number, when I called it Tom's daughter answered, letting me know that just that morning her father had been taken to the hospital. He would pass on only a few days later.

Dear Jerry,
The chores of early fatherhood took me away from my work for a bit. Happily, I'm back into the book project. My reason for writing, however, is to let you know that I was thinking about you when I heard the news of Tom Dowd's death. Someone in my position can only guess at the level of intimacy shared by the two of you, but I imagine it was considerable and the loss is deeply felt. My condolences go out to you as the friend and collaborator of a great talent.

I'm sending this to Florida because, if I recall, you drift South at some point in late October. I wouldn't mind doing that myself. When snow and cold happen, I have a difficult time thinking of them as necessary to my existence—though, using my favorite literary form, the complaint, I say the same thing about heat in the summer. I might have to learn a thing or two from Jerry Wexler's migratory patterns.

My son grows at a frightening rate. For a while there, he was referred to as The Milk Pig. In fact, my wife and I thought he was making every effort to eat her whole, that, like many chicken eaters, he merely preferred to start with the breast. Fortunately for her, he's calmed down a bit in his vigor. He's even managed to sleep through the night several times in the past week! For a while there, I would have felt the fool to even dream of such a possibility. So, the changes are all happening in good time, if too fast. Next thing I know, I'll be counseling him on the merits and methods of birth control. God forbid!

If you have a phone number down there, I'd love to have it. I'm looking forward to more conversations with you. Not every young man is afforded the chance to make actual contact with one who has imprinted his imagination as you have mine through music. My questions about Dusty's *Memphis* record now revolve around the studio situation, cutting tracks, the room itself and production methods. Chips Moman has never been reachable, but I'll keep trying. In the meantime, however, I hope you and your family are well. All the best to you.

Warren Zanes

The only trouble with talking to Jerry Wexler is that, again, he is a conversationalist of the old school. Which is to say, if as a professor I'm well-versed in digression, Jerry is fully capable of following me wherever I so digress. The topic of *Dusty in Memphis* could have taken us anywhere, and it did. But we'd return to the subject when my own sense of responsibility, sometimes dormant, was awakened—or when Jerry helped me to remember why I'd called in the first place. He did, after all, have other things to do.

As Jerry tells it, the story of *Dusty in Memphis* started when a lawyer working for Dusty contacted him in New York. Already an outspoken advocate of Dusty, her voice and what she did with it, he was quick to sign Dusty to a contract. Written into the contract was what is called a "key man clause." In this case, the "key man clause" stated that Dusty's contract was contingent on Jerry Wexler's involvement as producer. Were Jerry to be off the project, Dusty could walk, freely and without strings. This in itself says much about Dusty's attraction to Atlantic Records: a lover of the black music of the 1950s and 1960s, the best of which was often associated with Atlantic, Dusty wanted to draw herself closer to that musical environment and its legacy, which had been Jerry Wexler's obsession for decades already. Given Jerry's place in that world, Dusty made the strategic decision to name Jerry her "key man" in order to insure that the music she loved would be the reference point for her latest project.

WZ: It's no secret that Dusty loved the black music of the South—do you think part of your kinship with her had to do with a shared love for the music of the South?

Jerry Wexler: She was looking at this one step removed, as a worshiper of this kind of music. I was a promulgator of this music. I was in it.

If it all began in mutual admiration, the scene would grow complicated almost immediately. Jerry describes it thus in an article written for *The Oxford American*:

> And so it was arranged for Dusty to come to New York to begin preparing for the session. I began an intense hunt for songs that I could believe in—and that I prayed would please her. With the help of my assistants, Jerry Greenberg and Mark Myerson, we spent several months amassing a cornucopia of lead sheets, lyric sheets, and acetate demos (cassettes had yet to appear). In my zeal to provide her with the widest possible choice of material, we wound up with seventy or eighty songs.
>
> I thought it would be comfortable for her to come out to Great Neck, where we could work without the distractions of a frantic record office. Dusty showed up at my door, and we went into my living room. We soon found ourselves ass-deep in acetates—on tables, chairs, shelves, the floor. As I played her song after song, I was hoping for a response—would she like this one? If not, how about the next one?
>
> Most of the day, and well into the night, I became first fatigued, and then spastic, as I moved from floor to player, then back to the shelves, the chairs, and the tables, in what turned eventually into a ballet of despair.
>
> After going through my entire inventory, the box score was Wexler 80, Springfield 0. Out of my meticulously assembled treasure trove, the fair lady liked exactly none.

Dusty returned a few months later to hear a new batch of tracks. Jerry, with no fresh material to show her, selected twenty from the original eighty he had played that day in Great Neck. And Dusty loved them unequivocally. If *Dusty in Memphis* has the cohesive structure that distinguishes great albums, the lore attached to the project suggests that the actual making of the album sometimes lacked such structure. No matter how one views it, Dusty was a classic high-maintenance pop star, as insecure as any in the history of the pop star phenomenon. After Dusty rejected the original batch of eighty songs, the Muscle Shoals studio sessions that Jerry booked would have to be cancelled. Eventually Chips Moman's American Studios in Memphis would be home to the tracking sessions. But even then, settled in with an astounding band, Dusty would not sing. The band played without even a scratch vocal to guide them. Which is to say, while in Memphis to record *Dusty in Memphis*, Dusty recorded nothing.[2]

Arif Mardin: You got the story from Wexler that Dusty was extremely intimidated, right?

The band tracks that were recorded at American Studios, however, were more of what Atlantic had been associated with for years: riveting, in-the-pocket ensemble performances that had both ecomomy and a distinct emotional center. Of course, American, under the supervision of Chips Moman, was known for just this. On some level, the Dusty project was just another day in the mines for the folks at American. And Atlantic looked for just this kind of workaday consistency when they went hunting for production sites in the South.

From some perspectives, Jerry Wexler and Ahmet Ertugen's Atlantic Records were in the business of taking advantage, cashing in on the Southern scene and bringing the booty back north. And, indeed, there is no doubt that the label made enormous profits from its associations with Stax, Fame, and the Muscle Shoals scene, among others. In Robert Gordon's *It Came from Memphis*, Jim Dickinson, Memphis musician and producer, offers a wry perspective on the subject:

> I resented the exploitation aspect of the music business very deeply for a long time, until I started to understand it. A couple of years after I'd worked for Jerry Wexler at Atlantic in 1970, he came to Memphis for some event, and we ended up at this party, quite a party. Wexler, Sam Phillips, Betty Hayes—who'd booked bands with Ray Brown—my wife and I and Stanley Booth. Wexler had just produced an Aretha Franklin gospel record, and he was real proud of it. He had also, not that recently, done a Tony Joe White record. Well, after dinner everybody was kinda laidback and Wexler kept trying to play this Aretha Franklin record, but every time he'd start it, Sam would take it off and put on the Tony Joe White record. Sam kept playing the same cut over and over, "Got a Thing About Ya, Baby," which was a hit. And finally Wexler says, "Sam! Baby! You know, I'm really hurt that you're not listening to my Aretha record, baby!" Jerry plays it again and so one more time Sam gets up and takes the record off, puts on "Thing About Ya, Baby" and says, "Goddamn, Jerry, that's so good it don't sound paid for."
>
> I thought, by God, that's it. They can hear the difference. To somebody at the level of Sam Phillips and Jerry Wexler, that's what they get off

---

2 In talking with Arif Mardin, I did encounter a memory conflict among two of the producers. Contradicting Jerry Wexler's recollection, Arif insisted that while in Memphis Dusty did record guide or "scratch" vocals that the musicians could follow.

on. Not paying for it! . . . I had always taken it real personally when they didn't pay me. I'd say, Oh, the bastards didn't pay me again. Now I understand this sense of larceny as an element of production.

At times Jim Dickinson's commentary, in the above case and, for that matter, in many of his entertaining, anecdotal accounts, comes off as what might be called self-consciously quotable, as though he's just waiting for the next clown with a tape recorder. The recurring figure in Dickinson's accounts is, of course, Dickinson himself, emerging as either the carefree iconoclast or the somewhat gruff, certainly cynical underdog in (and against) the barbarities of the music business, the underdog who identifies more with the black man's position than with that of the cold-blooded money men sitting against a background of platinum records in their posh offices. Of course, the rhetorical structure at the heart of such self-portrayals is among the oldest in popular music culture: the record men, here reduced to caricature, represent Commerce, and Dickinson, by default and by suggestion, assumes the other pole, that of Art. Herein is a story about authenticity that is as old as popular music culture itself—the real of Art is opposed to the false of Commerce. But, however old, it's a story that makes great copy. Everybody loves to hear how the guy with the fattest wallet is the one who can't dance, is the one who has a six-figure abstract painting hanging upside-down in his living room. Good copy, yes, but it's too simple. And there's no reason to tell the story of Atlantic's Southern sojourn in terms too simple, even if, as regards the matter of exploitation, there are certain fundamental historical truths that reinforce Dickinson's basic point.

> **WZ:** In the 1950s and 1960s, the music industry was clearly a different beast than it is today. What freedoms did a record man have at that time that were eventually lost?
>
> **Jerry Wexler:** We'd go on the road with an acetate of a new Ruth Brown record. We'd see a transmitter, we'd walk in. The disc jockey would say, "Hey! Sure, what can I do for you?" He'd put the acetate right on! In other words, there was no music director, there were no committees. You had something new? "Here, here you go." And so we'd leave the guy a bottle of Jack or a sports shirt.

Among the record company personnel that came from the North to cut tracks, there is no doubt that many (most? all, of course!) had potential earnings on their minds in booking studio time down South. There was big money to be made, little of which would return to the South. And Jerry Wexler was certainly no exception. As he insisted in conversation, "The word 'commercial' is not a bad word." But in reducing that which

Wexler "got off on" when cutting tracks down South to "not paying for it," Dickinson is hardly what would be referred to as a "reliable narrator." Of course, that's just what makes Dickinson interesting. Rarely are the great storytellers Truth's ambassadors. My point is, however, that any story of Southern music that conveys only a narrative of the exploiter and exploited will reduce history to the one-dimensionality of the polemic. Was exploitation a part of the story? Yes, and arguably a very big part. But there is no doubt that Jerry Wexler, while earning a dreamy wage cutting hit records in the South, was "getting off" on a complicated amalgam of things, among which was the sound of a crack band playing that mixture of country and blues that came up out of the American South.

In fact, had Jerry Wexler not fallen in love with the music of the South, he might have followed a career trajectory more like that of his Atlantic partner Ahmet Ertugen, who knew when it was time to move on, to shift his focus from the raw sound of a hot band playing in the studio to—let's just say it—Foreigner. As a biography of Ertugen attests, Ahmet shed tears during a playback of "I Want to Know What Love Is" (if Jerry had done the same, likely it would have been for different reasons). If both men came to the record business as fans of the most obsessive variety, it's nonetheless hard to resist assessing their points of divergence. Risking oversimplification, it seems that Ahmet was perhaps the more brilliant record man, as fully capable of adapting to a fickle industry when necessary as he was of determining its course when such adaptation wasn't demanded of him. Jerry, if a brilliant record man for multiple decades, had at some point lost himself in something that happened down South.

Depending on your angle, Jerry Wexler's inability to go in the direction that Atlantic had to go in order to remain viable in the market is perhaps what makes him less the great record executive; but his commitment to a certain sound, his unabashed affection for it, also committed him to a certain standard, in effect kept him from being able to follow popular music down the road that it was at least temporarily going. Returning to Jim Dickinson's remarks, yes, Jerry Wexler knew how to exploit—taken in a broad sense, the word could be used to describe just what a producer does—but at the end of the day the fan inside of Jerry Wexler was perhaps master to the executive. So, when the music Jerry loved went on the back shelf, he went with it. But, before that, what a run he had.

Jerry Wexler: We signed people whose music we liked. There were two requisites: we had to really like it, and we had to imagine it could sell. I call that column A. Later on a column B came in: music which we didn't necessarily like but had to deal with to stay alive. And although I was instrumental in signing much of this other kind of act which we thought would sell, I never produced it. I never went into the studio unless the music spoke directly to me. As a result, if you look at my dossier, you'll see I dealt with very, very few rock and roll artists.

A romanticization of Jerry Wexler? Perhaps. But lesser men have been romanticized for lesser reasons. And there is no wrapping your brain around *Dusty in Memphis* without considering Jerry Wexler's role in the album's genesis. To Dusty's credit, she knew who she wanted. The "key man" clause is more than a clue to the whole situation—it's a statement of purpose on Dusty's part. Likely she had her own epiphanies while listening to Atlantic records and reading over and over the black typeface on the back. For a certain generation of music fans, that typeface is today capable of an effect Proustian in kind. And Jerry's was a name that appeared in all the right places. But there is more to be said about her choice.

* * *

Jerry Wexler was no different from Dusty in the sense that he, too, had grown up in a culture drawn to the myth of the South. The South was, like the American West, a fantastic elsewhere. But because it was also the place of incubation for the most crucial American music, the South was, for many who were drawn to its sounds, the ultimate fantastic elsewhere. The place had the best soundtrack. All the lore surrounding the region was as available and as enticing to Dusty as it was to Jerry. Furthering their common bond, there is no question that Jerry first arrived in Memphis as a creature out of his element, an alien, just as Dusty would years later. And, logically, her best guide to the South, her Virgil, would not be an insider but an outsider who had gotten in, a breed with no better representative than Jerry Wexler. The outsider-getting-in thing is, after all, one of the key sounds of *Dusty in Memphis*. The album's unique hybridity depends on just this. Peter Guralnick's *Sweet Soul Music*, without a doubt the best historical work on the subject of rhythm and blues in the Atlantic heyday, is rich in passages that describe Jerry's involvement in Memphis, Muscle Shoals, and elsewhere. Take, for instance, this description of Jerry Wexler's first contact with Stax records:

> At a time when Stax records was acquiring an aura and a legend all its own, no one at Stax—including Jim Stewart, Memphis bank manager who joined his sister, Estelle, to run Stax—had the slightest idea what was going on in the outside world. To them it was not Wilson Pickett who was the star; Wilson Pickett was just another rhythm and blues singer. It was Jerry Wexler and the Atlantic label, after which they patterned their whole sound, who were the stars. Jerry Wexler was an exotic presence; his very speech (a "Jewish brogue") was like a foreign tongue to Memphians who

had never even seen New York City. This was the ultimate validation.

The category of the exotic is, of course, notably open-ended, fluid. The exotic can be idealized but, just as easily, cast into the shadows of deep suspicion. As Guralnick goes on to describe, "when Jerry Wexler, venerated by Jim and perceived by all as the benevolent godfather who had beamed approvingly on all of Stax's successes to date, left in somewhat high dudgeon after the third Wilson Pickett session in December 1965, the entire Stax family rallied round and cast Wexler in a new light, as an exploiter or 'outside agitator' perhaps." Likely it is somewhere between the peaks of idealization and the valleys of suspicion that Jerry lived at that time and in those circumstances. The biggest trouble in sticking to the valleys when assessing Jerry's involvement down South comes in failing to recognize his deep devotion to both the region's music and the region itself.

As is suggested in his memoir, *Rhythm and the Blues*, throughout his teens and well into his twenties Jerry Wexler was a young man who, as the saying goes, had trouble applying himself. Distracted by the allure of jazz culture and all that went with it, he went about things in the classic style of the underachiever. He was, in his own words and sidestepping euphemism, a "cosmic fuck-up." Helping him along in this, it seems, was a doting mother. If labels are to be handed out, Elsa Wexler was what the language of self-help describes as a codependent. She managed to hold out hope against hope, giving her son repeated chances to prove himself in the world and fully believing that her golden boy was only temporarily under wraps, would soon shine for more than maternal eyes alone. But she'd be in for a wait. If the Wexler memoir is to be believed, Jerry's prolonged adolescence was perhaps his mother's greatest production. In that same volume Elsa responds to the suggestion that her bond with Jerry was so powerful as to be Oedipal in nature: "Freud, shmeud. I loved Gerald, but I never wanted to fuck him."

There was, of course, a period there, before the glory days of Atlantic, when it seemed that Elsa's faith would be redeemed. That was when Jerry applied himself to something other than music, showing promise not simply as a student of journalism but as a writer of short fiction. And while this story-within-the-story is nothing that needs full elaboration here—I recommend you get a copy of the memoir, which is a page-turner in the best sense—there is a point in considering this pre-Atlantic period. The Jerry Wexler that would be drawn to the South for its music was, in many ways, already gestating within Jerry Wexler the writer, as the fiction from that period suggests.

When I asked him if I could get my hands on any of his short fiction, Jerry was quick to send a few pieces to me, pieces we later discussed over the phone. In introducing Jerry Wexler as "extravagantly verbal," "his lexicon a mixture of the mean streets and the graduate library," coauthor of *Rhythm and the Blues* David Ritz begins to describe the seeming pleasure with which Jerry approaches the plasticity of language. Words that are decidedly archaic and often esoteric will emerge in Jerry's everyday speech, uncanny fragments, displaced and capable of producing the striking contrast upon which Ritz comments. The young Jerry Wexler's fiction, however, is more often marked by the stylistic economy one associates with American modernism, particularly Hemingway's short fiction.

In the story "Lost Summer," published in 1947 by *The Kansas Magazine*, a first-person narrator reflects on a season past, "the summer of Elaine and me and George the elevator boy of the building across the street." Weighing the awkward yet epiphanic passage from boyhood to manhood and the characters with whom he made that passage, this narrator quickly reminds one of William Styron's protagonist in *Sophie's Choice*, both in terms of the latter's entrance into adulthood and the complicated sexual /emotional triangle that serves to insure such an entrance. If the story follows the basic pattern of much coming-of-age writing and risks the sentimentality germane to any such retrospective narration, it still works. The author might tell you otherwise, of course. Though he published work in *Story* and *The New York Post*, among other publications, Jerry remains circumspect if not downright self-effacing about his then burgeoning career as a writer—"The truth is that I wasn't much of a worker or much of a writer." But while one gets from these stories the feeling that behind them stands a green author, stricken by the romanticism that so often plagues young people with quills and inkpots, there is evidence enough that Jerry learned his craft. The characters stand up, and conflict makes them move. Anyone who has taken a creative writing class knows that this isn't an everyday occurrence among the legions of people who hope to one day call themselves fiction writers.

That little bit of literary criticism aside, "Lost Summer" speaks directly to Jerry Wexler's interest in the South. The obsession that would indeed lead to a career permeates the story's content. Particularly in the character of George the elevator boy, one finds traces of the future Atlantic Records executive's fascination with the American South and its music. Not surprisingly, George the elevator boy is a musician from Memphis. The narrator speaks of him thus:

> I know now that what he played was the blues, the real old blues. I have never heard another white man play and sing the blues like George. That was before everyone knew about jazz, and George didn't know he was playing native American art, and of course I didn't either. He just played simple harmonies and sang in his rich Southern voice about the people who were flooded out and didn't have no place to go, or about the young

man lonesome in a strange northern city and with no money to pay the landlord.

On some level, George, the man who didn't even know that what he did was Art, is exactly the kind of person Jerry Wexler would go looking for when he cut tracks down South. An artist not conscious of his works as art, an art made with no market in mind, an art so close to the fact of nature that it doesn't yet know to parade as Culture: this is the sound with which the South has long been associated, the sound that has been described in a number of ways, many if not most of them hinging on the sanctified concept of "authenticity." Such a sound is, in fact, that to which Sam Phillips was referring when he described a Tony Joe White track as "so good it don't sound paid for."

If a gulf exists between what Jerry did at Atlantic and what a song collector like Alan Lomax did for the Library of Congress, both men were affected by what in American culture has been a longstanding fascination with the South as a land more directly tied to our agrarian past, as an almost pre-modern entity, certain pockets of which know a life that is raw, without effect. If in the early twentieth century European artists expressed a fascination with the "primitive," a fascination with Africa, with the West Indies or Tahiti, for instance, in the United States a related primitivism, perhaps more subtle because not born of colonialism, fixed on the South, a place where, it seemed, life was lived with instinct as guide. The collective vision of the South as a place of authenticity had it that in this place artists did what they did not because they thought they were artists making art but because their deepest impulses and needs lead them to do so. Such is one common primitivist myth that has left a deep mark on music culture.

In his memoir, Jerry includes a passage in which Ahmet Ertegun speaks, with an unabashed and almost surprising self-reflexivity, directly to the matter of American primitivism and the Southern romance that is so often at its heart. Ahmet describes an early Atlantic Records A&R trip to New Orleans taken with then partner Herb Abramson, a trip during which they "discover" the legendary Professor Longhair:

We asked around and finally found ourselves taking a ferry boat to the other side of the Mississippi, to Algiers, where a white taxi driver would deliver us only as far as an open field. "You're on your own," he said, pointing to the lights of a distant village. "I ain't going into that niggertown." Abandoned, we trudged across the field, lit only by the light of a crescent moon. The closer we came, the more distinct the sound of distant music—some big rocking band, the rhythm exciting us and pushing us on. Finally we came upon a nightclub—or, rather, a shack—which, like an animated cartoon, appeared to be expanding and deflating with the pulsation of the beat. The man at the door was skeptical. What did these two white men want? "We're from *LIFE* magazine," I lied. Inside, people scattered, thinking we were police. And instead of a full band, I saw only a single musician—Professor Longhair—playing these weird, wide harmonies, using the piano as both keyboard and bass drum, pounding a kick plate to keep time and singing in the open-throated style of the blues shouters of old.

"My God," I said to Herb, "We've discovered a primitive genius."

Afterwards I introduced myself. "You won't believe this," I said to the Professor, "but I want to record you."

"You won't believe this," he answered, "but I just signed with Mercury."

The anecdote itself, laced with irony, plays on the conventions of both ethnographic writing and the colonial-adventure-gone-weird one associates with Joseph Conrad. That open field, "lit only by the light of a crescent moon" and leading toward "the sound of distant music," all but requires a pith helmet.

Of course, in the modern West this is a crucial story genre. And without a doubt, it is also a story that has been grafted to the value systems at the heart of American music culture. If "authenticity" is a term commonly used to organize value in popular music culture, the South has long been mythologized as the place where authenticity lingers in the form of a people and a sound. The South, across that open field that Ertegun describes, is many things, among them America's garden. A statement made by bluesman Bukka White suggests that the Southern place of authenticity can very nearly be pointed to: "That's where the blues start from, back across them fields. . . . It started right behind one of them mules or one of them log houses, one of them log camps or the levee camp." The potency of the mythology that associates some place down South with authenticity has made that mythology a lasting one, as indicated by high-profile symptoms such as last year's article "White Man at the Door: Searching for the Last of the Bluesmen," published in *The New Yorker* and written by Jay McInerney.

There are, of course, all kinds of ways to tell the tale of authenticity. Bruce Springsteen's early street persona, for instance, developed with Asbury Park as the center of a rather self-consciously constructed mythscape, is structured with the streets of lower-middle class New Jersey as a place of both alienation and, subsequently, authenticity. Springsteen's credibility hinges on the fact that he speaks from the margins, from the wastelands of the American dream. Woody Guthrie's itinerant persona, itself a rather heavily worked-over construction, hinges on Guthrie's identification with dustbowl refugees, with the disenfranchised in general. Such stories tell us that there's a place, a place beyond or perhaps below where something more real is happening, something that transcends the commercial world's house of signs and mirrors, a house in which most of us, the stories insist, are living, living but lost.

Fans, when they've found a music maker who comes from that place of authenticity, will protect what they've found, declare his or her worth with an adamance, seemingly all out of proportion, that betrays how high the stakes are in this authenticity game. And of course they're very high; for finding that thing of authenticity which exists just beyond yet is approachable by those special enough to recognize its true value, is, of course, an act that becomes the finder. Which is to say, when one makes a statement regarding some trace of authenticity found, the moment of declaration—"Look what I've found!"—is as much about the speaker as it is about the authentic object discovered. Authenticity is conferred by association. Ahmet Ertegun makes good comedy of this exchange system but, at the same time, draws attention to the deep collective desire to find the "real thing."

Put simply, finding the real thing, the authentic, is one way of participating in it, of, in effect, being the real thing. And this search for authenticity becomes all the more crucial in a world that is terrified of its own artifice, which is to say a world like the modern world, unmoored from tradition and watching, numb, commerce's ever changing landscape of flashing signs and latest models. Perhaps it is no surprise, then, that modern man, dreading the artifice of his own surroundings, has always been game for a little ethnography. Elsewhere, he insists, slipping into his safari clothes, real life is being lived. It's there, across that field. Of course, when his finger points out at some more authentic plot of ground, he is making his implicit commentary on the diminished character of the place from which he comes. If the authentic is over there, across that field, the over here is, by contrast, a place of flimsy sets and actors working from scripts. Gauguin's idealization of Tahitian "primitive" life, for instance, was finally his way of speaking his criticisms of European culture, his two judgments intrinsically bound as one tightly woven fabric of argument.

* * *

There is no avoiding psychobiography when writing about Dusty Springfield. She was troubled, out of place in her world. The authorized Dusty Springfield biography portrays Dusty's life as one long, often sad if occasionally and curiously joyous, car crash of a life, a redemptive turn coming late in the game but almost too late. If one is to believe the biography—and why not?—Dusty was a good but deeply conflicted soul, more often settling for diversions from her torments rather than solutions to them. The vulnerability we hear in her voice, it seems, is not some fluke but the sound that pain makes when it comes out of a certain body. If both simplistic and romantic, this art-born-of-pain interpretation of the Dusty Springfield story remains the most viable version. Why banish such a reading simply because the story has been told too many times of too many people? In Dusty's case, it fits. It's hard to avoid the reasonable enough idea that singing was perhaps Dusty's one valve to let off a little of the pressure building inside. Well, singing and, as the biography seems to insist, throwing food.

Given all of this, her tangled, chaotic life story and her alienation from a public that at different times embraced her and forgot her, one can well imagine that the notion of an elsewhere, a more real other place, a place where something vaguely related to freedom could be experienced would prove a potent concept to Dusty. If children are forever off in some land of their own making, those adults who believe they have left some crucial part of themselves in childhood—and Dusty was unequivocal in thinking this—will often return to those landscapes of childhood for a lost object, will often become involved in transport as a way of life. And, indeed, it seems that the South, that imagined region of authenticity sitting just beyond that field, was one of the elsewheres to which Dusty often returned. She found something in the music and the magic of the South that gave her, if only in the imagination, a more satisfying home. The music she loved was merely the sound, the raw expression of a sense of freedom, that came out of that home. The South was her elsewhere. And *Dusty in Memphis*, whether consciously produced as such or not, is her tribute to just that place.

Forever Changes

by Andrew Hultkrans

Chapter 2
The Burden of (Hollywood) Babylon

My depression is the most faithful mistress I have known—no wonder,
then, that I return the love.

—Søren Kierkegaard, *Either/Or* (1843)

During the final months of his stay in Paris, when, having lost faith in everything, he was oppressed by hypochondria and ravaged by spleen, he had
reached such a pitch of nervous sensibility that the sight of a disagreeable
object or person would etch itself into his brain so deeply as to require several days for its imprint to be even slightly dulled; during that period the touch
of a human form, brushed against in the street, had been one of his most
excruciating torments.

—Joris-Karl Huysmans, *Against Nature* (1884)

Here we go alone, and like it better so . . . we cease to be soldiers in the army
of the upright; we become deserters. They march to battle. We float with the
sticks on the stream; helter-skelter with the dead leaves on the lawn, irrespon-
sible and disinterested and able, perhaps for the first time in years, to look
round, to look up-to look, for example, at the sky.

—Virginia Woolf, *On Being Ill* (1930)

The sun is a joke.

—Nathanael West, *The Day of the Locust* (1939)

My favorite professor in college was the great Canadian-born Americanist
Sacvan Bercovitch, who taught a yearlong course in the English department
called "The Myth of America." Beginning with Puritan sermons, the syllabus
moved through examples of early American literature, the Transcendentalists,

Hawthorne, Melville, Poe, Whitman, modernist American novels (Faulkner, Dos Passos, Nathanael West) and poetry, and culminated, in my year, with Pynchon's *The Crying of Lot 49*, on which I wrote my senior thesis. I was honored to have Bercovitch read and grade my work and sit on my oral defense committee. One of many Bercovitch quotes that sticks in my memory was his claim that "to be an American is to discover oneself by prophecy." While this maxim suggests multiple meanings, I understand it to mean that—because America was founded on prophecy, a prophecy of exceptionalism, John Winthrop's "City upon a Hill" sermon of 1630 being the obvious example— the contemporary American must not only acknowledge the foundational Puritan texts that gave the nation its identity, but must also take it upon himself to continue to render judgment on and prophesy against the failures of the American experiment, an experiment that originated with such impossibly high standards that its failure seemed almost certain. The stakes laid out by the Puritan settlers were so high that if they indeed failed, it was assumed that the skeptical onlookers of the Old World would revel in *schadenfreude*, seeing the entire enterprise as a pipe dream, as an instance of extreme hubris, or even, perhaps, as evidence of the death of God. As Winthrop warned:

> [T]he eyes of all people are upon us; so that if we shall deal falsely with our God in this work we have undertaken and so cause him to withdraw his present help from us, we shall be made a story and a byword through the world, we shall open the mouths of enemies to speak evil of the ways of God and all professors for God's sake; we shall shame the faces of many of God's worthy servants, and cause their prayers to be turned into Curses upon us till we be consumed out of the good land whither we are going.

Given this challenge, America was and always will be a blank canvas upon which the best picture of human civilization could be drawn; but conversely it is also the place where false prophets, mostly politicians, it turns out, could wreak havoc on its people and the world in the name of God and Manifest Destiny, and where the relative ahistoricism of the culture could enable man's lowest impulses to consume him and the land, as in the Wild West—or in Hollywood Babylon. What Bercovitch is getting at, in my view, is the responsibility of all Americans to speak out against the betrayal of the original promise of America itself, not necessarily in a religious sense—too many people have been mercilessly slaughtered in the name of God to make that position tenable—but in the sense of warning the people that they are heading in the wrong direction, whether it's in the direction of war mongering, of plutocracy, of racism, of mindless consumerism, of intolerance, of greed, of ignorance, of institutional corruption, of blind patriotism. Those who are called to this manner of prophecy in contemporary America must walk a lonely road. They are always in peril of incurring the wrath of the authorities, always one speech or action away from being reduced to that jabbering madman on the corner, or worse, from being muzzled and locked up, possibly executed.

Greil Marcus, another great Americanist, has, in the past few years, taught a seminar called "Prophecy and the American Voice" at Princeton and UC Berkeley, and his thoughts on the subject are useful here. In defining what he means by "prophecy" in the context of his class, he notes that for him the term "meant not prophecy in terms of predicting the future, but prophecy in the Old Testament sense, the prophet as one who delivers judgment on a society." In a recent talk he delivered at the New School for Social Research in New York City on Pere Ubu singer David Thomas, titled "Crank Prophet Bestride America, Grinning: The Case of David Thomas," Marcus elaborates:

> The prophetic figure may seem to predict or call forth the future, but if this is so it's not because he or she sees the future, but because he or she embodies his or her place and time—his or her commonality, and all those who make it up. This prophet looks at the present and the past, at promises made and promises broken—or perhaps worse, forgotten—and asks what fate is appropriate for such a people. More than that, the prophet may embody both the promise and the betrayal, embody the fate of his or her nation. . . . And here we get much closer to the crank prophet: the person standing on the street telling you what you don't want to hear, the person you pretend you don't hear, don't notice, never saw.

According to Marcus, the "crank" prophet is "an avatar of an American voice: you never know what he's going to say," and this characterization, I believe, applies as neatly to the Arthur Lee of *Forever Changes* as it does to Pere Ubu's David Thomas. Marcus continues:

> When he opens his mouth, you are sure you don't want to hear whatever he's got in it, but it's easier to decide to turn away than to do it. There is madness in his voice—a madness that gives off the odd feeling that it might be cultivated, that it might be a con, that it might be there to get you to buy something, even if you can't imagine what it is. There is authority in the voice—the authority of someone who really doesn't care if you listen, but knows that if you won't, the person behind you might, and you might be back. As a prophet he lays out the terms on which he, his audience, his city, and his country will be judged—by God, history, himself, ourselves. He embodies those terms: if we don't speak the truth as we know it, we will be forced into a life of self-hatred and self-denial, where suicide, fast or slow, is the only way out-and if you do tell the truth as you know it, you will be forced into the role of a crank. Your voice will become more and more strangled, more and more pinched, and you will have to struggle ever harder to believe the sound of the noise you

yourself make.

The charge that the crank prophet's voice "might be cultivated . . . a con" has been directed at Arthur Lee, particularly by nascent rock critics soon after the release of *Forever Changes*. Richard Meltzer, in his inimitably prolix, jive-philosopher style, put it this way: "To Arthur Lee, the great trans-soul spade trans-spade of Love, the soul symbol is a tool (imitations of Jagger imitating primal soul spades), but merely one among many, including the show music symbol, the orchestrality symbol, the plagiarism symbol, the language symbol, the symbol symbol, others too." For Sandy Pearlman, reviewing *Forever Changes* in the seminal rock zine *Crawdaddy*, Lee's elegantly daft but effective con extends to the record's music as well:

> *Forever Changes* is incredibly beautiful. But in its own very, very odd way. . . . And now the paradox. Because all this sounds really conventionally beautiful. The referents for conventional beauty are all obvious. . . . And yet . . . the album doesn't have the Muzak ring. But aren't all of this stuff's most signifi-cant referents Muzak? That they are, and that it doesn't sound like Muzak, is highly significant because it means that Love have come up with the neat trick of *The Internal-Muzak Denial Move*. Specifically, they've modularized the Muzak components available, in overwhelming quantity, in the cultural pool. But this makes for the subordination of these components (given their traditional role). The usual Muzak pop homogeneity has been short-circuited. . . . They have denuded Muzak of the soporific. Allowing even the words to be heard and enjoyed. And establishing a pretty gorgeous context that doesn't prevent cog-nition.

To be fair, I should note that during the late 60s the invocation of Muzak in assessing "serious" rock music was as damning as referring to someone as "plastic," words that do not carry the same polarizing resonance today. It is to Arthur's credit that the record was able to subvert and subsume what would ordinarily be the kiss of death in hip music circles, and to Pearlman's credit for coining the "The Internal-Muzak Denial Move" to account for it. (It would make a cracking band name, if it isn't one already.)

As for the crank prophet's voice, a voice that commands "the authority of someone who really doesn't care if you listen, but knows that if you won't, the person behind you might, and you might be back," Love drummer Michael Stuart-Ware's recollections speak volumes: "Arthur called his vocal style [on aggressive, pre-*Changes* songs like "My Flash on You" and "7&7 Is"] 'preach-ing.' It was more than that. Like film clips you've seen of Adolph Hitler pump-ing up the massive throngs of the Third Reich to a fever pitch, it was threat-eningly ferocious. More like 'inciting to riot' than 'preaching.'" And for Mar-cus's claim that "this prophet looks at the present and the past, at promises made and promises broken—or perhaps worse, forgotten—and asks what fate is appropriate for such a people," I'll go to the source himself, Arthur Lee, who in a 70s interview with Lenny Kaye maintained that:

> I write about my environment. That's what I constantly write about, what I see, what I think needs to be changed and what I think shouldn't. . . . That's my whole trip . . . "call them as you see them." . . . A melody or a tune or a whistle in your head sticks with you more than anything I've ever come across. So, I want to put a nursery rhyme in your head and tell you what I want you to hear with the nursery rhyme . . . let them hum the nursery rhyme that I wrote and then . . . maybe work a change in their life.

In later interviews, he added, of the songs on *Forever Changes*, "I think of everyone else when I write a song. Usually, I think of what other people are going through in this life. . . . I saw what I saw in my life and I wrote about the names and the people and the times and the things that were happening— and oddly enough, nothing has changed."

In 1967, according to the pocket jeremiads Lee delivered on *Forever Changes*, the changes he was advocating, however cryptically, for America were of eleventh-hour urgency, not least because he believed he might not live to see them through. This latter predicament is the other side of the prophet's role—that he is doomed by the very fact of having taken on the mantle of prophecy, doomed at best to madness, affliction, social marginalization, perhaps incarceration; at worst, doomed to follow in Jesus' footsteps toward humiliating public torture and ignoble death at the hands of the State. Hence, the mantle of prophecy is a burden, not only in the sense that the prophecy will come down as a great weight on the community being judged, as in "The Burden of Babylon" in the Book of Isaiah, but also that the prophecy itself, "the Word," is a burden on the shoulders and conscience of the prophet who must bear it to the people. An early scene in Martin Scorsese's *The Last Temptation of Christ* movingly illustrates the ordinary man's resistance to being chosen to carry the burden of prophecy. The young Jesus is shown as an average carpenter, content to build houses and fit in with his fellow woodworkers, but he is intermittently troubled by voices in his head, voices that tell him that he is special, that he must carry a message to the people of Israel, that he must be an extraordinary man, apart from all others, and that, last but not least, he must proclaim to the world that he is the Son of God. Naturally, as you or I might in a similar set of circumstances, Jesus initially rejects the call, telling the voices to begone, to leave him alone, leave him within his safe shell of anonymity where he can take simple pleasure in the light responsibilities of craftsmanship. Of course, God, holding all the cards as He is wont to do, eventually gets His way—and you know the rest of the story.

The Hebrew word for "prophecy" as it occurs in the Old Testament, *massa*, perhaps best captures the double-edged nature of prophecy. *Massa*, as rather poetically defined in Strong's *Hebrew Dictionary*, is "a burden; an utterance, chiefly a doom, especially singing; prophecy." It is a burden in the twin senses noted above, a heavy load on both the prophet and the community he addresses. Unlike the "good news" of the New Testament, an Old Testament prophecy is "chiefly a doom," very bad news indeed for those it is directed at—the prelude, typically, to a scourging of the entire population by a vengeful God. Paradoxically, *massa* also suggests singing, *especially* singing—a fetching, charismatic approach, perhaps, for delivering doom-laden judgments to terrified audiences, though it's hard to imagine the excruciatingly detailed PowerPoint presentation of hellfire and teeth-gnashing in Jonathan Edwards' "Sinners in the Hand of an Angry God" going over better in plainchant. For our subject, though, *massa*'s aberrant subdefinition seems more than appropriate. Arthur Lee characterizes his messages as "nursery rhymes" that he implants in the heads of his listeners, because "a melody or a tune or a whistle in your head sticks with you more than anything." Once his song is embedded in someone's mind, it becomes their own, part of them, something they will whistle, hum, sing, and in so doing, "maybe work a change in their life." Not a bad strategy for a modern-day prophet, especially one living in late 60s America, a time when singing, *especially* singing, seemed, more than anything, to carry the weight and wattage of prophecy.

> Many Arguments perswade us, that our glorious Lord, will have an Holy city in AMERICA, a City, the Street whereof will be Pure Gold.
>
> —Cotton Mather (1709)

If the notion that troubled rocker Arthur Lee—no saint by most accounts—donned the hairshirt of prophecy for *Forever Changes* seems a luffing kite on loose tether, let's rein it in by performing an informal exegesis of the record's second (and Arthur's first) song, "A House Is Not a Motel." On its surface, the title is a facile but odd pun on Bacharach/David's "A House Is Not a Home" (Arthur had misused Bacharach to great effect on Love's first single, "My Little Red Book," so the dig had precedence). But in light of Arthur's experience of living communally at "The Castle," where he had to step over prostrate bodies on his way to a midnight snack, the title also suggests a loner's irritation with a house full of overnight crashers and mooching hipsters. It also implies that a house is somehow sanctified, blessed by its very permanence and integrity, the antithesis of the transitory, potentially sleazy motel. But the more I think about it, the song's distinction between house and motel harbors a judgment, a condemnation, really, of far greater magnitude: the house is the House of God—a church, or perhaps the chosen community itself—and the motel, with its prefab pastel bungalows obscuring the barely suppressed bloodlust of its occupants, is what America has become. In this way, "A House

Is Not a Motel" can be heard as an inverted echo of The Stones' "Sympathy for the Devil"—a song in which the singer takes on the voice and the perspective of a deity. But unlike Mick-as-Satan, on the frontlines of the Blitzkrieg in a Nazi Panzer, Arthur is playing God, and he's here to clean house. In the first verse, he invites you into his holy sanctum, noting in the first line that, while dim and perhaps foreboding, it is not a dungeon, or a prison:

At my house I've got no shackles
You can come and look if you want to
Through the halls you'll see the mantels
Where the light shines dim all around you

This house sits on a hill, possibly Winthrop's Hill, and with its dimness, its halls and mantels (altars?), it could be a church. The next line tells you that this church is in America, perhaps Puritan America, as the image invoked comes straight from the mouth of Cotton Mather, three centuries earlier: "And the streets are paved with gold / And if someone asks you, you can call my name." The house, the church, is, it appears, in Mather's *City*, on Winthrop's Hill—but something has gone horribly wrong. This City upon a Hill, you see, is Hollywood, and while the streets may be nearly paved with gold (reflected sunshine, gold stars lining the "Walk of Fame"), they are awash in sin—narcissism, violence, lust, greed, murder. And when the singer stops singing, all the revulsion, the terror, the soul-scraping *guilt* that Gene Hackman experiences in his encounter with the fateful toilet of *The Conversation* will be visited upon the City's residents a millionfold. LA's streets may presently be paved with gold, but through the efficiency of Mulholland's ingeniously designed aqueducts, they are about to be flooded with blood:

And the water's turned to blood
And if you don't think so
Go turn on your tub
And if it's mixed with mud
You'll see it turn to grey

The mud, it seems, is the sand of the ever-encroaching desert, LA's long-suppressed nemesis, always eroding the city's foundations, always desperately thirsty. Arthur admitted to a friend that he got the image from a Vietnam vet, who told him that when blood is mixed with mud, it resolves to a deathly gray. By the end of the song, in the face of the plumbing plague, the sandstorms, the gold streets gone gray, the residents of this (Sin) City upon a Hill are ready to repent. After kindly offering his ear for the first two verses, Arthur-as-God finally, when it's already too late, hears the cries of his wayward flock: "I hear you calling my naaame!" Sorry, he says, Armageddon already been in effect.

The band then abruptly cedes the floor to a primal, tom-heavy drum break, a kind of martial warning, a preemptory strike, for the twin electric guitars that swoop in like howling divebombers, tearing up the skies in a furious dogfight that spirals upward into the stratosphere. Meanwhile, Arthur babbles beneath the firestorm like a Pentecostal speaking in tongues, or an Indian shaman, or both. Are you sure you want to live here?

Arthur was intimately familiar with a previous local cataclysm that many Angelenos viewed as the beginning of The End for their fair city—the Watts race riots of 1965. He had to drive into the district in the midst of the turmoil to check on the safety of his mother, Agnes, who was light-skinned enough to be mistaken for white. This experience—along with his awareness of being black in a white world, his innate sense that America's "streets of gold" had been paved with the bodies and blood of his ancestors, that the country had furthermore been "settled" by white colonists through the near genocide of its native residents, and that the descendents of those colonists were currently massacring people of color in Southeast Asia—more than likely contributed to the fervent, fire-and-brimstone rhetoric coursing throughout *Forever Changes*. As Jon Savage writes, "Lee was too much of a racial-social-chemical outsider not to boil inside at Watts, at the Vietnam war, at the ethnic cleansing of the Native American, about the nature of everyday life itself, dominated by the false perception of media and consumerism."

Arthur's outsider status, along with his near-agoraphobic hypersensitivity to the teeming masses of Angelenos surrounding him—masses who were burning down one side of the city, while, across town, the decadent classes of Hollywood slowly slid toward the "motel money murder madness" that would characterize the end of the decade—surely made him "boil inside," but it also made him ill, afflicted by the existential nausea that Jean-Paul Sartre thought to be the chronic condition of the truly aware individual. In the throes of this nausea, Sartre writes, "I am all alone, but I march like a regiment descending on a city . . . I am full of anguish: the slightest movement irks me. I can't imagine what they want with me." As in Arthur's LA, "Nothing seemed true; I felt surrounded by cardboard scenery which could quickly be removed," and the scenery embodies the sickness: "The Nausea is not inside me: I feel it out there in the wall, in the suspenders, everywhere around me. It makes itself one with the café, I am the one who is within it." But eventually, for Sartre and for the porous psyche of Arthur Lee, the subject becomes the very embodiment of the illness permeating the environment: "The Nausea has not left me and I don't believe it will leave me so soon; but I no longer have to bear it, it is no longer an illness or a passing fit: it is I."

Perhaps it was this nausea—the revulsion with one's surroundings, with other people, with existence itself, its intimations of meaninglessness, powerlessness, nihilism—that turned to messianic rage in the stomach of Arthur Lee, placing upon him the greatest weight: the burden of prophecy. For as Virginia Woolf wrote in her meditation on illness, "It is only the recumbent who know what, after all, nature is at no pains to conceal—that she in the end will conquer; heat will leave the world; stiff with frost we shall cease to drag ourselves about the fields; ice will lay thick upon factory and engine; the sun will go out." Perhaps it was this nausea that drove Arthur, like Huysmans' decadent anti-hero Des Esseintes, "oppressed by hypochondria and ravaged by spleen," to, as Woolf wrote, "cease to be [a soldier] in the army of the upright," to become a "deserter," to hole up in his hilltop manor where he could gaze down upon the city and from a safe distance pass judgment on its creeping rot, a sickness that had infected him to such a degree that it *was* him. And so if Jim Morrison would be cast as the charismatic antichrist for psychedelic LA's imminent "sea-change from jingle-jangle, Cuban-heel innocence into strange-days, Manson-era weirdness," as Barney Hoskyns put it, writing of *Forever Changes*, Arthur Lee was his John the Baptist—fringe, marginalized, possibly insane, but indisputably first—herald of the crowned and conquering child that LA occult circles believed was slouching toward the city, waiting to be born so to purify the land for the Golden Dawn of the Age of Aquarius.

Reluctantly accepting his mantle, his charge, Arthur realized that singing, *especially* singing, would be the best way to deliver his judgment on the corrupt city below. Unlike Moses, whose voice was weak, possibly due to a speech impediment, Arthur possessed a voice of commanding power and protean skill—not preaching, *inciting to riot*. And as in the countless novels and movies depicting (celebrating?) apocalypse in LA and its aftermath, Arthur would encase his revelation in the Trojan Horse of a popular mass-medium, the rock LP, a move that would have pleased Nathanael West. In West's novel *The Day of the Locust*, Hollywood studio sketch artist Tod Hackett privately labors over a mural-like painting called *The Burning of Los Angeles*, a work that will record for posterity his judgment on the beautiful and the damned, the bored and betrayed, the gray masses of resentment and rage that comprise, for him, a modern-day Babylon:

> For the faces of its members, he was using the innumerable sketches he had made of the people who come to California to die; the cultists of all sorts, economic as well as religious, the wave, airplane, funeral and preview watchers—all those poor devils who can only be stirred by the promise of miracles and then only to violence. A super "Dr. Know-All Pierce-All" had made the necessary promise and they were marching behind his banner in a great unified front of screwballs and screwboxes to purify the land. No longer bored, they sang and danced joyously in the red light of the flames.

"There are people wearing frowns / Who'll screw you up / But they would rather screw you down," Arthur would sing on "You Set the Scene," the final track on *Forever Changes*. And he was right—about heroin dealers, cops, rioters, Satanists, Scientologists, and other creeping denizens of the Strip—but could he have suspected that a "Dr. Know-All Pierce-All" named Charles Manson had already arrived in LA, promising to purify the land and busily recruiting the "unified front of screwballs and screwboxes" that would come to be known as "The Family" to do so? "People told me Manson used to come to my shows," Arthur revealed twenty years later to Barney Hoskyns in *Mojo*, hastening to add, "I never knew that." One is inclined to believe him, even if there were several coincidental instances of Arthur, through friends or acquaintances, being one degree of separation from Manson in LA during the years leading up the August '69 murders on Cielo Drive; in the first instance, the person had yet to meet Manson, but within three years he would be the Family's first killer, Bobby Beausoleil. Before settling on Bryan MacLean, Arthur had given Beausoleil a shot at being the rhythm guitarist for Love, when they were still known as the Grass Roots. Lead guitarist Johnny Echols recalls Beausoleil's stint with the band:

> Bobby Beausoleil was in the group briefly. He was a very good guitar player. I often wonder what if things had been different, if we had just kind of found a place for Bobby, if [the Manson murders] would have ever come down. Because Bobby was responsible for bringing 90 percent of the people together as the Family, because he met Charles Manson first. He was basically just a naïve kid, you know, he was not a criminal person like that. He just got carried away with this evil guy.

In truth, Manson had already amassed quite a flock of wayward women before he met Beausoleil, but given that Manson was an ambitious aspiring musician and Beausoleil, the former roommate of Satanist filmmaker Kenneth Anger, was a seasoned guitarist with hip Hollywood connections, some introductions must have ensued, if only to local rock stars and record producers. As Neil Young once told journalist Nick Kent, "A lot of pretty well-known musicians around LA knew [Manson], though they'd probably deny it now." Ed Sanders, in his sprawling beat reportage on the Manson murders, *The Family*, claims that "Very few—almost no one actually—in the years thereafter would admit to having anything to do with Manson and his Family during the flower power, folk and acid rock, commune-dwelling, 'free love' era of 1967-69. Yet, he was there, especially from late 1967 through the spring of 1969, a year and a half of hanging around, pushing his will, singing his songs and hungry for some of the glory." But Arthur's closest tie to Manson was his gregarious bandmate Bryan MacLean, who, unlike Arthur, *was* a "hang on the scene" along with David Crosby in rarefied, decadent Hollywood circles. "I went to parties at Roman Polanski's and Sharon Tate's," MacLean freely admitted in an interview years later in *Psychedelic Psounds*. "Roman Polanski's house was actually Terry Melcher's house . . . I was part of that whole scene. [Did you ever meet Charles Manson?] Nothing to really mention, but I was aware of 'Crazy Charlie' that Dennis Wilson brought around." (To note that there being "nothing to really mention" doesn't really mean that "nothing happened" would be oversuspicious—yellow journalism, really—but there it is.) In his indispensable history of the LA music industry, *Waiting for the Sun*, Barney Hoskyns fleshes out MacLean's "scene" up on Cielo Drive:

> Bobby Beausoleil contended that "Sharon Tate and that gang . . . picked up kids on the Strip and took them home and whipped them," while Dennis Hopper claimed that they'd "fallen into sadism and masochism and bestiality." . . . Terry Melcher . . . "presumed the murders had something to do with the weird film Polanski had made [*Rosemary's Baby*], and the equally weird people who were hanging around that house"—people who'd been "making a lot of homemade sadomasochistic-porno movies with quite a few recognizable Hollywood faces in them."

Hoskyns then goes on to note, in fairness, that within the LA music community of the late 60s, benign guilt-by-Manson-association was nearly unavoidable:

> The essence of the LA music community at this time was its manifold interconnections—and the fact that the boundaries between sanity and madness, pleasure and self-destruction, good and evil had become hopelessly blurred. How else could a group such as the Beach Boys, who only five years before had epitomized everything that was healthy and clean-cut about California youth, be mingling so perilously with the band of psychopathic hippie criminals who rampaged through California under the name "The Family"?

From his initial emergence on the Strip in 1965, Arthur Lee already seemed to embody how "the boundaries between sanity and madness, pleasure and self-destruction, good and evil" would become "hopelessly blurred" in LA within a few years. "Lee cut quite an imposing figure," recalled Three Dog Night's Jimmy Greenspoon, who was on the scene while Love were making a name for themselves on the Strip in 1966. "Dark glasses, a scarf around his neck, Edwardian shirts and—what was to become his trademark—an old pair of army boots with one unlaced. He had a mesmerizing presence. The audience became followers of King Arthur Lee. He was a Pied Piper who would lead them down the road to a different form of consciousness." David Anderle described Lee's dual nature this way: "Arthur was the first guy who had that LA look with the fringe jacket and the Levi's and the little glasses. I never thought of it at the time, but he was more of a punk than a hippie. It was gangster stuff, rule by intimidation, but at the same time he could be so sweet. Maybe that schizoid quality had something to do with being black in a white world, at a time when it was pretty unusual," later adding, "I don't want to say that Arthur was demonic, but he was very manipulative and destructive." According to Hoskyns, while Arthur and his bandmates walked under the banner of Love, they gave off an altogether different vibe:

> Many people found the band not just surly but intimidating, profoundly at odds with the prevailing spirit of peace and . . . well, love. LA music writer Jerry Hopkins, who briefly managed them, said they should have been called Fist, while in San Francisco they were regarded with even more opprobrium: the fanzine *Mojo Navigator* called them "a bunch of hoods," and Pete Albin of Big Brother and the Holding Company referred to them as Hate. . . . When KPIA Beat's Rochelle Reed interviewed them in June 1966 in the legendary "Castle" . . . they treated her abominably, psyching her out with mind games and telling her they'd met during a gang fight.

This dark streak, in what could have been superficially mistaken for yet another peace-and-love psychedelic band, seems to have affected members of Love itself. Original Love drummer Alban "Snoopy" Pfisterer, when prompted years later by a radio interviewer who said, "Well, it must have felt good to be such a part of the hippie era, helping to represent peace and love and all. My aunt told me all about it. She was one of your biggest fans," laughingly responded, "I'm sorry man, your aunt had it all wrong. There wasn't any love in that group. It had nothing whatsoever to do with love. It was all about hate. That should have been the name of the band." The experience even took a toll on his drumming, as he later told Barney Hoskyns: "I couldn't play drums worth a fuck when I joined Love, and I was even worse when I left . . . I mean, I got through that time with those fucking heavies—they were so fucking heavy with all their heavies that I got heavied out, man, and instead of improving over two years I regressed . . . I mean, there were some really heavy scenes went down there, man." (Not to deflate Snoopy's amusing posthippie hysteria, but as it happened, things would get *even heavier* after he left the band.) Ultimately, with regard to the radically mixed signals Love presented to the world, no one put it better than critic and fan Sandy Pearlman, who concluded that "Love looks good to people of Satanic imagination. Love's excess isn't wretched, it's plain corrupting. All corruption means is that meanings become questionable."

> It meant nothing that Hollywood was filled with great musicians, poets and philosophers. It was also filled with spiritualists, religious nuts and swindlers. It devoured everyone, and whoever was unable to save himself in time, would lose his identity, whether he thought so himself or not.
>
> —Erich Maria Remarque, *Shadows in Paradise* (1971)

For Arthur Lee, his band, and the late 60s itself, meanings indeed became questionable, just as identities became fluid, fragmented, or simply dissolved. The charged nexus of psychedelic drugs and quasi-Satanic mysticism in certain circles did much to destabilize all received truths, resulting in a generalized corruption of meaning that found its most extreme expression in the insane doomsday eschatology of the Manson Family. And Arthur Lee and Love, perhaps more than any band of the time, called bedrock meanings and recognizable identities into question. When Bryan MacLean first met Arthur, he recalled that Lee looked "so strange and unusual that at first sight I couldn't determine his gender." Later, when New Yorker Jac Holzman first saw Love perform in LA, with an eye toward signing them, he described the club, Bido Lito's, as "The Black Hole of Calcutta with a door charge. . . . It was a scene from one of the more amiable rings of Dante's inferno. Bodies crushing into each other, silken-clad girls with ironed blonde hair moving the kind of shapes you didn't see in New York, to a cadence part musical and all sexual. . . . Five guys of all colors, black, white, and psychedelic—that was a real first. My heart skipped a beat."

The band's confounding indeterminacy would find its expression in all of its music, but particularly on *Forever Changes*. As Craig Werner, author of *A Change Is Gonna Come: Music, Race and the Soul of America*, put it, "The songs on *Forever Changes* consistently hit the places where the political chaos of the time became indistinguishable from the psychic chaos." Jon Savage notes that the record is "full of bizarre juxtapositions, perceptual tricks, multiple viewpoint lyrics, lightning fast, almost schizoid changes of mood and topic, the personal fusing with the universal. . . . Its greatness lies in its very equipoise between light and dark: heaven and hell enacted over 45 minutes." Andrew Sandoval, who has overseen the remastering, beginning in 2001, of Love's first four albums for Rhino/Elektra, observes of *Forever Changes* that "You've got song structures that are not like any other songs. They're not verse-chorus songs, they've got stream-of-consciousness lyrics, orchestral interludes that are more like Herb Alpert and the Tijuana Brass than the heavier ones on *Sgt. Pepper* and *Pet Sounds*. It took me forever to understand the album. The songs were not hummable, but they were so melodic. It took so long to sink in, because it's so confusing." And Love fan Ewan Fairley, who wrote a song-by-song philosophical analysis of *Forever Changes* that is reprinted in *The Castle*, concluded, after only the first song, that "We are left with the assumption that nothing can be taken at face value, indeed the probability is that there remains hidden a deep and private code of meaning belonging to a deeply hidden inner world; this leitmotif continues throughout the album."

The cryptic nature of *Forever Changes* can be partly attributed to it being a uniquely representative product of its times—times when, as Todd Gitlin wrote in his *The Sixties: Years of Hope, Days of Rage*, "Developments broke so fast, who could absorb them, let alone insert them into the mind's polarities of left/right, politics/culture, rational/irrational? Extravagance was the common currency. Whatever was happening, it was far out, too much, out of sight." In *Against Nature* (a novel which, it should be noted, was a talismanic text in 60s bohemian circles), Huysmans' decadent isolate Des Esseintes, no stranger to extravagance, voices an extreme fondness for "the selected works of Jan van Ruysbroeck the Blessed, a thirteenth century mystic, whose prose offers an incomprehensible but appealing amalgam of mysterious ecstasy, sentimental effusions, and scathing outbursts." Had they been available in fin-de-siècle Paris, Des Esseintes probably would have treasured the works of Love as well. Though written in 1884, the latter half of his paean to Ruysbroeck could serve as a particularly elegant description of *Forever Changes*. The record, veiled in incomprehensibility and suffused with the ecstatic revelations of LSD, traffics in ominous mysticism; and while the sentimental reveries of Bryan MacLean's two songs briefly lighten the mood, they are surrounded on all sides by the scathing prophetic outbursts of Arthur Lee. That these outbursts do not, on first inspection, make sense, demonstrates the inherent linguistic challenge of prophecy, an affliction that the burden of a revelation, especially one that is "chiefly a doom," instills in the healthy, rational mind.

As Virginia Woolf puts it, in her assessment of the effects of illness, of affliction, on one's ability to speak plainly, "let a sufferer try to describe a pain in his head to a doctor and the language at once runs dry. There is nothing ready made for him. He is forced to coin words himself, and, taking his pain in one hand, and a lump of pure sound in the other (as perhaps the people of Babel did in the beginning), so to crush them together that a brand new word in the end drops out. . . . In illness words seem to possess a mystic quality." And so Arthur, in his attempt to give voice to his burden, crushes words together—"white/yellow," "hands/face," "high/face," "Andmoreagain," "free-dumb," "end-endend-end-end-end-end-end . . . and?"—because, as Greil Marcus notes, "If the prophetic figure cannot find the voice in the land, he or she makes the voice up," whether in the form of inscrutable wordplay, arcane argot, or unmitigated glossolalia. Woolf goes on to say that "Incomprehensibility has an enormous power over us in illness, more legitimately perhaps than the upright will allow. In health meaning has encroached upon sound. Our intelligence domineers over our senses. But in illness . . . the words give out their scent and distil their flavour, and then, if at last we grasp the meaning, it is all the richer for having come to us sensually first, by way of the palate and the nostrils, like some queer odour." In the liner notes of a recent Love bootleg, *Castle Walls*, the writer describes Lee's vocals on "The Red Telephone" thus: "This disturbing track manages to suggest its paranoia just through the phrasing. The staccato way of highlighting words has a strange, chanting, almost occult effect. It's been described as a kind of nursery rhyme rap." Another critic, echoing Woolf, once referred to Lee's clipped, portentously enunciated singing style as "sensual pronunciation," and its effects indeed border on the occult, adding to the general air of prophecy permeating *Forever Changes*.

> From Mount Hollywood, Los Angeles looks rather nice, enveloped in a haze of changing colors. Actually, it is a bad place—full of old, dying people, who were born old of tired pioneer parents, victims of America—full of curious wild and poisonous growths, decadent religious cults and fake science, and wildcat enterprises, which, with their aim for quick profit, are doomed to collapse and drag down multitudes of people . . . a jungle.
>
> —Louis Adamic

If Arthur Lee could be considered to be a prophet, or at least to be gripped, in 1967, by the prophetic urge while sitting on his hillside on Lookout Mountain, what was he prophesying against? On one level, he was casting judgment upon the banal, plastic excess of Los Angeles, its false promises of fame, glamour, and gold-paved streets creating an ever-growing population of increasingly bitter, disappointed dupes from middle America and South of the Border. Of course, there is a long tradition of this line of critique, finding its most contemporary voice in the nonfiction LA jeremiads of urban studies author Mike Davis, *City of Quartz* and *Ecology of Fear*, in particular. Earlier, in the mid-60s, Thomas Pynchon made a rare foray into journalism with an article titled "A Journey into the Mind of Watts," in which the novelist detailed LA's galling appearance/reality gap: "[Watts was] a country which lies, psychologically, uncounted miles further than most whites seem at present willing to travel. . . . [The whole LA scene] was basically a white scene . . . from the giant aerospace firms that flourish or retrench at the whims of Robert McNamara to the 'action' everybody mills along the Strip on weekends looking for, unaware that they and their search, which usually ends unfulfilled, are the only action in town. . . . [Watts was] a pocket of bitter reality." Having labored briefly as a technical writer at an LA aerospace firm, Pynchon knew of what he spoke, and it is indeed true that the military industries of aerospace and weapons research have always been deeply intertwined with the culture of Southern California. But the writer who perhaps best captured the combustibility of the legions of unfulfilled Angelenos was Nathanael West, who in *The Day of the Locust* described the grinding boredom and cynicism of the thousands of hopefuls who quickly found themselves at the bottom of Hollywood's "Dream Dump" and warned of their barely suppressed potential for violent retribution:

> Once there, they discover sunshine isn't enough. They get tired of oranges, even of avocado pears and passion fruit. Nothing happens. They don't know what to do with their time. . . . Their boredom becomes more and more terrible. They realize that they've been tricked and burn with resentment. Every

day of their lives they read the newspapers and went to the movies. Both fed them on lynchings, murder, sex crimes, explosions, wrecks, love nests, fires, miracles, revolutions, war. This daily diet made sophisticates of them. The sun is a joke. Oranges can't titillate their jaded palates. Nothing can ever be violent enough to make taut their slack minds and bodies. They have been cheated and betrayed.

In "The Daily Planet," the fourth track on *Forever Changes*, Arthur rather sarcastically takes us on a guided tour of the treadmill of banality that is everyday LA existence:

> *In the morning we arise and*
> *Start the day the same old way*
> *As yesterday the day before and*
> *For it all it's just a day like*
> *All the rest so do your best with*
> *Chewing gum and it is oh so*
> *Repetitious*
> *Waiting on the sun*

In the second verse, he evokes both West's hungry consumers of the "explosions, wrecks . . . fires . . . war" in the pages of the *Los Angeles Times*, the city's version of *The Daily Planet*, and Pynchon's observations on the self-perpetuating culture of LA's "giant aerospace firms" and "the 'action' everybody mills along the Strip on weekends looking for," the very Strip which Arthur claims inspired the first line:

> *Down on Go-Stop Boulevard*
> *It never fails to bring me down*
> *The sirens and the accidents and*
> *For a laugh there's Plastic Nancy*
> *She's real fancy with her children*
> *They'll go far, she*
> *Buys them toys to*
> *Keep in practice*
> *Waiting on the war*

By the end of the song, Arthur—echoing the Last Poets, whose "Run Nigger" began with the blunt pronouncement "I understand that time is running out"—intimates that a day will soon come that is not just "a day like all the rest," and that the oh-so-repetitious sun will become something altogether less benign and life-supporting. As Barney Hoskyns put it, writing of the later Doors song "Waiting for the Sun," "The sun they were awaiting was no longer the sun of the early Beach Boys records, it was a scorching god, an apocalyptic destroyer." During the last revolutions of "The Daily Planet," Arthur feels that time is indeed running out and that a "scorching god" will soon consume the earth:

I feel shivers in my spine
And the iceman, yes his ice is melting
Won't be there on time
Hope he finds a rhyme
For his little mind

Recall that Arthur considered his songs "nursery rhymes" designed to help people "make a change in their life," and that puzzling last couplet begins to make sense. It could be taken as a coded prophetic admonishment to "Repent Now, the End Is at Hand." And the implication that the Iceman—death himself—won't be able to complete his appointed rounds before the impending cataclysm is a coy literary allusion that darkens and redoubles the dire fate awaiting LA and Arthur himself.

Harvest

by Sam Inglis

Ready for the Country

In 1971, as it is now, the music industry was based around four cities: New York, Los Angeles, London, and Nashville. In England, or on the West or East Coast, you could find diversity. There were top-selling pop bands, but there were also world-class orchestras, jazz groups, and thriving underground rock communities. Nashville, by contrast, was built almost entirely upon one kind of music: country music.

The entire country music industry seemed to exist in a parallel universe. It had its own record labels, run from Nashville and kept under tight control by a few all-powerful owners and managers. It had its own chart system, where stars could be No. 1 for weeks without registering at all on the pop charts; and it had its own channels for promoting music, through country radio stations and TV shows.

In the late 60s and early 70s, the country music business retained many traditions that had vanished from pop and rock music. The goal in rock music was no longer hit singles, at least for their own sake: it was successful albums. Rock artists, unlike many country stars, were free to choose their own material and to record only their own songs. They were, moreover, becoming increasingly ambitious. The Beatles had demonstrated that pop and rock recordings need not simply be the literal record of a band's live performance, but could be confected through imaginative use of technology. This, naturally, was a difficult process, requiring months in the studio. The shift to albums as the primary format for selling music allowed bands to extend the idea of the pop song, from complex multipart pieces with pseudo-classical overtones to lengthy jams. A pop band like the Buffalo Springfield was more than just an assemblage of competent musicians thrown together to back a singer: it was a group of people working together as one unit, realizing a collective musical vision.

Country music in 1971 had taken on few of these new ideas. For the most part, record company bosses, producers and A&R men had effective control over what songs their artists recorded and how they should sound. Some artists had their own backup bands, but most of the playing on country records was done by professional session musicians—and it was done quickly. The specialty of Nashville was the mass production of records, and it had evolved a breed of musician whose professionalism was legendary. Studios were booked out in blocks of three hours, and it was expected that any given group of musicians would be able to set up their equipment, and learn and record at least four songs in any one session.

Nashville's unique musical culture was complemented by its recording facilities. Since the earliest days of music recording, all four major cities had evolved different conventions over studio design, recording technique and equipment. Every studio would have its share of homemade equipment, and engineers would learn that city's approach to recording, based on trying to achieve the best sound with the rooms and the gear available to them. By the late 60s, top artists like Dylan or the Rolling Stones were free to travel to their studio of choice, but the same was not true of most recording engineers. The idea that a mere engineer could be freelance, not bound by contract to a particular studio, was in its infancy, while the cross-pollination and eventual globalization of recording techniques was years away.

In the 60s it was highly unusual for an engineer trained in one city to have any contact at all with studios elsewhere. Many American man-hours were spent puzzling over the sources of the "British Sound," while engineers in London were equally fixated on the records coming out of New York or Memphis. Even today, when you can find the same equipment and the same recording techniques in every studio in the world, Nashville retains a certain individuality. "When I first recorded in London I was amazed at how different the studios were and they were amazed at how different my approach was about recording," says Elliot Mazer, who recorded and produced the bulk of the material on *Harvest*. "Nashville studios were built to get solid tight rhythm sounds and isolated vocals. They had good earphone systems and good-sounding echo. New York and LA studios were mostly medium or large rooms that worked well for jazz groups and big pop records, and the studios and engineers thumbed their noses at rock."

In 1971, times were just beginning to change, and Elliot Mazer was in the vanguard. Nearly all Nashville studios were owned and staffed by Nashville people, but Mazer was from New York, where he had begun his career in the early 60s as an A&R man for Prestige Records. Unusually, although he was a capable recording engineer, he'd been a record producer first, working on a lot of jazz and folk records and learning about recording technique from some of the best-known studio wizards in New York. As a producer, he'd had the opportunities to travel that were denied to most engineers, and had first visited Nashville in 1963. "I loved the feeling down there," he says. "The studios were great for rhythm sections, the sound was fantastic and the musicians were amazing."

Impressed, Mazer had eventually decided to settle in Nashville. "I started to engineer my own records when I began doing projects in Nashville," he explains. "The engineers in Nashville were good, but they were more limited in their scope as they had only recorded country and some R&B. In New York I got to work with engineers like Rudy Van Gelder, Bob Fine, George Piros, Bill Blachly, Fred Catero, Fred Plaut, Frank Laico, Joe Tarsia and many others as a producer, before I went to Nashville. Down there I learned from the guys at Bradley's Barn and some of the classic engineers at RCA and Columbia. I prefer working with a good engineer, but after a while, I wanted to use some of the ideas that I learned in New York in Nashville and the best way to do that was to do it myself."

The resulting combination of Mazer's New York engineering training and Nashville musical professionalism would, eventually, reach the ears of Neil Young and many other West Coast musicians. Mazer recorded some instrumental sessions with bassist Wayne Moss, drummer Kenny Buttrey, and sundry other session regulars. This band eventually took the name Area Code 615, and their album would become very influential in the burgeoning country-rock scene.

"I did a few projects at Wayne Moss' Cinderella Sound and Wayne let me engineer and I let him play bass," explains Mazer. "That room was a two-car garage and it sounded great. The Area Code 615 projects were done there. That experience taught me a lot about recording."

Mazer soon decided to build a studio of his own: "David Briggs, Norbert Putnam and I built Quadrafonic Studios around this time. We wanted to build a slightly bigger room that gave us a lot of control and sounded tight and fat like Cinderella. I had the opportunity to do a lot of my own engineering there." Mazer's partners in the project were record producer Norbert Putnam and session pianist David Briggs (not the same David Briggs who had produced *After the Goldrush*). Thirty years later Mazer would be called upon to remix *Harvest* in surround sound, but at that time, engineers and producers were still getting to grips with stereo. "We called it Quadrafonic as a joke," says Mazer, "although it did have four speakers in the control room. I did one quad mix there."

The differences between Nashville and LA or New York weren't just musical, they were political. To his audience, Neil Young was a figure of the hippie counterculture. The Buffalo Springfield had been prime movers in the alternative LA scene, embracing its drug culture and opposition to established authority. CSNY's very existence seemed to be a political statement, their every utterance scrutinized for its significance by fans and journalists. When four students were killed at Kent State University in 1970, Young documented his horror in "Ohio." Recorded by CSNY and rush-released within a month of the event, the resulting hit single was an unequivocal and powerful protest. Then, of course, there was "Southern Man," Young's polemic against Southern racism and the Ku Klux Klan.

But country music was the music of the Southern Man, and there was little in common between the country worldview and the hippie outlook. The hippies were anti-establishment: country music *was* an establishment, and one that was strongly allied with forces of conservatism. Country songwriters might romanticize the plight of the soldier, but not because they were opposed to the Vietnam war. Sensitive hippies at least paid lipservice to the rise of feminism; with a few exceptions, such as the remarkable Loretta Lynn, country music championed traditional, paternalistic family values. Even walking around with long hair was likely to get men beaten up in parts of the South, while open drug use was unheard of. Hippies and country music fans eyed one another from a great distance, with deep and mutual suspicion.

Embracing country music was thus a brave decision for someone who was a hero of the counterculture, an icon of radical thought and politics. At least it was when Bob Dylan did it. Dylan already had a track record for upsetting his fans, having caused consternation among serious young men when he "went electric" in 1965. His decision to cast aside the Hawks and use Nashville session musicians to back him on 1966's *Blonde on Blonde* must have seemed equally perverse, although there was little on the album that sounded "country." It was the professionalism of the musicians that had impressed Dylan and producer Bob Johnston: Nashville's finest had almost certainly never been faced with an epic like "Sad-Eyed Lady of the Lowlands" before, but they had no trouble picking it up and playing it, straight off the bat.

Having recovered from a near-fatal motorbike crash, Dylan spent much of 1967 recording with his live band. The results, universally known as the *Basement Tapes*, were widely circulated in the music business as a catalogue of new Dylan songs for other artists to record, but he chose not to make them available to the public. Instead, he returned to Nashville to make an album of new material called *John Wesley Harding*. The recordings were stark and unadorned, while the material had more of a clear country influence. Dylan's next album went even further. It was not only recorded in Nashville, but named after the city. It boasted a duet with Johnny Cash, perhaps the biggest star in country music. Dylan's songwriting had also undergone a seismic shift. Grandiose allegories and clever wordplay had given way to simple, almost banal lyrics, and the harsh musical landscape of *Blonde on Blonde* had softened to the point where Dylan's singing actually sounded tuneful. *Nashville Skyline* was not the first or the best meeting of pop and country traditions, but it was by far the most important. It was also the first to be a hit.

Bob Dylan was not the only pop artist to be ahead of his audience in liking country music. The West Coast cognoscenti got turned on to bands like the aforementioned Area Code 615, whose popularity was boosted by the fact that Kenny Buttrey had drummed on Dylan's albums. Artists like Johnny Cash and Merle Haggard had plenty of admirers in the wider music business, and there were points of contact between country and hippie ideologies. Self-important rock stars craved the air of authenticity that surrounded country, its status as an American folk music. Johnny Cash was seen as the champion of the downtrodden and the outcast, and also had a drug intake that any self-respecting pop star would struggle to match. Meanwhile, other country stars were struggling to break the yoke of artistic control exercised by record company bosses, and looked enviously at the pop stars who were free to make the records they wanted to.

Like many others in the hippie movement, Neil Young was appalled by racism and the other problems that blighted the American South. However, Young seems never to have felt the almost instinctive distaste for country music and its culture that others, such as David Crosby, had to overcome. Young had grown up in Canada, where there was no civil rights struggle, no bitter legacy of Civil War division and slavery. Country radio had come crackling through the ether over the Great Plains just as had pop stations and rock 'n' roll shows. All went to make up Young's childhood musical education. As a good hippie, he would protest indignantly about prejudice and injustice in the South, yet he was never the kind of rock star who would flinch at the sound of a pedal steel guitar. The gut-rooted association between country music and redneck politics never seems to have taken hold in Young.

By the time Neil Young made it to Nashville, the idea of a counterculture rock star collaborating with the redneck enemy had lost some of its political significance. *Nashville Skyline* was almost two years old, and its impact had been followed up by the likes of The Band. The city itself was becoming recognized as a place where musicians got things done, quickly and well, and artists of all shapes and sizes were flying there to record. Rock and country were beginning to build a shared audience thanks to syndicated TV extravaganzas like "The Johnny Cash Show," which showcased country's biggest acts alongside the likes of Dylan, Joni Mitchell, and James Taylor.

Although it could still provoke ill-feeling, in 1971 it was no longer automatically assumed that a pop star going to Nashville was about to become a poster child for the Republicans—in Young's case, that wouldn't happen for another ten years. Nor did it necessarily mean that he would come back with an album of country music. It could, however, be a comment on the state of rock music. Dylan's alignment with the Nashville music industry was a deliberate reaction against the more complex, experimental approach to record production that was becoming commonplace in pop and rock music. The Beatles' *Sgt. Pepper's Lonely Hearts Club Band* had triggered this rash of studio experimentation on its 1967 release. Many found it inspiring, but Bob Dylan was not among them. "I thought *Sergeant Pepper* was a very indulgent album," he later said. "I didn't think all that production was necessary."

Neil Young had contributed to his fair share of "studio as an instrument" recordings. Buffalo Springfield's most ambitious pieces, such as "Broken Arrow" and "Expecting to Fly," were Young compositions, elaborately layered and edited. His first solo album was similarly dense with overdubs and effects, while Crosby, Stills, and Nash became a byword for studio excess. With *After the Goldrush*, however, Young had turned decisively against this approach.

If Dylan went back to basics in the studio as a protest against rock star egotism, Neil Young's motivation seems to have been less high-minded. No rock star who chose to record with the London Symphony Orchestra could be too concerned to avoid accusations of self-indulgence, yet Young stuck to his new-found philosophy of recording even then, singing and playing live as the orchestra sawed away. The simple truth seems to be that Young felt he made better records that way. Young had struggled to find musicians in LA who shared his ideals, and had largely failed to persuade Crosby, Stills, and Nash to do so. In Nashville, it was the way records had always been made.

Nevertheless, when Young made his first visit there, he did so with no firm intention to record an album. The visit itself was the result of the mellowing relations between pop and country: Young had been invited to appear on "The Johnny Cash Show," alongside Linda Ronstadt, James Taylor, and Tony Joe White. He probably wasn't expecting to acquire a new band and a new producer at the same time.

Recording *Harvest*

With contacts from his New York days, Elliot Mazer was able to act as a bridge between Nashville and the rest of the world. One of these contacts was Neil Young's manager, Elliot Roberts, who also managed Joni Mitchell. Young's fellow guest artists on "The Johnny Cash Show" included singer Linda Ronstadt, who Elliot Mazer also knew, having produced her *Silk Purse* LP. Knowing that Roberts, Young, and Ronstadt were coming to Nashville, Mazer invited them and the other "Cash Show" guests to a dinner party.

Neil Young and Elliot Mazer fell to talking, and Young revealed that he had some new material he was hoping to record. He was familiar with the Area Code 615 albums, and asked Mazer whether he could get the band's rhythm section and steel player into the studio the next day to accompany him.

Although drummer Kenny Buttrey was available, bassist Norbert Putnam and pedal steel player Weldon Myrick had other commitments. Fortunately, good musicians were in plentiful supply in Nashville, and a band was swiftly assembled comprising Buttrey, songwriter Troy Seals on bass, and session guitarist Teddy Irwin. Seals' place was soon taken by Tim Drummond, who'd been told about the session that afternoon, and the band was completed by pedal steel guitarist Ben Keith. Young brought with him a freak Nashville snowstorm. Elliot recalls:

> When Neil played those songs, everything about the arrangements and sound seemed obvious. Neil was totally prepared with songs when he got to the studio. The songs were great and he had the feels and the basic arrangements worked out.
>
> Neil came in, sang the songs and looked at the studio. We set up the studio so that he could be right in between the members of the band. He asked if we could put him near the drums. I brought him in for his first playback and he was happy, and off we went. We had great sounds, great earphone mixes and we were ready to go a few minutes after he got to the studio. The studio never got in his way.
>
> Quad was a two-storey Victorian-era house. The control room was the porch, the playing rooms were the living room and the dining room which were connected by sliding doors. The living room had wood panels and was [acoustically] lively, the dining room was padded. Neil sat between the rooms in the doorway. Kenny was in the living room to his left and the rest were to his right—bass, steel, piano, second guitar, banjo.

This arrangement, with all the musicians in the same room, was not so far removed from the approach Young and David Briggs had adopted on *After the Goldrush*. Although each instrument had its own microphone and would have its own track on the 16-track recorder, it meant there was no way of maintaining absolute isolation. The sound of drums was bound to creep on to everything, while it would be impossible to maintain complete aural separation between all the instruments crammed into the dining room. Elliot Mazer knew that this might lead to trouble at the mixing stage, but it was the only way to capture a true live performance: "The leakage gave the record character and we knew we were not going to replace anything."

Like Dylan and so many others, Young had been attracted by the idea of recording in Nashville at least partly because of the quality of that city's musicians. Now that he had corralled some of the finest session men in the world into a room, he laid down the law about how he wanted them to arrange his songs. In Crazy Horse, he'd found a band who were willing to back him in the most basic style imaginable, playing nothing that was not absolutely necessary to get the song across. In the case of Crazy Horse, this was largely because that was the only way they could play: they made a virtue of their lack of proficiency.

Nashville's session musicians were nothing if not proficient. Unlike Crosby, Stills, and Nash, however, they were used to being treated as sidemen, never indulging in instrumental grandstanding unless that was what the client demanded. For the *Harvest* sessions, Young went in the opposite direction, insisting on the simplest of arrangements. It was almost as though he was trying to reduce these hugely talented and experienced players to the level of Crazy Horse. "Neil's songs dictated the arrangements," says Elliot Mazer. "We asked Kenny to not play any fills on some songs and no hihat on another. One on song he sat on his right hand."

The musicians Young and Mazer had assembled were professional enough to fulfil these demands to the letter, but doing so didn't make them sound like Crazy Horse. The Horse had displayed more subtlety in the *After the Goldrush* sessions than they had on *Everybody Knows This Is Nowhere*, but they were still fundamentally a garage band, constantly in danger of dropping the beat or fluffing a chord change. With the Stray Gators, as the new collection of musicians would eventually be known, things worked on a different level. Even though Young was placing severe limits on their freedom to interpret his material, they were able to use their experience and ability in countless small ways. "Kenny is a fantastic drummer," says Elliot Mazer by way of explanation. "He was great playing right with Neil, catching accents and making the songs come alive."

One significant difference between the *Harvest* band and any of Young's previous groups was the presence of Ben Keith on pedal steel guitar. Young's bare-bones arrangements on songs like "Out on the Weekend" boldly left acres of open space, and Ben Keith's playing did not so much fill these open spaces as emphasize their presence. His thin chords skirted around the edges of the songs, pointing up the sparseness of the music rather than padding it out. Keith would become one of Young's most constant musical collaborators in years to come, and it's easy to see why.

Other singers are described as having brassy or reedy singing voices, and it doesn't seem too fanciful to describe Neil Young as having a pedal-steely voice. Young's confidence in his singing had drastically improved since his Buffalo Springfield days, and its distinctiveness was only enhanced by his policy of recording everything live. Mournful, high-pitched, keening, never quite in tune, it was matched perfectly by the sound of pedal steel, to which all the same adjectives could be applied. Even *Rolling Stone*'s damning review had to admit that, on *Harvest*, "Neil Young still sings awful pretty," and the album contains some of his finest vocal performances.

For the first Nashville session in February 1971, Young also called on the services of his fellow "Cash Show" guests James Taylor and Linda Ronstadt. Their introduction to Young's recording methods took the form of a short, sharp shock. For the recording of "Old Man," Taylor was handed a six-string banjo, an instrument he'd never played before, while the pair contributed backing vocals in a rather more offhand manner than they were used to. Mazer threw up a microphone in the control room, Taylor and Ronstadt sang along, and that was that.

"Each song was cut in a few takes," says Elliot Mazer. "With Neil, you can tell from the start if a take is going to be magic. He lets that happen when he feels the band and the studio are ready. All of Neil's sessions feel like the music he is recording, and these sessions were warm and friendly. They had a great feel to them. The sessions felt like the way the music sounded."

This first session lasted a weekend and yielded *Harvest*'s two hit singles, "Heart of Gold" and "Old Man." A third song, "Bad Fog of Loneliness," was also recorded, but would not make it to the final track listing and remains unreleased. "That song did not stand up to the others," says Elliot Mazer. "It fell out the race early."

It was immediately obvious to both Mazer and Kenny Buttrey that "Heart of Gold" was destined to be a hit. Neil Young too was excited about the results of his first Nashville recording session, and what plans he might have had for a live album were shelved for good. According to his biographer Jimmy McDonough, Young was so taken with the Quadrafonic recordings that he didn't even listen to the tapes of the concerts he'd had recorded in Toronto.

Two songs, of course, were not enough to make an album, and a second session at Quadrafonic was booked, with the same musicians, for early April. In the meantime, Young was due to visit London to play at the Royal Festival Hall and record a solo live session for BBC TV's "The Old Grey Whistle Test." Most of the songs Young played for the BBC's invited audience were new, and several would end up on *Harvest*. "Out on the Weekend" was so new that he forgot the words.

He and Jack Nitzsche used the rest of their time in London to record the two songs for which Nitzsche had written orchestral arrangements. "A Man Needs a Maid"and "There's a World" were both cut in the Assembly Hall at Barking Town Hall with the London Symphony Orchestra. Young sang and played piano live, while hot-shot engineer Glyn Johns manned the controls in the Rolling Stones' mobile truck. (Located in an unprepossessing suburb of East London, the Assembly Hall doesn't sound like an obvious choice. It is, however, one of a number of out-of-the-way London halls that is highly regarded for its acoustics, and has often been used for orchestral recordings: it was a favorite of cult soundtrack composer Bernard Herrmann, who recorded many of his film scores there.)

According to the liner notes for Young's *Decade* compilation, the London trip also yielded a new song. "Harvest" would eventually provide the title for his album, and was one of the songs Young and the Stray Gators tackled on his return to Quadrafonic. Once again, Elliot Mazer engineered and sat in the producer's chair; and once again, a weekend's work yielded masters for two songs, "Out on the Weekend" and "Harvest." Attempts to record another song, "Alabama," were not so successful. Young realized that this, and another new song, "Words," needed more muscle than he could provide in his enforced sitting-down acoustic mode.

Young's back problems persisted, and he became increasingly frustrated with both the medication he was forced to take and his inability to play an electric guitar. Eventually, in August 1971, he had surgery to remove some discs from his back, and returned to his ranch to recuperate. The following month, Elliot Mazer and the Stray Gators joined him there, where they would complete *Harvest*. The band set up in an old barn full of bird shit, and a Wally Heider remote recording truck was hired to immortalize their output. Quadrafonic Studios had proved perfect for capturing the mellow feel of songs like "Heart of Gold," but it was a less ideal environment for recording noisier material. " 'Words,' 'Alabama' and 'Are You Ready for the Country' needed to be cut in a big room," says Elliot Mazer. "We had cut a quiet version of 'Alabama' at Quadrafonic, but it was not as good as the one we cut at the ranch." The DVD-A version of *Harvest* boasts a short film clip of Mazer "behind the barn" explaining how he set up microphones outdoors to record a fortuitous natural echo created by the shape of the land and buildings.

The photo on the back cover of *Harvest*, taken by Neil Young's archivist Joel Bernstein, shows the Stray Gators at work in the barn on Young's ranch, where they were augmented by Jack Nitzsche. The intention was that Nitzsche would play piano, as the session men who'd tinkled the ivories on "Harvest" and "Old Man" had remained in Nashville. This he did, but Young also repeated the trick he'd played on Nils Lofgren. Lofgren was a talented guitarist, and Young had forced him to play piano: now pianist Nitzsche was inveigled into playing slide guitar on "Are You Ready for the Country." Young himself had recovered from the operation enough to stand up and play a Gretsch White Falcon electric guitar instead of the acoustic he'd been forced to use for the previous year or so.

This time, backing vocal duties were undertaken by Young's more established collaborators Stephen Stills, David Crosby, and Graham Nash.

Nash's stay provided one of the more famous stories of Neil Young's eccentricity, when the Englishman received a sneak preview of the new album in a rowing boat on the lake that lay behind the barn. Young and Mazer had set up a giant outdoor stereo system, with one stack of speakers in the barn and another in Young's house. When Mazer came and stood on the shore to ask how it sounded, Young yelled back "More barn!" You can get an idea of the size of the sound rig from the interview with Young on the *Harvest* DVD, where a playback of "Words" rings out across the hills.

"Words," "Alabama," and "Are You Ready for the Country" were duly completed, and *Harvest*'s track listing was bulked out by the two orchestral pieces Young had completed with Jack Nitzsche and a fragment from the aborted live album. On January 30, 1971, the final American date of Neil Young's solo tour had taken him to Royce Hall at the University of California, Los Angeles, where it was taped by Henry Lewy in a Wally Heider mobile truck. One song from this concert, "The Needle and the Damage Done," wound up on *Harvest*. "No other Royce Hall recordings were considered," says Elliot Mazer. "Neil chose that one. Neil has a phenomenal memory and he can recall a particular take from years before."

Once the track listing had been decided, Young and Elliot Mazer set about mixing the album at Young's ranch. On the title track, no mixing was necessary: the stereo master they'd recorded at the time was deemed good enough to use. The other songs, however, needed a fair amount of work. "Trying to recapture the feeling of the original sessions was the challenge," says Mazer. Despite the lengthy mixing process, the results have a straightforward, pure quality to them. Most pop and rock records make use of a technique known as compression to even out the level of the different elements in a mix. This can give individual instruments and voices a thicker and more substantial sound, but if overused it can also leave recordings sounding flat and lacking in dynamics. Elliot Mazer deliberately avoided using compression anywhere on *Harvest*, and the resulting sound is open and spacious.

The idea that Young had "gone country" was reinforced by Tom Wilkes' sleeve design. The cover of *After the Goldrush* had seen Young lurking anonymously in a gray city street: here, the only image was a red disc, around which Young's name and the album title flowed in elaborate calligraphy. With its muted buff background, the results had a decidedly rustic air. Nowhere on *Harvest* did Young's face appear clearly, although Joel Bernstein's black-and-white photo for the back cover showed the Stray Gators getting down in the barn, Young was just a mess of hair. The inside of the gatefold sleeve was even more obscure, a blurred, distorted Neil Young reflected in a polished brass doorknob. It was easier to decipher the words by listening to the record than by struggling with Young's handwriting, but the lyric sheet was a thoughtful finishing touch. As a package, *Harvest* was understated, nicely crafted, touchingly self-effacing. It was a fine cover for what Young would come to see as his finest album.

The Kinks Are the Village Green Preservation Society
by Andy Miller

Chapter Two
The Kinks Are the Village Green Preservation Society

The English village green is a little patch of grassland that still strikes a chord in the hearts of most native men and women two hundred years after the Industrial Revolution changed the majority of us to urban dwellers. It represents rural peace and quiet, as well as a community spirit that does not obtain in towns, and sets up in most of us a yearning for that fondly imagined country paradise, lost by the growth of imperialism and capitalism which have made England an over-populated country of noisy and dirty towns and cities where the mass of men, as Thoreau put it, lead lives of quiet desperation.

—Brian Bailey, *The English Village Green* (1985)

By the summer of 1968, Ray Davies was still without a title for the forth-coming Kinks album. *Village Green*, the project's working title, seemed too narrow—the original Village Green concept had mutated as other, more personal songs joined the fray and, although the track "Village Green" remained essential to Davies' plan for the album, it would be two years old by the time the LP was released. Things had moved on.

"I was looking for a title for the album about three months ago, when we had finished most of the tracks," Davies told *Saturday Club*'s Brian Matthew in November, a few days before the record finally reached the shops, "and somebody said that one of the things The Kinks have been doing for the last three years is preserving." The suggestion was clearly enough to prompt Davies toward not just a title for his album, but also to compose what he subsequently described as its "national anthem"—"The Village Green Preservation Society." "This started out to be a solo album for me," he told Bob Dawbarn in *Melody Maker*, "but somebody mentioned to me that the Kinks do try to preserve things—we are all for that looking back thing. I thought it would be a nice idea to try and sum it up in one song."

At first glance, the basic elements of "The Village Green Preservation Society" seem to betray the speed with which it was manufactured—four strummed chords with a simple, circling melody, modulating from C major to D major at 1:12. However, its structure is unorthodox and unpredictable, the arrangement is pinsharp, and the performances are self-assured. And then there is Davies' deceptively acerbic lyric, which could so easily have been a showcase for resourceful use of the thesaurus (consortium, affinity, affiliate, er, vernacular . . .) and not much besides, but which transcends its own ingenuity to stand alongside its author's finest moments —heartfelt, whimsical, and recklessly unfashionable.

"The Village Green Preservation Society" is carefully set up as a slow burn, everything leading to Davies' seemingly off-the-cuff "God save the village green!" as the track begins to fade. Much of the credit for the success of this arrangement must go to Mick Avory, whose drumming is especially exuberant. The opening piano figure is similarly light and effortless.[1] Ray's close harmony vocal with Dave Davies is sustained throughout, dropping away for Ray to emphasise the last line before the modulation to D. Only at the song's close does Davies purposefully move center stage (literally, if you are listening in stereo), singing the last two lines solo with a backwash of falsetto harmonies. "God save the village green!" We're left in no doubt as to whose Preservation Society, and whose album, this is.

"All the things in the song are things are things I'd like to see preserved," said Davies at the time. "I like village greens and preservation societies," he told Jonathan Cott of *Rolling Stone*. "I like Donald Duck, Desperate Dan, draught beer." This is disingenuous and, as Davies belatedly realized, open to misinterpretation. "A lot of people accuse me in the song of being kind of fascist," he has said. "Traditional, you know? But it's not. It's a warm feeling, like a fantasy world that I can retreat to." As noted by Robert Christgau in his influential appraisal of the album in the *Village Voice*, "Does Davies really want to preserve virginity? Presumably not. But the fictional form allows him to remain ambivalent."

However, there is a satirical edge to "The Village Green Preservation Society" that has been dulled or lost in the years since its release. Nineteen sixty-eight was not a comfortable year for Britain and the

---

1 This may or may not be Nicky Hopkins. The slightly slower BBC version recorded on November 26, 1968 (and available on *BBC Sessions 1964–1977*), on which the piano part is definitely played by Davies, reveals a somewhat less steady hand on the keyboard.

British. The anti-Vietnam protests outside the American embassy in Grosvenor Square were the most violent manifestation of a general post-colonial unease with Britain's diminishing role in the world. The economic climate was deteriorating, causing the Labour government to launch its "I'm Backing Britain" initiative as a spur to the consumer to buy British-made goods and support British industry in the wake of devaluation of the pound. The entertainer Bruce Forsyth released a single on Pye called "I'm Backing Britain," cowritten by Pye's musical director Tony Hatch ("Let's keep it going / The good times are blowing our way").

Nineteen sixty-eight was also the year Conservative MP Enoch Powell urged the repatriation of African and West Indian immigrants in a speech which quickly passed into infamy: "As I look ahead I am filled with foreboding. Like the Romans, I seem to see the River Tiber foaming with blood." People marched against Powell, and for him. In a photograph from the time, an Asian woman balances her baby in one hand and a homemade placard in the other: WE ARE BACKING BRITAIN. Meanwhile a group of porters from Smithfield meat market demonstrate in their blood-spattered overalls, laughing and carrying a banner: SMITHFIELD SAYS: A GEORGE CROSS FOR ENOCH.

So 1968 was a year of anger and unrest, of fear of the future and nostalgia for a safer past, of preservation societies, affinities and affiliates, not all of them wholesome—something Davies was undoubtedly aware of. Early in the year, he had penned a satirical song called "We're Backing Britain" for the BBC TV program "At the Eleventh Hour."[2] In this context, the lyrics of "The Village Green Preservation Society" are less quaint,

---

2 Davies wrote at least nine songs for "At the Eleventh Hour," a late-night satire program in the mould of "That Was the Week That Was." As noted by Doug Hinman, they were performed in the show by jazz singer Jeannie Lamb with light orchestral backing, and included "You Can't Give More Than What You Have," "If Christmas Day Could Last Forever," "We're Backing Britain," "Could Be You're Getting Old," "This Is What the World Is All About," "The Man Who Conned Dinner from the Ritz," "Did You See His Name," "Poor Old Intellectual Sadie," and "Just a Poor Country Girl." None were recorded by the Kinks, with the exception of "Did You See His Name," which was cut during *TKATVGPS* sessions in May 1968 and finally released four years later on the Reprise compilation *The Kink Kronikles*. The following year, Davies repeated the stunt, writing five songs for the television series "Where Was Spring?" These were recorded by The Kinks, but only two have so far surfaced officially—"Where Did My Spring Go?" and "When I Turn Off the Living Room Light," both on *The Great Lost Kinks Album*. The remaining three—"Darling I Respect You," "Let's Take Off All Our Clothes," and (probably) "We Are Two of a Kind" are still missing, though a near-unlistenable off-air copy of the first of these is circulating on bootleg. In May 1971, it was announced in the music papers that an album containing some or all these songs—*Songs I Sang for Auntie/The Ray Davies Songbook*—was underway for release later that same year. Of course, it never appeared. Neither the BBC, nor Sanctuary, nor Reprise holds copies of the missing songs, in complete or demo form. We can only hope that, somewhere deep in the bowels of Konk Studios, Raymond Douglas Davies is keeping them safe.

less escapist; rather, they mock the certainties of protest with a list of utterly idiosyncratic demands, then make a personal plea for moderation: what more can we do? "I'm not particularly patriotic—perhaps I'm just selfish," Davies told Derek Boltwood six months after the album was released, "but I like these traditional British things to be there. I never go to watch cricket any more, but I like to know it's there. . . . It all sounds terribly serious, but it isn't really—I mean, I wouldn't die for this cause, but I think it's frightfully important."

It may lack the righteousness and glamour of "Street Fighting Man," but unlike the Rolling Stones' modish call to arms, Davies' quiet song of defiance is not a pose. Taken either as autobiography or satire, as a curtain raiser for the album, or as the world's gentlest and most oblique protest song, "The Village Green Preservation Society" is central to Davies' map of the Village Green, and the great theme of his songwriting at this time —the ambiguous allure of the past. The Kinks simply dusted it with magic and passed it on.

Do You Remember Walter

"The past is a curious thing," says George Bowling, the middle-aged narrator of George Orwell's *Coming Up for Air*. "It's with you all the time." Bowling, a dissatisfied insurance salesman, fat and washed up in a stagnating marriage, yearns for the landscape of his childhood. "What was it that people had in those days?" he wonders. "A feeling of security, even when they weren't secure. More exactly, it was a feeling of continuity." These could be the words of Ray Davies in 1968, contemplating a bygone age and all of 24 years old.

In *Coming Up for Air*, George Bowling contrives an escape from the routine and frustration of his day-to-day existence by returning to Lower Binfield, the small country town in which he grew up. The trip is a disaster. Lower Binfield has changed almost beyond recognition; Bowling's long-wished-for homecoming brings only disillusionment and despair, depriving him even of the safe haven of his memories. There is no return because, of course, there cannot be. Elsie, the sweetheart Bowling left behind 25 years earlier, is now married to a tobacconist. She is old at 47, her hair completely gray. More to the point, "She didn't know me from Adam. I was just a customer, a stranger, an uninteresting fat man . . . she didn't even recognize me. If I told her who I was, very likely she wouldn't remember."

If the title track is the national anthem of *TKATVGPS*, "Do You Remember Walter" is its lyrical heart. It is one of Davies' finest songs, a meditation on friendship and time which, in common with his best work, takes an everyday image or commonplace event (commuters at Waterloo, the stars on Hollywood Boulevard) and finds the universe within it. "Walter was a friend of mine, we used to play football together every Saturday," Davies told *Melody Maker* shortly before the album's release. "Then I met him again after about five years and we found out we didn't have anything to talk about." Davies transformed this awkwardness into art.

Five years, says Davies, yet Walter reminds him of "a world I knew *so long ago*," a world before the Kinks, before the hits, the screaming, and the breakdowns—hardly surprising there wasn't much to say, especially if the famous pop star only wanted to linger on the old times. They were going to be free, Ray and Walter; like Edward Lear's Owl and Pussycat, they were going to sail away to sea ("in a beautiful pea-green boat / They took some honey / And plenty of money . . .") but somehow they never did it. And yet, Davies seems to suggest, in the end neither man would wish for the other's fate—Walter is bored by the singer's reminiscing, while Davies scoffs at Walter's early bedtime (and conformity). In the final reckoning, that isn't what counts. "There's a line in the lyric—'People often change but memories of people remain'—which sums up what this is about," said Davies, and at the song's conclusion he slows everything down to emphasize the point. The awkwardness, the sadness of things, Davies says, is the price we pay for change, but we should try to preserve the memory regardless.

Davies matched the winding, conversational lyric of "Do You Remember Walter" with one of his most precocious melodies. The tune skips up and down the scale like a piano exercise (see also: "Picture Book," "People Take Pictures of Each Other"). That the finished track sounds neither precious nor pretentious is a tribute to Davies' single-minded arrangement —every instrument and production nuance has been made a slave to the lyric and the vocal. Against the measured pounding of the piano and bass (and Mick Avory's Boys' Brigade snare rolls), Davies sings with passionate restraint, his vocal track cleverly enhanced by some occasional double-tracking and a hazy Mellotron line that shadows the melody; like Walter, an echo. The effect is rousing at times, melancholic at others. Having paused to deliver the song's parting shot, the Mellotron line is left behind as the track fades, as if to bear it out—our memories are what remains long after names have been forgotten.[3]

---

3 As was the custom of the day, there are clear differences between the mono and stereo mixes of some *TKATVGPS* tracks, and indeed between a handful of numbers on the 12- and 15-track editions. At this stage, mono was still Ray Davies' preferred format. In the case of "Do You Remember Walter," the differences are minor: a little more of Dave's guitar, a little less Mellotron, and no tambourine. Both mixes are included on the current British edition of the album.

Picture Book

In 2002, Ray Davies was called upon to pen sleeve notes for his own various artists tribute album, *This Is Where I Belong: The Songs of Ray Davies & the Kinks*. There are three selections from *TKATVGPS* on the album, of which "Picture Book" is one; "brave" is how Davies describes Bill Lloyd and Tommy Womack's decision to tackle it. The song was not written for the Kinks. "They were songs that I should have consigned to my private collection," he writes. "Both songs ['Picture Book' and 'Muswell Hillbilly'] are inspired by my family and mention people that really existed."

Yet, from the beginning, "Picture Book" was always one of *TKATVG-PS*'s most visible and significant songs. Recorded in the spring of 1968, it was selected by Davies for the aborted *Four More Respected Gentlemen*, and for both twelve- and fifteen-track versions of the album where, as noted above, it falls in behind "The Village Green Preservation Society" and "Do You Remember Walter," the opening triumvirate that introduces the major themes and images of the LP. The Kinks also included "Picture Book" in their July 26th appearance on the "Colour Me Pop" strand of BBC 2's "Late Night Line-Up," a full five months ahead of the album's release. The group performed it again the following February on another BBC 2 music program "Once More with Felix," hosted by the folk singer Julie Felix.[4]

In other words, however Ray Davies may feel about it today, "Picture Book" was an important song to the Kinks and an important piece of the whole *Village Green* jigsaw. In the studio, Pete Quaife recalls being drilled through multiple takes of the track, as Davies struggled to get it finished to his satisfaction. "Picture Book" is a scruffier proposition than either of the songs that precede it, the final minute a mish-mash of assorted "yeah yeah yeah's," "na na na's," and even a "scooby dooby doo" or two, lifted from Sinatra's "Strangers in the Night," and crooned by Davies in suitably ironic fashion. Despite their reported fatigue, the Kinks' playing sounds enthusiastic. The track progresses so jauntily, in fact, that one can easily miss the grit at its center; these family photographs were taken "a long

---

4 Both these shows are missing from the BBC archives, presumed wiped. "Colour Me Pop" is the greater loss. The Kinks wore their colorful late-sixties stage outfits and performed some or all of "Dedicated Follower of Fashion," "A Well Respected Man," "Death of a Clown," "Sunny Afternoon," "Lincoln County," "Picture Book," "Sitting By the Riverside," "She's Got Everything" (filmed insert), "Two Sisters," and "Days." It is not known if this was a live or lipsynched performance, but note the inclusion of two tracks from *TKATVGPS* so far in advance of the album's release. It seems likely that these renditions varied from what appeared on the finished LP. The other song performed on "Once More with Felix" (recorded January 8, 1969, broadcast February 1st) was "Last of the Steam-Powered Trains."

time ago" and the happiness they represent—the happiness of childhood —has gone forever.

"No one could afford a bloody camera," Dave Davies told Bill Orton in 2001. "I didn't know anybody that had a camera, not even on our street. It wasn't a big thing, unless you went on holiday—Ramsgate or whatever. We had pictures of that . . . " Two such pictures are reproduced in Dave's autobiography. In one, Ray Davies, no more than twelve years old, stands on the beach between his brother Dave and their nephew Terry (the son of their sister Rosie and her husband, Arthur, both of whom would one day have songs, whole albums, written about them). Dave and Terry are on all fours, like dogs; Ray is holding them both by the hair, grinning from ear to ear.

The other snap is of Gwen and Rene, two more Davies sisters. Dave thinks the photos date from around June 1957. Within weeks, Ray would turn thirteen. For his birthday Rene would buy him a Spanish guitar. Then, against doctor's orders, she would go out dancing to the Lyceum Ballroom in the Strand, where she would collapse on the dance floor. She died that night. "What dreadful mixed feelings my brother must have experienced on that following morning," writes Dave Davies. "For months he had been on and on about that bloody guitar . . . " So the gaiety of "Picture Book"—"a paper hat, kiss-me-quick" song as Ray described it—masks an even greater sense of personal loss than that portrayed in "Do You Remember Walter." To Ray Davies, the photographs are reminders both of happier times and of time lost, an ambivalence more fully expressed in "People Take Pictures of Each Other" (on *This Is Where I Belong*, Bill Lloyd and Tommy Womack's "brave" cover version of "Picture Book" concludes with a snatch of the latter song). Also recorded by the Kinks at this time was the marvellous "Pictures in the Sand," released only briefly on *The Great Lost Kinks Album*. The song shares "Picture Book's" seaside setting and end-of-the-pier musical jollity, and also its quiet desperation; although these pictures aren't permanent like photographs, they still can't picture love, in the here and now, vanished or taken away.

* * *

The opening trio of tracks on *TKATVGPS* had no equivalent in the pop scene of 1968, chart or underground, in either sound or subject. This wasn't merely unfashionable; it was anathema to the prevailing rock culture of the time, one that embraced Concepts but struggled with ideas. In a year when musicianship for its own sake was on the rise and "feel" was all, when people could conceive of nothing finer than to boogie with Canned Heat, Davies makes it plain that everything on *TKATVGPS*—arrangement, performance, production—will be the servant of the song, and the songs will be about ordinary things and everyday people: "I go out of my way to like ordinary things. I cling on to the simple values . . . I think 'ordinary' people are quite complex enough without looking for greater sophistication. . . . We do a lot of stompy things. The rhythms are reminiscent of the twenties. I like the old days. Everybody does—in song." Ignoring what was happening around him, Ray Davies pursued his particular vision to its conclusion and in doing so consigned the LP to swift obscurity and broke the Kinks.

But what more could he do?

Johnny Thunder

Another track selected for *Four More Respected Gentlemen* and both incarnations of *TKATVGPS*, "Johnny Thunder" neatly fits Davies' original "town and the people who live there" conception of *Village Green*, as LP, stage musical, or whatever. "It's about a rocker," he told *Melody Maker*. "I wrote it after *Wild One* was released." László Benedek's 1954 film *The Wild One*, starring Marlon Brando and Lee Marvin as the leaders of rival biker gangs, had been reissued to London cinemas in early 1968. Brando's character is called Johnny, and it may be Brando that Davies had in mind as his model for Johnny Thunder (try swapping the names around the next time you're singing along).[5] "He's the local hound—a real swine," Dave told *Disc* and *Music Echo*, before reassuring readers, "but he's inside at the moment!"

"Johnny Thunder" is one of the more straightforward songs on *TKATVGPS*, with few production tricks and a rare solo vocal from Ray, his first on the album not to be double-tracked at any point. Acoustic guitars, bass, and drums are joined by Dave Davies' treated and tidy guitar part, mixed almost out of earshot—a shame, as the countermelody that accompanies the chorus and "thunder and lightning" refrain is delightful. The brass-bandlike wordless vocal line provides a melodic flourish, while once again the rhythm section has been given some space to stretch out and the Kinks' harmonies are characteristically imaginative (if a little ragged).

Davies' portrait of the rebel motorcyclist who rides alone, subsisting on nothing but the elements, is so idealized as to be untrustworthy (an unreliable narrator is another literary aspect of the songs on *TKATVGPS*, notably "Village Green" itself). The inhabitants may not be able to reach Johnny, but he is a much-loved feature of the town nevertheless—he is even in Helena's prayers. Johnny, like Walter, has sworn to be free, and in the process has been turned into a perfectly preserved—and thus

---

5 Rock historians please note: the rival gangs of *The Wild One* have now supplied two bands with names—the Beetles have been joined by the Black Rebel Motorcycle Club.

neutered—icon of rebellion, just as pictures of Marlon Brando in *The Wild One* eventually decorated a million bedroom walls. God bless him indeed (and tudor houses, china cups, virginity, etc.). The character, fleshed out somewhat, reappears as "One of the Survivors" on *Preservation Act 1*.

According to Dave Davies, the original "Johnny Thunder" attracted the attention of a longstanding Kinks' admirer: Pete Townshend of the Who. Davies alleges Townshend so liked the song's dramatic opening riff that he quickly recycled it in his own work—after all, The Who's guitarist had form where the Kinks were concerned. He openly admitted to modelling "I Can't Explain" on the Kinks' first few hits, and Dave suspected Ray and Pete's mutual friend Barry Fantoni of "conveying our ideas to Townshend." Dave declines to say exactly where this new "tribute" occurred, but listeners to *Tommy*, released just six months after *TKATVG-PS*, may detect some similarity between "Johnny Thunder" and parts of "Overture" and "Go to the Mirror!"

Ray may have agreed with his brother. Speaking to *Rolling Stone* in November 1969, by which time *Tommy*, rock's much-hyped first opera, had become a sensation and turned Townshend and his group into superstars, Davies had this to say on the subject of "Johnny Thunder": "It's not a cowboy song," he told Jonathan Cott, pleasantly. "It would be nice to hear The Who sing it."

Last of the Steam-Powered Trains

From thunder and lightning to "Smokestack Lightnin'." "Last of the Steam-Powered Trains" was a very late addition to *TKATVGPS* and evidence suggests it was probably the last song to be composed for the album. Like "Big Sky," it was recorded in October 1968, after the cancellation of the original twelve-track edition. In several respects, the song is uncharacteristic of the album as a whole—its R&B derivation, its live-sounding performance, and its four-minute length are all atypical[6]—but in another, it is the quintessence of Davies' writing for this project. On a LP full of deceptively acidic songs, "Last of the Steam-Powered Trains" may well be the most corrosive of them all.

The Kinks, in common with many of the pop era's finest groups, emerged from the rhythm and blues boom of the early sixties. Among the most totemic R&B favorites was a sinister, sensual half-shuffle called "Smokestack Lightnin'" by Chester Burnett, aka the Howlin' Wolf. By 1963, the song was a staple of every self-respecting British R&B band's act. The High Numbers performed "Smokestack Lightnin'" at their

---

6 No other song on *TKATVGPS* exceeds three minutes, let alone four.

unsuccessful Abbey Road audition in October 1964. In Southampton, there was even a group called the Howlin' Wolves (later to change their name and find brief fame as reluctant psychedelic nabobs Simon Dupree and the Big Sound).

It may be nearly fifty years old, but the original "Smokestack Light-nin'" is a jawdropping record, a despatch from some sweltering, moonlit chamber, sung with the kind of elemental, roaring fervor that only Don Van Vliet, alias Captain Beefheart, has ever seemed able to match. In comparison, recorded British beat boom versions of the song tend to be either long on fretwork and short on menace (the Yardbirds) or well intentioned but hopelessly callow (Manfred Mann).

By late 1963, Howlin' Wolf's original recording of "Smokestack Light-nin'" was in such demand that Pye issued it as the lead track of a moderately successful EP. Six months later—around the time the Kinks were fighting with the same label to get "You Really Got Me" rerecorded with more power and atmosphere—the company issued "Smokestack Light-nin'" again, this time as a single. Howlin' Wolf, six-foot-three and nearly three hundred pounds, made a memorable appearance as the surprise guest on BBC TV's "Jukebox Jury," where he towered over the suddenly quaking members of a panel who had just voted his greatest hit a "miss."

By mid-1965, however, the R&B scene was in decline as pop proliferated and groups increasingly came under pressure, often from their own management, to compete with the Beatles and write their own pop-orientated material. Out went the repertoire. In *X-Ray*, Davies recounts Hal Carter's advice to the Kinks about tailoring their stage act: "Cut out that 'Smokestack Lightning' number. You're not doing yourselves and anybody else any favours by playing that." Meanwhile, the High Numbers, now with a new name and a record deal, were changing their tune(s). "The Who are having serious doubts about the state of R&B," their manager Kit Lambert told *Disc*. "Now the LP material [for *My Generation*] will consist of hard pop. They've finished with 'Smokestack Lightning'."

So in 1968, by basing "Last of the Steam-Powered Trains" on an instantly recognizable riff from four or five years earlier, Ray Davies was blowing the whistle both on himself and his R&B contemporaries. There are jokes and allusions to "Smokestack Lightnin'," and the scene in general, scattered throughout the song. Like Howlin' Wolf's original track and subsequent covers of it, "Last of the Steam-Powered Trains" chugs along in E major. At 2:21, Ray Davies can distantly be heard emitting a scrawny falsetto howl, more afghan hound than wolf. From 3:41 to 3:44, the Kinks double the tempo for two bars, Pete Quaife leaping an octave to play a distinctly Chuck Berry-like bass line. In the third verse there is a lyrical allusion to "Train Kept a-Rollin'," recorded by the Yardbirds and famously performed by the Jeff Beck/Jimmy Page lineup of the group in Michelangelo Antonioni's *Blow-Up* (1966).[7] And throughout, there is Ray, huffing and puffing away on the harmonica—double-tracked in places: how else do you blow lead and rhythm simultaneously?—like it was 1963 again and the Kinks were back in the pubs and youth clubs of Muswell Hill and East Finchley.

"This was a case of the idea coming before the song," Ray Davies told *Melody Maker* when the album was released. "Again, like the 'Walter' song it's really about not having anything in common with people. Everybody wanted to know about steam trains a couple of years ago, but they don't any more. It's about me being the last of the renegades. All my friends are middle class now. They've all stopped playing in clubs. They've all made money and have happy faces. Oddly enough I never did like steam trains much."

The correlation of steam trains and R&B in "Last of the Steam-Powered Trains" is inspired, both in its witty juxtaposition of such distinctly English and American archetypes, and in the hesitancy it expresses on behalf of its author. *Look,* Davies says, *you, we, loved this music but there is something increasingly ridiculous and misplaced about our love—an English middle-class, middle-aged "Smokestack Lightnin'" is about as authentically bluesy as the Titfield Thunderbolt. I am the last renegade; how absurd that is.*

Accordingly, on record the track hovers between paying homage to the R&B sound and spoofing it. Although the Kinks play it straight, some aptly locomotive touches have been added to the arrangement. The group locks into the well-worn groove, picking up speed (and handclaps) as they go. After throwing some ascending chords onto the fire (2:56 to 3:05), they race through the song's final minute, grinding to a halt with a final puff of smoke from Mick Avory's cymbals and kick drum.

It should be too contrived for words; what prevents it from collapsing into novelty is, once again, Davies' lyric and the despair that runs just beneath its surface jocularity and pride. Like Johnny Thunder, the Last of the Steam-Powered Trains is a rebel, a survivor, who has avoided becoming bourgeois and gray like his friends. Sweat and blood, soot and scum. But such freedom comes at a cost. He is kept in a museum; preservation is driving him mad. By the time he composed the song, Ray Davies had been writing *Village Green* material for two years, and "Last of the Steam-Powered Trains" reiterates its central dilemmas with wit and assurance. How do you reconcile your past and present? How do you stop the weight of experience from dragging you under? How do you keep rollin' when all you want to do is stop?

Reports of the death of British R&B would prove to be greatly exaggerated. In the same month that the Kinks cut "Last of the Steam-Powered Trains," thereby bringing to a close the protracted sessions for

---

7 For copyright reasons, the song was quickly rewritten on the film's set as "Stroll On."

TKATVGPS, south of the river at Olympic Studios in Barnes, Yardbirds guitarist Jimmy Page's new group was recording its debut LP. In a mere thirty-six hours, the irresistible force of Led Zeppelin remade rhythm and blues as hard rock and, in doing so, invented the 1970s. The first song the group ever played together was "Train Kept a-Rollin'."

"Last of the Steam-Powered Trains" became a fixture of the Kinks' live act when they returned to America in October 1969; at the Boston Tea Party on the 23rd it was their opening number. Tapes reveal that the record's ironies and nuances have all been ditched in favor of some fully fledged and unfortunate Zep-like noodling. The song has become the sort of blues workout Davies originally sought to lampoon. By the end of the tour, on the stage of the Fillmore West, San Francisco, it stretches to seven tedious minutes; at the same venue a year later it has swollen to a mind-numbing eleven. Ray bellows the words, jumbling and repeating the lyrics; Dave gives full rein to his incipient guitar heroics. "I was walking in a field one day," yells Dave Davies at one point, bafflingly, "and I happened to look up at the sky. And man, you know what I saw? I SAW AN ALBA-TROSS!!!" Cue seven minutes of maximum heaviosity (and boredom). It must have sounded great if you were stoned, or one of the musicians, or both. Coincidentally, Bay Area extemporizers the Grateful Dead regularly featured "Smokestack Lightnin'" in their interminable concerts. It would be nice to think that the Kinks' "coals to Newcastle" live performances of "Last of the Steam-Powered Trains" in San Francisco were extending the song's satirical reach; in fact, they were just playing to the long-haired, droopy-lidded gallery. By chance, the song fitted the back-to-rock-basics mood of the times.

One last thought: in its acknowledgment of pop's inevitable graying, "Last of the Steam-Powered Trains" has proved to be gloriously predic-tive. Magazines like *Mojo* and *Classic Rock*, with their emphasis on classi-cism and authenticity—even iconoclastic movements like punk and tech-no are now revered for their classicism and authenticity—are like muse-ums of rock music, with figures like Ray Davies and albums like *TKATVGPS* their prize exhibits.

Big Sky

Ray Davies wrote the immortal "Big Sky" on the balcony of the Carlton Hotel in Cannes. "I spent an evening with all these people doing deals," he said. "The next morning at the Carlton Hotel I watched the sun come up and I looked at them all down there, all going out to do their deals. That's where I got the 'Big Sky looking down on all the people' line. It started from there." In his liner notes for *This Is Where I Belong*, Davies says he watched the sun set, not rise: whatever, the combination of the awe-inspiring skies above the Mediterranean and the businessmen below in their suits and ties was enough to make him consider the existence of "a being somewhat bigger than all of the hustlers around me." He completed the resulting song quickly, boarded a plane, and brought it back to London.[8]

"Big Sky" is not a song about God, but about how human beings cope in a world where God is seemingly unconcerned at their plight. The Big Sky is not dead but preoccupied, benign but indifferent. For Ray Davies, this is a cause for celebration, or at least consolation. The Big Sky is so big, our troubles are small in comparison—and these too shall pass. Freedom comes to everyone in the end, whether we want it or not. Until then, don't let your sorrow get the better of you. The song is a memo both to himself and the Big Sky over his head. It is as good as anything written in the 1960s, by Lennon and McCartney, Bob Dylan, or anyone else.

As noted above, "Big Sky" was recorded in October 1968, just weeks before the final version of the LP reached the shops. As such, it represents the high point of Davies' creativity in the *Village Green* period and also its final flowering. He would go on to write great songs, and the Kinks would continue to make good records, occasionally great ones, but the rhapsodic, sweeping "Big Sky" is the last in a line of Kinks classics that began with "Sunny Afternoon" in 1966 and which, because of the fundamental change in the way Davies viewed his writing and career after the failure of *TKATVGPS*, the group never quite regained.

Why did Davies wait nine months before cutting "Big Sky" with the Kinks? The simple answer may be that this pillar of . . . *The Village Green Preservation Society* is not really a *Village Green* number at all (unless you think the Big Sky is looking down on Johnny Thunder, Walter, Wicked Annabella, et al.). It shares few of the LP's preoccupations with memory and desire and may, like "Picture Book," have been intended only for Davies' "private collection"; alternatively, it may have been earmarked for the solo album which, in early 1968, Davies still hoped to make. However, by the autumn, with his solo project a distant memory and Pye rejecting his request for a double album of the songs he and the Kinks had been safeguarding for nearly a year, Davies seems to have realized that if "Big Sky" were to be heard at all, it would have to be on *TKATVGPS*, and that a new Kinks LP could only benefit from its inclusion. So, at the last minute, the Kinks returned to Pye Studio 2.

A fittingly divine inspiration seems to have visited them there, for the Kinks' version of "Big Sky" contains some of the most beautiful, thunderous music they ever recorded, aligned to a vulnerability and warmth no other group—and I mean no other group—could ever hope to equal. It is a perfectly balanced production. On the one hand, the mesh of clattering

---

8 Davies may also have copped the title from Howard Hawks' 1952 movie *The Big Sky*.

drums and electric guitar never threatens to overwhelm the melody; on the other, the gossamer-light harmonies, Ray and Dave's vocal line traced by Rasa Davies' wordless falsetto, are bursting with emotion. When most of the instruments drop away at 1:20, the effect is effortlessly vivid—two lines where Davies' performance is both nonchalant and impassioned. The result is wonderfully, enchantingly sad, made more so perhaps by the knowledge that the Kinks will never again sound so refined or so right.

Twenty years later, Davies told Jon Savage that although "Big Sky" was one of his favorite songs, he was dissatisfied with the Kinks' recording of it. "Maybe I wasn't the right person to sing it," he said.[9] "Knowing I got the image across and the fact that a lot of people like the song is enough. But my performance is really bad. . . . It just wasn't recorded properly . . ." Davies has habitually deflected attention away from the personal nature and commercial failure of *TKATVGPS* by claiming either that the songs suffered from his inexperience behind the mixing desk ("those songs are demos really, pure demos. . . . They're good ideas but not executed properly. I was lacking a producer . . .") or that he deliberately under-recorded them ("I wanted a record that would not necessarily get airplay but would be played for friends and at parties—just play the record like playing a demo. I achieved that and it didn't get any airplay at all. It became a cult record as a result."). "Big Sky," so scintillating in design and execution, gives the lie to both these evasions.

Coincidentally, the final two songs recorded for *TKATVGPS* were also the only two the Kinks carried over into their live set at the time, where they would be introduced as numbers from "an LP we had out but few people bought" or "an album we had out called *The Village Green Preservation Society*. I don't know if you've ever heard of it." (The scattered, half-hearted applause that usually followed these announcements indicates most gig-goers had not). Live, "Big Sky" ("as opposed to pig sty") received the same kind of heavy rock punishment meted out to "Last of the Steam-Powered Trains." At the Fillmore West in 1970 the song resembles Hendrix's "Hey Joe," with its lethargic power chords and longwinded rolls across the tom-toms. Ray Davies shouts over the din, struggling to make those beautiful words heard above his brother, who is busy kilowatting the song to death with his guitar. Horrible.

Sadly, this was the end of the road for "Big Sky." After 1972 the Kinks dropped it from their live set, never to return. Neither Ray Davies nor Dave Davies has sung it since. A pity; it is one of the Kinks'—and the pop era's—finest two minutes and fifty seconds, eternally fresh and, like the Big Sky himself, ultimately consoling and inspiring.

---

9 Davies told Jonathan Cott he would like to hear "Big Sky" intoned by the rather more messianic sounding Burt Lancaster.

Meat Is Murder

by Joe Pernice

Allison smelled like Halsa brand shampoo. It has a very distinct scent. Not the green apple or orange kind, but the brown henna kind that comes in the bottle with the Swiss mountain scene on the label. I'd say I catch a whiff of that scent on other people no less than once a month, and it never fails to shake me a little. She wore her hair in a short black bob during what was the heyday of colossal styles, and I was clobbered. At that age I learned a hairdo has magical powers.

I don't remember exactly when it happened, but sometime during that spring she got under my skin. A simple turn of her head could liberate in me a bolt of libidinous energy powerful enough to shoot my satellite from the sky. Our last names were close in spelling and we were both in the "accelerated class," as they liked to call it, so to my discomfort and delight, she always sat close by.

When she sat in front of me, I'd stare at her through the prison lattice of her chair back and try to make out the lines of her underclothes. Her blue pastel uniform blouse covered the mystery of her skin like a palimpsest. I wanted to scrape away the cheap paint and reveal the hidden pornographic landscape.

When she sat beside me, I'd gaze at her out of the corners of my eyes, straining them to the point of headache, until curlicue floaters sailed through my frame of vision. When she'd shift in her seat, so would I, but self-consciously, carefully.

I was becoming a more horrible student by the minute, and a smoker. Allison smoked like a starlet, Merit Lights, so I took it up and practiced harder than a future Olympian to impress her at "The Lung"—a benchless, concrete slab of a patio near the dumpster behind the cafeteria. On rainy mornings I'd hang out at the Lung before school and chain-smoke beneath the impotent tin awning that hung over the door, listening to a tape of *Hatful of Hollow* or *All Mod Cons* on my walkman.

I played it out in my head countless times: Allison soaking wet, pushing against me to fit beneath the awning while streams of rainwater pour down around us . . . *when she cycles by* . . . Her smokes soggy, contaminated, she says, and her lips kiss the air. I offer her one of mine . . . *there go all my dreams* . . . She holds it in her fingers like the bone of a saint. Raises it to her lips, wordless. Her eyes so giant, I look at each individually. I light her smoke . . . *is she still there or has she gone away?* . . . She smokes. She blinks. We fuck.

What I felt for her then was real and big enough to eclipse the memory of an old dead friend, and I refused to hate myself for it. Danny who? When she sat behind me, it frustrated me that I couldn't see her. It had a physically painful quality to it. I did some frantic calculations that verified what I already knew: there were not many minutes left in the semester. I'd have to work quickly and efficiently, though I wasn't really sure what that meant.

Allison knew I was alive, but that was about it, and it troubled me to no end. I wanted to stick myself with something sharp, the way a dermatologist lances a painful cyst. I wanted to loosen my own teeth for her. Instead I listened endlessly to "Reel Around the Fountain" and withdrew into the reliable and disturbing comfort of longing.

* * *

MTV was already in full swing by '85, but my family didn't have cable TV. I'd seen it a couple times at my cousin's house and was transfixed. It was intoxicating. It was numbing. And it was hot, hot, hot. But my old man said there was no way in hell he was going to pay good money to watch bad television and that was the end of that. So I pined away in my room at night with a purple black light on the job, listening to the Smiths and blowing tidy pillars of cigarette smoke into the backyard. I did my best to draw pictures of Allison, but I had—and still have—zero artistic ability.

Some nights in bed I'd fire up a transistor radio (manufactured in the shape of Popeye's head) in hopes of hearing "How Soon Is Now" and thus feeling vaguely connected to the outside world. Radio was only a few synapses away from brain dead, but they kept the poor vegetable on life support for years. Once in a great while, a station on the North Shore called Y95 would play my favorite song or "Hand in Glove" or something by the Cure or New Order.

The problem was Y95's transmitter was so weak—powered by a monkey pedaling a miniature bicycle—that its broadcast was always going in and out. It was as frustrating as anything I can remember. I'd micro tune like a madman, trying to catch a clear-sounding verse or chorus before the song ended. And if I missed the song I tried to pick up the disc jockey's back announcement. It was that important to connect. To this day, even the slightest bit of static peppering a broadcast makes me anxious.

But tweaking the Popeye transistor caused Y95's signal to vanish completely, and that of a powerful mainstream station would paint over the smaller station's bandwidth. I suffered through countless surprising flourishes of Wang Chung and Phil Collins and Van Halen and that "Total Eclipse of the Heart" song. The one about riding on the freeway of love; man, that was deplorable. Pure fucking misery.

That summer the little monkey died in a hostile corporate takeover, and Y95 went away for good.

I had a twelve-inch black-and-white TV made by a company called Admiral. If I moved the TV to the northernmost point of my bedroom and taped a disfigured wire coat hanger to the end of the antenna, and if the weather was just right then maybe, just maybe, I could pick up a grainy broadcast music video station called V68. It was like I was trying to receive secretly coded messages from the French Underground. Actually, Polish Underground is more accurate: I discovered V68 by accident one Friday night. I was twisting the VHF dial looking for a movie with lots of implicit sex, when I happened upon the video for "Minus Zero" by Lady Pank. They were driving around in a white battle tank I later found out was actually pink. I was looking at the black-and-white world.

I saw the video for "How Soon Is Now" within an hour of picking up the channel for the first time. I recognized the tremelo guitar but couldn't believe it was actually happening. The Smiths on regular TV? I felt hopeful and victorious. Anyone who watched V68 at that moment had to be watching the Smiths. It was like my world went from black-and-white to a thousand shades of gray.

For me, the Smiths were the great pasty white hope. R.E.M. ran a close second (until late '86 when they lost me), but the Brits had an emotional edge. It was like Morrissey was given the key to the city of morbid, romantic angst. He tiptoed over a suspension bridge of glass blown by Marr and Co. It was pop music and ultra-melodic, with lyrics that penetrated my quietest fears with a diamond-tipped bummer.

"Why don't you listen to something else . . . like jazz? That Smith Family is so depressing," offered my mother, simply doing her best to help, and I blamed her for it. "No wonder you don't feel like getting up," she added, leaving a basket of folded laundry inside my room without coming in. "Their poor mother and father." I rolled over on the bed so that if she had anything else to say, it would be to my back. Even as I was acting like a hateful little shit, I knew I loved her, but I could not stop myself from excluding her from my life in a hurtful way. It's endearing now, the way she thought the Smiths were a real dysfunctional family. But then I was embarrassed both for her and for myself.

"They're not related. It's just a band name, like the Dead Kennedys," I snapped (though at that time the Dead Kennedys were a band I knew by name alone), and closed the door hard in her face with my foot. "Besides, it makes me feel good."

She stood outside for a few seconds, then she sighed. I could hear her footsteps moving down the hardwood hallway until I jacked up the volume knob on the tape player. Once again, thankfully, I was alone. I took a pen and some paper from my bag and started to write Allison yet another note I would never send. I flipped the tape from front to back as I imagined her on her bed, listening to a girlfriend on the phone, with her feet against the wall.

* * *

Denise was a knockout right out of *The Last Picture Show*. She was so beautiful that she could drive a teenage boy (or a man) into a state of complete lovesick ruination from which he might never, and I mean never, recover. But Jesus H. Christ, our Lord and Salvation, took pity on me, and I felt no inklings of love for her. Instead I suffered over Allison, played bass guitar, and was trying to put a band together. In a school as small as Saint Longinus (eight hundred inmates strong), a cool tidbit—like you're in a band—travels fast. Even the rumor of possibly wanting to form a band carried with it a speck of social clout, and I took it.

Denise was already known among the student body for being not only absolutely mint, but also an artist of notable talent. Her charcoals of a windswept Bryan Adams looked real enough to earn her first prize (four free movie tickets to the of-the-moment Jeff Bridges vehicle) in the all-school art fair. Anyway, her artistic ability and my fledgling musical ambitions made us kindred spirits in the eyes of the talentless. Therefore it was okay and kind of expected of us to have short conversations or wave to each other in passing. And though it never grew beyond that, we were known as friends bound by a shared insight into "some pretty deep shit."

She was from a wealthy beach town, known as the Irish Riviera, on the South Shore of Boston that was closer to Cape Cod than to Southie or Dorchester. Her suntans lasted well into October and resurfaced by the middle of March. At the start of April, she and three of her hometown friends (a girl and two guys) killed themselves by crashing her Swedish car through a pharmacy at the sufficient speed. The paper ran a photo of the remnants of what was once a fully functioning automobile, all smashed up and twisted, jutting out of a fresh breach in the wall, blocking the sidewalk. Four o'clock in the afternoon. They died just as a syndicated episode of "Magnum P.I." lit up my tiny black-and-white TV.

A newspaper article said an employee's leg was broken by one of the victims who had been ejected from the car. They were pretty wasted (on "vocka" as they say in the suburban Boston vernacular), but there was no mistaking their intentions. They all signed a suicide note, and fixed it to the other girl's refrigerator with a souvenir magnet, probably from Sea World or Freeport, Maine. The quadruple wake had already come and gone before anyone discovered it, camouflaged by the usual refrigerator clutter accumulated by a family of six.

There was a lot of speculation among the kids at school as to the contents of the suicide note. Me, I was more interested in knowing exactly who wrote it and when and where. Did they all write a paragraph? Did they vote on the method? Were they concerned with the possibility of surviving and spending the rest of their lives crippled, unable to, among other things, have sex, wipe, or cut up their own chicken? I was still waiting for my maiden voyage on the *SS Intercourse*. At the time, suicide was not so high on my to-do list, and Denise the person faded from my consciousness like a much-hyped TV serial canceled during its first season.

"They did it because they were in a cult," or "Nobody would ever accept them for what they were, a gay/lesbian foursome." People were really saying things like that. My favorite came from this balding sixteen-year-old named Flaherty who later joined—and was subsequently asked to leave—the seminary: "They did it because of despair." No fucking shit.

Anyway, all of the talk got the higher-ups at school concerned. Monkey-see, monkey-do, and all that. Monkey-lawsuit is more like it. I was mildly sad and all, but I couldn't help thinking of Allison. Death and mourning made me want to marry her. I was alive. She was alive. Add it up.

Outlandish schemes of exodus and teenage codependency began to seem possible and worthy of goal-like status after I'd found myself alone with her in the Lung one day, during lunch period. It was a sunny afternoon following a heavy morning shower. You could still smell the rain. Allison was standing at the edge of a puddle that was as big as a black Crown Victoria. Her reflection grooved languidly, reclining on what would be the hood. I positioned myself so that I could see both of her.

The bell signaling the end of lunch had sounded. Kids scrambled for the door, flicking their heaters against the ash-blackened wall and blowing huge gulps of smoke back into the cafeteria just to piss off anyone inside who might take offense. Allison stayed behind to work on a brand-new dart. I could taste the filter burning in my mouth, but I made it last while my glances shifted quickly from the real her to the reflected her, to the real her.

"How's the band?" she asked while exhaling a long drag. It was so quiet in the Lung with everyone else gone, and her voice and cigarette smoke were one and the same. I was momentarily, for obvious reasons, breathless. Then I leaned in toward the secondhand cloud and inhaled some of her words as if they were kisses. It was all terribly romantic, at least for me.

What had been in her was now in me. I kept it there until I couldn't stand it anymore. Danny who? Denise who? And then I doubled over, coughing uncontrollably.

"Are you okay?" she asked, moving closer to me. I could see the white leather fringe on her boots approaching. I could hear the little bells on their zippers tinkle then go quiet.

"Fine," I choked. Tears streamed down my face, and clear phlegm worked its way from my nose to my saliva-wet lips. God, I loved her. I continued hacking in the silence. "I have asthma, but it's not so bad," I told her, trying to subdue the coughing fit and mopping up a medley of fluids with my shirtsleeve. I was still hunched over, my hands on my knees. She gently touched my upper back with one hand, and used the other to carefully pick the smoldering filter from my fingers.

"You might catch on fire," she said in a tone that I wanted so badly to interpret as seductive.

"I swear, I'm fine. Really." Her hand grazed my rusty corduroys just above the knee. One of her Echo and the Bunnymen pins fell from her denim jacket, and whether she noticed it or not, she made no effort to pick it up. I distracted her with an outrageously dramatic cough, and with the firm but gentle precision of a hen setting up shop on her egg, I covered the pin with my foot. It was the first time I had been touched below the waist by a female who wasn't a relative or in the medical profession. And I had the badge to commemorate it. (I still have it.) She kept her hand on my back for a minute, rubbing me lightly while my breathing evened out.

"You really shouldn't smoke," she said sympathetically, though sure of herself. I loved the complexity of her tone. The sleeve of her jacket worked its way up her arm and collected in a bunch near her elbow, exposing an orange day-glow Swatch. "Jesus, I'm fucking late for Bloody's class. She has it in for me already. Fuck, she's going to fuckin' kill me. You're sure you're okay, right?" she asked, flicking her butt and scrambling to collect her bag.

"I'm great," I assured her, which was partially true.

"See you in calc," she said anxiously and was gone. I scooped the Echo pin up off the ground of the Lung and held it in my hand for the rest of the day and for a lot of days after that. I looked at it in bed at night. I studied it. I smelled it for traces of her. I threaded it through my callused fingertips after long hours of practicing bass in my room, and pulled on it until it broke free through my bloodless skin. I scratched a small A on the inside of my right thigh and picked at it so that it wouldn't heal before she might see it.

Few things were certain in my mind, but one of them was that I had to start a band.

* * *

Death, more precisely suicide, became the hot topic with the kids. Some of the girls in school cried a lot in the hallways, and they decorated Denise's locker with all sorts of notes, flowers, stickers, and mementos until it too looked like a refrigerator door. Some genius saw the parallel and stuck a phony suicide note to the locker with chewing gum. It said something about going to the big auto body shop in the sky. (I have to admit I thought it was funny in a way, but wasn't exactly sure why.)

A Spanish teacher named Ms. (Margaret) Kirkwood took the note down without making any big deal of it. Very cool and very unlike your typical high school teacher who would have pursued it like a wolverine until someone, if not everyone, paid. Kirkwood was probably in her mid-thirties, and she knew full well we were all fucked. The guys stood around and watched her crumple the note, then looked at each other, nodding our heads up and down in accord. Yes, we agreed without speaking, Kirkwood was cool.

Later that day I was in the front row of her conversational Spanish class. She came running in a few minutes after the bell, and everyone was going berserk. Kirkwood was in no mood and took charge of the room. Her put-on disciplinarian's tone got me fantasizing about her.

As she spoke passionately about irregular verbs, I slowly looked her up and down through the sweaty headrest of my fingers—as if I needed any more unsettling stimulae. My eyes scanned her left leg bent slightly at the knee—Audrey Hepburn/*Roman Holiday* style—and stopped at her calf.

The sanitary napkin was stuck there but dangling, crimson side up. I stiffened in my seat, repulsed, nervous, and intrigued. My eyes caught Allison's, and she whispered, as loud as breathing out, "Yikes." A bulging, Marty Feldman-like quality to her expression filled me with an amusing ease. And heightened by the potential catastrophe, the significance of sharing a secret with her was not lost on me then.

But, oh, will the crossroads never end? I mused. At hand was the setup of a rare, legend-making scenario of the sort that can transform the remainder of a teacher's tenure into hell on earth. Certainly there were teachers who deserved it, but Kirkwood wasn't one of them.

McManus, the steak-faced jarhead sitting next to me, took a hard look toward the bloody mess flapping against her nylons (he could smell the blood), then straight ahead at the chalkboard. Either he had an epiphany of some kind, resulting in an act of low-level compassion, or he was just so fucking thick, he lost his grip on what had momentarily, tenuously, and miraculously occupied his mind. He made no motion for a long minute, then just slid lower in his seat and went back to the important work of drawing sombreros on the photos of people in the Spanish book.

After class, Allison hurried to the front of the room and, placing her hand on Kirkwood's forearm, whispered something in her ear.

* * *

This kid Paul wasn't really in any grade. He had cystic fibrosis and missed about eighty percent of school. Everyone said he was supposed to be a genius, though no one I knew actually knew him. Kids protected themselves from the inexplicable mindfuck that comes with knowing a dying kid by cloaking the tragic reality of Paul's condition in some kind of super-genius/loner mystery: "Yeah, I guess he's sick or something. But he's so smart he hardly ever comes to school, the lucky bastard."

When he was well enough to show up, he had a private teacher and took all of his classes in the library so he wouldn't risk overexerting himself by moving around too much. He didn't have to wear a uniform like the rest of us. He was known by little more than his disease. Already a ghost.

During a convulsive nor'easter of an asthma attack brought on by allergies from the north and bronchitis from the south, I collapsed onto—and nearly crushed—the tiny card catalogue in the pathetically underfunded library. The entire Dewey decimal system was thrown into complete chaos as the maple drawers spilled onto the carpet, and reference cards scattered like money from a blown safe.

The librarian was a deacon (in other words a priest wannabe) who resembled a comically diminutive Charles Nelson Riley. He was a horrible little Hitler of a Napoleon. He knew everyone called him Little Big Man behind his back. He also knew we sometimes covered our mouths and coughed "Little Big Man, Little Big Man" to his face. But he was bitter for other reasons that ran deep and were known only to him. And on this occasion my asthma attack was genuine.

"What did you just call me? What did you just call me? I order you to repeat what you just called me!" He was snarling. As I struggled for breath I frantically patted my pockets to locate my inhaler. But before I could grab it, Little Big Man got hold of my arm and started trying to shake some of God's good sense back into me.

"I'll teach you some respect, you moron!" he hissed, dragging me toward the door. As he pulled me through the petrified forest of furniture legs and human legs, kicking up reference cards that hadn't seen the light of day in decades, the eye of my coughing fit was passing directly overhead. I thought I was going to dry heave at his feet. Instead I threw up on his shoes, which had an instantly calming effect both of us. Outside of a groan or two from the weak of stomach, the library (which was a classroom littered—in every sense of the word—with McCarthy-era books) was quiet.

Then Paul, the kid with cystic fibrosis, started in with some wheezy, plangent, high-pitched laughter, like a castrato soloist singing through a didgeridoo. His voice had an inhumanly consistent warble to it, and the pitch of his laughter fluctuated uniformly around a stable root note, the way an electron from the tightest shell buzzes around a nucleus. And then he started to really sing. As in a song. In French. I didn't have any idea what the song was, but it was definitely French and doleful and minor in key.

By the start of the third verse I was thinking of Allison and wondering if she ever considered marrying me and having a kid instead of doing something really stupid like going to college? I pictured her, baby Simone, and myself living happily, simply, on a houseboat in Paris. Apparently, one of us has just been commissioned to paint a soon-to-be-legendary mural (it must be Allison because I don't paint). And just in the nick of time. Both scenes, the imagined and the real, got me choked up.

Little Big Man affectionately lifted his meathooks from my arm and listened as Paul's voice rallied unconventionally through a coda that he faded on naturally. You could have heard a pin drop, even on the carpet. Through the kaleidoscope of my tears I could see that Paul was crying. Then he got up, apologized to Little Big Man, and left the room for the remainder of the semester.

* * *

They herded the students, one class at a time, into the main assembly hall for a talk about suicide. They served up the pedestrian stuff about looking for signs of depression in our friends, how we should turn to God for strength in prayer, and how we shouldn't hesitate to tell a teacher or another "grown-up" if we thought someone was "not okay." Shit, I didn't know anyone who was really okay, but I wasn't talking.

Ms. Duchampe, a crunchy leftover Jesus freak from the 70s, emceed the assembly. We were just glad to be missing class. I could feel Allison somewhere close to me even before I spotted her. She was resting her ear on her hand, and I could make out the wire from a single earphone running along her fingers, vanishing into her shirtsleeve. Oh, to be that wire upon her gloved hand. Her head and shoulders swayed ever so slightly as she flexed and relaxed her thigh muscles to—I could have sworn—the rhythm of an ultra-tinny "How Soon Is Now."

The panel onstage was peopled by our principal, Father Clarey (whose talk was interrupted here and there by his own winces and audible grunts of pain, just some of the perks from a recent and tricky urological procedure), Miss Hall (the ambiguously sexual, ambiguously qualified gym/health teacher), and a phantom corpse of a nun known only as Mumbles (who was apparently the school nurse).

Duchampe was kind of hot for a hippie. She looked like an oily skinned, blond-haired version of Gloria Steinem's stunt double. She had far-reaching bad breath that was, for lack of a better word, arousing. Something was changing in me, because before that semester, I would have thought a glimpse (or sniff) of Duchampe's humanness would have been an instant attraction killer, the way an otherwise fine person's ugly laugh can disqualify them from the list of those worthy of being loved. But her terrible breath made her sexy and I was learning to go with it.

A couple of the girls in class considered Duchampe their buddy and told her she'd be gorgeous with some newer clothes, an updated hairstyle, and a little help from Miss Clairol or Maybelline. Duchampe had been to Altamont, and that meant she was open-minded. I got to sleep more than once jerking off to a fictional, innuendo-heavy rendition of a very real talking-to she'd dealt my way.

"We're going to have to do something about your tardiness, now aren't we?" In reality, it was worded quite differently, and she did not chew her eyeglasses which were textbook John Denver wire jobs, not tortoise.

"Oh, yes we are," I'd pant toward the ceiling, at the luminescent constellation of sticker stars left over from my childhood, as bare feet interrupted the lamplight that slipped in beneath my bedroom door.

For months after the suicide pep rally, my friend Ray would greet me in person with some variation of the following: "I want you to have my car. I don't need it where I'm going." To which I'd reply with as straight a face as I could keep, removing the watch from my wrist, "Here, take this. It used to mean a lot to me, but now . . . I don't know. I'd like you to have it. Something to remember me by." Then we'd laugh until we were choking and bond over references to obscure Borscht Belt comedians we knew about only because we had siblings who were much older than us. Once he telephoned to say he had just begun the lengthy self-basting process necessary to ensure a successful immolation, and that there was a large parcel of cash (unmarked, except for my name) in the trunk of his malignant Dodge Dart Swinger.

* * *

My eyes were really starting to go bad that spring, and to be honest, I was afraid to get behind the wheel of a car. Though I liked the freedom that driving represented, I was almost nineteen (an old man by American standards) when I got my license. Until then I bummed rides off of friends or slummed it on the bus.

In the mornings I'd get off at the Braintree station if it was before eight thirty and wait for Ray to cruise through the "bus only" lane as a matter of course and pick me up. Then we'd stop for take-out coffee, and we'd smoke, fantasize about girls (though I confess, I did most of the talk-ing), and listen to tapes. Ray had an eight-track player in his car with one of those converters that lets you play normal cassettes. He was a total freak for the Smiths and the Clash, and it's his fault for making me the same. Actually, he was a card-carrying Anglophile when it came to music, but the Smiths and the Clash, in that order, ruled all.

Compared to where I lived, Manchester, England, seemed exotic. I've been lucky enough to go to Manchester a few times, and compared to where I grew up, it *is* exotic. (My town has the dubious honor of produc-ing a famous hazardous waste dump and a Republican cabinet member.)

Ray and I would navigate the boring streets of middle-class suburbia, past the early-70s pre-fab storefronts that were home to tax preparers, car-pet sample outlets, independent savings banks, and insurance agents. On to the pothole-pocked side streets where the awful, vinyl-sided house con-verted to a "professional building" was king. And there were a lot of kings. At any given time, some kid was being dragged against his will into a "pro-fessional building" for his booster shot, or to have the wires on his braces tightened.

Fluorescent-lit rooms were filled with former hairdressers with pluck who now analyzed the urine of old people for a living. This was the life we were striving for? We couldn't understand how they did it, and yet they did. Thousands of them. We talked at length about there having to be anoth-er way of living, and how we'd rather die than sell out.

A tallboy of bewilderment, disgust, anxiety, and a bit of admiration did its dirty numbers inside me as we'd drive past the vibrant South Shore Blood Laboratory, or Dynamic Actuaries, Inc. Past their anemic, spare-every-expense landscaping and dog-shit brown strips of lawn. The idea of working in such a place for twenty-five years was enough to make anyone consider suicide.

And the traffic was murder. Bumper to bumper every morning and every evening. People were moving to the area in record numbers. It made no sense to any of us who were dying to get out.

"We should just blow off all this shit and drive out West . . . right now." It would take me some years to take that good advice. I had just seen *Easy Rider* for the first time. At that point both Ray and I knew his shitty car would be lucky to make Hartford. And neither of us wanted to end up in Hartford.

We'd slow down at the ranch-style house converted to a professional building where my older sister's dentist, Dr. Aranow—in his mid-thir-ties—had recently killed himself. He locked the doors and windows after the last patient left. He gassed himself silly with nitrous oxide, set the wait-ing room on fire, and blew his head off with a shotgun while seated in the dental chair.

For several months after his suicide, the house and yard were left untouched. Overgrown tufts of yellowing crabgrass dominated the yard and cracks in the walkway. Internal fire and water damage caused the scorched outer clapboards to bow and lift from their joists, leaving the house looking like a poorly constructed, failing boat.

Ray thought the back yard might be a cool place to hang out at night and drink. It was going to be summer in a matter of weeks. Drinking season. Our alcohol intake would increase in direct proportion to the temperature, peak by the middle of August, and taper off by Labor Day. Finding a reliable buyer and a safe outdoor drinking spot (and by that I mean safe from the police) were top priorities. Virtually every kid on the South Shore who has ever been drunk has been so in a field or in the woods or near the beach.

When I was eighteen, still three years shy of the legal age in Massachusetts, Ray's first cousin Caroline helped me score my first (and only) fake ID in glorious fashion. For an underage music/booze lover in suburban Boston, having a foolproof fake ID—especially one with your own picture on it—was better than having a winning Wonka Bar (probably still is).

Anyway, Caroline had a deluxe scam going, but she was smart not to overdo it and kill the golden goose. I was one of the lucky few who were brought into the inner sanctum. Caroline worked at the Registry of Motor Vehicles in Quincy, taking photos of people and fixing them to their freshly minted licenses. With a gig like that she might as well have been the First Lady of America. *Just Say No*, my ass! *Just Stay Shitfaced* was a better idea. Back then I was a staunch conservative when it came to trickle down alcoholics.

So I was instructed to show up on a Wednesday around four-thirty, get in line with a blank application, and look twenty-one. My skin had cleared up and I was shaving pretty regularly, so illegally passing for the legal age wasn't that much of a stretch. Until my twenty-first birthday I went by the name Steven Morrissey when I drank. People in-the-know called me Steve-o.

* * *

I was late for school so many times that spring they almost didn't advance me to the next grade. If I missed my connection with Ray in the mornings that meant I was really late and would have to run the remaining half a mile or so. This involved taking the life-threatening shortcut across the Route Three Overpass. Eight years earlier, a kid in my older brother's class got hit by a motorcycle there, so they tried to crack down on pedestrians. You'd get suspended for two days if school caught you. I probably ran that section of road no fewer than fifty times, and never once got caught nor killed.

One morning as I was jogging my way past the bronze plaque commemorating the deaths of one student and one motorcyclist, my necktie flapping like a windsock, Ray floored the brake pedal of his Dodge as he closed in on me. Fifty-mile-an-hour traffic came to a screeching, nearly murderous halt behind him.

He leaned over and rolled down the passenger side window in one fluid motion. He dispensed with formalities while I marveled at the audacity of his driving and, tossing something at me, he winked and said, "Here. I'm going to kill myself." He pegged the gas, leaving a surprisingly good patch of rubber for such a shitty car.

In the gutter, sugared with sand put down during the winter's last snow, I saw written in red felt ink on masking tape stuck to a smoky-clear cassette: "Smiths: Meat."

I got a lot of my music back then from Ray. I never had much money to spend on records, or anything else for that matter. I didn't even own a record player. I had my parents' old top-loading single speaker cassette player from the late 60s. So Ray would give me tapes of albums he thought were important. Tapes, but no cases, and rarely any writing on them. A band name and album title at best, and always abbreviated. It was his trademark. "Clash: Rope," "U2: Oct," "Costello: Aim." I'd break his balls and say it was his way of making me earn it, meaning I'd have to do the legwork to learn more about an album or band. Maybe it was.

Of the few store-bought cassette tapes I owned, at least half of them fell into the category of birthday present or Christmas present. Album art, liner notes, and the simple pleasure of "reading" an album while it played would remain for the most part unknown to me until I got a decent job. Until then I'd rifle through the stacks of albums at Ray's house or take the bus to Musicland in Quincy and scribble down song titles and credits.

On the rare occasion, I'd splurge for a month-old *NME* or *Melody Maker*. Which was fitting because in many ways I was always a good distance behind. Plus, it was 1985, and information oozed. The internet as we know it was probably being drawn up on a napkin somewhere.

I'd make my own J-cards with Union Jacks and pictures of bands with London Bridge or Big Ben floating in the background. I drew Hitler moustaches on assorted Reagans and Bushes. I was so green and into it, I wrote "Anarchy in the USA" on a Sex Pistols tape, and for weeks secretly thought I had coined a new phrase.

We (meaning Ray and I, with emphasis on the I) felt like we lived in the middle of nowhere, a place where a comeback radio single could make Yes or Deep Purple kings of the airwaves again. An overwhelming majority of the kids I grew up with were weaned off their mothers onto classic Styx and Stones rock blocks.

Did the small group of us who liked "faggot" British music feel like we were any better than them? Of course we did. Amen to that, brother. The following exchange illustrates the nearly religious and potentially violent musical loyalty of some of my peers:

"I think the Smiths are a much better band than Kansas."

"You better not say that up at the park on a Friday night, or you'll get your fuckin' ass kicked. What are you, a fag?"

No, I was not a fag, and thankfully "the park" was not one of my usual haunts.

Getting our hands on a new Smiths' record (and issued on a major label no less—another victory) reassured us that there was a lot more out there than the cock rock our older brothers tried to score to. Sure, we were trying to score too, but we were younger, and the Smiths were new. Youth beats tradition, like rock beats scissors, or paper covers rock.

If suicide, AIDS, or the bomb didn't get us, we'd outlive our elders and cash in on the benefits (and misfortunes) of having a greater amount of history to learn from. It gave some of us a perspective that made the rock titans of yesteryear look, well, dumb. And whether it was true or not, Morrissey sang like he was as miserable, terrified, and poorly designed as the rest of us. He captured it perfectly. We figured any teenage kid living through those Reagan years who said the Smiths were too miserable for them was either a liar, an imbecile, or so thoroughly fucked up they had no idea just how miserable they were.

Every once in a while, Ray would get his hands on an imported British bootleg, or a ten-inch maxi-single or an EP. They were—figuratively and literally—foreign to me. And much more exciting than the domestic store-bought releases. Even for an active record buyer like Ray, it was hard back then to know exactly where a recording fell in a particular band's discography, or how huge the gaps in one's collection were. Since I had mostly tapes Ray made for me, I was almost completely in the dark. My "collection" was made up of gaps.

The Piper at the Gates of Dawn
by John Cavanagh

1
The Run-in Groove

"That light you can see has taken 36 years to reach Earth," my brother told me as we looked toward Arcturus on a hot July night in 1975. I focused on the star and became mesmerized with the idea that the trajectory of this orangey-yellow glow across space had begun so long ago, or so it seemed to me as a ten-year-old.

Back inside our post-War end terrace house on the outskirts of Scotland's biggest city, Glasgow, I heard something on the radio that night which seemed as remote and otherworldly as Arcturus. To those who have grown up in the era of the CD and the easy availability of just about any sort of music from the back catalogue, I should explain something about 1975. As the glitter of glam rock became faded grandeur, 1975 was surely the year of the sharpest division between buyers of singles and buyers of albums. Novelty records, country dirges, and weak imitations of reggae music filled the Top Forty and if anyone put out an exciting single (and the likes of Be Bop Deluxe and Brian Eno tried), then the chance of it getting anywhere was approximately nil. Many "albums bands" didn't even bother to issue singles at all. I mean bands like Led Zeppelin and, of course, Pink Floyd. I already loved the Floyd's *Meddle*, one of the first half-dozen LPs I owned, but the thing I heard that night took me somewhere else entirely. Unlike anything I'd heard before, it was called "Astronomy Domine."

It was an event, a discovery. One moment I was looking at distant constellations, the next I was hearing a voice, like the sound of Apollo astronauts hailing the president from the moon, but more remote; a chugging incessant guitar; massive drums; a jagged bass riff and a song which name-checked planets and satellites, seemed to sweep the higher reaches of the infinite, then cascaded downward toward "the icy waters underground."

This was Pink Floyd? It didn't sound anything like *Dark Side of the Moon*, that was for sure. Then the DJ explained that this was from their first album, that Syd Barrett had fronted the band in those days, and that he now lived in a cellar in Cambridge.

With my vivid imagination, I was off and running. He wasn't out in LA making dull AOR music and he wasn't a dead rock star, like Jimi Hendrix. He'd named this first Floyd album after a chapter in *The Wind in the Willows* by Kenneth Grahame (a favorite of mine!) and now he lived in an underground lair. Was he rock's answer to Mr. Badger, who lived right in the heart of the woods and preferred to see others before he was seen? This Syd Barrett was clearly unique and someone I wanted to know more about. The next day, I looked at the rack of Floyd LPs in Listen Records (the sort of shop where a picture of Zappa appeared on their carrier bags under the slogan FRANKLY CHEAPER!) and found *The Piper at the Gates of Dawn*. It was full price and I noticed that the more affordable *Relics* compilation album had "See Emily Play" on it. That would do to start.

Relics, "a bizarre collection of antiques and curios," boasted a couple of amazing tracks from Pink Floyd's debut album: "Interstellar Overdrive" and "Bike." Once I got into those, I had further incentive to own a copy of *Piper*. I'm quite sure that these sounds would have impacted on my world whenever I found them, but there was something about the arid musical landscape of the mid-70s which made them even more poignant. *Piper* has served as a form of musical escapism for many people across time, and an escape from 1975 was most welcome to me.

In time I learned more about Syd Barrett and realized that his journey back to a life in Cambridge had been a harrowing one. The stories of Syd's difficult latter days with Pink Floyd, his lifestyle, and his solo albums have been told and retold, sometimes with due regard for accuracy and sympathy for the subject and, sadly, on other occasions where the urge to print a spicy story overrides any other consideration. I am not a journalist.

This fact was helpful when approaching those who had been stitched up by hungry hacks many times before, people like Duggie Fields, who still lives in a flat he once shared with Syd—his workspace as an artist is the room which features on the sleeve of *The Madcap Laughs*. Over thirty years after Barrett left that address, Duggie still finds unexpected callers on his doorstep, people who are searching for . . . what? A rock 'n' roll myth or a man called Roger Barrett who has had nothing to do with the music industry for many years?

The Piper at the Gates of Dawn is a wondrous creation often seen through the distorted view of later events. These things have served to overshadow the achievement of the Pink Floyd on their debut album; an outstanding group performance; a milestone in record production; and something made in much happier circumstances than I had expected to find.

When I was, let's say, fourteen, I imagined myself going to Cambridge, meeting Mr. Barrett, and becoming his friend. Of course, like many fans who had similar notions, I never did and wouldn't entertain the idea of disturbing him now. . . . I'll leave that sort of crassness to the journalists who still bang on his door and snoop a photograph of him at the local shops or a view through his front window.

This is *not* another book about "mad Syd." This, instead, is a celebration of a moment when everything seemed possible, when creative worlds and forces converged, when an album spoke with an entirely new voice. "Such music I never dreamed of," as Rat said to Mole.

* * *

"We didn't start out trying to get anything new, it just entirely happened. We originally started as an R & B group," Roger Waters told a reporter from the Canadian Broadcasting Corporation (CBC), around the turn of the year 1966–67. Syd Barrett continued, "Sometimes we just let loose a bit and started hitting the guitar a bit harder and not worrying quite so much about the chords . . . " Roger: "It stopped being sort of third rate academic rock and started being intuitive groove." Syd: "It's free-form."

By that time, Roger Keith "Syd" Barrett, Nicholas Berkeley Mason (known as "Nicky" at the time), George Roger Waters, and Richard William Wright were only weeks away from signing a record deal with EMI and had rapidly built up a fan base for their live shows where improvised sound and light melded together. According to the (sadly nameless) girl who compiled the CBC feature, they had "stupefied audiences . . . [with] an array of equipment sadistically designed to shatter the strongest nerves. . . . " She pondered, "Is this the music destined to replace the Beatles? Are the melodic harmonies, poetic lyrics and soulful rhythms of today to be swept into the archives, totally undermined by a psychotic sweep of sound and visions such as this? Large pockets of enthusiasts from all over the country are determined that it shall, despite the powerful opposition of the majority of leading disc jockeys." On hearing this remarkable piece of prose, Canadian radio listeners could easily have been forgiven for thinking that Pink Floyd were causing anarchy on British streets, although listening now I ask myself why these powerful DJs would be so opposed to a band who had, as our trusty reporter says, "yet to make their debut on records"?

What the Pink Floyd were doing live was a unique evolution for a band who had started playing R&B covers. Two songs recorded in 1965 and widely circulated among Floyd fans illustrate their early sound with lead guitarist Bob Klose. "Lucy Leave" is an original composition, with a strong vocal by Syd Barrett; the other title is the old Slim Harpo number "I'm a King Bee," which the Rolling Stones covered. Bob appeared on *Crazy Diamond*, a BBC TV documentary devoted to Syd Barrett in 2001 and recalled:

"You heard the early things, you thought maybe it's the Stones . . . and you recognize Syd's voice, but it's not Pink Floyd sound yet. It needed me to leave to do that. You know, that was quite an important step."

With Bob Klose off the scene (and pursuing a career as a photographer) Pink Floyd gradually moved away from jamming on "Louie Louie" to create highly original new sounds. David Gale had grown up with Syd Barrett and Roger Waters in Cambridge: "I was present in Syd's bedroom in Hills Road, before we moved up to London, when he produced a Zippo lighter that he may well have got off an American serviceman and began running it up and down the neck of his guitar and saying, "What do you think of that?" He was not playing as if it were a bottleneck. In Cambridge people were already taking LSD in the nexus that circulated around Storm Thorgerson's house and Syd was among the people doing that. It may be that that made him impatient with doing Chuck Berry and Bo Diddley covers and made him experiment with other ways of getting sounds out of an electric guitar. He had two areas in which he could be experimental: guitar playing and painting. His painting had certain affinities with the pop art that Jim Dine was doing in the States, cloth appliquéd to canvas and heavily treated with oil paint."

Pink Floyd played at four events, a series of happenings called The Spontaneous Underground, held at the Marquee Club on Sunday afternoons between late February and early April 1966. John "Hoppy" Hopkins, photographer and key figure in the emergent counterculture, had his first experience of the band at one of these shows: "A lot of people who were around at that time were open to new or experimental sounds, pictures and movies, whatever was going down. They had a light show of sorts and the combination of that and the sound they were making really was very exciting. They were playing sheets of sound, sometimes similar to the way that AMM were treating the boundary between sound and music."

AMM were—and remain—a particularly innovative improv group with a floating lineup. Their first album, *AMMUSIC* 1966, was made by DNA, a small production company which involved both Hoppy and the man who was about to become Pink Floyd's comanager, Peter Jenner (in partnership with his friend Andrew King). AMM took their cue from artists like Marcel Duchamp and the Dada movement, dispensing with conventional ideas of technique. Even today, guitarist Keith Rowe neither rehearses nor tunes his guitar, preferring to apply different objects to the pickups and strings and use it as a sound generator.

Duchamp and Dada aside, it seems Pink Floyd's transformation had more practical roots. Bob Klose had been, in conventional terms, the most skilled musician in the lineup. Without him it was difficult to achieve a good standard repertoire for live shows. Better R&B bands were in abundance, so the competition was hot. Storm Thorgerson was one of the

Cambridge boys who moved to London to study art. He told me: "When they were playing at the Marquee, they were booked in for longer than they had a set. In order to get paid properly, they had to play longer. They extended their songs in a rambling kind of fashion and it turned out very popular and got more people! They stopped doing blues and Syd was instrumental, literally, in turning them around."

John Whiteley, a former Buckingham Palace guardsman, was living at the same address as Syd in late 1966: "We went to see them at the Hornsey Art School and I'd expected a really super together band, but Syd was on stage shouting the chords to play to the other guys!" In July 1967, Peter Jenner talked to *Disc* and *Music Echo* magazines about the way Pink Floyd had arrived at their style: "My guess is that this was not even intentional. They are a lazy bunch and could never be bothered to practice, so they probably had to improvise to get away with it." Reflecting on their evolving style, Hoppy said, "I was trying to figure out what the pathways were and one of the key people in that was Joe Boyd. Joe was their first producer, he also produced the Incredible String Band and the recording that we made of AMM. The people in the Floyd were part of the receptive participant audience for everything else that was going on, as we were to them. John Cage had come over round about that time and he had a show at the Saddle Theatre in Shaftesbury Avenue. Cage used silence as much as he used sound and we were all up for it, ready and excited, the place was full. The general context of people being ready for it, by some magical confluence of energies is what a lot of that rests on: all the cross-influences." Peter Jenner: "I think that things like AMM had an influence and, just generally, improvised music, whether it was jazz or whatever, but in songwriting, the influence was much more pop songs." Anna Murray was a close friend of Syd's. She says: "We were listening to the Beatles, Doors, Bob Dylan and then a lot of blues and jazz . . . Miles Davis, Thelonious Monk, Charlie Parker. . . . "

"The next time I saw them, after Spontaneous Underground," says Hoppy, "was in Notting Hill. We called ourselves the London Free School. For my sins, I was the person paying for the printing of the newsletter and we were so disorganised that I was getting more and more in debt. I decided to hold a benefit at the local church hall [All Saints, Powis Gardens]. One of the bands that played was the Floyd and a few people turned up. The following week, the Floyd played again and a few more people turned up and by the third week it was quite obvious that we were sitting on some kind of tinderbox, because the queues were round the block! I have a muted memory of some sort of pleasure to do with having solved my financial problems, so the benefit was successful." Pink Floyd played ten London Free School shows between the end of September and late November 1966. Duggie Fields attended these events: "A group of friends was their audience first, then suddenly they got an enormous following within a very short space of time, shorter than it took for the Rolling Stones to happen."

Contemporary recordings of Pink Floyd speaking about their music are very rare, but they described their approach in that CBC interview. First, Syd: "In terms of construction, it's almost like jazz where you start off with a riff and then you improvise on that . . . " Roger cut in: "Where it differs from jazz is that if you're improvising around a jazz number and it's a sixteen bar number, you stick to sixteen bar choruses, you take sixteen bar solos, whereas with us, it starts and we may play three choruses of something that lasts for seventeen and a half bars each chorus and then it'll start happening and it'll stop happening when it stops happening and it may be four hundred and twenty three bars later, or it may be four!"

A set list from a Free School event on October 14, 1966 closed with "Astronomy Domine" and also included "The Gnome," "Interstellar Overdrive," "Stethoscope," "Matilda Mother," and "Pow R Toc H," six of the eleven titles which would end up on *The Piper at the Gates of Dawn*. "Lucy Leave" was still there; a couple of Bo Diddley numbers were the only nonoriginal material played that night.

Writer Jenny Fabian's impression of the live Floyd experience was intense: "The first time they had less impact on me than later on, when I was on acid. It was at All Saints Hall and it was just—wow!—they're really weird and quite interesting looking." As the Free School events got busier, Hoppy knew it was time to step up a gear: "Joe Boyd said to me, 'If I can find a venue, why don't we take this West and run a club?' which was how UFO started and, of course, the first people to play there were the Pink Floyd." The opening night of UFO (pronounced "U-Fo" by the cognoscente) was two days before Christmas 1966 in the basement ballroom of the Blarney, an Irish pub on Tottenham Court Road. Jenny Fabian recalls: "The UFO things are imprinted forever on my consciousness. Kaftans, blobs . . . wonderful! You couldn't have asked for anything better than to be out of your head at UFO." Fittingly, for a club in an old ballroom, the audience was no longer static, as Duggie Fields remembers: "The first person I ever saw dancing to them was at All Saints Hall. All the projections and all the visuals were going on and everyone was laid back, except for one person who was dancing on his own and he was amazing! At UFO people would dance, that was just evolution." As Syd Barrett told the CBC reporter, "We play for people to dance to . . . they don't seem to dance much now, but that's the initial idea. So we play loudly and we're playing with electric guitars, so we're utilising all the volume and all the effects you can get." Roger Waters added: "But now we're trying to develop this by using the light." Jenny Fabian: "They did play music for our kind of dancing that was evolving. There was a very heavy rhythm thudding away, with these cosmic bleeps on top and then it would go off into something. If you're on acid, you just drift in that bit of music and gradually the rhythm seeps from underneath and you're taken over by the rhythm and it really used to enter into our bodies. Everybody danced, obviously plenty were flat on the floor! There were people floating around to it and people bopping to it quite nicely. I could do anything to their music."

The handful of UFO events crystallised a scene of cross-culture creativity, where Pink Floyd would appear with the Soft Machine, Marilyn Monroe films, or AMM. Aside from UFO, the club circuit was vibrant: a look at Pink Floyd's live schedule from early 1967 finds them appearing, variously, with Cream, the Who, Alexis Korner, belly dancers, and . . . Tuppence the TV Dancer. In addition to music, the incursion of Beat writers meant that Pink Floyd might share a bill with, for example, the Scottish poet Alex Trocchi. This movement was propelled by a poetry event at the Albert Hall in 1965 (more of which later) and the efforts of people like Hoppy and Barry Miles to put more free thoughts into print. Jenny Fabian: "It was quite a London scene of underground thoughts and hedonism. People say now that it was a time when we were having all these thoughts of peace and love, but there was anarchy involved as well. The Floyd just fed that for us. They were opening the doors of musical perception and we felt they belonged to us. There were other people . . . there was Dylan, but he was far away and sort of God-like, the Beatles had evolved, but they didn't play live. So the Floyd were like our local consciousness come to life. It was as though they'd always been there . . . poets from the cosmos."

The Pink Floyd had gathered so much momentum with their live show that interest from record companies was inevitable. Both the band and their managers were fans of artists on the American label Elektra, founded in the 1950s by folk enthusiast and recording pioneer Jac Holzman, which had lately branched out from its New York HQ to sign some of the most exciting acts emerging on the West Coast. Peter Jenner: "We did audition for Jac Holzman, who turned us down. We did a showcase in the afternoon at the Marquee and he wasn't impressed. He did come more from a folky thing and I think it was a bit too loud and weird. If you think about the people he had—Arthur Lee and Love, proper songs and things, and the Doors were a band he would've found easier to relate to, whereas he had trouble later with the Stooges and the MC5 when David Anderle signed them. He couldn't quite handle that stuff. But we gave him all the waffle. He got the full ten minute rambles! I'm sure he thought, 'I'll never get this band on radio in America'—and we were probably out of tune."

Joe Boyd had worked for Elektra, branching out to form Witchseason Productions, which licensed his recordings of the Incredible String Band to Holzman's label. He hoped to sign the Floyd to Witchseason and was lining up a deal for releasing their music through Polydor. Meanwhile,

Andrew King and Peter Jenner were shopping for an agent. "Richard Armitage was a big mainstream agent in Denmark Street and the people in his office wore morning suits," Andrew said. "Then round the corner at 142 Charing Cross Road was Bryan Morrison with Steve O'Rourke and Tony Howard. He was booking the Pretty Things and all the bands that played at the Speakeasy, it was just groovier and the main reason for signing with Morrison was that he only wanted ten percent commission and Armitage wanted to take fifteen percent."

The Floyd didn't demo for EMI. Instead, they arrived with finished masters of two tracks which would form their first single. Joe Boyd produced these with engineer John Wood at his favored studio, Sound Techniques, and it says a great deal for Boyd that he had anything to do with this session at all. With the realization that he was losing the band, coupled with the knowledge that EMI had a strict policy regarding the use of "in-house" producers, he was creating a sweetener for a deal which was about to cut him out of the picture. Peter Jenner: "I was talking recently with Joe and I'd forgotten, but we completely stitched him up and fucked him off terribly. Apparently, the deal was all ready to go with Polydor and we backed away from it when EMI came in with a better deal with more money and better points. Polydor was, at that stage, a very new thing and we were advised by Bryan Morrison that we should go with EMI because of their distribution, they were much stronger in the market."

"More money" meant £5,000. When a decent wage in the UK was still less than £20 per week and £2,000 a year was a dream for most, it seemed a lot. The naïve Jenner and King were soon to find otherwise when they bought some new kit for the band. A Binson echo unit cost nearly £180 alone and, as these were the main effects used on both Syd's guitar and Rick's Farfisa Compact Duo organ, it didn't take long for the bill to add up to £2,000.

There was another reason for signing to EMI—perhaps the most important for the band: it was the home of the Beatles. "Wow, man!" says Peter Jenner. "You looked up the stairs at where the Beatles had their photo taken and then you went to Abbey Road where the Beatles were recording. Technical people wore brown coats, you had tea brought to you, one felt one was in a big family. It was a very comforting, institutional place. Altogether EMI was very reassuring, down to the commissionaires in uniform on the door, both at Manchester Square and Abbey Road. It was a bit like going to the BBC. There was Beecher Stevens, who signed the deal and then Norman [Smith] was our link with everything and subsequently, when records came out, we were involved with Roy Featherstone and, to some extent, Ron White and Ken East. We never, ever met [EMI chairman] Sir Joseph Lockwood. One *heard* Sir Joseph!"

* * *

Arnold Layne
Had a strange hobby
Collecting clothes
Moonshine washing line
They suit him fine!

The practice of hyping new artists onto the charts has been around as long as there have been charts. A shady area, yes, but commonplace. Even Jimi Hendrix's first single had a little "assistance" to help it on the way. In the mid-60s the BBC's monopoly on radio in the UK was challenged by off-shore pirate ships, which operated for a prosperous couple of years until a legal loophole was closed. While the BBC made small concessions to the beat group boom with a couple of (admittedly excellent) shows, "Pick of the Pops" and "Saturday Club," the pirates offered a constant stream of fresh pop sounds and made the BBC's "Light Programme" service sound very dated. Radio London pirate DJ Kenny Everett coined the word "Beeb" and portrayed the BBC as a stuffy maiden aunt and yet, while the BBC played Pink Floyd's song about a clothes fetishist, Radio London refused. "We spent a couple of hundred quid, which was quite a lot of money in those days," said Andrew King, "trying to buy it into the charts. The management did that, not EMI. It was the pirates that banned us. They were in the process of trying to get licenses and proving that they were respectable, so they were trying to be more 'Auntie Beeb-ish' than the Beeb. At the time I couldn't believe it. We were all reading William Burroughs and the idea that 'Arnold Layne' was naughty was weird to us!"

"Arnold Layne" b/w "Candy and a Currant Bun" was a commercial breakthrough for Joe Boyd. It was also his last recording with Pink Floyd. Boyd's greatest skill as a producer lies in his ability to create an atmosphere which has allowed talents as diverse as Nick Drake, John Martyn, and Vashti Bunyan to shine in the studio. His partnership with the outstanding engineer John Wood has endured and brought awards for their recent work with Toumani Diabate, but Peter Jenner is philosophical when he compares Boyd to the producer Pink Floyd were assigned by EMI, Norman Smith: "Syd did essentially write standard pop song structures, but then live they would improvise these long instrumental breaks. When Norman got hold of them, he thought this ain't gonna work and I don't think anybody minded because they all—especially Syd—listened to pop music. Live, they were all like 'Interstellar Overdrive.' Norman heard the songs and he made sure the songs came through. Joe would've had much more difficulty, I suspect, in getting them to chop the songs down in the studio, because he probably had much more of the status of a mate. I think Norman had that status of being the man from EMI, the man who'd worked with the Beatles, the guy who really knew what was going on. Joe had a lot of that, relatively, compared to us, but we instinctively felt he was one of us, whereas Norman was a real pro. He really knew what a hit record was."

* * *

My early memory of Norman, sorry, "Hurricane," Smith is of him having hit records (like "Don't Let It Die" in July 1971) rather than producing them. With bright floral shirts and a big moustache he looked to me like TV detective Jason King, as played by Peter Wyngarde, when I saw him on "Top of the Pops." In the teenybop era of the Osmonds, Smith was an unlikely figure for chart success, but in his mid-late forties he enjoyed Top Five hits with annoyingly catchy songs and a rasping style, the vocal equivalent of Earl Bostic's saxophone playing. Peter Jenner had him marked out as "pretty groovy in an older way! He was a dapper dresser."

To get into EMI Studios as a recording assistant in 1959, Norman Smith had to shave six years off his age. Luckily his claim to be 28 (the age ceiling) was not challenged and he was one of a trio to be taken on from a pool of around two hundred who had applied. His previous studio experience, allied to his ability as a player of brass, piano, and drums, carried him through to a world where strict guidelines governed the way records were made. Studios were places where "as live" performances were captured on tape. The idea of using any form of experimental recording technique was alien to most producers, as maverick engineer Joe Meek discovered. When he broke free of these formal constraints and created the unique sound world of "Telstar," a global number one hit written and recorded in a small London flat, the industry was rattled.

The arrival of another force was about to change the rules completely and Norman Smith was with it from the beginning. Jeff Jarratt, who began working at EMI in autumn 1966 (and was tape op. on most of the *Piper* sessions), explains: "Norman was the engineer on Beatles recordings from when they first started at Abbey Road. He did their audition and followed through, working with them for several albums. He was well versed in the sort of lateral thinking one had to have if you were working with the Beatles. They would always be coming up with new ideas. In their own way, the Floyd had that same thirst for trying to do things which were a little different from anything going on at the time: he was the right person to have around, to be open-minded about how you could rethink the normal recording process." Peter Jenner: "We were the first pop band that EMI signed to an album deal. That was part of the thing we were holding out for, because we wanted to do our long rambles, we wanted to be free, man! We didn't want to be held down, man! But I think Norman quietly and craftily got them to record a pop album." Andrew King: "He was not at all conservative; he never said 'You can't do that because that's not the way we do things.' Norman did it with a very light hand. [He] didn't tell them how they had to do it. They'd say what they wanted to do and he enabled them to do what they wanted."

Norman Smith chooses not to discuss his work with Pink Floyd these days, which is a great pity as his early involvement with the band has suffered some revisionism, becoming tarnished by events farther down the line. When I started on this book, I viewed Smith as a jazz snob, someone who was not in tune with the band. I imagined that *Piper* was good in spite of him. An oft-quoted line from a 1973 edition of *ZigZag* magazine fuelled this perception: Roger Waters described "Apples and Oranges" (a single from late 1967) as "a fucking good song . . . destroyed by the production." My impression was quite clearly wrong. Peter Jenner offered his perspective: "It all became more fraught later on, after 'See Emily Play.' From there on in the pressure built up. . . . We need another hit, Syd, we need a new single and then when Syd had gone it all became much, much more difficult. I recall *Piper at the Gates of Dawn* being really exciting and fun. Hard work, but positive. I can't remember people storming out. Being uptight or worried was definitely something which came subsequently."

Waters wasn't the only one with a few sharp words. Smith talked about his career to *Studio Sound* magazine for its May 1998 issue: "I can't in all honesty say that the music meant anything at all to me. In fact, I could barely call it music, given my background as a jazz musician and the musical experience that I'd had with the Beatles. After all, with the Beatles we're talking about something really melodic, whereas with Pink Floyd, bless them, I can't really say the same thing for the majority of their material. A mood creation through sound is the best way that I could describe the Floyd. . . . Nevertheless, we got along as well as anybody could with Syd Barrett. He really was in control. He was the only one doing any writing, he was the only one who I, as a producer, had to convince if I had any ideas, but the trouble with Syd was that he would agree with almost everything I said and then go back in and do exactly the same bloody thing again. I was really getting nowhere."

While that's certainly true of later sessions, it was not the case with the *Piper* recordings. Jeff Jarratt: "When I was asked to do the album, I went down to see them at the Regent Polytechnic, to know what it was all about before we started working and their performance onstage was quite fantastic. It was literally just a matter of capturing that when they came into the studio. Sure, they would do a few takes, but that's normal. They were extremely efficient. Most of what you hear on that album was done on the basic recording. Obviously, there would be some overdubs." The session sheets for all the early Floyd work with Norman Smith were unearthed by David Parker for his book *Random Precision* and the facts are clear: two songs on *Piper* needed only a single take to achieve a master recording.

Jeff Jarratt's credits range from the Beatles to Barbra Streisand. He describes Norman Smith as "absolutely fantastic. Nobody knew how the studio worked better than him . . . one of the best people I've ever worked with." In an internet interview with Richie Unterberger, Phil May of the Pretty Things said, "If there hadn't been Norman Smith, the Floyd wouldn't have been able to develop what they were trying to do. There was nobody with ears like Norman." Nick Mason put the situation in context: "Our split with Norman came further down the line when it became apparent that he would've liked to have stuck with what one might call the classic pop music style and length and so on. Norman felt, very strongly, that that's how records should be made. I think he was less interested in the ramblings of the band. To some extent history proved him wrong, but at the time it was the recordings that gave us some popularity. We were popular at the UFO and the few underground clubs, but basically our long improvisations didn't work that well when we went up to the north, or indeed further east or west. He was a lovely man and I was very fond of him. We, more or less, managed to part as friends rather than any other way, which is nice."

The other key member of the production team was the late Peter Bown. "He started off as a classical engineer," said Jeff Jarratt, "but he crossed over all the different genres that came into the studio. His personality was such that he lived for recording and was a fun person to be around." Andrew King recalled: "He said the faders were wearing out the ends of his fingers and he'd sit at the desk painting the ends of his fingers with this little pot of plastic skin which you'd put on sores and cracks." Ken Townsend, fondly remembered for his time as manager of Abbey Road, says Peter had a crew-cut hairstyle and "nearly married [50s singing star] Ruby Murray, but his mother didn't approve, then he went a bit 'the other way' later on." The straight side of Mr. Bown wasn't obvious to Peter Jenner: "He was as bent as a nine bob note! So quite florid, but he was sweet and very supportive. I think he liked the band and would help them along, but every now and then the eyebrows would raise—'Oh my God, what are they doing now?' sort of thing. He helped hold the sound together. It was a good team."

While it was alright for Syd Barrett to kick off his shoes in EMI studio 3, it wasn't so free and easy for employees like Jeff Jarratt: "Technical chaps always wore white coats on sessions and engineers had to wear ties, which was pretty silly. I got sent home one day for not wearing a tie!" Nick Mason recalled the session structure: "They were fairly formalised, EMI had specific three hour sessions, nine until twelve or two until five. We might do two sessions in a day, or go from afternoon to evening and the evening ones would run late, but it wouldn't be unheard of for us to be out of there at five to make way for someone else." Jeff Jarratt: "The amazing thing about working at Abbey Road was that, in the morning, you could be working with Sir Adrian Boult, Sir John Barbirolli or Otto Klemperer and then Victor Sylvester and his ballroom band in the afternoon and in the evening you could be doing the Beatles or the Pink Floyd. We used to finish at three or four in the morning and you could be back in there at a quarter to ten for a session the next morning and I did this seven days a week for several years!"

It's often assumed that the Beatles were the first artists to record through the night and that late sessions were a bonanza for producers and engineers. Ken Townsend clarified that point: "The very first person to work late night was Adam Faith. I did midnight to three AM sessions with him in 1958–59 when John Barry was the musical director. The Musicians Union specified an excessive payment if you worked beyond, say, ten o'clock at night [for artists]. Nothing to do with studio staff: they got flat rate."

Abba Gold

by Elisabeth Vincentelli

1992: The World Is Ready for Abba . . . Again

Between 1973 and 1982, Abba sold millions of albums globally. However, it took only ten years to bury that impeccable track record and by the early 1990s the band's above-ground legacy endured mostly in bargain bins. The Swedish quartet had become a victim of its own success: it incarnated a dated decade, a dated look, and a dated type of pop. The music world had moved on, and Abba had been left behind. It didn't help that none of its four members had kept a high media profile: Benny Andersson and Björn Ulvaeus, the men who wrote Abba's songs, were focusing on musical theater; after releasing middlingly successful solo albums in the early and mid-80s, singers Agnetha Fältskog and Anni-Frid "Frida" Lyngstad had progressively abandoned the music scene. Both couples—Benny and Frida, Björn and Agnetha—had divorced and it felt as if they all had lost interest in preserving their band's legacy. "We have little in common and it's seldom that we meet," Agnetha said in 1985. It was hard to fathom that, just ten years before, their faces had adorned mugs and socks from Melbourne to Manchester.

By now, the saga of the little Swedish band that could has become a fairly well-known chapter in pop history; still, certain elements bear repeating. While many think that the band exploded out of nowhere in 1974, when its song "Waterloo" won the Eurovision Song Contest, the four musicians who made up Abba already had quite a rich past in their home country. In the 60s, Björn was a member of a popular folk outfit, the Hootenanny Singers, while Benny was in the Hep Stars, a Beatles-influenced pop combo that was the biggest Swedish group at the time. Both groups toured relentlessly and built up extensive stage experience from the very beginning. Indeed, Benny and Björn had met when their respective bands crossed paths on the Swedish *Folkpark* circuit in 1966. The two hit it off immediately and started collaborating, playing on each others' records and writing songs together. At roughly the same time, in 1967, Agnetha and Frida were (separately) doing the rounds of Swedish cabarets and talent contests; both started cutting singles in the late 60s, though Agnetha met with more success than Frida, who plied her trade on small-town stages with small-town bands. The two couples were formed in 1969, and immediately established relationships in which the romantic and the professional were intricately interwoven. After several false starts, Abba was chosen to represent Sweden at the 1974 Eurovision Song Contest. Its song, "Waterloo," won and became a European hit: it topped the charts in the UK, Belgium, Finland, Ireland, West Germany, and Switzerland. More surprisingly, it reached number six in the United States, a country in which awareness of the Eurovision extravaganza hovers somewhere between nil and zilch. With the help of manager and label head Stig Anderson (who also contributed lyrics to many early songs), Abba became a habitual presence on European television screens, radios, and magazine covers all through the 70s. The group's reach extended to Australia, where a 1977 tour provoked astonishing scenes of hysteria, and Latin America, where Spanish versions of some of the songs helped open the market.

During the years framed by its 1974 victory and its last studio recording in 1982, Abba was a worldwide superstar band, selling records by the truckload and scoring dozens of number one hits in as many countries. It managed to have ten Top Twenty singles in America, and that's one of the countries where the group was the least popular: the quartet scored almost twenty Top Ten singles in the UK, for instance. In addition to records, Abba was pervasive enough to be plastered over T-shirts, lunchboxes, and trading cards; famous enough to have its own mockumentary, 1977's *Abba—The Movie*; and infamous enough to embody the excessively gaudy side of the 70s.

And yet all these achievements had gradually receded from public consciousness in the decade following the band's demise (it never officially broke up). As Carl Magnus Palm put it, with a certain sense of understatement, "When the eighties were over, it was clear that none of the former Abba members had any relevance whatsoever in the international pop landscape." The release of 1986's *Abba Live* (which included material from 1977, 1979, and 1981) felt like a frustrating afterthought and marked the nadir of the group's story: the album spent a couple of weeks in the Swedish Top Fifty, and it wasn't even released in some of the countries in which the band had previously been successful. While it did cover most of the group's phases, *Abba Live* didn't present it at its best—let's just say there was a reason Abba, like all good pop bands, had studiously avoided guitar solos on its studio efforts.

At the same time, the music world had evolved in a direction that didn't leave much space for hit-making Swedes perceived to tread the thin line between wholesome and campy. Punk had become a force to be reckoned with in 1977; electronic music was growing in leaps and bounds thanks to the development of house and techno; hip-hop came into its own, eclipsing pop—and, to a lesser degree, mainstream rock, which went through a slump only to be electroshocked back to life in 1992, when Nirvana's *Nevermind* hit full force. That album sent a tremor through popular music, redefining indie and mainstream rock—and their connection with each other—for the following decade. *Nevermind*'s impact was global, despite Kurt Cobain's reluctant relationship with fame and its trappings, an ambivalence partly explained by what he believed to be an irreconcilable difference between artistic and commercial successes. Yet Cobain was an avowed admirer of Abba, a group that bridged the gap between art and commerce with ease; he even asked for a goofy (and fairly successful) Abba cover band called Björn Again to open for Nirvana at the Reading Festival in 1992.

But if 1992 was Nirvana's year, it also witnessed the eruption of a worldwide phenomenon that would redraw the pop landscape as much as the Seattle grunge band had redrawn the rock one. Forerunning signs could be glimpsed as early as 1987, when the Justified Ancients of Mu Mu—aka English quasi-situationist pranksters the KLF—sampled large chunks of a nine-year-old Abba hit called "Dancing Queen" for a track titled "The Queen and I"; Abba's publishers suggested the JAMM destroy all copies of the album, elegantly titled *1987 What the Fuck's Going On?* A couple of years later, the aforementioned Björn Again performed its first show in Melbourne in May 1989; by the time it was a guest of Cobain's at Reading, the band was selling out club dates around the globe.

In the summer of 1992, U2 included a cover of "Dancing Queen" in the set of its Zoo Tour (at the time, the peak of the Irish group's half-ironic, half-earnest exploration of pop tropes). To top it all off, U2 was joined on stage by Benny and Björn when it performed the song in Stockholm in July. But the most significant indicator of what was to come was the release of Erasure's *Abba-esque* EP in June. Erasure had toyed with the idea of doing an entire album of Abba songs but because time was at a premium (the group was in production rehearsals for its Phantasmagorical Entertainment Tour), it only covered four: "Lay All Your Love on Me," "SOS," "Take a Chance on Me," and "Voulez-Vous." The British synth-pop duo had been around since 1986, winning critical praise and a fair amount of sales, but it wasn't until *Abba-esque* that it topped the UK charts. In addition to going to number one in England, *Abba-esque* also did surprisingly well in the US, the one country in which the Swedes had struggled to establish a solid foothold. The EP reached the *Billboard* Top 100, which doesn't seem that impressive now but at the time was quite an accomplishment for a British electro-pop band fronted by an openly gay singer.

Erasure wasn't new to Abba, having already tested the waters by putting a cover of "Gimme! Gimme! Gimme! (A Man After Midnight)" on the B side of "Oh L'Amour" in the spring of 1986. The duo was the perfect mongrel act to help usher in the Abba renaissance: po-faced synth master and composer Vince Clark had been in an early incarnation of Depeche Mode and in the short-lived Yazoo, while the adjectives used to describe singer Andy Bell never failed to include "flamboyant" (he describes playing Frida in the "Take a Chance on Me" video as "a particular highlight" of his life). The combination was a knowing, liberated mirror of the division of labor adopted by the Swedish quartet itself. Erasure was signed to Mute Records, home to the dark side of synth-pop and an unlikely but oddly fitting place to release a tribute to a 70s pop band. Erasure's success was the biggest clue that Abba's popularity had not evaporated in the 80s, but simply gone underground.

As if this weren't enough, in October of 1992 Björn Again put out a single titled Erasure-ish ("A Little Respect" b/w "Stop"). If Erasure put a face on Abba's gay following, Björn Again examplified one of the main elements that would mark the Swedish group's revival: from the very beginning, Björn Again teetered between homage and parody. Always in character on stage, its four leads—Agnetha Falstart, Frida Longstokin, Björn Volvo—us and Benny Anderwear—performed sets made up exclusively of Abba material, complete with Abba-inspired costume, choreography, and groan-inducing stage banter in caricatural Swedish accents. But the humor didn't completely obscure the affection and faithfulness with which the Abba catalog was performed, and Björn Again, for better or for worse, paved the way for what would become a cottage industry of Abba tribute bands.

The combination of these factors suggested that the Abba momentum was increasing throughout 1992. The band's "heritage" produced the tidy sum of $4 million a year in publishing and mechanical income. The back catalog had remained a steady seller, even while its members had mostly deserted the pop field: in addition to Erasure, off-the-wall projects flourished and even an album in which Abba's material was performed by the Munich Symphony Orchestra managed to sell 130,000 copies. Still, the attention of the group members was focused somewhere else. Björn and Benny's musical theater career was taking off (their first effort, *Chess*, came out as a concept album in 1984, preceding a proper stage production by two years), while Frida and Agnetha had gradually retired from the pop life. So it was left to a new record company to make a move, and it so happened that the way was suddenly clear.

In May 1989, Stig Anderson had sold Sweden Music, the publishing company he led, to the multinational behemoth Polygram; one of Sweden Music's assets was Polar, the label that had been associated with Abba from the very beginning (and even before that, since the Hootenanny Singers had signed on it in 1963). The purchase was estimated at 300 million kronor ($25 million) and included, among other things, Abba's songs and masters. By then, the band members had strained relations with Anderson. Frida herself had already sold her shares, but in early 1990, the financial representative of Benny and Agnetha found out that for several years the band members had received less royalties than they were owed. The matter went to court, which, needless to say, didn't improve things between the musicians and Stig. The lawsuit felt final nail: this time, the Abba book was closed for good, as least as far as the main participants in the saga were concerned.

Once everything was sorted out and it had retrieved all the rights previously spread out over various countries, Polygram decided to release a greatest hits collection, undaunted by the fact that there had been a flock of similar releases in the past fifteen years or so. *Greatest Hits* had come out in November 1975 (only three albums into the band's career), followed by *Greatest Hits Vol. 2* in October 1979 and the optimistically titled *The Singles—The First Ten Years* in 1982. Variations on the 1975 album came out in several countries—one titled *The Best of Abba* was number one for four weeks in Germany. In addition, there were several various budget collections that were often tailor-made for the countries in which they were released. But the main difference between these releases and *Gold* is that Polygram's acquisition marked the first time the catalog was owned by one company. According to Tobler, "When Polygram acquired worldwide rights to the Abba catalog in the early 1990s, Abba records could be released worldwide for the first time. Any record company that can release a 'Greatest Hits' album of an act that has enjoyed worldwide success will do so, not least to recoup some of their outlay in buying the catalog. I suspect that there was no one individual who suggested the idea of *Abba Gold*, but rather Polygram's marketing department."

Once the Abba catalog was brought under control, Polygram's London office decided to go ahead with *Gold*. According to Ingemar Bergman, who helped put the album together, the British-based conglomerate "'sucked the market dry' of Abba records and 'killed' all contracts Anderson had made with everyone everywhere. In a record landscape devoid of any traces of old Abba compilations put out by more or less respectable record companies, Abba Gold was finally launched."

Apparently, the original plan was to go for a box set but it was scaled down to one disc. Long-time Abba expert Ian Cole recalls that "in the months before *Abba Gold* was released, there was a group of fans campaigning for the release of the box set instead of the compilation, and they were writing to other fans, encouraging them to write to Polygram in protest." A box set, of course, is to a regular compilation what a Rolls-

Royce is to a Hyundai: it's more prestigious, and that prestige makes the label, the band, and the buyer feel good about themselves. Still, in 1992 nobody was sure that Abba warranted a deluxe treatment and Polygram was hesitant about the presence of a market (two years later, the label would change its tune and put out the four-CD box set *Thank You for the Music*). As head of Polygram Music Publishing, David Hockman had worked on the deal with Polar. In a 2000 interview, he explains that "Abba were actually considered a bit passé at that time [the early 90s], no one cared about them. Björn and Benny were involved in other things, and neither they nor anyone else believed Abba had much glitter left. Even Stig thought it was all over. We ourselves were taken unaware when *Abba Gold* did so well." According to Palm, "the record company was fortuitous in that they were preparing this compilation album at exactly the same time as this interest in Abba was reawakened."

Abba Gold was first released in Europe in September 1992; the US version followed a year later, on September 21, 1993, by which time the international release had already spawned 5.1 million copies and thirteen number one hits in countries such as the UK, Sweden, France, Israel, Singapore, and Argentina. As Polygram prepared the box set's release in 1994, a German retailer remembers *Gold*'s impact well: "It was absolutely crazy. Everything remotely connected with Abba—printed music as well as the records—was bought up straight away. Within a short space of time, there was an Abba boom here among the general public." The boom was only bolstered when two Australian movies with a big Abba presence, *Muriel's Wedding* and *The Adventures of Priscilla, Queen of the Desert*, came out in 1994. Both served as echo chambers to the Abba revival, which by 1994 had turned into a worldwide phenomenon. Abba was a bit of a running joke in *Priscilla*, but it played an integral part in *Muriel*, with symbolic and aesthetic implications on which I will return to later. Taken together, the movies underline that numbers alone don't explain *Gold* and its impact: whatever the cause, what happened in 1992–1994 was nothing less than an artistic resurrection—and that's something that sets *Gold* apart from even its megaselling rivals (their *Greatest Hits* didn't make Eagles any cooler). If yet another definition of an album is that it allows us to gauge a band's impact, then *Gold* is the most important entry in the Abba canon: it single-handedly retooled the band's image and symbolized the moment when it became acceptable to take Abba seriously. And the critical reevaluation started right with the compilation's cover art.

The covers of Abba's studio albums all displayed portraits of the group. Some of them were relatively straightforward (1973's *Ring Ring* and its smiling couples; 1979's *Voulez-Vous*, with the group ready to go to an upscale discotheque) while others were dramatically staged (the four band members crammed into a helicopter for 1976's *Arrival*; the Fellini-esque

crowd scene of 1980's *Super Trouper*). But *Abba Gold* came out under a relatively dignified black cover, in an obvious, deliberate attempt to dissoci-
ate the music from what was perceived as a dated image, and thus win over
a new generation of fans. Type was laid out on a black field, with the
band's name taking up the upper third, the word *Gold* below it and, in
smaller font size, *Greatest Hits* neatly tucked under the stylized crown that
would become the symbol of the "Gold" family of releases. By all
accounts this was a conservative choice, particularly when compared to,
say, the original Swedish version of the 1975 *Greatest Hits*, which boasts
one of the ugliest pieces of cover art in the history of the recording industry (including the entire hair-metal canon). That cover depicted Frida
singing and Benny at the piano, except the drawing was a nightmarish mix
of Hieronymus Bosch and Salvador Dalí, a surrealist take on the group as
half-human, half-mythical creatures. It was a long way from the group shot
on the back cover of the *Abba Gold* booklet: the four bandmembers wear
what can be described as casual-smart outfits and hold a board featuring
the band's logo (except that it looks as if they're holding a blank board on
which the logo was later Photoshopped). They look like proud parents
holding their kids' science-fair results, not pop stars.

The inside front cover of the booklet reproduced the artwork of
Abba's eight studio records as well as its posthumous live album; the track
listing was on the right page. It didn't say when songs came out or which
album they had been on, so if you wanted to track down a particular
song's album of origin, you had to do some homework. It felt as if the
compilation wasn't meant to help move the back catalog but rather function as its own, independent entity.

Following the track listing came liner notes written by John Tobler, by
then a long-time associate of the band's. Tobler had become press officer
at CBS in London on April 1, 1974, only to learn that his first assignment
would be to work with the three CBS acts competing in the Eurovision
Contest, held five days later in Brighton. Tobler would remain the group's
British publicist until early 1975; he then wrote *ABBA Gold—The Complete
Story*. Tobler recalls that he "was contacted by Chris Griffin, whose project it was to exploit [the Abba] catalogue. I was involved with Chris and
with George McManus in compiling the album (although it mostly chose
itself—they had nineteen Top 10 hits in Britain), and writing a sleeve note
which put it all into context."

In his essay, Tobler retold the group's history in a straightforward manner that didn't match the chronologically jumbled sequencing. The notes
have been criticized by some fans, who have pointed out some factual
errors and what could be described as enthusiastic exaggerations. For
instance, Tobler said that both Agnetha and Frida had successful solo
careers before being in Abba; Agnetha was indeed successful in the 60s,

but Frida struggled quite a bit and didn't make "several big-selling albums in Sweden." Tobler also wrote that 1973's "Ring Ring" was released by Abba, whereas the group took that name only the following year.

But in many parts of the world, those notes are now gone. *Abba Gold* has been so commercially successful that it has been given the reissue treatment usually awarded to, well, classic albums: it was rereleased in 1999 with a new set of liner notes by Carl Magnus Palm, who had emerged in the 1990s as the Abba expert. The 1999 version was freakishly successful in England, considering that the 1992 compilation had already sold huge numbers and the track listing was unchanged; *Billboard* chart expert Fred Bronson noted that "even I didn't dream that the greatest-hits collection would leap 8-1 in its 218th [UK] chart week. Given that London is being swept by Abba-fever, it shouldn't be such a shock that the 1992 release is back on top." A tenth anniversary edition followed in 2002; Palm slightly updated his 1999 notes while the booklet was redone. The cover art remained the same, except that the correct font was used for the famous reversed-B logo. Unfortunately, America is still stuck with the 1992 version, which is widely considered by fans to be imperfect, especially compared to the subsequent ones. (Because the original version of *Gold* had the most impact, it's the one I'm focusing on in this book.)

Tobler's notes were dense, unadorned by any photos; the latter were grouped, collage-like, on three pages: a spread in the middle of the booklet and the inside back cover. The group members were portrayed in street clothes, performing live in rather demure outfits, working out songs in the studio. Most of the photos were medium to close-up shots. The third collage even depicted the quartet at the peak of some kind of Scandinavian health trip: in one photo they positively shone—not with lip gloss for a change but with what looked like a healthy ski glow. In another, Frida wore a shirt bearing a logo for something called "Hobie Sports Center." It would take the advent of golfer Annika Sorenstam to see another Swedish woman so proudly harboring a logo-ed shirt. The aura of wholesomeness—as opposed to cheesiness—permeating the illustrations was unmistakeable. As with the cover, the photo selection tried to disassociate the band from its oft-garish image: there were no oversize T-shirts adorned with cartoonish, grinning cats; there were no unflattering, way-too-tight bell bottoms or body-hugging, *white what-were-they-thinking?* catsuits. But Polygram's effort to clean up Abba's image would have been pointless if the music on *Gold* had stayed stuck in the 70s. What *Gold* showed was that it had passed the test of time, and even acquired a new resonance.

Unlike a band's regular studio albums, a compilation is characterized as much by what is there as by what is not there. As far as what was included, Abba had racked up so many hits that gathering them on one CD was a no-brainer. "The track selection was virtually automatic," Tobler says.

"When the act in question has had nineteen Top Ten hits, most of which have been Top Five and nine of which had been number one, there can be very little argument. *The Visitors* was the divorce album, without many hit singles, and *Waterloo* was released before Abba were established, but *Voulez-Vous* had been loaded with hits. The title was *Gold*, but the concept was *Greatest Hits*." Palm agrees: "I seem to remember that they consulted the various Polygram offices around the world to find out which tracks they wanted on the album," he says. "But basically I believe the track listing was simply meant to reflect the biggest hits, globally, and that's pretty much what you have on *Abba Gold*. The exception is 'Thank You for the Music,' which was never a big hit, but which is certainly well-known."

Abba Gold included nineteen tracks, four fewer than there were on *The Singles*. There are songs pulled from all the studio albums, as well as "Fernando" and "Gimme! Gimme! Gimme! (A Man After Midnight)," two singles that didn't originally appear on full-lengths. The only records not represented are the much-decried live album and the 1973 debut, *Ring Ring* (which had been released when the group still went by the cumbersome name of *Björn & Benny, Agnetha & Frida*). This underlines the UK-centric nature of the compilation, because "Ring Ring" had been Abba's first stab at the spot at the Eurovision Song Contest; it didn't make it past the Swedish selection process but was still a hit there. But it didn't do well in England, where *Gold* was conceived, and so it wasn't included.

This is not to say that the compilers' selection was completely consistent: a great single such as 1978's "Summer Night City" reached number five in England and did very well in several other countries, but it's not on *Gold*. The 1992 version of *Gold* also took out a few seconds of music within selected tracks: two of the songs—"The Name of the Game" and "Voulez-Vous"—were edited down, the consensus now being that it was a simple mistake, one that was corrected on subsequent reissues. (Still, tampering with two tracks is exactly the kind of thing that feeds into the hang-ups of those who have little faith in the artistic integrity of compilations.) But *Gold* didn't dwell on the absences: *Ring Ring* and *Abba Live* were among the album sleeves reproduced on the inside front cover of the compilation's booklet, and the fact that two tracks were edited wasn't acknowledged by Tobler.

There were no extras to make up for the missing stuff, either. Even *Greatest Hits* (with "Fernando") and *Greatest Hits Vol. 2* (with "Gimme! Gimme! Gimme! (A Man After Midnight)" and "Summer Night City") included songs that had been previously available only as singles. *The Singles—The First Ten Years* boasted a brand-new tune, "The Day Before You Came," which was released as a single at the same time the compilation came out, in October 1982. There was no such thing with *Abba Gold*, even though it could conceivably have included a late single such as "Under

Attack," one of the two new tracks on *The Singles*. All the extra goodies you could wish for ended up tucked away on the fourth disc of the 1994 box set *Thank You for the Music*. (Whatever new packaging the label could come up with now wouldn't be of much use, anyway: as Björn noted in an interview, "Benny has made a calculation that over the period that Abba was active we wrote only twelve songs a year. And we recorded everything so there's nothing more in the can.")

As for the sequencing, it looked as if it resulted from uncertainty on the part of the label, which wasn't quite ready to make the leap into serious documentation. *The Singles—The First Ten Years* did follow a chronological order, but that model wasn't adopted for *Gold*. The latter was an old-school collection, jamming the biggest hits together and throwing them out to the public. Had it come a couple of years later, it may have acquired cachet and a veneer of scholarly respectability—and it would have been called an anthology instead of a compilation. The 1999 and 2002 reissues, with their updated essays, actually reflect that evolution— except that the unchronological track listing was maintained. Palm remembers "Chris [Griffin] telling me that when he sequenced the album, he was trying to program it as if it was a radio show." And so *Gold* begins with what has become the band's signature song, "Dancing Queen," and concludes with Abba's first international success, "Waterloo." In between these two tracks, the sequencing is all over the map, jumping back and forth in time, alternating slow and fast numbers.

As I pored over *Gold* again and again, I realized I would have to organize the songs in some kind of order. And so I grouped them according to which album they first appeared on. Starting with "Dancing Queen" felt as if it was just meant to be: not only does it start off *Gold* but it first appeared on a 1976 album titled *Arrival*.

Electric Ladyland

by John Perry

3
Live

I saw Jimi play many times but the most memorable shows, for different reasons, were the first and the last. When I first saw him I was a fourteen-year-old bedroom guitarist, *just* capable of playing the five root-position chords that make "Hey Joe." Chords were as far as I went. Lead guitar, especially the blues-based phrasing that Hendrix flung around, was way beyond me. I hadn't the first idea how it was done.

A rainy Monday lunchtime in a concrete school playground, early in February '67. Boys kicking around footballs, others sheltering beneath a line of poplars, reading *Disc* and *Music Echo*. A friend came up and asked if I wanted to go "down the Locarno" that evening to see "some American bloke play with his teeth." This didn't sound especially promising. For one thing, I'd seen most of the good bands there—Cream, the Who, Small Faces—and then there were other, rival attractions to consider, too. Was it worth risking a valuable Monday evening on some unknown American guitarist when I could be throwing stones up at the disused airfield we disputed with hill-tribes from the council estates behind it?

At 7:30 I climbed the concrete stairs leading to the Bristol Locarno, one of a chain of indistinguishable provincial ballrooms plonked down in towns like Coventry, Stevenage, and Sunderland. Decorated in halfwitted Polynesian chic—plastic palm trees grew in the dimly lit Bali-Hai bar—it featured a DJ who played Tamla Motown singles to the young Mods until it was time for the revolving stage to bring round the night's live band. Groups only appeared midweek, possibly because the weekends were strict-tempo nights, the sacred province of ballroom dancing to the sophisticated sound of the Denis Mann Orchestra, but more likely because groups could be booked for half the price of a Friday or Saturday night.

The DJ stopped his records, the lights dimmed, and the stage revolved, bringing round a left-handed guitar player with a black military jacket and a white Stratocaster. He chewed *furiously*. He stood in his usual spot, stage right (on the left, from the audience viewpoint), in front of a single Marshall stack, the upper of the two speaker cabinets draped with a large, colorful beach towel. I'd seen Townshend cover his speaker cabinets with a Union Jack but I'd never before seen anyone use a Marshall stack as a towel rack. How sensible! Anyone speeding as hard as this bloke seemed to be would work up a fair sweat. My first impressions were the towel and the jacket (the same gold-braided number he would wear on the *Are You Experienced* cover).[1] The black coat was nicely set off by the white, upside-down Strat, while a second Strat, a spare, also white, leaned up against the Marshall. I'd never seen anyone with *two* guitars before. He must be *really* good.

Of the other two geezers, the drummer looked like he might still be at school, and the bass player wore glasses. All three had frizzed-out hair. They played as loud as Cream, though the performance was less aggressive than the Who. There was a different tone altogether. It's not that they lacked attack, just that the atmosphere was different: good-natured where the Who were menacing. The left-handed guitarist in particular seemed to be really enjoying himself. Clearly getting off on the music, he grinned a lot and every so often waved his left arm in invitation, as though beckoning the audience to join him in the fun. There was something engaging about this—and he was clearly a pretty tasty guitarist—so I thought I'd better wander down to the front and have a good, close look.

After a couple of numbers I began to get the hang of his unusual demeanor. (English blues guitarists of that era generally stood still looking *extremely* serious—their audiences even more so.) Hendrix wasn't mucking about, it was just that his technique was so assured he had time to play brilliantly *and* do all this other stuff with his arms. Sometimes he only had one hand on the guitar, and it still sounded great. It was similar to that quality seen in those rare sportsmen who come along once or twice in a decade: they seem to have fractionally more time than their peers, time in which they can choose their shot, or adjust it without ever looking hurried, time which makes their play seem effortless and their companions or opponents look clumsy.

As far as I can remember, there wasn't a great deal of original material in the forty-five-minute set. "Hey Joe," "Stone Free," and "Can You See Me" were fleshed out with blues, "Rock Me Baby," "Killin' Floor," and soul standards like "Mercy Mercy," which Jimi announced, in his characteristic halting delivery:

---

[1] The jacket, which Hendrix loved, came from Lord Kitcheners Valet. He later discovered it bore the insignia of the (noncombatant) Veterinary Surgeons Unit or, as Chas put it, "donkey-tenders."

A little toon . . . a very straight . . . a-huh . . . Top 40 R&B . . . rock'n'roll record . . . a little thing called Have Mercy . . . have-mercy-on-me . . . BABY.

The only live recording I know of "Mercy" is found on a tape from the Flamingo, London. Recorded just five days before the Locarno show, it's a fair representation of the content, if not the atmosphere of that show. Jimi scythes through the guitar intro with throwaway virtuosity, taking its corners at speed—yet somehow, he still retains soul.[2]

After a race through "Can You See Me in the Key of F sharp," Jimi drops into an extended opening instrumental passage from "Like a Rollin' Stone," played with such delicacy—even by comparison with the better-known Monterey version—that it's touching. The calm after the storm. What I call his "Little Wing" major-key guitar style is present and fully formed, even here, right at the start of the career. Once again, the dexterity is breathtaking.

The Bristol set definitely ended with "Wild Thing." I have an abiding memory that he played "Third Stone from the Sun"—though how I would have known (months before the first album was issued) or could possibly have remembered doesn't bear close examination. False-memory syndrome, I suspect. Yet when I asked Mitch Mitchell if it was possible, he said yes. I'm still skeptical, though.

I recognized the intro of "Hey Joe," and knew from "Ready Steady Go" that this would be the "teeth number." With devastating schoolboy logic my pal and I moved round to the side of the platform, where we enjoyed an uninterrupted view across stage, to see if he *really* played with his teeth, or if we were being had.

In the solo, he first pulled the Strat behind his head (grinning, and playing the break much as it is on record), then brought it back over his head and lifted it up to his face, to play the second half of the break with his teeth. Then he whipped the instrument back into the normal position for the unison passage with the bass. We were close. But we still couldn't be sure. There did seem something distinctly *dental* about the sound. It had the right sort of attack—toothy—but at the crucial moment his face was hidden by the guitar. I admired his cunning.

That show was on February 9, 1967, and though I saw half a dozen more shows over the next three years, nothing compared with this initial exposure, when I had no preconceptions. For a brief period—January until the end of March 1967—English audiences could see Hendrix in a

---

2 Compare Jimi's guitar intro on Don Covay's Atlantic single "Mercy Mercy" with that of his own composition "Remember" (from the UK *Are You Experienced* album). For Steve Cropper's thoughts on "Mercy," see chapter 5 of John Perry's *Electric Ladyland*.

way that would never again be possible. Why? Two factors: proximity and our own lack of preparation. I'll explain those in a moment. Why those dates? Well, Jimi arrived in London in September 1966. Once he'd recruited a rhythm section he set off to mainland Europe for a couple of warm-up gigs—France in October and Germany in November. In December, the band played just five or six club dates around London, and a New Year's Eve show at a tiny social club in Noel's hometown of Folkestone. Regular gigging around England didn't begin until January 4, 1967, after which they played almost every night of the week.

The first factor was simple proximity. Most of those shows were in ballrooms and clubs so small you could have reached out and strummed his guitar yourself (or bitten it, had you felt that to be more appropriate). At the Bristol show I was perhaps six feet away; a picture taken two nights later at the Blue Moon club in Cheltenham shows audience members seated as though riding a busy subway train with Jimi standing in the aisle. When you have that sort of physical proximity to somebody with unique skills, it leaves a profound impression.

The second element (as long as it lasted) was surprise. Few people attending those gigs had any idea what to expect. Hendrix arrived unheralded—in a manner that's all but vanished from today's entertainment industry. No videos, no albums forewarned us—just a sole 45 ("Hey Joe") and one TV appearance miming the song on "Ready Steady Go." We were quite unprepared. It's rare, in any era, to come across an artist of supreme quality. To stumble across one playing in your local dancehall is great good fortune.

Good as they were, none of the English players I'd seen—Clapton, Beck, Townshend—prepared one for Hendrix. It wasn't a question of *degrees* of ability but a qualitative difference: the English guys all seemed like highly skilled workers *applying* themselves to a task while Hendrix seemed a natural. Ferocious power and great delicacy side by side—delivered with equal nonchalance. They seemed to cost him nothing. Jimi had mastered technique so totally it was transparent, which allowed his playing to become a direct expression of personality rather than a brilliantly executed performance.

But people become accustomed to even the most radical breakthroughs very, very quickly. The extraordinary becomes the commonplace in matter of weeks. Subsequently, when you went to see Jimi, you knew just what to expect. He didn't disappoint, but you knew what was coming.

The "age of innocence" was never going to last long with a star of Jimi's magnitude and by the end of March '67 it had passed. This is not an entirely arbitrary date: by then his second hit single, "Purple Haze," was heading toward number three, Jimi was all over TV and the radio, and the publicity machine was generating plenty of column inches in the press. It was improbable that many people would now see Jimi without having heard the records and read the reviews.

March 31st was also the opening night of Jimi's first major UK package tour, appearing in the unlikely company of Englebert Humperdink, Cat Stevens, and the Walker Brothers,[3] on large theater stages before seated audiences. He had moved up a rung as far as venues went, and many more rungs in his personal fame. The American bloke who played with his teeth had become the well-known artist Jimi Hendrix—and the possibility of any accidental encounter had gone.

* * *

It's not surprising that those who saw the early shows formed similar impressions. In his book *Give the Anarchist a Cigarette*, Mick Farren writes about his first sighting of Hendrix, at the Marquee in Wardour St. He saw a show in late January '67, just a week or so before mine, and like me, he watched from a distance of a few feet. Hendrix's magnetism worked on adult and schoolboy alike:

> Anything one might say about Hendrix on stage has to be essentially redundant. For more than thirty years we've listened to the recordings and watched the film and video clips and it is almost impossible to re-create the absolute awe . . . at seeing him play. . . . He loved what he was doing to such a quantum degree that it encompassed the entire audience. His blatant sexuality was, of course, supremely evident but to interpret it as sinister you'd have to be either a monstrous prude or a pathetic racist. His dirty boogie had no mean streak and his technique was so effortless that he was able to take time out to joke, frolic and tease. Most critics concentrate on the flamboyant showboating . . . but I was more impressed by the smaller moves, the simple hammering of the strings with his fluent right hand . . . the actual flexing of the neck against his body to produce slight variations of tone and nuance. It might seem odd to use the word "nuance" in the context of such wildly aggressive music played at deafening volume, but Hendrix's attention to detail amid the maelstrom was uncanny . . . (in) the more introspective parts of his solos I could almost see his mind working as he eased through the magnetic fields of the Marshall stack, exploiting each unique fluctuation between the speaker coil and the pickups on his guitar . . . I would see Jimi many more times, but never with the proximity or the real (or imagined) insight of that night at the Marquee.

---

3 It was Keith Altham who suggested livening up opening night (March 31st, at the Astoria in London) by getting Jimi to burn his guitar. He did—though Jimi was more excited by the idea of setting fire to the Walker Brothers.

That's as concise a description of early Hendrix as I've come across. Farren typifies the first reactions of both the English fans and the press— so why then did the first American critics respond so differently?

When Jimi burst on them at Monterey, six months later, he was as unknown to most Americans as he'd been to English audiences. Yet it was as though they were reviewing a different performer. Critics wrote of an "undignified," "psychedelic Uncle Tom" whose "gimmick-laden" act was a "second-rate copy of the Who's destruction." Even his speech annoyed them with its "superspade jive." The shrewd reader may feel a common theme underlies all those responses. . . .

The liberal American press from *Esquire* to the *Village Voice* was perplexed by Hendrix in a way that the English never were. It seems extraordinary that the hippest American papers lined up with views found only in the English tabloids ("Wildman of Borneo" etc.). Nobody expected English papers like the *Mirror* to get anything right, least of all music, but one hoped for more from the American underground press. Filtering their reviews through a whole complex of self-consciously "radical" Vietnam-era attitudes to race relations, they managed to miss the music almost entirely.

My purpose is not to flay the American press—they were quite busy enough flaying themselves. Behind a whole raft of complaints about Hendrix's undignified performance and his irritating failure to fit existing critical categories for black performers lay the essential point that his songs mysteriously failed to punish the audience for being white. Hendrix didn't play the wounded, angry black man, or the dignified bearer of oppression; he didn't provide white critics with a handy receptacle for their guilt. They didn't know quite *what* role he fulfilled. But they knew they didn't like it.

Reviewing Monterey for *Esquire*, the "Dean of American Rock Critics," Robert Christgau, first distinguished himself by calling the Grateful Dead "the standout improvisers of the Festival." (In fact, the performance was so awful that the Dead refused to allow even ten seconds to be used in the film or the soundtrack album.) Garcia was very funny when he spoke about this, years later in London. He told me:

> We blew Monterey *and* Woodstock. I dunno that big festivals ever really suited us. At Monterey we were sandwiched between the Who and Hendrix . . . first the Who—bang crash roar—smashed everything . . . then Hendrix—huge sound, set fire to everything . . . whooooosh . . . then *we* came out and played our little music. . . .

But as Christgau saw it:

> [The Dead's] performance was quickly obscured by the Jimi Hendrix Experience. Hendrix is a Negro from Seattle who was brought from

Greenwich Village to England by ex-Animal Chas Chandler in January. It was a smart move. England, like all of Europe, thirsts for the Real Thing, as performers from Howlin' Wolf to Muhammad Ali have discovered. Hendrix picked up two good English sidemen and crashed the scene. He came to Monterey recommended by the likes of Paul McCartney. He was terrible.

Hendrix is a psychedelic Uncle Tom. Don't believe me, believe Sam Silver of *The East Village Other*: "Jimi did a beautiful Spade routine." . . . He also played what everybody seems to call "heavy" guitar; in this case, that means he was loud. . . . The destructiveness of the Who is consistent theater, deriving directly from the group's defiant, lower-class stance. I suppose Hendrix's act can be seen as a consistently vulgar parody of rock theatrics, but I don't feel I have to like it. Anyhow, he can't sing.

It's not my intention to single out Christgau. Clearly he represented one definite strain of US opinion (not necessarily restricted to white reviewers) and to his credit, he continues to stand by his original impression: a good polemicist should oppose the prevailing orthodoxy.[4] But the disparity between UK and US opinion remains deeply puzzling. Hendrix's offences (apart from being unnecessarily black in an American context) appear to be:

(1) Coming on after the Grateful Dead (A dirty job but someone's got to do it)
(2) Going to England (Thereby reinforcing the deplorable European taste or Real Things)
(3) Crashing the scene (!)
(4) Being terrible (!!)
(5) *Seeming* to be "heavy" (?)
(6) Consistent vulgarity
(7) Inability to sing

Well. Add tone deafness and poor microphone technique, and you've got a pretty damning case.

* * *

Hendrix spent almost all of 1968, the year of *Electric Ladyland*, in America.

The only English sighting was a TV duet with Dusty, singing "Mockingbird" on the "Dusty Springfield Show." By the time he returned to

---

4 You can find the review in its full context online at www.robertchristgau.com/xg/music/monterey-69.php

European stages he was a different performer, more assured, less nervous, and keen to please—and also the highest paid act in rock 'n' roll.

My final sight of Jimi was as memorable as the first—though for all the wrong reasons. In 1969, Dylan came to England to play a festival on the Isle of Wight, not least as a means of escaping the crowds spilling out from another, larger festival and threatening to swamp his home in Woodstock. The Isle of Wight organizers decided to repeat their success the following year, booking an impressive bill with Jimi headlining. Thus in August 1970 what turned out to be Hendrix's last-ever English show took place on a small holiday island off the south coast of England.

An estimated 250,000 people packed onto the ferries that run across the Solent from Southampton. Arriving at the site after dark, I found myself inching through gaps in the double-fencing opened by some bikers, who were letting people through at ten bob a pop (about a fifth of the official ticket price). Later on, a squad of French Anarchists, rationally, skeptically demolished a whole section of fence, declaring the festival free, though they first had to repel a mixed company of bikers and official security guards who'd combined against the foreign threat to their mutual financial interests—a textbook example of late-capitalist flexibility in exploiting the false-consciousness of the proletariat.

As Mick Farren notes, in retrospect this festival marks the end of the sixties and the start of the seventies. Having observed the festival's preparations and judged them more suitable for a prison camp, Farren set out to disrupt the event. In the pages of *International Times*, he leaked news that the festival could be viewed for free from a large hill overlooking the site. Sure enough, those who didn't slide through the fence sat up on the hill.

In those days, festivals always ran monstrously late, and it was one or two AM by the time Hendrix took the stage. Trying to stay awake through what seemed like six or seven hours of Joan Baez took some doing. I lay back and dozed, and when I opened my eyes the sky was full of shooting stars—the annual Perseids meteor shower. Everything augured well.

Hendrix mumbled a greeting in that familiar self-effacing, speedy manner and launched into "Sergeant Pepper," by way of a salute. Almost at once you could feel something was wrong, even from fifty yards back in the crowd. The Experience sounded tired, Mitch drumming furiously but not always keeping the steadiest time, like a man working doubly hard to keep the ship from sinking. Billy Cox, who'd replaced Noel Redding, did his job so anonymously you hardly noticed that he was far from well, having been spiked at an earlier gig. And Hendrix—of all people, Hendrix, who'd always seemed invulnerable in his confidence and exuberance—was clearly fighting a losing battle against something: what, I couldn't quite tell.

Instead of his usual warmth, the vibe from the stage was distant, variable, and at times seemed close to panic. At that time in the morning, I wasn't sure at first if it was just me: the crowd yelled and cheered and seemed happy enough. But the music felt edgy, nervy, possessed of some quality that, at the time, I couldn't place. Here was another harbinger of the seventies, because that sound, or something like it, would become familiar as the decade wore on: the brittle, jangly tone of musicians playing outside their skins on way too much coke.

What Hendrix had actually taken, I couldn't say (apparently he'd been up for days, celebrating the opening of his Electric Lady studio) but anyone even half listening could hear something was seriously off. So could he, because after a couple of songs he called a halt. He mumbled an apology and walked offstage, returning after a few minutes to announce he'd start again.

He tried, he tried hard, but it wasn't happening. The music kept getting away from him. Whatever the problem was, it could be solved by effort. The first thing I noticed was that his feedback was off. He'd always been a master of controlling onstage feedback, incorporating its accidentals into his music. Here, instead of those lovely warm, bluesy tones, the feedback was shrill and jarring. Instead of catching on melodic notes and coming in as it should, an octave or an octave and a fifth above the fundamental, the notes were off-key and impossible to use.

Usually Hendrix controlled volume so well it was never painful—he always made a distinction between "good loud" which was powerful and "bad loud" which just hurt your ears—but that night nothing would work for him. His amps picked up crackly shortwave announcements from the security guards' radios—and at one point, if memory serves, even the stage above him caught fire.

If he hadn't died so shortly afterward, the Isle of Wight would have just been a bad gig, but the feeling from the stage was so strange, the sense of joy so lacking that when I heard news of his death a couple of weeks later, it somehow came as less than a complete shock. Hendrix was such an open performer that his mood came right out—as Johnny Winter put it, "he didn't hide behind a show, he just played"—so what came across was a true expression of his feeling in the moment.

* * *

Some critics argued that the onstage showmanship detracted from Jimi as a "serious" player. It's a question about which Jimi himself was ambivalent. He complained of being viewed as a "circus act"—though in practice this seems to have meant he resented being expected to smash the equipment about *when he didn't feel like it.*

His routines—tongue, teeth, splits, guitar behind the head, etc.—were present at every stage of his career—they got him sacked from Little

Richard's band for upstaging the principal—and they form a part of his musical character just as valid as his taste for Chicago blues or Beck-era Yardbirds experimentation. Performance was his element. When you attempt to introduce a distinction between performing and some ideal state of "pure" musicianship (especially with so *natural* a performer), you wind up chasing your tail. Consider Hendrix's use of feedback.

At its simplest, feedback can mean anything, from the screech of a microphone held too close to a speaker to the unwanted shrieks that plague semi-acoustic electric guitars at high volume. But the deliberate use of *melodic* feedback is something different. It's the harnessing of an accidental electronic side-effect to a musical end.

When you play a note on an electric guitar, the pickup detects the string movement and sends a signal to the amplifier. It's amplified and a stronger signal is sent to the loudspeaker, from which the sound emerges. At high volume, loudspeakers move the air around—you can feel it if you stand close. So when an electric guitar is played at sufficiently high volume, a new element enters the picture. Feedback. Instead of needing to *pick* the strings to produce a note, the force of sound coming from the speaker causes the string to vibrate on its own, producing a loop.

If you stand right in front of the loudspeaker, feedback is encouraged. Thus your physical position becomes a factor. You might get one note when you face the speaker and a different one (perhaps an octave higher) when you stand at right angles. Simple movements change the pitch of the feedback. The electric guitarist has several variations to play with, and Jimi used them all.

(1) The simplest form of feedback recycles the note you strike (the fundamental), catches it, and loops it. The note will sustain as long as you like.
(2) The next stage is the note that catches, then feeds back on a note one octave above the fundamental. This sounds wonderfully dramatic, as there's no sharp division between the two notes; the higher note seems to grow out of the lower.
(3) A variant on (2) produces a note an octave and a half higher.
(4) The last form is, by far, the hardest to pull off, being a very controlled form of feedback. Other variants sound *wild*, whereas this sounds like a bowed instrument, a cello or viola; more like measured sustain than the giant swell that makes simple feedback sound so dramatic. To invoke it, you play a note, it catches, starts to feedback. Next, you slide your (fretting) finger up or down the neck to a different fret, changing the pitch. And that note feeds back too. To the observer, the guitarist appears to be playing tunes on a single string without ever picking a note. A commercial device called the E-bow produces a similar effect, but you can hear the sound done by hand on Jimi's song "Drifting" (another Water ballad,

found on the *Cry of Love* or *First Rays* albums). Starting at the 2:23 minute mark of "Drifting," there's a high note that swells for a couple of seconds (peaking at 2:25) then runs into a descending phrase through to 2:31. The tone is celestial, and for me it's Jimi's single most beautiful recorded sound.

Once you start playing at the sort of volume the Experience used, the entire stage becomes sensitive to feedback, and the experienced player knows that moving about—even facing in certain directions—will change the quality or the pitch of the feedback. Think of those illustrations that use color to show the variations in magnetic fields. When you can control feedback as well as Hendrix, you can literally "play the stage": every movement affects the sound being produced. As Tom Nordlie wrote in *Spin*, Jimi's "body language was impossible to separate from his technique."

* * *

One final memory comes from a couple of years after Hendrix's death. Certain pieces of music, even on record, will always evoke certain memories. One hearing of "All Along the Watchtower" remains with me above all. In July 1973, I played the Trentishoe Festival in North Devon, set in fields hundreds of feet up on cliffs overlooking the Bristol Channel, with the Welsh coast and the Gower visible twenty miles across the water.

Setting out a day ahead of the official start, we arrived in the afternoon to find the PA still being erected. By eight PM it still hadn't made a useful sound. Just before sunset it emitted some high-frequency squeals, then sank back into a sullen silence. These days a 20,000-watt PA is no big deal but in 1973 this was a huge rig. The system (lent by Joe Cocker, we were told) was not only powerful but clean and efficient, as advanced a PA as you'd find at any European festival of that time. Maybe that was the problem. By midnight we'd given up expecting it to work. As the riggers swarmed over the scaffolding, supporting banks of speakers on either side of the stage, we set out for a stroll around the perimeter.

Overhead the stars were clear. The lights of Swansea and the distant Welsh coast shimmered across the sea. Closer at hand, the night was dotted with campfires and the glow of tents—brightest among them, the Pink Fairies Casino and Off-License, a venture operated by Boss Goodman, the Fairies, and (once again) Mick Farren, who hoped to fleece unsuspecting hippies with a weighted roulette wheel. Those not already out of their heads on acid would be sold canned lager till they were too stoned to notice their lost wagers. Sound Vegas principles, really—and in fact they might have worked if the Fairies weren't all tripping themselves and hadn't drunk all the lager.

As we turned back along the cliff path and came over a low ridge we were again in sight of the stage, picked out with rudimentary lighting and the flicker of the crew's torch beams in the scaffolding. Suddenly, the night burst into life. The PA system was up. The full stage-lighting came on, filling the night with color, and at absolute top volume, in stunning clarity—from nowhere!—came "All Along the Watchtower." It sounded wonderful. As if that wasn't enough, an offshore breeze blew the sound waves around, occasionally adding an effect that resembled "natural" phasing.

Powerful electric music, projected over a distance at night, sounds like nothing else on earth. Ships four or five miles out in the channel started hooting.

4
The Cover

Jimi hated the English cover art for *Electric Ladyland*—and who can blame him? A singularly unpleasant photograph, it fails from all angles: it's neither good art nor attractive pornography. The only sense in which it can be called successful is in its stunning irrelevance to the record.

The cover was put together by Chris Stamp and Track Records art director David King while Hendrix was in the US. Stamp sent King and photographer David Montgomery down to the Speakeasy to round up some girls, with the brief to make them look like "real people." At £5 a head (or £10 with their knickers off) this sounds like authentic Stamp. Jimi returned to England and a *fait accompli*. He took one look at the artwork and distanced himself as far as possible, telling interviewers it was "nothing to do with him." Mitch too thought the cover "a load of rubbish."

How far the result—blamed at various times on "bad lighting," "cheap ink," or "poor-quality paper"—succeeded in depicting "real people" is arguable but it undoubtedly succeeded in removing any shred of glamour. One of the models, Reine Sutcliffe, told *Melody Maker*:

> It makes us look like a load of old tarts. It's rotten. Everyone looked great but the picture makes us look old and tired. We were trying to look to sexy—but it didn't work out.

Reine is right. Even teenage boys, proverbially undiscerning consumers of the female form, failed to find anything worth getting to grips with in this image.

Clearly Track Records had acted without consulting Jimi, but there must have been some plan. What was the thinking? They hoped, I suppose, that the picture (a feeble pun on the album's title) might prove sufficiently controversial to stir up some free tabloid publicity. They'd tried a similar stunt the preceding summer when a collection of saucy Victorian/Edwardian postcards were used to advertise the label's second single, the Who's "Pictures of Lily" (Track's first single was "Purple Haze"). Stamp had found the postcards whilst trawling market stalls on the Portobello Road, and eight of them were arranged to make a Who poster that was witty and visually attractive—neither attributes that anyone would claim for the *Electric Ladyland* sleeve. The "Lily" poster scored on all fronts; it managed to be hip whilst still keeping step with mainstream UK fashions in graphic art. Victoriana was a familiar genre in mid-60s England and the poster failed to make any waves at all—though in America, where tastes were more cautious, Decca Records substituted a cartoon of the band members.

Hopes of "stirring it" are the only credible explanation I can see for the *Electric Ladyland* sleeve. Track Records was set up by the Who's managers as an outlet for their band but it can't be said that Track ever favored the Who over Hendrix; at Monterey, for instance, there'd been a fearful row when Track shared the expense of air-freighting Hendrix's Marshall amps over to California yet insisted that the Who must make do with locally rented American Vox amps. Both bands depended on the Marshall "roar" and the Who's set, though it was—as we've seen—better received by US reviewers than Jimi's, was seriously weakened.

Track's hoped-for controversy amounted to little more than seeing the cover banned from a few provincial record shops in York, Hull, and Bristol. In the tabloid newspapers, the *Mirror* bore fruit—of a sort. In early November it reported:

20 NUDES DISC IS BANNED

Two record dealers have banned a new pop disc—because they are shocked by the record sleeve. The LP, *Electric Ladyland*, by the Jimi Hendrix Experience, has on its cover eight lounging nude girls. The other side of the sleeve shows twelve more in similar pose.

The owner of one of the York shops which has banned the record, Mr. Hugh Robertson, declared yesterday: "This has gone too far. There is no need for covers like this."

If this was the sort of controversy Track hoped for, one fails to see how it would convert into record sales—least of all for an artist like Hendrix. Few of Hendrix's target audience were natural *Mirror* readers, or at least readers likely to set much store by the *Mirror's* opinions on Hendrix. The paper reported Track's response:

ARTISTIC

A spokesman for the company which designed the sleeve, Track Records, of London, replied: "The cover should be looked at from an artistic point of view."

Track's comment is so lame one almost suspects the usually prosaic *Mirror* of dry humor. "Artistic" indeed. Three weeks later, those who weren't too busy re-examining the album cover from an artistic point of view could read in the *Sunday Mirror*:

DISC DEALERS HIT AT SEXY COVERS

Britain's disc dealers hit out last night at the trend towards "vulgarity" on pop record covers.

Mr. Christopher Foss, secretary of the Gramophone Retailers' Committee, said the trend could only lower the industry's image in the eyes of the public.

He claimed that twenty-one naked girls pictured on the cover of Jimi Hendrix's new LP, *Electric Ladyland*, were unnecessary. "This type of album sleeve is almost certain to reduce the sales of records," said Foss.

But a spokesman for the Jimi Hendrix Experience said last night that more than 35,000 copies were sold within four days of its release in Britain.

The body count was now up to twenty-one but the most interesting detail lies in the final paragraph. Even allowing for exaggerated figures, the album sold as soon as it hit the shelves. Of course it did. Staunch Hendrix fans bought it in the first week—and would have bought it wrapped in sandpaper, newspaper ,or without any paper at all. They had been waiting a year for the new record and Hendrix had a large, loyal fan base. This was a long-awaited release by a major artist and, as Track's own figures show, the last thing it needed was (what we'd now think of as) a Pistols-style rumpus to grab mainstream media attention.

No wonder Hendrix was so disgusted; apart from anything else, the disagreement neatly symbolized the widening gap between his and the label's views of his status as an artist. From this point on, the defining movement of Jimi's final years became the establishment of his own studio (in New York City, not in London) as a place where he could withdraw and work undisturbed by the jive that seemed constantly to surround him.

After seeing the mess Track had made, Jimi submitted his own cover art to Warners in the US. He sent clear instructions and sketches along with Linda Eastman's photographs of the band in Central Park. Amid the spare, characteristically polite wording of his accompanying letter is a poignant sense of frustration, perhaps even disgust, with Track:

Please use ALL the pictures . . . any other drastic change from these directions would not be appropriate according to the music . . . we have enough *personal* problems without having to worry about this simple yet effective layout.[5]

Inevitably, the art department at Warners felt no obligation to follow Jimi's directions (except where these coincided with their own intentions) but the US cover emerged looking, at least in part, as Hendrix had hoped. And it was free of leprous-looking nudes . . .

---

5 Jimi's sketches are reproduced on pp. 306–7 of Harry Shapiro's book *Electric Gypsy*.

Unknown Pleasures

by Chris Ott

Chapter 3
The Record Is Alive, as That Which It Recorded Is Alive

In April of 1979, Joy Division finally committed to tape the frantic performances on which they'd built a modest but critically impressive reputation. At the posh, thirty-six-track Strawberry Studios in Stockport—lined with gold records—Martin Hannett produced the set of fifteen songs they'd built up during months of rehearsals at TJ Davidson's. It was during these sessions that the band first realized the depths of Martin Hannett's mercurial personality, increasing drug use, and impatient, cerebral hyperactivity. While his temper was bearable during the single day of recording for *A Factory Sample*, Factory had hired out Strawberry Studios for three weeks to record and mix *Unknown Pleasures*. Joy Division endured Martin's inexplicable recording techniques, drug-fueled irrationality, and inherently abusive personality for five straight days, then fought for weeks to be present for the off-hours mixing. On the third day of recording, Hannett famously disassembled Stephen Morris' drum kit down to its metal rims, searching for a rattle that was bleeding through due to his brilliant technique: the output from the drum room was lined down to an Auratone speaker that sat perched on the seat of a tiny basement toilet, removing all reverberation.

In the kind of dead silence you'd only find in a basement, Stephen Morris was playing to ghosts, who in the form of a single microphone breathed back his muted wooden thuds to Martin Hannett's fantastic little black box. Just weeks before recording "Digital" and "Glass," Hannett had gleaned a prototype of a digital delay rig from friends within AMS Neve, a cutting-edge electronic audio company based in Burnley, Lancashire. Though the digital delay line had been invented in the 60s and large technology companies were already trading the technology, binary digital delay hadn't yet been captured in a separate device that could be selectively applied—post-effected—to live sound. Wah-wah and distortion pedals were already commonplace in rock, but they modified sound as it traveled from the guitar to the amp. Digital delay was the first device that could reproduce that sound exactly. Reverb was a series of reflections with limited and diminished frequency response: it had a uniform sound and any tracks using it would bleed together in a Joe Meek racket. Charge coupled (CCD) analog "tape echo" had been available, but it produced unmanageable line noise and increasing distortion with each bounce. Binary digital delay translated its input into electronic data—1s and 0s—before bouncing it back, completely intact, as frequently as the operator chose. Hannett chose a miniscule report time, as Factory staple Vini Reilly of the Durutti Column—who were inextricably linked with guitar delay—later explained: "Martin used that digital delay not as a repeat echo delay but to make a tiny millisecond that came so close to the drum it was impossible to hear. I would never have thought of doing that. Nobody else would. I don't know how he could have possibly envisaged the final sound."

The urgent, alien thwack of Stephen Morris' processed snare drum as it bounced from the left to right channel was so arresting, one could have listened to that opening bar for hours trying to figure how on *earth* someone made such sounds. Like John Bonham's ludicrous, mansion-backed stomp at the start of "When the Levee Breaks"—only far less expensive— the crisp, trebly snare sound Martin Hannett would make his career on announced *Unknown Pleasures* as a finessed, foreboding masterpiece. Peter Hook's compressed, somewhat flat bass line rides up front in the mix, and it's not until the hugely reverbed, minor-note guitar line crashes through that you can understand the need for such a warm, analog treatment. Layering a few tracks together to create a six-string shriek on par with Siouxsie & the Banshees' *The Scream*, Hannett's equalization cuts the brunt of Sumner's fuller live sound down to an echoing squeal. In search of vocal clarity and space for delay and reverb to ring out, Hannett relegates the guitar to hard-panned stereo placement in later tracks, and thins the robust double-humbucker sound of Sumner's Gibson SG. And that's what Bernard Sumner's dissatisfaction boils down to: he still heard guitar attack and fury. From the *Heart and Soul* liner notes: "We played the album live. The music was loud and heavy, and we felt that Martin had toned it down, especially with the guitars. The production inflicted this dark, doomy mood over the album: we'd drawn this picture in black and white, and Martin had coloured it in for us."

As Sumner often says, the band were always more aggressive in concert, but Ian Curtis was very impressed with the icy, evocative sound of *Unknown Pleasures*. His approach to lyrics had been steadily evolving, and by the time of the group entered the studio he had moved beyond storytelling and condemnation into expressionist pleading: "I've been waiting for a guide to come and take me by the hand / Could these sensations make me feel the pleasures of a normal man?" The album's opening lines, from "Disorder," suggest Curtis is lamenting his depression and alienation. The song's very name seems to invoke the epilepsy that was, along with the powerful medications he had to take, preventing Curtis from pursuing the late nights, casual alcohol intake, and cathartic stage shows he enjoyed so much with Joy Division. The booming, climactic finale spins out of control as Curtis bellows "I've got the spirit / But lose the feeling." "Disorder" is so arresting, cathartic, and novel, it's hard to fathom there are even more potent moments beyond its collapsing explosion of snare drum and cymbals.

Few lyric poets are as readily dissected as Ian Curtis, whose every word seems to have layered meanings entwining personal struggles—his disease, ensuing success, possible failure, and the ultimate futility of either—with more universal pleas for honesty and conviction. Regret and self-doubt would rule the rest of his short life, but on *Unknown Pleasures* he's still asking questions, wondering if his affliction would subside, and whether he'd find happiness as Joy Division continued to make bold strides. "*Where will it end?*" he screams, during the surprisingly laconic dirge "Day of the Lords" (named for a discarded early lyric sheet that included the phrase). By this point, Joy Division have clearly laid punk's quickly consumed fire to rest, concentrating instead on atmosphere and the severity of slower tempos: hammering chords ring out into stretched silence; during lulls, there's space for more complex guitar progressions, menacing feedback, and eerie, monotonous keyboards. Like all the material written in advance of *Unknown Pleasures*, "Day of the Lords" confronts uncertainty, the onset of adulthood, and the death of youth's romantic abandon, building to a pulsating crescendo with each despondent, imploring refrain from Curtis. "Candidate" is even more subdued, a barely there backdrop of repetitive bass broken by drum fills. Haphazard, creeping guitar squeals rise and fall in the distance, swirling between both channels; Hannett's snare treatment is at its most exposed, punching with first contact and quickly dispersing as controlled, shimmering high-end decay. In "Disorder" and "Day of the Lords," Curtis' voice is sonically flush with the song's palette, a mostly realistic re-creation of their performance, but on "Candidate," Hannett increases the treble to the vocal track, creating a throaty, tremulous timbre shattered by hissing consonant inflections. The lyrics are perhaps the album's most egregiously morose: "Corrupted from memory, no longer the power / It's creeping up slowly, that last fatal hour."

Sumner and Hook's instant dissatisfaction with Hannett's production is easiest to appreciate during "Insight," which is hugely diminished on record in comparison to the song's in-concert power (and even compared with the Peel Session performance in January). Hannett's focus on drums, vocals and electronic noises to the exclusion of guitars reduces this driving, climactic composition to a nervy, tame mid-tempo ballad, staging the electronic drum breakdown toward the end too dramatically. Lyrically, the song is perhaps the most telling document of Curtis's fermenting internal resignation and fatalistic outlook:

> *Guess the dreams always end*
> *They don't rise up just descend*
> *But I don't care anymore*
> *I've lost the will to want more*
> *I'm not afraid not at all*
> *I watch them all as they fall*
> *But I remember when we were young*

His debilitating epilepsy and impending fatherhood—Deborah gave birth to a daughter as Martin Hannett was finishing the mix for *Unknown Pleasures*—weighed heavily on such a dramatic young soul. The shift in tone from the band's simpler first wave of punk songs was undeniable, but it was art, and so artistic, so outstanding that Curtis' fellow band members were excited by the seriousness it lent their already brooding music. Knowing he was suffering through frequent seizures and was affected by the heavy medication he was taking, it seems obvious that someone should have pried into his mental state right away, but as Deborah Curtis would later write, "it was too incredible to comprehend that he would use such a public method to cry for help." Indeed, photographer Kevin Cummins has dozens of prints from early 1979 of Curtis laughing and messing around like schoolboys with his band mates outside their rehearsal space. To people who knew him, Ian Curtis was a fun if explosively temperamental character. Whatever self-obsessed fatalism he was beginning to harbor was kept secret, revealed only in his lyrics and denied outside their context as poetry and art.

Though *Unknown Pleasures* remains a début album of unparalleled drama and scope, the central passage from side one (titled "Outside") to two ("Inside") is where it makes its most powerful first impression. "New Dawn Fades" closes the first side at a faster tempo than "Candidate" or "Day of the Lords," but it's definitely of the same monolithic, stately stock as these newer tracks. Sumner plucks a series of notes through the first half, distantly chiming behind Hook's hard downstrokes before the song's explosion at the 2:30 mark, Curtis bellowing in a cracking, full-torso scream, "The strain's too much / Can't take much more / I've walked on water, run through fire / Can't seem to feel it anymore / It was me / Waiting for me / Hoping for something more."

Deborah Curtis was rightly unsettled by such grave lyrics and their depressed delivery—especially audible in "Insight"—and questioned her husband about the morbid, flailing finale of "New Dawn Fades." Her justifiable consternation only drew protestations and slight denials: the pair fell into a fight, and Ian stormed off in a frustrated huff. It's an incident that betrays Curtis's increasingly solipsistic, self-absorbed outlook after acquiring a disease he had studied just over a year earlier. While working as the Assistant Disablement Resettlement Officer at Macclesfield's Employment Exchange in late 1977, Curtis was required to take a course on epilepsy to better understand its impact on the people he was helping. That he could then succumb to such a dramatic case of the disease was a bizarre coincidence. But, using the anomalous adolescent incidents and Ian's description of feeling "flashbacks" as a teen—most likely preseizing "auras" that never fomented, or only culminated in easily ignored "absence seizures"—it seems obvious epilepsy was lurking in the background, waiting to manifest itself until Curtis reached his twenties, when so many neurological maladies assert themselves.

Ian's experiences with the mentally ill informed the band's defining track to this point: "She's Lost Control," the band's first-ever hit with audiences. It was written about an epileptic woman who would often turn up at the Macclesfield Employment Exchange looking for work; when she stopped coming in, Curtis wrote the comparatively normal, descriptive lyrics about her, but as his own epilepsy took hold, the song grew to have awful implications, especially after he learned she'd died. Joy Division would glossily rerecord it in 1980 as Curtis himself spiraled out of control; a side-by-side comparison of his vocals just nine months apart reveals defeated, desperate slurring, made all the more unsettling by delay, which only accented the inaccuracies of his delivery.

The *Unknown Pleasures* recording of "She's Lost Control" is far superior in its compact, tense drumming and demented vocal effects, but neither studio version captures the overwhelming volume of Bernard Sumner's bare chord progression in concert. The analog, muted treatment of the bass is also a problem, as without the slight distortion—or at least the trebly ring—of his live rig, Peter Hook's lead line is disconnected, too isolated from the rest of the tracks. Though it approaches in concert intensity toward its end, Hannett's production again defers to the electronic percussion elements and the subtly mixed but complex effects on Ian Curtis' vocals.

For punk and heavy metal fans, "Shadowplay" was the gateway track that sold them on Joy Division's jet-black album. A swelling, churning industrial portrait—Morris even accents the beat with an electronic percussion hit that approximates gasping machine valves opening and shutting—it's the one moment on *Unknown Pleasures* where Bernard Sumner is given his due, allowed to dominate the song with two huge, deafening tracks of guitar, ringing out over all else. "Shadowplay," like "Interzone," was a more familiar, older track, and as such the lyrics are notably less morose, appreciable for their lyric beauty rather than any morbid revisionist analysis. Still, "Shadowplay" hides one of Curtis' most salient first-person lyrics: "In a room with no window in the corner, I found truth."

"Wilderness" shoulders the most overt use of Hannett's digital delay, Stephen Morris' snare ricocheting from speaker to speaker like a heavy dub reggae track. A precursor to their later masterpiece "Dead Souls," "Wilderness" is the weakest track on *Unknown Pleasures*, with obvious religious lyrics based in fantasy and mythology, and a guitar progression that's too repetitive. But it's quickly forgotten when the surprisingly traditional rock riffing of "Interzone" starts up, a holdover from the band's 1978 RCA session. For the *Unknown Pleasures* version, Ian adds a second track in the right channel, a spoken-word counter to his surprisingly high-pitched, smooth main verses. His fluttering, whooping choral yodel is still audible, but it's nowhere near as arresting or up front as on the original RCA demo, which—for its raw performance and flat sound—is of huge interest to fans and was wisely included on *Heart and Soul*.

Following what—relative to the surroundings—amounts to a lull, the album's finale serves as a devastating rejoinder to the more easily absorbed, instant, and danceable pair of songs that precede it. "I Remember Nothing" uses the same hollowed-out template previewed on "Candidate," ripping a hole in its own tense fabric with the jarring sounds of breaking glass and shrill electronic crashes, all disintegrating rapidly inside Hannett's box. Like the earlier dirges on *Unknown Pleasures*, "I Remember Nothing" props up Ian Curtis' alternately timid and commanding voice, belting out a message almost certainly aimed at his wife, cruelly focusing on the line "We were strangers / For way too long." As with "Disorder," the very title refers to his affliction: epileptic seizures occur because of chemical and/or neuron disruptions in the brain, sometimes referred to as "electrical storms." As a result, sufferers never remember them. The violence Curtis intimates in his rasping, barked delivery is also tied to his seizures: "Violent, more violent / His hand cracks the chair / Moves on reaction, then slumps in despair." His pregnant wife tried to stifle these attacks so that he wouldn't hurt himself: the image is too painful to envision, but with Ian's unflinching use of his tumultuous home life as a source of poetic inspiration, he left his spouse no choice but to replay these incidents. Devastated, Deborah Curtis was forced to ask herself agonizing questions about her husband's intentions, even at this early stage. Her memoir, *Touching from a Distance*, is uncomfortably, brutally honest in places, but owing to love, respect, and her laudable awareness of its impact, she put more than a decade of distance between her feelings and her husband's emotionally devastating death before writing about their life together. While his band mates and producers heard drama, potent lyricism, and mounting vocal tal-

CHRIS OTT

ent, the person closest to Ian Curtis heard the actual words.

To this day, the surviving members of Joy Division complain about Hannett's hand in the sound of *Unknown Pleasures*, which they immediately felt weakened their deafening live sound. Of the recording process, Bernard Sumner later recalled: "Martin didn't give a fuck about making a pop record. All he wanted to do was experiment; his attitude was that you get a load of drugs, lock the door of the studio and you stay in there all night and you see what you've got the next morning. And you keep doing that until it's done. That's how all our records were made. We were on speed, Martin was into smack." Joy Division still identified with punk's urgency, having seen every first-wave British punk band in person and performed with many of them. Hannett's forward-thinking obsession with digital delay and the distant, warehouse guitars he favored created a sound too studio-processed, too close to the excesses their generation was still burning at the stake. "She's Lost Control" and "Insight" incorporated an electronic drum pad from the beginning, but both songs were driven as much by Bernard Sumner's overblown guitar and Peter Hook's unforgettable treble bass riffs. Though all parties would come around to Hannett's approach and the use of more ambient and electronic sounds, much of Joy Division's music was, at this point, still in line with punk rock's evolution. Bernard Sumner summarized his and Hook's initial feelings in the *Heart and Soul* box set: "We resented it, but Rob loved it, Wilson loved it, and the press loved it, and the public loved it: we were just the poor stupid musicians who wrote it! We swallowed our pride and went with it." Oddly, Stephen Morris has never complained much about the production, considering his performance was the most affected by Hannett's techniques.

"I mean Martin did teach us a lot—he taught us to look at music and our songs and our sounds in a totally different way. We had a very narrow vision of them, we'd just turn our amps on and that was it. When we got in the studio we couldn't understand why the monitors didn't sound like our amps. He taught us to make allowances for certain things like that," admitted Peter Hook in Charles Neal's *Tape Delay*, but he also complained that Hannett "took it right down"; one wonders how their newer, slower tunes like "Candidate" and the majestic "I Remember Nothing" could have been "rocky," as he put it, even in concert. If not as grievously tortured as the anthems they'd record for *Closer*, they were romantic, bleak tunes. Bernard Sumner has been humbly forthcoming about Curtis' central role in Joy Division: "He was a catalyst for the rest of us. We would write all the music, but Ian would direct us. He'd say, 'I like that bit of guitar, I like that bass line, I like that drum riff.' He brought our ideas together in his own way, really."

As such, Curtis loved *Unknown Pleasures*. Hannett had taken their dark rock and roll and infused it with the kind of confrontational, novel soundscapes Ian so admired in groups like Throbbing Gristle and Kraftwerk. Hannett had made Joy Division's debut as formidable and unique as the records Curtis admired. It seems clear that Joy Division was changing again, in Ian's mind if not Hook's and Sumner's, and Hannett shepherded that change at a speed that left the guitarists feeling the record was taken away from them a bit. Which, in one literal sense, it was: Hannett didn't want the band members present while he mixed *Unknown Pleasures*, and would head to Strawberry at all hours of the morning hoping to avoid them. Peter Hook: "The scene was stupid from the word go. Martin never understood that he was working *for us*. We were paying him and so he should have done the mixing when we said so . . . he should have done what we said at all times."

For his part, Hannett later claimed they ran out of time at Strawberry and that he would have changed some aspects of his mix if he had more time, and this is backed up by the post-production recording and remixing of "Walked in Line" for *Still* in 1981. That version was a little over the top in the midranges—so much so that it would be released in its original state for the *Heart and Soul* anthology—but even in the original mix from the *Unknown Pleasures* recordings, Hannett used distorted electronic squeals to approximate clapping.

True to Hook's and Sumner's fears, the synthesizers, electronic percussion, and smashing glass would leave the most immediate impression on critics and listeners, though these effects only featured notably in the first and last songs on *Unknown Pleasures*. And the noises themselves weren't Hannett's idea: the group were becoming increasingly fascinated with Kraftwerk, whose *Trans Europe Express* and *Autobahn* LPs were always around, and they'd also taken some cues from Roxy Music and Brian Eno's solo work. But they were only toying with keyboards and electronics at this stage, as accents; it was down to Hannett's hollow mix and digital delay box that the electronic and industrial noises had such an impact and changed the perception of Joy Division instantly.

Hannett's most extreme use of the nascent AMS delay technology wouldn't even end up on *Unknown Pleasures*: the six-minute "Autosuggestion" was as close to dub as Joy Division ever came on record, although Hook later claimed that Hannett had done dub mixes of "Digital" and "Glass" as a way of learning the device. (In a rueful instance of neglect, Peter Hook's partner in Suite Sixteen—they had purchased Cargo Studios and renamed it—sold all the master reels when he left, including these dub mixes, at fifty pence each.) The sprawling, experimental "Autosuggestion" would indicate Hannett had a sustained interest in dub production techniques at the time, so we can only regret the loss of those artifacts.

Something of a jam, "Autosuggestion" is nonetheless engaging—a slow, echoing anthem in the vein of "Day of the Lords" and "New Dawn

Fades," if somewhat sparser. Unlike the more bleating tracks on *Unknown Pleasures*, "Autosuggestion" bursts to a frenzied doubletime finale of rare and inspiring hope. Much like the superlative single "Transmission" that would follow in the album's wake, "Autosuggestion" appears to be a work of self-reprimand, Curtis fighting his new fears of unpredictable seizures and his much older habit of living within his mind. He urges himself (and, more universally, anyone) to "take a chance and step outside," to "lose some sleep and say you tried."

The upbeat "From Safety to Where . . . ?" is decorated with brightly flickering beams of delay and brilliant—if subtly mixed—acoustic guitars. Though only two slight minutes of liquid strings (and the earliest precursor to New Order's sound), "From Safety to Where . . . ?" contains the most explicit, direct discussion of Curtis' sense of paralysis, debating his future fame—"I got this ticket to use"—and the domestic promise he'd made at eighteen: "Just passing through, 'til we reach the next stage / But just to where, well it's all been arranged / Just passing through but the break must be made / Should we move on or stay safely away?" With the exception of "Walked in Line," any of the discarded tracks could have been released to acclaim, but it's this pair that were made available to Scottish new-wave label FAST, which included "Autosuggestion" and "From Safety to Where . . . ?" on its *Earcom 2: Contradiction* 12-inch, released in October 1979.

"The Only Mistake" was unfortunately sequestered in the vaults—like all but two of the April 1979 tracks left off *Unknown Pleasures*—until the posthumous May 1981 rarities collection *Still*. Apart from the band's most haunting track "Atmosphere," "The Only Mistake" is the most ambient composition the band ever recorded. Sumner's doubled guitar tracks are layered with an almost breathing delay that calls the listener deeper into its hypnotic, swirling gaze. Morris has a few drum fills to break up the oppressive bass line, climbing the same four notes over and over. Repetition, meditation, and atmosphere come together in a wintry, defining moment of Gothic austerity. Lyrically, the song is from the first spate of self-loathing that produced "Autosuggestion" and "Transmission"; not yet resigned to his fate or failure, Curtis condemns his selfishness: "Made the fatal mistake / Like I did once before / A tendency just to take / 'til the purpose turned sour." The band perfected "Exercise One" with Hannett, but except for its excellent guitar line and Curtis' pointed lyrics, it never evolved beyond a single progression. In many ways, it's a precursor to the more accomplished, impossibly honest "Passover" from *Closer*. "The Kill" is barely recognizable in comparison to the Warsaw tune of the same name, though some of the melodies are similar enough. Dominated by keyboards, the song is a frantic, coursing dart, overtly indebted to Siouxsie & the Banshees. The song features one of Curtis's more simple verses, its refrain "through it all I kept my eyes on you" a potential nod to his possessiveness. Recycling the title "The Kill" may have had nothing to do with their earlier punk tune: for Ian Curtis' dramatic lyrics and their powerful music, Joy Division usually paid little attention to song titles. Later, Bernard Sumner would reveal: "We did a concert in Berlin with Joy Division in an old cinema, and in the dressing room there was this old, old film poster on the wall. And we stole it, and took it back to our rehearsal room and it listed every film that was gonna be on for, like, the next five years at this German cinema. And every time we wanted a title, we'd look at this film poster and pick two or three titles. Like 'The Eternal' came from a film called *The Eternal Flame.*"

The famous *Unknown Pleasures* sleeve design of a Fourier analysis on a black background was done by Peter Saville. Bernard Sumner is reputed to have found the image "100 consecutive pulses from the pulsar CP 1919" in a textbook, but in *From Joy Division to New Order: The Factory Story,* author Mick Middles recalls that, after he picked up the prints of the artwork for Rob Gretton in exchange for one of the closely guarded promo copies, he asked Bernard where the cover image came from. "Fucked if I know" was his response. Whatever the source, this framed industrial line drawing of the sound of a dying star is perfectly emblematic of the digitally precise, spiraling music inside.

The title *Unknown Pleasures* in all likelihood refers to Proust's *Remembrance of Things Past,* a divisive, drawnout autobiography of the author's willful, self-absorbed youth. While *Remembrance of Things Past* is widely considered an embellishment if not egomaniacal revisionism, the series invariably appeals to self-determinate young men, who savor its unapologetic solipsism. But as personal and emotional as Curtis' lyrics were, the sense of despair and frustration they conveyed had broad implications in the England of the late 1970s, where hopelessness was a very real sensation. The economic downturn resulted in labor strikes ranging from garbage workers to nurses to gravediggers. The working-class boys in Joy Division found decent jobs—and kept them, never unrealistically leaping for the indentured servitude of a major label advance—but Manchester was in a state of economic stasis, and—as in London—tower-block living and dole queues were a grim reality for most.

Adding to this stagnation, the promising fire of punk rock was almost totally consumed, and disco still ruled the radio in its fourth straight year of saturation: Blondie's "Heart of Glass" and Amii Stewart's remake of the Eddie Floyd classic "Knock on Wood" were chart-toppers while Joy Division recorded *Unknown Pleasures.* As hope for real musical progress began to fade, the Sex Pistols disintegrated into Public Image Limited, while many of their contemporaries became darker and more distant.

Sign 'O' the Times

by Michaelangelo Matos

Side Three
Play

The cover of *Sign 'O' the Times* depicts an ornately decorated stage. In the middle, on a raised platform atop a Cadillac's front grille (with a Minnesota license plate; the right headlight has been removed, the left apparently painted over in yellow), there's an enormously kitted-out drum set, obviously belonging to Sheila E., who'd replaced Bobby Z. in Prince's band when he broke up the Revolution, and who had already recorded two albums under Prince's watch. The drums are vaguely peach-colored; if it weren't for the fact that the colors of rest of the images come through perfectly you'd be forgiven for mistaking the cover photograph for having been run through a peach tint. A large pink plasma ball, the kind you see in old science fiction movies—you put your hand on it, colorful electricity patterns follow your touch—sits between the kit and a Hammond organ with bench; a white, horizontal neon lamp glows over the keyboard. Tall plants and flowers festoon the platform, and there's a giant bouquet in the bottom left corner. In the bottom center is a bright peach guitar with an elongated spermatozoa-looking fin that rests against his body when he plays, and a matching strap; it's laying on the floor, the neck facing downward at a 45-degree angle, very phallic. A large guitar amplifier, about three-quarters of the way on the right, is decorated with what looks like a face carved in stone, surrounded by leaves—very Roman Catholic.

In the background, there's a nighttime city lightscape. The middle is solid peach, and it moves up and out from the middle of the drum kit like a cartoon lightning bolt, à la old Captain Marvel/Shazam! logo. Surrounding it are a crazy quilt of signs—BAR GRILL, ARCADE, R_X DRUGS, HOTEL ROOM, SNOOKER, LOAN, GIRLS GIRLS GIRLS, POOL ALL NITE, TANGO—each dotted by light bulbs and arranged on top of each other in arresting art decoish patterns. The signs themselves look like they're from the thirties and forties; so are the curiously old-fashioned street lamps on either side of the tableaux, with their crooked, sloped-overhanged lights. It isn't until you concentrate your eye on it that you realize that the signs are false, and that the entire background has been screened onto a curtain.

In the bottom right corner, we see Prince, cleanshaven for the first time in his career, his hair in roughly the same pompadour as on the cover of *Controversy*, only a bit shorter. He's wearing a peach turtleneck under a collarless black leather jacket; big, round, gold-framed eyeglasses (I vividly remember reading Jon Bream saying they were nonprescription in the *Strib*); a dangling earring; and a stone stare. He's looking straight ahead, i.e. not at the camera, and crucially, he is turned away from the visual bounty behind him. The implication seems to be that he's had enough of the party lifestyle and is walking away from it all—that, unlike the hedonist who partied in the face of the impending apocalypse, he's stepping away from the center of celebration in favor of, let us assume, something more mature. Which turned out to be both true and untrue.

* * *

Sign 'O' the Times underwent a busy production history. At one point or another, five different albums—two of them doubles, one a triple—were set for release containing part or all of the music that would eventually make its way onto the final *Sign*. According to Per Nilsen's *Dancemusicsexromance: Prince: The First Decade* (London: Firefly, 1999), an exhaustive sessionography/professional history, the first, eleven-song version of *Dream Factory* was pieced together in April 1986. On June 3, he resequenced it into a nineteen-track double LP. After another furious round of recording, he remade the double set with eighteen songs.

During a European tour on which his already rocky relationship with the Revolution deteriorated, Prince taped a soundcheck and concert at Paris's 6,000-capacity Le Zenith with a mobile truck; this is the source of "It's Gonna Be a Beautiful Night," a white-hot big-band jam that would end up on the final *Sign* after being considerably overdubbed. He also recorded some miscellaneous cuts—including the drop-dead gorgeous "Crucial," a ballad that, according to *Dancemusicsexromance*, was intended not for an album but a stage musical Prince was working on, whose "plot" would later be recycled for the 1990 movie *Graffiti Bridge*, the soundtrack of which also made use of the hypnotic, dirgey "Joy in Repetition." But according to the liner notes for the 1998 NPG Records compilation *Crystal Ball*—which contained the first official release of "Crucial"—the song was going to be included on the album Prince was working on, and was pulled in favor of "Adore." That makes sense: in many ways, "Crucial" sounds like a dress rehearsal for "Adore," which was recorded two months later. It's a terrific ballad, sort of "The Beautiful Ones" minus the anguish, a show-stopper on which Prince uses the growlier side of his falsetto, shrieking and belting more than crooning, and it ends with a lengthy, though not especially inspired, guitar solo. (No wonder it was meant for a stage musical.) (For simplicity's sake, *Crystal Ball* will refer to the aborted 1987 album enumerated below and "the NPG *Crystal Ball*" to the 1998 compilation.)

On October 7, Prince fired most of the original Revolution—Wendy Melvoin, Lisa Coleman, drummer Bobby Z. Rivkin, bassist Mark Brown— retaining keyboardist "Dr." Matt Fink. By this point, Prince had expanded the band's live lineup by appending several members of the Family (saxophonist Eric Leeds, dancers and backing vocalists Wally Safford, Greg Brooks, and ex-Time man Jerome Benton), Sheila E.'s guitarist Miko Weaver, and trumpeter Matt Blistan. These new members, save Jerome Benton, were added to his band, as were dancer/backing vocalist Cat Glover, Sheila E.'s bassist Levi Seacer, Jr., and keyboardist/vocalist Boni Boyer, and, on drums, Sheila E. herself.

The day after firing the Revolution, October 8, Prince went back into the studio by himself and recorded "Housequake." Like "Shockadelica," which he'd recorded three weeks earlier as a love tap aimed at former Time guitarist Jesse Johnson, who had recorded an album of the same title but neglected to write a song to go with it, "Housequake" utilized an odd, sped-up vocal that turned his voice into an androgynous twitter, less a woman than a neuter. ("Shockadelica" became the B-side of "If I Was Your Girlfriend" and was included on *The Hits/The B-Sides* box set.) Prince liked the effect so much that within a month he recorded more material like it and sequenced an eight-song album credited to and titled *Camille*. With the Family broken, the Time run out, and Vanity 6/Apollonia 6 gone the way of all old lingerie, Prince needed a side project; here was one without the bother of other folks' egos getting in the way. He also recorded a jazz-funk fusion album with Sheila E. and Eric Leeds around this time, under the name Madhouse, titled *8*.

Soon Prince decided to incorporate all the sides of his newly (musically) single self and put together a *triple* album that incorporated all but one of the *Camille* songs ("Feel U Up," later the B-side of the 1989 single "Partyman" and included on *The Hits/The B-Sides*) as well as—you guessed it— even more new material. The new album was called *Crystal Ball*, and was front-loaded with more recent material—the kicky rock number "Play in the Sunshine," the drop-dead gorgeous ballad "Adore," the mournful gospel-rock "The Cross," a downbeat electro-blues called "Sign 'O' the Times"— that pushed out many of the tracks that bore Wendy and Lisa's direct prints. The new disc was sequenced on the last day of November 1986.

Aside from the astonishing amount of first-rate material he had put together since wrapping *Parade*, Prince wanted *Crystal Ball* to be a three-disc set out of sheer cussed embattlement. After *Under the Cherry Moon*'s hard belly-flop, mass-media backlash, sliding album sales, and declining fortunes with music critics, he wanted to prove his mettle. Releasing *Crystal Ball* would certainly have been ballsy; no major rock artist had released a three-disc set of original studio material since 1981, when the Clash put out *Sandanista!* Unfortunately for Prince's ego, Warner Bros. refused the gamble—the album would have to be a double, or nothing. (Thank you, I'll be here all week.)

Cutting seven of *Crystal Ball*'s tracks away—including the title track and "Dream Factory," as well as four of the *Camille* numbers—Prince was left with fifteen songs. Soon there was a sixteenth. In Los Angeles, on December 21, Prince recorded "U Got the Look," which according to Alan Leeds's *The Hits/The B-Sides* liner notes was a calculated exercise in commercial songwriting: "[The song] was conceived as a private test for a Prince companion whose taste was usually determined by how familiar a record was. Curious to see if she'd take to a commercial sounding song before it actually became well known, Prince labored for hours over the structure and tempo of 'U Got the Look.' Finally reworking the vocals as a duet with Sheena Easton, he produced as mainstream a record as any in his career. I suspect the friend still didn't like it until the rest of the world showed its approval." Easton, with whom Prince was already acquainted, had walked into the studio while he was working on the song, and he invited her to sing. "U Got the Look" had originally been recorded at a slower tempo, but when Prince sped up the tape he got the tempo he desired, and it took his voice up with it, giving the song a semi-cartoony quality that enhanced its pop appeal. (See also Bruce Springsteen's "Hungry Heart" and James Brown's "Papa's Got a Brand New Bag.") "Camille" is credited on the final album as co-lead vocalist, even though "U Got the Look" was never intended for the *Camille* album.

* * *

Some of the outtakes from this period point in a direction that *Sign 'O' the Times* in its finished form hints at but doesn't quite take. "Dream Factory" was the first song Prince recorded for the project, in December 1985, and like most of the material he was cutting around this time (including the finished *Parade*), the song was a collaboration with the Revolution. As with "Around the World in a Day," "Dream Factory" seemed to signal a new direction for Prince's next album. It opens with a minute of droning organ, backward female vocals that take on a quasi-Arabic cast, and a smattering of backward electric guitar that sounds a bit like a revving motorcycle playing the "Let's Go Crazy" solo before moving into an electronically modified Prince, whose voice is sped up till it sounds like Donald Duck. The first half-minute of "Dream Factory" would later be recycled for the opening of the *Sign 'O' the Times* concert movie; the song itself would eventually show up in remixed form on the NPG *Crystal Ball*.

Prince also began recording solo again at his home studio. The first song he cut was the murky, cryptic, entrancing "The Ballad of Dorothy Parker," whose unusual sound was due to a blackout caused by a snowstorm: the power failure had disabled the tape machine, causing it to run at half-speed and robbing the song of its high end. Prince liked the results and left the song alone. Soon after, the Revolution gathered at his house and cut "Power Fantastic," a jazzy ballad cowritten with Wendy and Lisa (they wrote the music, Prince the lyrics) that has a heavy, muted-Ellington feel. (The brief solo-piano "Visions," written and performed by Lisa, is similarly ruminative.) According to Alan Leeds's liner notes to *The Hits/The B-Sides* box set, on which the song eventually appeared (minus Wendy and Lisa's writing credit),

> Lisa Coleman found herself playing the grand piano in the upstairs living room while the rest of the band huddled into the crowded basement studio. Connected only by mics and ear phones, the Revolution still managed to pull off the exquisite song in a single take—even the jazzy intro that Prince suggested just as the tape was ready to roll. "Power Fantastic" also serves to introduce the newest dimension in Prince's music—the only instrument that he couldn't play himself—horns.

The most immediately striking thing about *Sign 'O' the Times* is the jazzy sensibility running through it. Prince's father was a jazz musician, his mother a vocalist; he'd been a fan of chops-heavy jazz-fusion as well as rock and R&B growing up. But when Prince began recording for Warner Bros., he abjured the brass sections that dominated groups like Earth, Wind & Fire and Parliament-Funkadelic, opting instead for stacked synthesizer patterns and a spare, cold feel that markedly contrasted with lush, overarranged disco and the wild, thick underbrush of the era's giant funk ensembles; Rickey Vincent, author of *Funk: The Music, the People, and the Rhythm of the One*, dubbed it "naked funk." Getting away from traditional R&B instrumentation is an underappreciated aspect of Prince's crossover success; Prince is also said to have actively disliked the sound of horns early in his career.

Like most things with Prince—his musical direction, his name, the sense-to-words ratio of his public statements—this changed. His first significant dabbling with horns came on Sheila E.'s 1984 single, "The Glamorous Life," where they seem like a nod to Sheila's background in Latin jazz, where she, like her father, Coke Escovedo, was a star percussionist, playing with Azteca and George Duke. But they don't feel tacked on: the horn figures are as Princely as the bounding synth runs and quirked-out lyrics, and fit the busy, hooky music like a lace glove. Ditto the sax/trumpet lines on *Parade*'s "Mountains." *Sign 'O' the Times* is where he dives in completely, and he has continued using horns in his music: with the exception of Najee's treacly saxophone, which helps torpedo 2001's already torpid *The Rainbow Children*, Prince's writing for horns is probably the most consistently intriguing feature of his post-*Sign* work, particularly on 1996's *Emancipation* and 1992's *I'm Gonna Change My Name to the Title of This Album*.

Eric Leeds and Matt Blistan appear on five *Sign* tracks: "Housequake," "Slow Love," "Hot Thing," "It's Gonna Be a Beautiful Night," and "Adore." Fifteen years after first listening to the album, I'd guessed the number was higher until I actually sat down and counted. But five songs are enough to color our perception of the rest of the album. Excepting "Adore," where the trumpet and sax help thicken the overall sound without necessarily differentiating themselves from it, the *Sign* tracks with Leeds and Blistan feature horns as both foundation and icing: it's impossible to imagine "Housequake" or "It's Gonna Be a Beautiful Night" without their stuttering James Brown-redux riffs; "Hot Thing" takes off during Leeds's hot-and-sleazy soloing, and "Slow Love" is practically a duet between Prince and the horn charts. The easy fluidity of *Sign*'s bulk might not necessarily by itself suggest jazz, but add those four songs and the album is colored differently, the same way that Moby's *Play* works off the strength of its blues and gospel vocal samples even though they're only used on about a third of the album.

Much of the discarded Revolution material from this period is even more overtly jazzy—see the horn charts that dot "Last Heart," "Train," and "Witness 4 the Prosecution." But those songs are also more overtly rocky, overly funky, and overtly experimental, all at once. Simon Reynolds once wrote, "Prince doesn't so much build bridges between categories as create music that exceeds each category simultaneously," and that's a lot of what's happening here. Take "Crystal Ball," which starts as a tightly wound funk jam in the "Kiss"/"New Position" mode, then gradually turns into something looser and more overtly P-Funky, only with Prince's coyly coded apocalyptic/spiritual concerns in the place of George Clinton and Co.'s alien or underwater fantasias. It also once again features Prince's voice sped up to a semi-androgynous twitter, this time a little closer to his real voice than on "Dream Factory." "Crystal Ball" is a multipartite, nine-and-a-half-minute epic, but it's also endlessly playful, taking the bite-sized quirks of *Parade* and expanding them without losing their snap.

"And That Says What?" was a live jam session given a title and slated for inclusion on the first version of *Dream Factory*. "A Place in Heaven," like "Starfish and Coffee" and "Pop Life," has a sing-song melody and childlike, open-hearted lyrics, only they're sung entirely by Wendy. "All My

Dreams" is similar, seven minutes of schoolyard-ready kiddie psychedelia ("Don't ever lose your dreams," Prince sings impassionedly at the end) that had originally been meant to be the final track on *Parade*. According to the liner notes of the NPG *Crystal Ball*, "Movie Star" was a Time demo—and it sounds like one, with Prince in total Morris Day mode both vocally and lyrically ("Everybody at the club freaked / When I stepped out my limousine / They said, 'Ooh, it's good to see you' / I said, 'It's good to be seen, you know what I mean?'"), complete with spoken-word asides between verses: "Man, I hate making movies, but I like that money." (Wishful thinking ahoy!) These are the kind of songs Prince would have given to other artists or saved for side projects earlier and later on; it's a measure of how open the give-and-take between Prince and band was at this point—how willing he was to flux his own identity with others'—that he'd even have considered putting them out on his own album.

"Strange Relationship" is another case in point. Prince first tried the song in 1982; in 1985, he gave that song and another, "Teacher, Teacher," to Wendy and Lisa to revamp. "Strange Relationship" already had a bluesy feel, and in Wendy and Lisa's hands it took on a downcast, heavily psychedelic tinge with overdubs of wooden flute, hand-drums, and sitar; the droning intro led into a darkly etched, hard-downbeat groove; forty seconds in, the main riff enters, played on high-pitched synthesizer and echoed by a squelching bass that sounds like it's being dragged through the mud. The melody is as bright and pop as any Prince had written, but his vocal, sung in his lower reaches (even his falsetto registers as a growl), sounds mournful. That's appropriate, since the lyrics are about how the singer willfully fucks up his relationship with passive-aggressive behavior. As the song trails off, with Prince muttering "What's this strange relationship," the hand-drums and sitar regain their earlier prominence; the song conveys a muddled confusion, an interior dialogue that's as desolate as the lyric.

* * *

That's not how the song appears on *Sign 'O' the Times*, though. The final version of "Strange Relationship" tones down Wendy and Lisa's contributions considerably, refocusing the track on melody and rhythm rather than harmonic color. The results have an appealing sonic crunch—the chomping bassline sounds like Pac Man eating one on-the-beat pellet after the other, or a slow-and-low record scratch. Minus the aural clutter, Prince gets an amazing amount of propulsion from rudimentary rhythms; except for the occasional cymbal splashes and hand-drums, the beat basically doesn't get modified much here; everything stays in lockstep.

The biggest change to "Strange Relationship" is the vocal, which is completely different from the *Dream Factory* version—the lead is slightly tweaked, somewhere between Prince's normal voice and Camille's (the original vocal tracks remain in the background). There's a slight lyrical difference, too, with the still-unrepentant "I'll take the blame, but I'm only human / I didn't like the way u were so I had 2 make u mine" changed to the far more remorseful "I'll take all the blame, yo, baby, I'm sorry." That switch sums up the difference between the vocals' emotional import as well. On the earlier "Strange Relationship," Prince sounded like he was in the midst of his cruel actions; now he sounds like he's stepped back from them, is slightly horrified at the monster he's become, and his determination to find his way out of it has given him a spiritual lift—or a sense of panic, depending on how you hear it. Earlier, the line "Honey if you let me, I just might do something rash" registered as a blunt statement of fact; now, it comes across with a mixture of schoolmarm tut-tutting that he'd think such a thing and pure, upbeat performance.

The vocal's incongruous brashness is what makes it work, by complicating the song's emotional tone. Paradoxically, he makes the song more serious by making it more pop. The singer—the song's narrator—is a creep who wants to hurt you out of nothing but sheer boredom and habit, and worse, he knows you'll let him get away with it until he finally dumps you. That in itself doesn't change. What does change is that the new vocal makes this creep attractive and charismatic; you can understand why someone might be drawn to this guy, despite his bad habits, because the melody is so bright and Prince's singing is so emotionally identifiable. He's a fuck-up who wants to do better—anyone can relate to that. The doo-woppish scatting near the fade redoubles this effect—a happy-go-lucky bit of vocalese stuck at the end of a searching lyric, signaling that things are going to get better. Except the lyric signals the exact opposite—it never resolves itself, just keeps on going in circles, the cycle of abuse continuing nonchalantly along. Prince scrunches up his voice for a final "I think you and I got a"—pause, reverts to a mannered (pseudo-English accented) speaking voice—"strange relationship"—then dips into the same low tenor he'd mostly sung the song with the first time around—"What's this strange relationship?" The song's ultimate kick comes not from some kind of denouement but from the fact that its singer ends up just throwing his hands in the air. He's sung his sad song unsadly, and it hasn't done him a damn bit of good.

A lot of critics, then and now, saw *Sign 'O' the Times* as Prince's most serious album, and it is, but what a lot of them seem to have meant was that the title cut was a semiprotest song. "Strange Relationship" is far closer to the nut of *Sign*'s maturity: it deals with relationships—sexual and otherwise—with more nuance than anything Prince had done before, and it does so with the canniest music he'd ever devise. *Sign* is certainly kaleidoscopic, moving from minimalist funk to big-band ballads to raw, gut-level rock to whatever the hell "The Ballad of Dorothy Parker" is. But it's emotionally prismatic as well: even the fuck-machine stuff is shaded deeper than his previous work. Not so much something like the "I could read you poetry" line from "Hot Thing," either—more like the way his vocal in that song moves from cocksure monotone strut to overwhelmed craving. Check the way he sings the opening verse against the way he sings the third: "Maybe you should give your folks a call / Hot thing—tell them you're going 2 the Crystal Ball / Hot thing—tell them you're coming home late/If you're coming home at all / Hot thing—tell them u found a brand new baby doll." In that space, he moves from impatiently beseeching her to melting with desire. He's working every conceivable angle, partly out of his hustler's instinct, partly because of the old sexual-spiritual twinhood he's spent so much of his career outlining and falling into and back upon.

"Hot Thing" is hardly new territory for Prince, which may be one reason it's so good: he knows the terrain so well he can work new changes on it at will. One of the things that lends *Sign 'O' the Times* its coherence is its recurrent thematic pairings, of which "Hot Thing" and "It" are prime examples. Both are versions of Prince as funky erotomaniac, an obsessive cocksman exercising his libido the way a Berklee School of Music grad practices her scales. On the surface, neither song seems all that remarkable. "Hey, everybody," they proclaim, "I sing about sex all the time, quite often in the exact way I'm about to right now. *Two, three, four. . . .*" "It" certainly *begins* predictably, with stiff funk drums and an even stiffer eight-note bassline straight out of the *1999* songbook.

But in truth, having lived through *Diamonds & Pearls* and *Rave Un2 the Joy Fantastic*, not only do we know what Prince listlessly copying himself is really like, but "It" is more like a generic exercise that sums up and stands in for the genre. (Rough rock-geek equivalent: the Rolling Stones' "Monkey Man," from 1969's *Let It Bleed*.) There's more juice in "It" than you'd expect at first, and again, that's because of the singing. On paper, the lyric is perfectly blunt—"With you, I swear, I'm a maniac, all right / You see it ain't no joke, just a natural fact-uh, all right"—but there's a sweetly hesitant edge to Prince's singing that's enormously appealing. He sounds like he's at the end of his tether, confessing his sins, real and perceived, to his lover, coming clean, a kind of Sexaholics Anonymous meeting set to a machine beat; he gets caught up in the moment and falls into it, the drama accentuated by a brief, piercing guitar solo. And the song's rising-tide arrangement slowly but steadily piles on parts—sampled orchestral "hits" from the Fairlight sampler, deadpan background vocals droning "I could be guilty for my honesty" with robotic coldness before taunting "Think about it all the *tiiiime*," gong splashes—while Prince in the foreground gives into his libido, with the odd effect being that instead of getting it up he slowly recedes in the face of his sex-addict dilemma. His singing gets softer, feyer, finally dropping to a whisper, lost in a prison of his own making; by the end, he's tunneled so deep into his neuroses (and groove) that he comes out the other side, quietly. It's like James Brown's old cape-and-suitcase routine, except Prince never returns to the stage.

"Hot Thing," on the other hand, is like "It" taken past the point of no return. "It" cops to the singer's sexual obsession, and even indulges it a little (vocally, I mean—the groove embodies it). What "Hot Thing" does is accept that obsession as a precondition of existence, and work from there. Although I thought differently at first, "Hot Thing's" placement three songs after "It" is a programming masterstroke: the two very different songs separating them give Prince-the-sex-machine time to marinate in his own juices. (A more minor but equally crucial programming stroke is putting "Hot Thing" after "Slow Love," for reasons obvious from the titles.)

Marinate he does, and even better, he takes the sax player with him. Nothing Eric Leeds plays on "Hot Thing" breaks any ground—you wouldn't even get any argument out of me for saying all he does is recapitulate every honking R&B sax cliché in the book. What matters is how much, and how evidently, he savors those clichés, the thoroughness with which he utilizes them. Contrast this with the album's contemporaries. R&B's approach to saxophone in the mid-80s can generally be summed up in a series of terrifying two-word combinations: David Sanborn, Kenny G, quiet storm. I'm about to praise the lyrics of "Adore," so you'd better believe I have a high threshold for this type of shit. But even the lover in me has his limits. Then there is what we shall call beer-commercial saxophone, or BCS, which dominated the decade's rock/pop starting from Foreigner's "Urgent" (1981) on, and consisted of either Staxish "punch" (Peter Gabriel's "Sledgehammer," Steve Winwood's "Roll with It") or "Me and Mrs. Jones"–style noodling (Simply Red's "Holding Back the Years"). BCS was yet more 60s nostalgia, for, you know, a time when *real* music reigned supreme. Which has never explained why everything else on these records sounds panned and big-drummy just like every other 80s record, but hey.

Leeds' sax model is Maceo Parker, just as, throughout *Sign 'O' the Times*, more than on any Prince album before it, the purple guy's model is Parker's old paymaster, James Brown. He wasn't alone. If 1987 reached me, as a suburban midwestern teenager, as a 60s-redux kind of year, it reached urban America—particularly black New York—the same way, only different, because hip-hop was spearheading a full-blown J.B. revival. In 1986, hip-hop was coming out of its drum machine era, and producers were starting to rely heavily upon digital samples of prerecorded funk nuggets. Take Eric B. & Rakim's debut single, "Eric B. Is President," on which producer Marley Marl utilized snippets of Fonda Rae's "Over Like a Fat Rat," Mountain's "Long Red," the Mohawks' "Champ," and James Brown's "Funky President" to construct the track. Overnight, every rap producer who wanted to make a hot record ran to their crates and began cutting up beats. And nobody's beats, then or now, were funkier than James Brown's.

Brown's label, Polydor, had already begun its massive (and still in progress) J.B. reissue series with some period compilations, but they caught the wave and, with the 1986 compilation *In the Jungle Groove*, rode it. The bulk of *Jungle Groove*—eight tracks averaging eight minutes apiece, spread over two pieces of thick-grooved vinyl—was enticement enough for DJs, but the real bait was "Funky Drummer (Bonus Beat Reprise)," three cut-up minutes of that classic's infernally elastic percussion break-down that essentially did the sampling for you. "Funky Drummer" would have been well on its way to being a sampling cottage industry even without the *Jungle Groove* bonus, but it certainly didn't hurt: at press time, www.the-breaks.com lists 183 songs that sample it.

James Brown, of course, had a profound impact on the young Prince, from the show he saw (and briefly participated in) at age ten forward; he would later mention in several interviews bicycling to Minneapolis record shops as a kid every week to pick up new James Brown singles. Prince's 1986 "Hit & Run" shows—sporadic, last-minute-announcement concerts in a handful of American cities—and the subsequent *Parade* tour in Europe and Japan were heavily modeled on Brown's revue-style shows. And he's long thrown Brown covers into his live concerts, frequently jamming on "Mother Popcorn" and "Cold Sweat" during after-show club gigs and, during the *Sign 'O' the Times* tour, incorporating "Cold Sweat" into "It's Gonna Be a Beautiful Night."

So it makes sense that "Housequake" is, in content, the most direct J.B. homage Prince had recorded to that point (five years later, "Sexy MF" would sound even more Brownian). But "Housequake" is a meta-James Brown record in a different way from, say, Public Enemy's "Rebel without a Pause" or Eric B. & Rakim's "I Know You Got Soul" or Rob Base & DJ E-Z Rock's "It Takes Two." Hip-hop's take on Brown was micro-as-macro. Those records find the ultimate James Brown grooves by taking the most explosive portions of already existing ones and isolating and magnifying them till they shatter the windows. What Prince does is macro-as-micro, filling in the basic casing of a James Brown song—all-subsuming funk beat, chicken-scratch guitar, guttural utterances about dance crazes, call-and-response of simple phrases with his backup singers, post-bop horns rubbing against and pushing the groove, organ rumble—with stuff that's intrinsically his: the B-3 is replaced by an ever-present uncanny unsteady synthtone in the background that undulates like a rock about to fall off a cliff, the warmth is replaced by brittle, electronic atmosphere, the squeals are done by a neuter eunuch (this is one of the Camille songs), the backing vocals overdubbed and slowed down into near-parodies of R&B masculinity. Even the titular dance craze is artificial. (Brown sang about *real* dance crazes like the Mashed Potato and the Popcorn, damn it.) In a way, Prince's version of J.B. was far more up-to-date than the rappers'; the problem is that theirs was the way of the future, and Prince's methods, in hindsight, are pretty time-bound.

This hardly matters when "Housequake" is playing, though. One of Prince's underrated traits is how funny he is, a perception he hasn't helped by suing fans who put up websites about him and generally being a humorless prick in other areas. But as I began to prepare this book, I put *Sign 'O' the Times* on for the first time in what had probably been two or three years and was surprised to find myself laughing out loud, especially during "Housequake"—usually at specific lines (his cries of "Bullshit," and the "Shocka-locka-*boom!*" "What was that?" "Aftershock" exchange between lead and background vocal), but moreover at how audaciously energetic it was. For instance, there's a saxophone squiggle about three-quarters of the way through the song (following "And the saxophone is the fault, check it out"). Clearly, the shout-out and responsive lines are a nod to Maceo Parker's solos on James Brown's records, though here the odd, almost Eastern tonality is more like a (probably accidental) tribute to Robert McCollough's squawking blurts on 1970's "Super Bad." ("'Trane, brother!" J.B. shouted in encouragement, but, as Robert Christgau pointed out, McCollough's gusts were closer to Albert Ayler.) The squiggle is only a couple of bars long, but it's long enough to function as both homage and parody. So is the song's intro and outro, a record scratch with Prince shouting, "Shut up, already! Damn!" The first time it's an announcement that the singer and band are here (a nice touch after the busy, bustling "Play in the Sunshine," which winds down into an odd little dialogue that sounds like it wandered in from the movie constantly playing in Prince's head). The second time, it's Prince-as-listener, sounding older and haggard, yelling at the neighbor's kids to cut the racket out—he's trying to get some sleep. (For a nice recent analogue to this, see the ending of Sean Paul's "Get Busy" video.)

Is Prince yelling at the kids with their that's-not-music-that's-noise rap? You could certainly suspect so. "Housequake's" singer could just as easily be heard as a piss-take of a young MC (though not, ha ha, Young MC, who hadn't started yet) or a twittery-voiced J.B. clone. And Prince was a vocal critic of hip-hop: "Dead on It," from *The Black Album*, set for release in late 1987 and shelved until 1994, was a rather dim-witted rap parody in which Prince claims that "The only good rapper is one that's dead-on it" (rimshot!) and that "The rapper's problem usually stems from being tone deaf / Pack the house then try 2 sing, there won't be no one left," which misstates—and misses—the point completely. (Phrasing like "the rapper" doesn't help Professor Prince's case, either. And what's this "usually"? What about the rest of the time?)

The Velvet Underground and Nico

by Joe Harvard

Part One
The Setting

Our Heroes Meet...

Moe Tucker: I didn't like that love-peace shit.

John Cale: By 1965 Lou Reed had already written "Heroin" and "Waiting for the Man.". . . At the time I was playing with LaMonte Young in the Dream Syndicate and the concept of the group was to sustain notes for two hours at a time.

Sterling Morrison: I was a very unsensitive young person and played very unsensitive, uncaring music. Which is Wham, Bam, Pow! Let's Rock Out! What I expected my audience to do was tear the house down, beat me up, whatever. Lou and I came from the identical environment of Long Island rock 'n' roll bars, where you can drink anything at 18, everybody has phony proof at 16; I was a night crawler in high school and played some of the sleaziest bars.

David Fricke, author of the excellent little book that passes as liner notes for *Peel Slowly and See*, writes: "In 1965 rock and roll was a very young, carefree and essentially teenage music—everything Reed, Cale, Morrison and Tucker had outgrown by the time they became the Velvet Underground." A year after the Beatles released *A Hard Day's Night*, and the year they recorded *Rubber Soul*, former electroshock patient, drug dealer, and Syracuse English major Lou Reed graduated, having been nurtured under the mentorship of poet Delmore Schwartz (for his literary skills), and under the influence of every drug conceivable (for his songwriting). Reed got a hack songwriting job at Pickwick Records—a sort of poor man's Brill Building gig, writing songs for nonexistent bands made up of Pickwick personnel so the label could cash in on the latest musical fads. Loaded to the gills one night, Reed wrote a dance song called "The Ostrich," credited upon release to the fictitious Primitives. When sales of the record starting taking off, the label scrambled to form a band that could support it playing live dates; because he looked like a rock musician, John Cale was approached at a party and asked to "audition." For laughs—and because someone mentioned a salary—John attended.

Cale was a classical composer and prodigy from Wales, whose first composition was reportedly written on a piece of plywood. A graduate of London's prestigious Goldsmith College, a Leonard Bernstein Scholarship had brought him to the US. Plainly speaking, he was One Badass Classical Dude. He studied at Tanglewood Music Center under Iannis Xenakis, a former member of Le Corbusier's architectural group whose 1954 Metastasis, a work based on architectural design, had been enormously influential. Cale disliked the stuffy atmosphere of Tanglewood, however, and soon moved to Manhattan to explore the avant-garde. There, he played with LaMonte Young, proponent of the held notes called drones found in Indian and Arabic music.

At the Pickwick audition, Cale was flabbergasted to discover that "The Ostrich" was based on an open-tuned guitar part played by Lou Reed; with all the strings tuned to the same note (A#), the effect produced was the very same drone that Cale's associates had been working with! Having instantly formed a very low opinion of the Pickwick operation, and having come to expect such technique only within his rarefied avant-garde circle, this was a shock akin to finding a monkey tuning his viola. His attention thus captured, Cale joined the Primitives. They played just a few shows, but the experience of standing on a stage with a bunch of teenage girls screaming at him had its effect on the young Welshman: he was hooked. Infected with the rock bug, chumming around with Lou Reed, Cale finally listened to some of the "real" songs Reed had been pestering him about. Once again, he was more than pleasantly surprised. The Primitives' demise notwithstanding, the two musicians drew closer.

When fellow ex-Primitive Tony Conrad moved out of Cale's Lower East Side apartment, Reed moved in. Typical high-spirited lads, they shared their love for music and chemically assisted recreation . . . principally opiates. Sensing the need for a band, and an opportunity to do something truly different and important, they recruited Angus MacLise, a neighbor who provided percussion along with electricity for their amps. A true bohemian, he would die of malnutrition in Katmandu in 1979.

Soon, Reed ran into an old Syracuse acquaintance, Sterling Morrison. Sterling was a former trumpet player, a brilliant guitarist, and he shared Lou's tastes in rock 'n' roll. He believed rock music should make folks want to tear shit up, God bless him, and Reed immediately enlisted him. Together the four worked on songs throughout the summer of 1965, calling themselves the Warlocks, and then the Falling Spikes. When MacLise left the group, Morrison contacted the sister of an old friend, Jim Tucker, and Maureen

"Moe" Tucker entered the picture. A keypunch operator who played to Bo Diddley and Stones records after work, Moe had developed a unique style, playing a bass drum on its side with mallets and a tom-tom, eschewing cymbals and busy parts for a super-simple, relentlessly pulsing beat. Tucker was on her way to becoming one of the few completely original drummers in rock. Over the next year she played a tambourine (and nothing else), then a set of well-used garbage cans turned upside down, before reverting to her own weird-ass setup. The Velvet Underground was born.

The group agreed to a handshake management deal with pioneer rock journalist Al Aronowitz, whose middle name was "the man who introduced the Beatles to Dylan." Aronowitz booked them as house band at a tourist trap, Café Bizarre, where they got to play six sets a night for five bucks a member. Success! People hated them. Just as another pain-fest loomed, in the form of six New Year's Eve sets, in through the door walked Gerard Malanga, future whip dancer, and Paul Morrissey, business manager for Andy Warhol's Factory.

Erupting, Exploding, Etcetera

In the 1960s, an intriguing "art groupie" and critic, Barbara Rubin, began introducing talented people to one another with missionary zeal. It was on her advice that Paul Morrissey went to see the Velvets. Morrissey had just been given an opportunity to book a club—under the aegis of the Warhol name—and was seeking a house band for the venture. After seeing the Velvets he believed he had found one. The die was cast, and the next night Warhol himself returned to catch the band's set. After some cat-and-mouse between Reed and Morrissey—the Velvets, after all, had already accepted Aronowitz as their manager—a deal was struck, and Warhol and Morrissey became managers of the Velvet Underground, eventually forming a corporation called Warvel under which to operate.

The band soon became part of the multimedia "happenings" that Warhol had been planning, but which had yet to materialize. The concept of showing films, adding live music, and bathing it all in psychedelic light did not originate with Andy. Jonas Mekas had already featured the band playing behind a movie screen during shows at Cinemateque—but it was left to Warhol to develop an idea fully, incorporating confrontational theater techniques as well. His concept evolved from a film-plus-band appearance at a psychiatrist convention, into the successful *Andy Warhol, Uptight* show at Cinemateque (including an Edie Sedgwick film retrospective). It was then further refined into the *Exploding Plastic Inevitable* (EPI), a format without precedent, which eventually included a dozen-plus members. Norman Dolph recalls:

The final decision on a name came during a meeting in my living room. I believe it was Paul [Morrissey] who ultimately chose *"Exploding"* as more suitable than the name that nearly stuck—the *Erupting Plastic Inevitable*.

The *Exploding Plastic Inevitable* owed its existence to the public's interest in Warhol. Andy was expected to appear at the shows, and with the level of interest in the pop artists at its peak, high fees could be sought and got. But with art and film projects putting constant demands on his time, Andy eventually (and inevitably) began to lose interest in the extravaganzas. The *EPI* strobe lights dimmed, and the first cracks appeared in the Velvets' relationship with the Warhol/Morrissey team, leading to their break-up the next year.

Management and the Album

Much might be said regarding Warhol and Paul Morrissey's performance as managers, but we'll stick to aspects that affected this particular album. Their most significant capital outlay to the band—i.e., as a group and not as part of the *EPI*—went toward the recording process. The outlay was probably around $3,000, though John Cale has named the sum of $1,500 more than once.

Warvel's ability to put the group into the studio early on, capturing their still-fresh sound intact, was no doubt their most important and successful managerial act. Ironically, they paid their share of the studio bill with money from a triumph that ended their managerial nadir: the Dom. The *EPI* shows at the Dom, a former Polish social club on St. Mark's Place, were the hottest ticket in New York in the spring of '66. In just a month, the *EPI* brought in $18,000, and a permanent club was planned. However, before they secured the lease on the Dom space, the team decided to accept a month-long gig in Los Angeles.

The West Coast tour was a bust. The logistics of traveling with the troupe's dozen-plus members was formidable enough, but then the anticipated monthlong booking evaporated when the club closed after only three days. The trip simply magnified the Velvets' already healthy disdain for the West Coast. The only highlight was that the band was able to record for two days with Tom Wilson. After a demoralizing month, the group returned to New York, itching to regain the invigorating momentum of the Dom shows. On their arrival they discovered that the lease had been finessed out from under them by Bob Dylan's manager—an associate of the very person who booked them on the LA trip. The decision to go west, which Warhol was sure was a perfect place for the Velvets, had been an unmitigated disaster. "Their" club, renamed the Balloon Farm (later the Electric Circus), rapidly provided their rivals with industry clout which the Velvets would never possess. It also made scads of dough for the new owners, and the lease was later sold for a small fortune.

While the failure to book a European tour or capitalize on tentative overtures from Brian Epstein stand out as other lost management opportunities, the loss of the Dom was a body blow, in hindsight, to the first album. The lost income could have funded marketing and promotional activities independent of MGM/Verve's lackluster efforts: efforts so half-hearted that they all but guaranteed the commercial failure of the album. Without a reasonable budget, getting the record into stores and publicizing it was beyond the group's abilities.

Despite the depressing conclusion to the Dom adventure, there were two significant consequences of their involvement in the venue. First, it was there that the band's role grew from being just one element among many within the *EPI*'s chaotic framework, to becoming a central feature recognized as a viable entity in and of itself. Second, it was through the Dom that soon-to-be-producer Norman Dolph was drawn into the band's orbit . . . and along with him came the connection to the studio that the album would be recorded in.

How do Warhol and Morrissey, as managers, come out on the balance sheet, particularly with regard to *The Velvet Underground and Nico*? David Fricke evaluates the association this way:

> In the early years the band had the perfect manager and fan in Andy Warhol, someone who kept the biz wolves at bay through the sheer force of his own celebrity and who vigorously encouraged the band's high-minded purism at the expense of his own investment.

To his credit, Warhol created a bubble the band could grow in, and he never saw a dime from sales of *The Velvet Underground and Nico*. However, being utterly inexperienced at navigating record label politics, Warvel made rookie mistakes and proved unable to prevent delays or resolve problems that produced disastrous results. Many of the hold-ups in the release of the record were caused by fairly small issues—all of which could have been solved speedily if the arm that held the checkbook had been twisted sufficiently. But Warhol and Morrissey were either too green to realize this or simply unwilling to do the twisting.

Warhol recognized that he could only offer the band limited aid in the specialized world of record companies, lawyers, and publishers. He asked Reed if the band was really satisfied playing nothing but the art museums and school auditoriums Warvel could offer. Having long sensed Warhol's waning interest, and painfully aware of the dismal treatment the album was receiving from MGM/Verve, Reed saw no future with Warvel, and responded by firing Warhol. He then hired a genuine rock manager named Steve Sesnick, who'd been courting the group—with Reed's approval—for some time.

Overall, any evaluation of Warhol's managerial tenure has to acknowledge the dual role he played. His administrative shortcomings were certainly counterbalanced by the creative stimulus he provided the band. It was in that role that he was of inestimable value to them, and to their first album.

At the Board:
Andy, Norman, John & Tom

In "Andy Warhol" David Bowie sang, "Andy Warhol, Silver Screen, can't tell them apart at all." Bowie, a dedicated fan of all things Velvet and Warhol, describes a man whose desire was to surround himself with the interesting, the vibrant, and the talented, projecting them through his art and his films back on the world:

> Like to take a cement fix / Be a standing cinema
> Dress my friends up just for show / See them as they really are . . .
> Put a peephole in my brain / Two New Pence to have a go
> I'd like to be a gallery / Put you all inside my show

Warhol was immersed in—and becoming known for—his underground filmmaking when he met the Velvets, and his personal and professional attraction to the subjects of his films (largely Factory regulars) was apparent in his work. He did "see them as they really are," distilling on film the essence of the Superstar persona, revealing the face they most desired to show the public. He would help the Velvets do the same with their music. After their first meeting, Reed himself became a regular feature in the psychological theater of Warhol's Factory, part of the scene yet detached from it. Like the journalist he studied to be, he could always step back and watch, becoming more an observer than a participant, and around Andy there was always much to see—and wonder at. Reed's admiration for Warhol would be lifelong, and justly so. Warhol had a strong influence on the Velvets' music. But he was no Svengali.

One hot day in June, as we raked leaves in my back yard, I asked Jonathan Richman about Andy Warhol. He answered: "You know that Doors movie, the one by Oliver Stone? Well, Andy was nothing like that whatsoever"—his tone clearly indicating how offensive he found the caricature of Warhol as an effeminate fop. "For one thing, he was . . . if there's one word you'd use to describe him it would be 'dignified'"; adding, "he didn't talk a lot . . . he used very few words, very Zen." Jonathan described a man who was generous with his time and his ideas. Upon first meeting him at the Boston Tea Party rock club, Richman—then an aspiring artist himself—confessed that he did not really understand Andy's artwork. Warhol replied: "Yes you do." The world-famous artist then engaged in an unhurried conversation with the sixteen-year-old from the suburbs, discussing his work and art in general. "He was the perfect person for a sixteen-year-old to talk to," Jonathan told me.

Warhol really did listen, even to an unknown kid. Some time later, Jonathan visited the Factory, making the climb up to the loft space via the stairs instead of the elevator. Remembering the kid from their Boston meeting, Warhol asked him, "Why did you take the stairs?" Richman replied: "I like to exercise." At each subsequent meeting—three months, then three years later—Andy would eventually get around to asking him, "So did you take the stairs again?" The picture that forms certainly isn't one of a cynical, catty creep, but of a considerate, compassionate, understated individual who genuinely liked people and had a healthy sense of humor: Bodhidharma with a twinkle in his eye.

Norman Dolph also describes Warhol in similar terms. "He wasn't what I'd call a mover and a shaker, he was never loud or in your face. He'd be sitting quietly in the back of the room, observing, making the occasional wry comment . . . he was more of a presence, really."

As for Warhol's reputation as a manipulator (for which former rivals, disgruntled Factory Superstars with tarnished auras, and the media are mainly responsible), it should be said that he almost certainly lost money on most—if not all—of his film work with the Superstars, and definitely when it came to the Velvets. When the band was about to be signed to MGM/Verve, Lou Reed suddenly announced that he wouldn't sign the contract unless all monies went straight to the band, who would then distribute the agreed-upon twenty-five percent manager's share to Warhol and Morrissey. Preoccupied perhaps with this *coup d'état*, Reed neglected to have the rewritten contract stipulate what the band's share of royalties would be, and consequently it was many years before anyone received anything from the sales of the first album. Andy himself never saw a cent from the record, and the degree of goodwill he felt for the group can be gauged by the fact that—despite Reed's machinations—he immediately released them from their contract when they asked.

The Means of Production

What does a producer do on an album? A producer can be anything from a hand-holder who babysits a band in the studio to an overseer who micromanages every aspect of an album including the choice of songs, the final arrangements of those songs, the studio to use, even who gets to play what (if at all) on the project. An open-ended job description, it spans those who mix records, and those who mainly sit around mixing drinks. There are certain general types. My personal favorite is the transparent variety: the producer who adds little personal coloration, letting the band's sound take precedence. Some producers are transformers, taking every song apart, bar by bar; then there are the fashionable star producers, the Phil Spectors and Trevor Horns, who mark their work with their own immediately discernible brand. My least favorite variety I call "dog-ballers": producers who can't resist tinkering with a song, simply because they have the record company's authority to do so. (The name comes from an old joke: "Why do dogs lick their balls?" "Because they can!") The best producers select the approach most suited to emphasizing the unique strengths of a band, fulfilling the prime directive of their profession: making the best possible record. In that respect, Andy Warhol—with no engineering or production experience, but buoyed by a solid team who did have experience—would prove to be a great producer.

In terms of a traditional production role (i.e., sitting at the mixing board, getting good sounds, and choosing the best performances), for *The Velvet Underground and Nico* the Velvets worked with both a novice, Norman Dolph, and an experienced, transparent pro, Tom Wilson. The original LP credits read "edited and remixed under the supervision of Tom Wilson by Gene Radice and David Greene. Recording engineers: Omi Haden—T.T.G. Hollywood." Neither Dolph nor John Licata, the engineer he worked with, is mentioned—a travesty considering that they recorded the bulk of the record.

In 1966 Norman Dolph was twenty-seven, four years out of Yale with a degree in electrical engineering. Although he'd given his notice he was still a Columbia Records sales executive (the job lasted six years) at the time of the sessions. Dolph worked in the Customs Labels Division, which handled the plastic moulding for scores of small record labels that had no pressing plant of their own. One of Dolph's accounts was the independent Scepter Records. Scepter had moved into a new building the year before, and on one of his visits Dolph noticed that it included a new feature of its own: a recording studio.

In his spare time, Dolph had applied his engineering knowledge to a side venture:

> I operated a mobile discothèque, if not the first then at least the second one in New York. I was an art buff, and my thing was I'd provide the music at art galleries, for shows and openings, but I'd ask for a piece of art as payment, instead of cash. That's how I met Andy Warhol. Then one day I got a call, saying he was opening a new club—the Dom—and how would I like to provide the sound for it? We met at my apartment a few times to discuss it, but the main thing was going to be the records, we never even discussed the band. At the Dom—at first—the band were regarded as just one more thing happening in the room, but then there was so much going on. They'd show Andy's films, and they actually had a 16mm projector that Gerard

(Malanga) would carry around, flashing the movies on the audience, the band, all over . . . and this was no lightweight machine, either!

With the amount of speed being taken by Warhol's retinue at that time they could probably have juggled a couple 16mm projectors, but drugging was decidedly not Norman's scene: "My life was as far removed from heroin in the veins as it was possible to be." Fortunately for the Velvets, his musical habits were more akin to theirs, and when Warhol mentioned that they were planning on making a record, Dolph signed on ("I was moonlighting, really"). The plan was that he would book the studio, help cover costs, produce, and when the project was done he'd use his connections at Columbia to help the band get signed. He accomplished three of those four tasks, and began by getting in touch with John Licata at Scepter.

Licata may have been one of the few engineers at that time who could have done the job for the album—a time of which Lou Reed says, "engineers would walk out on us . . . 'I didn't become an engineer so I could listen to you guys jerk off! This is noise and garbage.' We ran into a lot of that." By contrast, Dolph says Licata was a seasoned pro:

> He was Scepter's full-time studio engineer. As a perk, he did custom jobs when the studio wasn't booked. He could engineer material he couldn't stand, but he would give it his all. He'd give the client what the client wanted. John would be over there doing soul–R&B acts one day and Dionne Warwick–Burt Bacharach orchestral stuff the next . . . "It's two o'clock so it must be a gospel session" . . . he was a journeyman engineer, with no "star attitude" that I imagine some engineers have now, but he gave it his all. He was a pro. HE would not treat the material with any disdain or "what the fuck!?"

Fair is fair; with Warhol in and out of the studio, only Dolph and Licata were present in the control room for the entire time the album was being made. This record wouldn't have happened without them. Dolph tips his hat to Licata and Cale though, saying: "Great credit for the sound of the record itself has to go to John Licata . . . I was more what you today call a line producer. The job of creative producer I would say was Cale's; anything to do with music or arrangements, Cale was in charge." (Author's note: I once did a session with the late Stones' producer Jimmy Miller, a beautiful and brilliant cat, and he brought along a line producer . . . the guy just kept producing lines.)

Dolph remained in music, as a lyricist and music publisher, "mostly during the disco era," placing songs with Isaac Hayes and KC and the Sunshine Band. He wrote the lyrics for Joey Levine's 1974 hit "Life Is a Rock (But the Radio Rolled Me)," a swank bit of bubblegum rapping, in which he managed the impressive feat of mentioning Dr. John the Night Tripper, Doris Day, and Jack the Ripper in one line; he also worked in Johnny Thunders, Bowie, and J.J.—but not John—Cale.

Little is known about the role of the recording engineer credited in LA, Omi Haden, also listed in credits as Ami Hadani. Haden engineered on the Mothers of Invention LPs *Freak Out* and *Absolutely Free*, and the Animals' *Animalism*, all done at TTG Studios. He also worked on Lowell George's Factory auditions for Zappa, at Original Sound in LA, in the fall of 1966. All but the last are Tom Wilson projects, and every one of these projects has a Zappa connection, so he may have been either TTG's house engineer, or the LA go-to guy for Zappa or Tom Wilson in '66 and '67.

Tom Wilson had been primarily a jazz producer, working with late 50s and early 60s progressive artists Sun Ra, John Coltrane, Cecil Taylor, and others until a 1963 management power play forced Columbia Records to hire him as Bob Dylan's producer, replacing the more staid John Hammond. Wilson, who held an economics degree from Harvard, was neither folkie nor rocker, but he was impressed enough by Dylan to assume control of sessions for *The Freewheelin' Bob Dylan*. Wilson's experiments with placing electric guitar on some tracks Dylan had laid down in '62, and his production on *Bringing It All Back Home* and "Like a Rolling Stone," make him a pioneer of the new folk-rock sound, a style he helped further define through his work with Simon and Garfunkel (who were on the verge of disbanding when Wilson's drum and guitar treatment propelled "Sound of Silence" into a reborn number one hit). Richie Unterberger has written:

> Overall, Wilson's stay at Columbia had turned into one of those "only in America, and only in rock and roll" scenarios: an African-American jazz producer, who professed not even to like folk music when he began recording it, turned out to be a main agent of folk's transition into folk-rock.

Wilson would later work with the Soft Machine and the Blues Project, but it was his move to MGM/Verve that paved the way for his involvement in avant-garde rock. In 1966 he produced the Animals, the Mothers of Invention, and Burt Ward—all at TTG Studios in Los Angeles, where he worked with the Velvets in May, and where he edited, remixed, and remastered the "Banana" album using engineers David Greene and Gene Radice. He later produced "Sunday Morning" in New York.

But it's Andy Warhol whose name appears on the record's spine, and he resembles neither Dolph nor Wilson. In hands-on terms Cale has said, "Andy Warhol didn't do anything." Warhol's unique style might disqualify him from the title of "producer" at all, making him effectively an executive producer. But Warhol's role, and his effect as producer, cannot be denied. You could say he produced the producers as well as the band.

Longtime friend of the band, rock manager and A&R legend Danny Fields spoke eloquently on the subject in *Uptight: The Velvet Underground Story*:

> Andy doesn't know how to translated ideas into musical terms . . . Andy. . . was making them sound like he knew they sounded at the Factory. That's what I would do if I were an amateur at production. . . . What Andy did was very generously reproduce . . . the way it sounded to him when he first fell in love with it.

The group had their sound together before meeting Warhol. They had Lou Reed's experience at Pickwick to prepare them for the studio's technical challenges, and the good fortune to luck into Dolph and Licata at the right moment. In Los Angeles, fortune smiled again, and they added Tom Wilson's expertise as well. So there was no need at all for Warhol to be a knob twiddler—which he clearly wasn't.

> **Reed:** Andy was the producer and Andy was in fact behind the board gazing with rap fascination.
> **Cale:** . . . at all the blinking lights.
> **Reed:** . . . At all the blinking lights. He just made it possible for us to be ourselves and go right ahead with it because he was Andy Warhol. In a sense he really did produce it, because he was this umbrella that absorbed all the attacks when we weren't large enough to be attacked . . . as a consequence of him being the producer, we'd just walk in and set up and do what we always did and no one would stop it because Andy was the producer. Of course, he didn't know anything about record production—but he didn't have to. He just sat there and said, "Oooh, that's fantastic," and the engineer would say, "Oh yeah! Right! It is fantastic, isn't it?"

This alone made Warhol indispensable to the album. But, of course, he did more than that. Fricke calls Warhol "a specialist in subtly engineering collisions of people and ideas," and in that role Warhol (with help from Paul Morrissey) coaxed the group into accepting Nico as a vocalist, completing the chemistry that makes the album so amazing. He was also the umbrella under which Dolph in New York and Wilson in LA (and later New York) worked, unfettered by label interference. And he got the album heard, for even if Dolph and Wilson had done brilliant work, without the carte blanche Warhol provided it's doubtful the recording would have made it onto vinyl. Thus, Warhol did precisely what a great producer should: he achieved an effective translation of the sound that the band heard in their heads onto tape, and then he got it out into the world intact.

A trade-off of Warhol's inexperience in the studio could have been a disastrous loss in sonic clarity. Cale also claimed that Norman Dolph "didn't understand the first fucking thing about recording . . . he didn't know what the hell he had on his hands," and while Dolph didn't dispute the charges (he responds "nobody knew what they were doing"), I think Cale's criticism is way off the mark. First of all, with Cale filling the role of creative producer without portfolio, Dolph says:

> I never felt I had the authority to pick takes, or veto them—that, to me, was clearly up to Cale, Reed and Morrison . . . Lou Reed was more the one who'd say "this needs to be a little hotter," he made decisions about technical things . . . and the mixing was really between Cale, Sterling and John Licata, 'cause that was all again, done in real time.

As for sound quality, oversaturated tapes caused some audible distortion, and noise from less-than-perfect overdubs is also in evidence. But considering the unprecedented sonic attack in songs like "European Son" and "Black Angel's Death Song," which few engineers would have been comfortable capturing (or tolerating) in 1966, you have to agree that the Dolph–Licata team performed brilliantly. Any doubts on that score can be dispelled with a few "this is what might have been" moments of comparative listening to Reed's primitive-sounding Pickwick recordings, which aren't even in the same ballpark as Licata's engineering work. And any noise/distortion issues on the LP detract little from the overall listening experience. Moreover, the band happily accepted these slight technical shortfalls at the time, and—whether by their own design or Warhol's—band and producer shared an aesthetic that made errors part of the *modus operandi*. Reed noted:

> No one wants it to sound professional. It's so much nicer to play into one very cheap mike. That's the way it sounds when you hear it live and that's the way it should sound on the record.

Warhol elaborated:

> I was worried that it would all come out sounding too professional . . . one of the things that was so great about them was they always sounded so raw and crude. Raw and crude was the way I liked our movies to look, and there's a similarity between sound in that album and the texture of *Chelsea Girls*, which came out at the same time.

The studio approach they took, as recalled by Dolph, left little threat of things sounding too professional:

> From a take-wise point of view you weren't presented with many options. They either got it right, or broke down, or did a couple of takes; but it was-

n't as though you got seventeen takes . . . either you chose this one or you chose that one and then you went on and did the next one. Usually they'd do a piece of one and then come in and listen to it. If one got largely through and it broke down, they'd come in and listen to it and say "yeah that sounds like we got it right"; or, if one got all the way through, they'd come in and either buy it, or adjust the mix or do it again. But there were not a whole lot of complete takes.

I'm Sticking with You

To a man or a Moe, the Velvets themselves have never wavered in their appreciation of Warhol's key role in their careers and on the first album. When personalities as disparate and intelligent (not to mention picky) as the Velvets all agree that they owe a huge debt of gratitude to Warhol, you have to take it at face value: after all, they were there. Cale and Reed would bury their oft-sharpened hatchet to write *Songs for Drella* together in 1989, an homage full of love and respect. (It's also a strong LP, which gets better with each listening, and among the more vital works by either writer since the Velvets dissolved.) Sterling Morrison offered his own tribute, citing Warhol as the most important influence on his own life, saying, "It sounds crazy, but on reflection I've decided he was never wrong. He gave us the confidence to keep doing what we were doing."

Confidence was precisely what the band needed most in 1966. They were about to go into the recording studio—in those days, still a place with a rarefied atmosphere. It would be another twenty years before musician-run, independent studios such as Athens, Georgia's Drive-In and Boston's Fort Apache (my place—our credo was "the nuts should run the nuthouse") became common. Some studios, like Abbey Road, had technicians in white lab coats, and even the less formal studios usually had actual engineering graduates behind the consoles. Studios were still more about science than art. Clients who dared make technical suggestions were treated with bemusement, derision, or hostility. The Velvets were a young band under constant critical attack, and the pressure to conform in order to gain acceptance must have been tremendous. Most bands of that era compromised with their record companies, through wholesale revamping of their image from wardrobe to musical style, changing or omitting lyrics, creating drastically edited versions for radio airplay, or eliminating songs entirely from their sets and records. With Andy Warhol in the band's corner, such threats were minimized.

The group often cites Andy's advice just before the first sessions that "everything's really great, just make sure you keep the dirty words in." The phrase, which even appears in *Songs for Drella*, was understood by the band to mean "keep it rough . . . don't let them tame it down so it doesn't disturb anyone." Thus bolstered, they had the courage to stick to the way they knew it should go: "Don't make it slick. Don't make it smooth and ruin it." Lou Reed has recounted how, before they entered the recording studio:

> Andy made a point of trying to make sure that on our first album the language remained intact . . . "don't change the words just because it's a record." I think Andy was interested in shocking, in giving people a jolt and not letting them talk us into taking that stuff out in the interest of popularity or easy airplay. The best things never got on record . . . he was adamant about that. He didn't want it to be cleaned up, and because he was there it wasn't.

The band had everyone in their corner on this, the point where their goals dovetailed with those of Warhol and Dolph. When we spoke, Norman downplayed his role in the sessions in all but one respect, and that was his effort to keep the sessions moving at a pace that would allow the group to achieve a goal so simple it was nearly impossible in 1966:

> They knew what they wanted, and nobody got off the path of that. They wanted it to sound like it had the night before, at the Dom, and . . . the money supply was finite and predetermined . . . I kept it on the rails, doing what had to be done under the constraints of time and money . . . beyond that I don't want to try to take any more credit.

For once, Danny Fields may have got it wrong when he says, "Andy had no influence on the sound of the band whatsoever." It's true that the band had their sound together before they met Warhol, but Warhol's creative input was felt outside of the recording studio, conceptually and creatively. It was Warhol's comment that the band should just rehearse onstage that helped push them toward their flights of improvised daring. He suggested that Reed write or make (sometimes small but significant) changes to "I'll Be Your Mirror," "Femme Fatale," "All Tomorrow's Parties," and "Sunday Morning." Sometimes it was just a simple statement to Lou that triggered the change, or inspired a part. At other times it was a more direct involvement, as with "Femme Fatale." Were it not for Warhol, of course, Nico would never have joined the group, and that in and of itself gives him a colossal role in the sound on the first album, and by extension the band.

Let It Be

by Steve Matteo

Chapter Three
We're on Our Way Home

The Beatles were to begin recording in the basement of Apple Studios on Monday, January 20. In fact, recording finally began on Wednesday, January 22. As at Twickenham, the sessions would be filmed.

George Harrison had recently attended a Ray Charles concert with Eric Clapton at the Royal Festival Hall on London's South Bank. One of the members of Charles' group was the also the opening act. He was a tall black man who was singing and dancing—and he quickly seized the attention of Harrison. It took a little bit of time, but to Harrison's delight, he finally figured out that it was Billy Preston.

The Beatles had become friendly with Preston when they made their second successive trip in 1962 to Hamburg, West Germany, for a two-week engagement at the Star-Club from November 1 through 14. At that time, the Beatles were sharing the bill with one of their American musical heroes, Little Richard, as they had done twice in Liverpool. Over those two weeks they met and befriended Little Richard's keyboardist, Billy Preston. They even asked him to play with them, but he rebuffed them, thinking that it would annoy Little Richard. Preston, then only sixteen years old, hailed from Houston, Texas. He would go on to play with Sam Cooke before working with Ray Charles in the studio in 1965 and touring with him starting in 1967.

George was able to get a message to Preston to call him. When he called, George told him to drop by Apple and say hello. Preston, having no idea what was about to happen, simply came to Apple on the 22nd at George's urging. Just after lunch, George found out that Preston was in the reception area of Apple. Without hesitation, he invited Preston to come in and jam. That day, Preston eventually played on the songs "Don't Let Me Down" and "She Came in Through the Bathroom Window."

Paralleling their time at Twickenham, the Beatles' first day at Apple would be a day of rehearsals. Why the Beatles would need any more rehearsing at that point seems hard to understand. Preston immediately brought a new élan to the session. The Beatles were considerably happier after abandoning Twickenham and clearing up the initial technical problems at Apple.

Also, they clearly enjoyed the cozy confines of Apple. Preston essentially became a guest in their home, putting everyone on their best behavior. They treated him right away as a musical equal after the measurable success of his brief input. At the end of the first day, he was officially asked to join the group for the rest of the January recordings at Apple.

Whereas the imminent departure from the project of Ringo—and, to a lesser extent, of Glyn Johns—served to limit the ultimate length of the recording to be done at Apple, other factors added to the pressure to bring the project to a timely conclusion. Specifically, the group had virtually no usable material from Twickenham, and Billy Preston was scheduled to do a tour of Texas in February.

That first day of rehearsals was not all that different from Twickenham, musically. The group played some oldies, including "New Orleans," "Hi-Heeled Sneakers," "My Baby Left Me/That's All Right," and "Good Rockin' Tonight." "Don't Let Me Down" was performed and "I've Got a Feeling" was fleshed out with seven near-complete takes. One of the last run-throughs of "Dig a Pony" was later included on the double-CD *Anthology 3*. Also, near the end of the day, two takes of "She Came in Through the Bathroom Window" were done, neither of which was very exciting. Nonetheless, the second one was also included on *Anthology 3*. Paul brought out "Every Night" for the first time during the "Get Back"/"Let It Be" project. The first version of it was short, poorly performed, incomplete as a song, and marred by technical problems. Paul would perform it again in a rather more fleshed out (yet still incomplete) fashion on the 24th.

The next day saw a major change in scheduling: the group did only a four-hour session during the day and then returned in the evening without the film crew to work on a complete take each of "Dig a Pony" and "I've Got a Feeling." That day also marked the debut for future superstar producer and recording artist Alan Parsons as tape-op. Parsons, of course, would go on to engineer Pink Floyd's *Dark Side of the Moon*, recorded at Abbey Road, in 1973. Parsons talked about the sessions: "My first impression was how unhappy they were. They were not very pleased with what they were hearing. I think Paul had a vision for it. I think the others didn't really go with that vision; that was my impression."

Activity increased on Friday the 24th and became more varied. The early part of the day was marked by the first discussion about having some kind of booklet accompanying the album. Ethan Russell, an American photographer, had been shooting photos for the past three days. When he showed his pictures to Neil Aspinall and the Beatles, he was asked to stay for the rest of the sessions and do a book to be included with the album. At some point there had been discussions about having über-photographer David Bailey shoot some photos of the filming and sessions. There had also been some serious consideration, particularly by John, about having Billy Preston join the group as a permanent member. In the end, Paul decided the idea was not so good after all. Four of them were quite enough at that point, thank you!

An early, half-hearted attempt at "Get Back" was made. The song was not worked on further, however, because of Billy Preston's absence until the afternoon. "Two of Us" and "Teddy Boy" were then worked on. "Two of Us" was given a sweeter, more acoustic, and slower tempo feel. "Teddy Boy" was brought back after a brief attempt at on the 9th at Twickenham. Paul had written it, along with "Junk," in India in 1968. Like "Junk," it would end up on Paul's solo debut. The Beatles had done a demo of it in 1968, which appeared on *Anthology 3*. Also, part of one of the versions of "Teddy Boy" done on that day, coupled with part of the song that would be performed on the 28th, were included on *Anthology 3*.

"Maggie Mae" turned up out of the blue for the first time on the 24th. While the song's origin derives from a minstrel song from 1856 entitled "Darling Nellie Gray," written by an American named Benjamin Russell Hanby, the version Paul and John would have been familiar with was the one recorded in 1957 by a Liverpool skiffle group called the Vipers. Three short snippets of the song were played on that day; the third ended up on the original *Let It Be* album. The song would be the last non-original song to appear on a Beatles album.

The 24th would also mark the first occasion at Apple when time was spent listening to playbacks. "Her Majesty" was recorded on that day as well. Other songs done by Paul that day included "There You Are Eddie," "Every Night," and "Pillow for Your Head." The group returned to jamming on some oldies with "I Lost My Little Girl," an oldies medley, and "Singin' the Blues." After running through "Dig It" with Billy Preston now back in tow, the group did many takes of "Get Back." More oldies followed, including "Bad Boy" and "Stand by Me/Where Have You Been." Geoff Emerick and engineer Neil Richmond may have also been present on the 24th, alongside Glyn Johns. That evening Johns headed to Olympic and spent ninety minutes or so working on some rough stereo mixes, thus accelerating the notion that there was actually the possibility of an album to come.

On Saturday, the group produced a finished take of a song, George's "For You Blue." Entitled "For You Blues" when George originally wrote it, the song had been briefly called "George's Blues" when the group was working on it at Twickenham.

The group's return to Apple on Sunday marked the first time in a year that it would work right through an entire weekend. The day began with George demoing "Isn't It a Pity." There were several takes of "Octopus's Garden," along with another slew of oldies, including "Great Balls of Fire," an oldies medley; "Blue Suede Shoes," and "You Really Got a Hold On Me." Just before the oldies medley, a long take of "Dig It" was done. A short snippet of it was destined to appear on the finished album. Heather Eastman, Linda's daughter, joined in on vocals on the song, and George Martin contributed on shaker.

At one point in the day, Mal Evans and some of the others ventured up to the roof for some fresh air and the idea of playing the live concert on the roof started to be formulated. Although it is hard to trace the progression of the idea exactly, later in the day everyone had decided to do the rooftop concert as a way to realize the idea of performing live and as a climax for the television film.

While Michael Lindsay-Hogg was not quite able to pinpoint it either, he believes that Saturday may have been the day that the idea for the rooftop concert was first proposed. "After lunch," he began, "Paul and I and Mal Evans went up on the roof and we looked around and jumped up and down on the boards and tried to figure out whether we would have to shore it up." "I think we were originally going to do it on a Wednesday," he continued, "but it was too cloudy and dull, so we did it on Thursday."

Monday the 27th began with "Strawberry Fields Forever." "Oh! Darling" was given a fairly long take and "Get Back," nearly ready, was done several times, as was "I've Got a Feeling." That would be the last time that the Beatles would do "Oh! Darling" during the "Get Back" project, and that loose version would be included on *Anthology 3*. The day ended on a high note for John, as he received word that Yoko's divorce was now final (it wouldn't be officially finalized until the following month).

That evening, John and Yoko met Allen Klein in the Harlequin suite (where Klein always stayed when in London) at the Dorchester Hotel on Park Lane. Klein, who had managed the Rolling Stones, had heard of the Beatles' unstable management situation and was interested in managing the group. The meeting came about as a result of Derek Taylor giving John's number to Klein. Klein had previously met with Peter Brown, but Brown didn't like him. John was immediately impressed with Klein and subsequently wrote a letter to Sir Joseph Lockwood, then the chairman of EMI, advising him that he wanted to officially appoint Klein as his manager. The letter John wrote simply said, "Dear Sir Joe, From now on Allen Klein handles all my stuff." That one meeting and hastily scribbled note very likely sparked the chain of events that would precipitate one of the most acrimonious splits in pop music history.

On the following day, the group finally came up with finished takes of both "Get Back" and "Don't Let Me Down," now destined to become the A and B sides of its next single. "One After 909" was brought back after having been resurrected at Twickenham and "The Long and Winding Road" was given another workout.

George continued to bring new songs to the project. "Old Brown Shoe" and "Something" were both introduced on that day, and "Let It Down" was revived after it had appeared early on at Twickenham. "Something," lyrically influenced by "Something in the Way She Moves," a song from James Taylor's self-titled Apple debut (which would be released on February 17), had been written by George during the *White Album* sessions. It was introduced too late to be included on that album, and appeared for the first time on January 28. The group did two very tentative versions of it, the first with very incomplete lyrics.

Two songs, loosely entitled "Billy's Song 1" and "Billy's Song 2," were also performed. Although it was a very productive day, there was still a great deal of uncertainty at the end of it about what exactly the group was going to do with regard to the album, the film, the rooftop performance, and the television show.

Wednesday the 29th saw the group go through a couple of tries at "All Things Must Pass," one more go at "Let It Down," a run-through of an oldies medley, and a rendition of two Buddy Holly covers. On that day, it was confirmed that the rooftop performance would indeed take place. It was also confirmed that the group would rehearse for it, but without Billy Preston.

The penultimate day of recording for the "Get Back" project, Thursday, January 30, has passed into Beatles lore as the day of the rooftop concert. The focus of the day would be a roughly 42-minute concert that the group would give on the roof of the Apple building, overlooking Burlington Gardens. For some of the people involved in putting on the concert, the day began very early in the morning.

Dave Harries and Keith Slaughter began the day at 4AM Harries said, "We had to collect all the stuff from Abbey Road and get it up on the roof, and it was all highly secret as well—and no one had to know about this." Harries said they had to "get it all up there and working by lunch time." "We had very, very little notice," he explained, "that this was going to happen."

Although not captured on film, but befitting the cinematic undertaking and in splendid Keystone Cops fashion, Harries and Slaughter nearly didn't make it to Apple with the much-needed equipment. Harries explained the not-very-auspicious start to such a historic day:

We got pulled over by the police in Kings Langley—Keith and I—and we couldn't tell them where we were going. We had funny caps on and loads of rope and lots of gear piled up, and it was four in the morning. We must have looked like we were out burglarizing someone. The police said,

"Where are you going?" and we said, "We can't tell you," and we thought, "Oh, God, they're going to lock us up and we'll never get to Savile Row." We said, "This is an EMI car," and they checked that. They found out it was an EMI pool car and they let us go.

While preparing the roof for the concert after their arrival, Harries and Slaughter, together with Alan Parsons, who was also helping set up the equipment, ran into another problem. Alan Parsons found the solution at the nearest branch of Marks and Spencer. "Glyn sent me out when we had a wind noise problem," he recalled. "So I just went round the corner to Regent St. and picked up a pair of stockings. They asked me what size and I said, 'It doesn't matter.' The store person thought I was either going to rob a bank or cross-dress."

Paul used his 1963 Hofner bass played through a silverface Fender Bass rig. John played a stripped Ephiphone Casino guitar, and George played a Fender Rosewood Telecaster guitar. They both played their guitars through silverface Fender Twin Reverb amps. Ringo played a Ludwig Hollywood five-piece multicolored drum kit with three cymbals. Billy Preston played a Fender Rhodes Seventy-Three keyboard, which had its own amplification. Vox speaker columns were used as makeshift monitors for the band. In order to allow the sound to be heard in the street below, a Fender Solid-State PA system with the speaker columns tilted slightly downward to face the street, was used for the vocals. Just as they had been using in their makeshift basement studio, the microphones they chose to use on the roof were the Neumann KM84i model.

During the concert George Martin was in the basement and Glyn Johns primarily engineered the live recording. Derek Taylor was in his office while the concert went on, and almost as soon as it started, the press started phoning. Peter Brown and Denis O'Dell were both on the roof.

Although the Beatles added more cameras to the film shoot when they moved from Twickenham to Apple, they added even more for the rooftop concert. Multiple cameras were also positioned on nearby rooftops and in the street. Finally, there was one in Apple's reception area. Les Parrott said that there were probably eleven cameras in total.

The plan to execute the concert itself was uncertain the day before it was to happen. In fact, it remained shaky right up until the time it had been scheduled to begin. Michael Lindsay-Hogg recalled the last-minute mood of the Beatles: "We planned to do it at about 12:30 to get the lunchtime crowds. They didn't agree to do it as a group until about twenty to one. Paul wanted to do it and George didn't. Ringo would go either way. Then John said, 'Oh fuck, let's do it,' and they went up and did it."

It was a cloud-covered day, with a washed-out gray sky and a chilling wind blowing. "The day was cold in a very London fashion," recalled Les

Parrott. "It's a cold that doesn't bother you too much as long as you're moving. However, if you stand still or don't have food and warm drink regularly and it attacks, you become very miserable very quick." Alan Parsons, who was also on the roof that day, said, "It was just a dreary wintry London day. It was certainly cold. Everyone was freezing their ass off."

The Beatles appeared slowly and tentatively from the stairwell of 3 Savile Row and emerged on the rooftop of the building. It was the beginning of another mundane lunchtime in London. Unbeknown to the few early lunchtime stragglers on the street and those imperviously going about their business in offices and shops in the area, the Beatles were about to play their last live concert together.

The four Beatles and Billy Preston arranged themselves around Ringo's drums. Billy Preston was perched in front of the stairwell wall, on Ringo's right, with Paul nearly in front of Billy. John was in the middle and George was to John's left and just a little behind him, facing sideways so he could see just about everyone. Paul seemed ready to make it a good show and was not overly animated to start. John looked very comfortable and happy. He often glanced at Paul when they sang harmonies together and smiled frequently. There was a sense that he really enjoyed being on a stage with his little band and there was an almost shy sweetness about him early on that belied any of the infighting, bad feelings, or odd behavior that had come about over the past weeks. Ringo was solid and—without even trying—he was the picture of cool. George seemed the most uncomfortable, hanging back, singing very little, and acting as if he was an aloof captive of this silly show. While Paul was smartly dressed in a dark suit and an open collar shirt, ignoring the cold, George wore green slacks, black, low-cut Converse sneakers, and a furry black jacket over his shirt. To confront the cold elements, Ringo had borrowed his wife Maureen's mod red raincoat, while John had borrowed Yoko's fur coat, which looked great with his white sneakers.

The group immediately launched into "Get Back," making all those weeks of playing together not such a big waste of time after all. Preston contributed a loose, funky keyboard to "Get Back," which further lubricated the rollicking, boogie feel of the song and added a much-needed bright punch. Even in the cold and with the dodgy sound setup, it sounded great. "Don't Let Me Down" sounded equally good and John's inability to get all the words right only added a disarming charm to the whole proceedings. John, Paul, and George harmonized well together and John and Paul frequently exchanged pleased glances. "I've Got a Feeling" really rocked and during it Paul finally became more animated. Ringo was superb, and even George had to smile. "One After 909" gave all those too young to have seen the Beatles play the Cavern a glimpse of the simple rockin' sound that had launched the group only a few short years ago. "Dig a Pony" began after some tentative starts, and Lennon's words cut through the biting winds.

During a second rendition of "Get Back," the increase in the number of people in the street and on adjacent roofs, combined with the hovering presence of the police, helped to create a sense that the concert could potentially break down at any minute. Dave Harries fondly remembered the police that day:

> There was a policeman knocking on the door saying if we didn't open the door he'd arrest everyone in the building, and George (Martin) looked a bit worried then. Then the policeman came in and all they did was stand around and watch. They didn't stop it—we thought they were going to try and stop it and we said, "No, don't stop it—leave it; everyone's enjoying it, it's all right. No problem, is it?" The policeman said, "Well, providing we can watch then." When they found out who it was, they didn't want to stop it.

With "Get Back" finished, including Paul's ad-lib that made reference to the police in attendance and John's singing of a snatch of "Danny Boy," there was a lot of applause. Paul thanked Ringo's wife, Maureen, for cheering so enthusiastically and then John made his famous comment: "I'd like to say thank you on behalf of the group and ourselves and I hope we passed the audition."

The above were the performances shown in the *Let It Be* film. There were several additional performances, including two more takes of "Get Back." There was also nearly two minutes of "I Want You (She's So Heavy)." "Don't Let Me Down" was also done again. A little over a minute of another run-through of "Dig a Pony," a couple of minutes of "God Save the Queen," and another fairly long run-through of "I've Got a Feeling" were also done.

It's hard to say for how long the Beatles would have played if the police hadn't arrived. It would have been fascinating to see them play in a more controlled environment, with proper sound and without having to battle the weather. They certainly played well and selected takes from the performance formed some of the basic tracks for the finished *Let It Be* album.

In summing up the rooftop concert, Michael Lindsay-Hogg said, "When they were doing it, they were happy. They actually kind of enjoyed it and had a lot of fun with it and each other."

Dave Harries reflected on some of the challenges of staging the rooftop concert. "Of course it was very hard in those days. You couldn't really have big PA rigs. You had to just use all the PA stuff that was at EMI and rig it so it was as loud as possible going down into the street. It worked quite well, actually—quite surprisingly, considering."

Alan Parsons, who was behind the camera in the stage-right corner, felt that everything went very smoothly, although he admitted that there were "possible conflicts between the film crew and the sound crew."

In the evening, Glyn Johns again returned to Olympic Sound Studios for a 7:30 to 10 PM session, at which he mixed some songs from the concert into stereo and cut acetates of them. The acetates were given to the Beatles.

The day after the rooftop concert, Friday, January 31, would be the last official day of filming and recording. With the more upbeat, electric rockers such as "Get Back," "Don't Let Me Down," "I've Got a Feeling," and "One After 909" having been tackled the day before on the roof, the more acoustic numbers were left to be recorded. Filming on the final day was unlike all previous filming in that the performances were staged specifically for the cameras.

The three songs the group focused on were the acoustic "Two of Us," and the two piano songs, "The Long and Winding Road" and "Let It Be," in that order. The day started out very lighthearted, with some joking obviously influenced by the old "Laugh-In" television show. John was heard muttering, "Goodnight, Dick." It was clear, though, that the Beatles were very focused on getting some final takes. There was little chatter and only a few moments of musical ad-libs. One of the most telling moments of the day, of the whole project, and maybe of the group's final months together, occurred after one of the takes of "Let It Be": John turned to Paul and said, "Let it be. Hey, I know what you mean." It was almost as if he was thankful that Paul was in some way acknowledging that it would be a good idea to just let the group end. Of course, that was not the central or complete meaning of the song. Yet, considering the ongoing tension and the group's awareness that the recording phase of the album was ending that day, John's quip succinctly summarized the entire project.

Alan Parsons reflected on the end of the sessions at Apple: "On the basis that they had a film they probably also had a record. I'm not really sure that they thought they had anything else other than a soundtrack for the film. I think probably they came away thinking that they hadn't made a record and it was just going to get put on the shelf."

At the end of the day, Billy Preston was officially signed to Apple Records.

So concluded all the filming and nearly all the recording related to the "Get Back" project.

Live at the Apollo

by Douglas Wolk

Yvonne Fair

Since 1960, there's almost always been a featured female vocalist with the James Brown show; for most of 1962, that singer was Yvonne Fair, a twenty-year-old R&B singer from Virginia. The October 20 issue of the *Amsterdam News* ran a publicity photo of her (posed like a Greek statue in a tight dress and spike heels, smiling, one knee lifted a bit, gesturing with her hands as if holding a large trophy); the caption claimed that she was "a native New Yorker and attended Janes Addams Vocational High" [*sic*]. James Brown had produced and played on three singles for her that year, notably "I Found You," which he'd remake a few years later as "I Got You (I Feel Good)."

At the time of the Apollo show, Yvonne's latest single was a cover of Gene Allison's 1958 hit "You Can Make It If You Try," reworked with a little sermonette at the beginning. Brown plays the organ on the single, as well as yelling constant encouragement; he might have turned up on stage to play it with her, too. King ran an ad in *Billboard* that month, with a picture of a grinning James Brown in front of a map of the US. In banner type, it read "JAMES BROWN and his Famous Flames - AN ALL U.S.A. Hit - King 5672 - MASHED POTATOES U.S.A." Down at the bottom, in much smaller type: "DON'T FORGET - You Can Make It If You Try - It Hurts To Be In Love - Yvonne Fair - King 5687."

What else might she have sung in her three-song spotlight? Maybe "Say So Long" or "If I Knew," from her earlier singles. At least one of her songs, though, was probably a cover of some then-current R&B hit; James Brown has always had an unfortunate habit of making people in his revue with perfectly good repertoires of their own do Motown or Stax karaoke.

Photographer Gordon Anderson made a montage of pictures he took at that week's Apollo shows. Yvonne Fair appears three times in it, including a big cameo-shaped image in its center. She's wearing a blond wig, for some reason, and a dress with a complicated print. Her makeup makes thick-rimmed almonds of her eyes. In one picture, she's looking up and to one side, her lips pursed, making a little wish. The middle photo is positioned so she looks like she's looking at her other image, smiling professionally but ruefully.

In any case, the night after *Live at the Apollo* was recorded was the last time Yvonne Fair sang onstage to James Brown's audience, because of something she wasn't about to tell them.

Freddie King

1961 had been Texas-born blues guitarist/singer Freddie, or Freddy, King's *annus mirabilis*. He'd placed six songs in the R&B charts (three of them, and one other single, went pop, too)—all released on King Records' subsidiary Federal, maybe so that nobody would think that Syd Nathan's label belonged to a blues guitarist! He never had another hit, but the chitlin circuit took care of its own: once you'd established your name on the network of little venues where black musicians played to mostly black audiences, you could keep playing there forever. That's essentially what King did until his death in 1976—he had, and still has, a cult following among hardcore blues buffs, but is little remembered otherwise.

King's singles usually had a blues vocal on one side and an instrumental on the other—he tried to showcase both sides of his talent whenever possible. The Apollo's ad that week listed his relatively recent single "I'm on My Way to Atlanta" under his name. His three-song set probably included "Hide Away," his long-lived instrumental hit, featuring a bridge that quotes the "Peter Gunn" theme (a riff that the Apollo audience would be hearing a bit later that night, too), and either the instrumental "San-Ho-Zay" or the jaunty blues "I'm Tore Down," which let him both sing and play guitar.

At around the same time that Freddie King was playing "Hide Away," a B-52 bomber took off from Westover Air Force Base in Massachusetts, heading north. The plane had nuclear bombs on board; the understanding was that it was to head over the North Pole and drop them on Russia, unless it got the order to turn back.

Solomon Burke

Solomon Burke's career has matched Brown's for longevity, if not for glory. He'd been appearing at the Apollo Theater in various capacities since the 50s (when Apollo Records released his first few records, credited to the "Boy Preacher"); he'd had R&B hits with "Just Out of Reach" in 1961 and "Cry to Me" in early 1962, and had spent July touring the South with Brown and his group. "Down in the Valley," its flip side "I'm Hanging Up My Heart for You," and "I Really Don't Want to Know" all hovered around the lower reaches of the pop charts that summer. The ad for the Apollo shows that appeared in the *Amsterdam News* credits him with singing "Tonight My Heart Is Crying," by which it probably means "Cry to Me," rather than the 1957 Shirley Bassey song that Burke never recorded. He most likely sang three songs, too.

Pigmeat Markham & Co.

Comedian Dewey "Pigmeat" Markham started playing at the Apollo in the 30s and never stopped—he appeared there more than any other act. (A vaudeville performer of the old school, he continued to perform in blackface right up into the 50s.) Curiously, he cut a live album at the Apollo the same week as James Brown. Chess Records recorded Markham's performances on Saturday and Sunday, October 20 and 21, and got six sketches out of it, which ended up being released on his album *The World's Greatest Clown*: "Go Ahead and Sing," "Frisco Kate," "Miss Monzell," "Hello Bill," "Ritz Service," and "Restaurant Scene." We can assume that those were from six different performances—the *Amsterdam News* plug for the show notes that Markham and crew would present "two comedy sketches, one the very popular 'judge' scene."

That would be the "Here Comes the Judge" routine that was Markham's greatest hit. It first turned up on record in 1961 or so—"The Judge," as it was then called, appeared on his early album *Pigmeat Markham at the Party*. In 1968, Markham broke out to the American mainstream with a series of appearances on the TV comedy show "Laugh-In," where "Here come the judge!" became a catchphrase. Soul singer Shorty Long adapted "Here Comes the Judge" into a hit funk single that May (No. 4 R&B); Markham, not about to let anyone steal his fire, recorded a danceable "Here Come the Judge" of his own, which followed it up the charts in June (No. 4 R&B, No. 19 pop), as did versions by the Magistrates and the Buena Vistas.

Then: Star Time.

Star Time

But back a moment to "Fats" Gonder's introduction, all one-minute-on-the-button of it. It's his star turn before Star Time, and he works it like a carnival barker, throwing in five-dollar turns of phrase but dropping vowels to talk more country. "Thank you, and thank you very kindly. It is indeed a great pleasure to present to you at THIS partic'lar time—national and *inter*national known—as the HHHardest Workin' Man in Show Binness—"

The Hardest Working Man in Show Business

You thought that was just a slogan. *Live at the Apollo* was at least James Brown's *twenty-fourth* show of that week. The Apollo Theater had four or sometimes even five shows a day, starting in the early afternoon, and the revue had been playing there since Friday the 19th. At that point, and through most of the 60s, the James Brown revue was playing around three hundred days a year. (Three hundred days a year. Four or five shows a day.) No venue was too tiny, no drive between gigs that was physically possible to make was too long. This particular leg of their endless tour had started October 9, at the Rainbow Gardens in Denver, Colorado. They worked their way across Texas, then stopped off for a one-off engagement at a gymnasium in Jackson, Mississippi, before the Apollo gigs.

Thursday, October 18, was evidently spent rehearsing in New York. (Trombonist Dicky Wells, a veteran of Count Basie's orchestra, had been brought into the band specifically for the Apollo shows.) Traditionally, the outgoing and incoming shows would have a Thursday-night "wrap party" at the Palm Cafe, a bar and restaurant down the street from the Apollo; between midnight and 3 AM, Major Robinson would broadcast over WWRL from the Palm, although the 18th was his final night there. The show that had just closed at the Apollo had been a gospel revue, featuring the Soul Stirrers (Sam Cooke's former group, who were still among the biggest stars of gospel) and the Swanee Quintet (friends of Brown's from Augusta, Georgia).

After *Live at the Apollo* was recorded, the Brown revue wandered up and down the East Coast, playing armories and arenas, darting west to play at an Odd Fellows Hall in Steubenville, Ohio, on October 30, then spending November in the mid-Atlantic, including ten-day engagements in Baltimore's Royal Theater and Washington, D.C.'s Howard Theater.

By modern standards, James Brown's tour promotions were pretty haphazard. Posters advertising his shows would often say "tickets available in the usual places": record stores, barber shops, drugstores. The Brown organization tended to promote shows themselves, or co-promoted them with local DJs. A smart move: the DJs would get part of the take, so they'd plug the show on the air and play James Brown records whenever they could. This was not really considered an ethical problem in those days. (King Records used to deduct their payola costs as a declared business expense. "Some [DJs] wanted cash only," Syd Nathan said in 1959, "but I told them if they wanted payola they'd have to take a check.")

The Bus

Never one to pass up free advertising, Brown covered the sides of his revue's fifty-passenger tour bus with plugs for every act it carried. His own name appeared biggest of all below the back window, with a little sign below it that read "TRY ME" "BEWILDERED" "YOU'VE GOT THE POWER" "PLEASE, PLEASE, PLEASE." Under the driver's side window was the contact information for his booking agency, Universal Attractions.

On December 7, 1962, the bus was destroyed in an accident in Hagerstown, Maryland—James Brown wasn't on board, but a few members of the band were injured. (Brown generally skipped the bus and drove ahead to wherever the next gig was in his Cadillac, in order to do promotional interviews and plug his records at every radio station within range of the venue.) The accident only knocked out a few dates before their scheduled vacation; everybody got seventeen days off before they resumed the endless string of one-nighters with a gig at a high school auditorium in Florence, South Carolina.

The Catalogue of Hits

Fats Gonder ramps up his delivery from a salesmanlike incantation to rabid enthusiasm. He's got a singer to sell. What's the man he's introducing done with all that hard work? "Man that sang, 'I Go CRAZY'!" The snare smacks as the horn section blares a G chord. It's really "I'll Go Crazy," but Gonder's determined to outcountry JB's enunciation. "Try ME!" G-sharp. "YOU've Got the Power!" A. "THINK!" A-sharp. "If You Want Me!" B—except, oh dear, problem in the trumpet section, either Teddy Washington or Mack Johnson hits a bad note. (What was this "If You Want Me"? Not a hit, really—it had been the flip-side of "Bewildered." What was it doing in the list of hits? It sounded good.) "I Don't Mind!" C. "Be-WIL-dered!" C-sharp. (At this point, there's what sounds like the first bit we've lost from the tape—just a tiny dropout, but perhaps there was something edited out there.) "Million-dolla sella 'LOST Someone'!" Not just a million-seller, mind you, but a million-*dollar* seller, at a time when a single usually cost 79 cents. "Lost Someone" had been a No. 2 R&B hit, but given that it only got up to No. 48 on the pop charts, that particular distinction is unlikely. The band hits a D. "The very latest release, 'NIGHT Train'!" Well, no—"Shout and Shimmy" and "Mashed Potatoes U.S.A." had come out since "Night Train"—but it had been his biggest hit that year. D-sharp. "It's everybody 'Shout and SHIMMY'!" We'll be hearing more about that in a minute. E.

Gold

"Brown has perhaps a dozen 'gold' records to his credit," the little unbylined puff piece in that week's *New York Amsterdam News* announced. That was pushing it—he'd only had fifteen chart singles by that point. James Brown didn't have a certified gold single until 1972's "Get on the Good Foot," although King evidently didn't bother with RIAA gold and platinum certification. Still, for an Apollo audience, Gonder had a lot of familiar song titles to mention.

There are an awful lot of citations of chart numbers and dates in this book. Live with them. They are an essential part of James Brown's art. His genius is the genius of rolls of tickets torn off one by one, of money handed over for records, of the *hit*. The great James Brown songs are popular, the popular James Brown songs are great. As George W.S. Trow wrote in another, darker context, "It's a Hit! Love it! It's a Hit. It loves you because you love it because it's a Hit!" "You come to see my show," Brown sang. "That's why James Brown loves you so." "This is a *hit!*" he declared as the tape rolled for "Papa's Got a Brand New Bag"; he cut it out of the released record, but persuaded some of the other artists whose records he produced around that time to yell the same thing, so it might work its magic for them too.

Look at his singles discography, and ignore the instrumentals, the duets, the reissues, the throwaways on King's subsidiary label Bethlehem, the Christmas and novelty records—just concentrate on the songs he threw his weight behind. A pattern emerges, or rather an unbroken block: between "Money Won't Change You" in July 1966 and "Hot (I Need To Be Loved, Loved, Loved, Loved)" nine years later, James Brown had over *sixty consecutive* chart hits. On his own terms, he was an unstoppable champion, and those terms were people paying to hear him sing, and being reassured that what they were paying for was *popular*.

That's why he wanted to make *Live at the Apollo* so badly: he could demonstrate that being James Brown was *itself* a hit. All he had to do was get it on tape.

The Catalogue of Hits

Back at the Apollo, Gonder's speech has been setting up a couple of subliminal effects. Starting with "You've Got the Power," and running through "Bewildered," there's a steady 6/8 rhythm to the words he accents and the band's stabs—a tick-tock swing that's at pretty much the same tempo as Brown's ballads. There's also a hidden message in those emphases—Crazy-Me-You-Think-Want-Mind-Be-WILL-Lost-Night-Shimmy! This is a night for total abandon, the suggestion goes; for thoughts to become desires and then to simply be, through sheer will; a night to be lost to shimmying.

(A young man named Danny Ray was waiting in the wings. He'd just been hired, that week, as James Brown's valet; a few years later, he'd take over the emcee job, which he still holds today, and his introductions to the James Brown show have been patterned on Gonder's ever since.)

Gonder's still going. "Mr. Dynamite"—*Mr. Dynamite* had been the title of two movies, one from 1935, adapted from Dashiell Hammett's story "On the Make," and the other from 1941, starring Lloyd Nolan as Tommy N. Thornton (nice initials)—"the amazing Mr. Please, Please himself, the star of the show"—as if there could be any doubt, as Gonder is almost erupting with conviction—"JAMES BROWN AND the FAMOUS FLAMES!"

The Scratch

The horns buck—one, two, three, four, five, all on a G chord that's climbed up an octave since Gonder started his litany. It's the beginning of a fanfare to announce the Hardest Working Man in Show Business's arrival: three choruses of a perky little blues riff. Brown glides onto stage during the third, and probably does some high-powered footwork, judging by the screams. Twenty-nine years old and as flexible as a piece of yarn, he can dance faster and harder than anyone, rippling his body, floating over a wooden floor as if it's waterslicked ice.

The perky little blues riff has a name, although it was never credited on any edition of *Live at the Apollo* until 2004: it's "The Scratch." Brown and his band (including Les Buie on guitar and Hubert Perry on bass, still with the band at the Apollo) had recorded it as an instrumental on October 4, 1960. ("The Scratch" is also a close cousin of Henry Mancini's "Peter Gunn" theme, which had been a hit for Ray Anthony in 1959; Duane Eddy's version charted for the first time on October 10, 1960.) Brown's version appeared as the B-side of "Hold It" in January 1961, and the band played it as his entrance music at least through mid-1963.

As the band bats down the last note again and again, you can almost see James Brown's feet slide frictionlessly into position behind the microphone.

I'll Go Crazy

James Brown steps up to the front of the Apollo stage, gazes out over 1,500 thoroughly warmed-up faces, and assesses matters with a huge holler. He feels all right, and he wants to make sure everybody knows it. The third time he announces it, he gives the "all" an enormous melismatic rush, swooping around at least twelve notes just to prove he can; then, as he takes a breath, guitarist Les Buie whacks sharply at his strings, and we're into "I'll Go Crazy."

The Missing Song

Except we're not: there's almost certainly at least one song missing from the set on *Live at the Apollo*. In those days, JB usually opened his shows with his latest hit. In October 1962, that was "Shout and Shimmy," which had made No. 16 on the R&B chart (No. 61 pop) back in August. Recorded February 9, 1961 (the same day as "Lost Someone" and "Night Train"), it starts with the I-feel-all-right routine, and then proceeds to a truly shameless rip-off of the Isley Brothers' 1959 hit "Shout."

(Really, truly shameless. The "I feel all right" business is derived from the beginning of the second half of the Isleys' record, and the rest of the record is basically the fast parts of "Shout," with the gospel inflections removed and the word "shimmy" added. It wasn't the last time JB would appropriate the Isleys' work as his own, either: "It's My Thing," his protégé Marva Whitney's 1969 single, credited to J. Brown/M. Whitney, could be charitably described as an answer song to the Isleys' "It's Your Thing." It could be less charitably described as a cover that changes the pronouns.)

Those who wonder what "Shout and Shimmy" might have sounded like here are directed to the chaotic live follow-up album, *Pure Dynamite!* (recorded, for the most part, at the Royal Theatre in Philadelphia in 1963 and released in 1964; it'll be discussed more later on). It mostly covers the part of Brown's concert repertoire that hadn't ended up on *Live at the Apollo*; "Shout and Shimmy" opens the show with a minute and a half of thunderous frenzy, followed by a strange little singspeech on which Brown declares, "I'm tired but I'm clean" and goofs around with a comedian.

Why was "Shout and Shimmy" omitted from *Live at the Apollo*? Alan Leeds suggests that it might have been excised at the request of King Records president Syd Nathan, who was uneasy enough about the live album as it was, and might not have wanted it to compete with the song's studio incarnation. It might also be that the performance didn't seem quite appropriate for the beginning of an album—the Pure Dynamite version sure doesn't.

There might be more missing from the *Apollo* performance, in fact. "This album is the actual recording of the midnight show and includes the actual forty minutes of James Brown on stage," Hal Neely wrote in his liner notes to the original album. But *Live at the Apollo* is under thirty-two minutes long—a little bit skimpy for Star Time. Maybe Gonder was mentioning "If You Want Me" because JB intended to sing it (although it's one of his vaguest, most unconvincing ballads). Maybe Brown also sang "I've Got Money," a wild rocker that he'd recorded back in May, although the single wouldn't see release for a few weeks yet. Or maybe "Please, Please, Please" was abridged, for reasons that will be explained later.

This is all guesswork. As far as Leeds and Polygram Records' Harry Weinger know, none of the outtake material still exists. In 1971, James Brown moved from King Records to the much bigger label Polydor, and took his back catalogue's master tapes with him; King subsequently sold its archive to Gusto Records in Nashville. There are rumors that a box or two accidentally ended up in Gusto's vault in 1971, but that's not likely, and Gusto's not talking. The 2000 fire that destroyed the offices of James Brown Enterprises in Augusta, Georgia, was sometimes reported to have burned the master tapes of an Apollo concert, but almost certainly not this one. And the outtakes, if they existed, were probably not stored by Brown: "During the time I worked for Brown in Cincinnati (1969–1971) and Augusta (1971–1973), I never saw or heard any evidence that suggested he had any substantial collection of tape in his homes or businesses," Leeds writes.

In any case, it's a smart edit. The introduction to "Shout and Shimmy" dovetails neatly with "I'll Go Crazy"; the flow of the show might have been imperfect in real life, but you'd never guess it from the way the album fits together. *Live at the Apollo* was edited by Gene Redd, a big-band trumpeter who'd gone on to be a staff producer at King Records—he'd played on a couple of Freddie King's sessions, in fact. Redd later edited a few more James Brown live albums: *Live at the Garden* (1967) and *Live at the Apollo, Vol. II* (1968).

I'll Go Crazy

James hasn't even started singing yet, and the crowd is already shrieking—maybe he's executing one of his improbable dance moves. The rhythm section is swinging into something like the 6/8-time ballads that were Brown's bread and butter through the late 50s, except they're playing this one fairly fast and very hard, with Clayton Fillyau bashing at the cymbal on every single beat. The trumpet blasts at the end of the intro are more enthusiastic than accurate, as JB reaches for the microphone. (He'd never just stand in front of the mic—he always has one hand on it, as a sign of intimacy.) The snare and cymbal detonate six times, rushing the beat just enough to suggest that something too exciting to wait for is about to happen.

(Incidentally, there's a longstanding debate over whether or not Clayton Fillyau was the only drummer at the Apollo shows: Brown often toured with two drummers, although his old standby Nat Kendrick didn't rejoin the group until mid-November. The CD edition of *LATA* lists Sam Latham as an additional drummer, but it turns out he didn't join the band until 1963. The one extant photo of the full band at the Apollo engagement—that blurry dance-contest shot—has two drum kits in it, one on a riser behind the other. Fillyau's playing the front kit, and the back kit is empty. George Sims, from Greensboro, North Carolina, may have been the second drummer.)

The band cuts out for a second, and Brown's voice erupts. "If you leave me," he sings, accusatorily, and the well-dressed men behind him on the stage echo him: "Leave meeee!"

Flames

This is the first we've heard from the Famous Flames. Contrary to popular belief, the Flames weren't JB's backup band—they were his backup singers. The lineup of Famous Flames varied over the years, although they almost always included Bobby Byrd. The others present for the Apollo gig were Eugene "Baby Lloyd" Stallworth and Bobby Bennett. Both had originally joined the group in 1959, having initially been hired as valets for Brown and for his then-bandleader J.C. Davis, respectively. Stallworth was replaced by first-generation Flame Johnny Terry (who'd served time and sung with James Brown in Georgia Juvenile Training Institute, and was credited with cowriting "Please, Please, Please") in early 1962, and replaced him in turn a few weeks before the Apollo shows. The group, in one form or another, continued to appear on stage with Brown through the 60s, but "Maybe the Last Time," released less than two years after *LATA* was recorded, was the last James Brown studio recording that featured them.

Stallworth made occasional half-hearted attempts at a solo career, though always as a Brown hanger-on. "Baby Lloyd" was one of the featured performers on the revue's July 1962 tour of the South, before he rejoined the Famous Flames proper; *The James Brown Show*, a 1966 recording of Brown's entourage, features Stallworth's nondescript performances of "(I Can't Get No) Satisfaction" and Rufus Thomas' "The Dog," spruced up by the high-powered band. He even got two singles of his own: "I Need Love (I've Got Money)" in 1960 (Brown would do much better by it two years later), and a verbatim imitation of Bobby Marchan's hit variation on Big Jay McNeely's "There Is Something on Your Mind."

A record credited solely to the Famous Flames didn't appear until the end of 1970—a pretty good one-off deep-soul single, "Who Am I," written and primarily sung by Johnny Terry, who was basically never heard from again. Bobby Byrd, though, was the Flame who got to emerge, at least partly, from James Brown's shadow. More on him later.

I'll Go Crazy

"I'll Go Crazy," recorded November 11, 1959, at the same session as the minor hit "This Old Heart," had originally been Brown's first single of 1960 (it made No. 15 on the R&B chart). It's a little sleepy in its studio incarnation. You can't say that about the live version, which revs the tempo up considerably—Les Buie detonates every note of his lead guitar part, and James Brown is springing off the faithful Flames like a diving board. They've had to attenuate what they're singing to keep up, too—the "oh yeah"s on the original recording become a crisp little "oyp!" here.

The other big difference, though, is that on the studio recording, JB is decidedly singing a lyric—a very simple lyric, but still a piece of text with a meaning. Here, he's often just showing off what his voice can do: alternating between an R&B shout and a rough croon (isolate every time he sings "I'll go crazy" in your head, and it sounds like he's singing the emphatic parts of a slow, quiet song rather than swinging and belting), leaping up to yelp, getting so caught up in the performance that he strays from the microphone on the second bridge: "You gotta live for yourself . . . yeah? AAAA! . . . eeee, I'll go crazy . . . " The madness is starting to come over him.

Madness

James Brown screams and sweats and implores. His path is a jagged slash. He flies off the text of the song, flits from one song to another, begins and ends when he pleases. As long as he works hard and can be seen working hard, he is almost unbounded by the responsibility of sticking to the program. Nobody else in his band can even break a sweat: they are required to work impossibly hard, too, but they are not to be seen with a hair out of place. James Brown is a vector of chaos, and chaos only means something by comparison with order. So the rest of his band is architecturally orderly, shoes shined and suits crisp, holding steady while he plays with phrasing, beats, song structure. They're at his mercy.

The Famous Flames become the voices in the head of a madman. He argues with them, or lets them complete his thoughts. "I'll Go Crazy" is the first statement here of his great theme: *you must not leave him.* If he stops commanding your attention, the craziness that makes him yowl and moan will consume everything. But, of course, the bridge of the song (where the Flames do more singing than he does) slyly adds, do what you like, you can't live for him.

It would be possible to sing "I'll Go Crazy" in a genuinely abject, desperate way—and we'll hear plenty of that kind of singing later—but that's not how Brown sings it. His singing here is flashy, even cocky, as if he's toying with the object of the song, daring her to leave him so he can demonstrate just how crazy he can be. There's a cruel, devouring side to both his madness and his need.

As James Brown swings the microphone back toward himself, a bulky, shadowy figure climbs the security fence at an Air Force base in Duluth, Minnesota. A guard shoots at it; thinking that it might be a saboteur, he sets off an alarm.

I'll Go Crazy

The Apollo version of "I'll Go Crazy," with a verse and "you gotta live" bridge repeated to pad it out to a more singlelike two minutes and ten seconds, was released as the B-side of "Lost Someone" (edited down from the *LATA* recording) in early 1966. The live "Lost Someone" went to No. 94 on the pop chart; "I'll Go Crazy" was No. 38 R&B and No. 73 pop. They may have ridden the coattails of Brown's previous single, the massive smash "I Got You (I Feel Good)," but it's still not a bad performance for two chopped-up live tracks in a style he'd almost abandoned by that point.

Abandoning Styles

"The King of the One-Nighters" was one of his nicknames, and the Apollo was as good as the chitlin circuit got, but James Brown was already aspiring to move beyond it. *LATA* was, arguably, meant as Brown's farewell to the raw R&B phase of his career; less than two months later, he was recording "Prisoner of Love" with an orchestra and chorus. Ray Charles had started a long series of string-sweetened country crossover hits in May 1962, driven by songs from his smash album *Modern Sounds in Country & Western Music*. JB had followed the example of Charles' live album *In Person*; now he wanted credit in the pop world as a balladeer. The *Prisoner of Love* album included versions of "Try Me" and "Lost Someone," with strings added for the easy-listening audience.

It didn't quite work: he couldn't entirely pull off the lounge act, and the "new direction" of his career got derailed by a record company mess that took up most of the next few years. By the time he got back into the swing of things, it was 1965, and his breakthrough record was the distinctly unsmooth "Papa's Got a Brand New Bag." But it took him a long time to give up on the crossover dream: in 1968 and 1969, he recorded albums with a cocktail jazz trio and the Louie Bellson Orchestra, and played the International Hotel in Las Vegas, singing "If I Ruled the World" and "September Song." Again, it failed to catch on. His subsequent foray into acid-rock was even shorter: a pretty good single (the original version of "Talkin' Loud and Sayin' Nothing"), which was withdrawn almost immediately, and an awful instrumental album, *Sho Is Funky Down Here*.

Try Me

Back at the Apollo, the horn riff at the end of "I'll Go Crazy" slows down and slides perfectly into the first word of "Try Me"—a flawless key change with no audible cue, the kind of trick JB will be pulling off throughout the show. That word, "try," is all the girls up front need to start screaming like a descending horde of locusts.

That instant recognition has to have been a relief for James Brown. "Please, Please, Please" had been a hit, but its follow-up singles weren't. Nine flops in a row came out in 1956, 1957, and 1958; Brown lost his original band and his original Flames as his name failed to appear on chart after chart. After an October 1957 session, King Records pretty much gave up recording him.

(Consider for a moment what might have happened if James Brown had left the music business at the end of his two-and-a-half-year losing streak. Somebody might have put out a retrospective CD in the 90s, when all sorts of R&B obscurities were getting reissued; "Just Won't Do Right" and the B-side, "Messing with the Blues," might even have been played a few times on specialty radio shows.)

"Try Me" probably saved his career. Released in October 1958, after radio play for Brown's own demo convinced King's Syd Nathan to record it for real, it was his first No. 1 R&B hit, and stayed on the Top 100 for 22 weeks (longer than any other Brown single ever has), even making it to No. 14 on the pop chart. "I had heard 'Raindrops' by Dee Clark and 'For Your Precious Love' by Jerry Butler and the Impressions," he notes in his autobiography, "so I wrote my song to fit between them."

Well, that's one possible story of where "Try Me" comes from, but it's not exactly in Brown's songwriting style. "James found the song down in Florida while he was working The Palms in Hallandale," Bobby Byrd told interviewer Cliff White. "I'm pretty sure it was really written by some other guy who just gave it away to James to record; either that or James developed it out of something he heard down there."

A January 1961 article in *Sepia* magazine, by Stella Comeaux, most of which appears to be totally fictional, suggests a third origin for "Try Me":

"A scout for the Chicago White Sox once tried to sign me up for their farm team," James explained. "But about this time I met a man named Andy Gibson—now my repertoire man. He tried me out with the song 'Try Me' and that was it. Andy told me I had what it took to become a top singer. That was good enough for me. He has been handling my music and arranging ever since."

Andy Gibson was a songwriter, arranger, and producer at King Records; he'd cowritten the much-covered Paul Williams hit "The Hucklebuck," produced the "Try Me" session, and cowrote a couple of songs with Brown under his pseudonym Albert Shubert. Here's Brown on Gibson's role in the making of "Try Me," in *The Godfather of Soul*: "Andy stayed out of my way, and that's what I wanted."

Wherever the song came from, it worked. "Try Me" was a minor hit for Brown again in 1965, this time as an organ-led instrumental (No. 34 R&B, No. 63 pop). He was apparently convinced for a while that it could work for anyone in his circle, too. The short-lived 1963 record label that released various JB productions was Try Me Records. In 1966, producing his old friends the Swanee Quintet, he gave them the barely altered "Try Me, Father" (as well as "That's the Spirit," a rewrite of his recent hit "Ain't That a Groove"). Gospel singer Kay Robinson got "Try Me, Father" in 1968, too. Wendy Lynn had a one-off single with "Try Me" in 1970. Martha High, who sang with Brown for twenty-seven years, only got one single of her own for the first seven of those years—"Try Me," in 1973. None of them charted.

The *LATA* version is closer to its studio incarnation than any other song in the show, down to the nearly identical instrumental break (with what sounds like both drummers playing at once). It's a little faster, definitely, but that does good things for the song. After the beginning, the screams largely subside, with intermittent outbreaks. The mix of the band is so precise you can hear the Flames' unison clap on every sixteenth beat, although James' microphone is acting up—it cuts out a couple of times. You can't blame it: he's almost sleepwalking through the performance, at least by his standards, and the band speeds up bit by bit, as if they just want to get to the other end of the hit they always have to play. Even so, "Try Me" is valuable in the context of *LATA*, because it acts in the service of the album's pace: if "I'll Go Crazy" were followed directly by "Think," it would be practically numbing.

The sabotage alarm in Duluth sets off other alarms at other military locations nearby. At Volk Field in Wisconsin, the alarm that goes off is the wrong one—it's the signal for F-106s, with Falcon air-to-air nuclear missiles, to scramble. At DEFCON 3 or higher, there are no practice alert drills, and the Strategic Air Command had switched to DEFCON 2 that day. As far as the pilots in Wisconsin know, the war has just started.

Aqualung

by Allan F. Moore

1

Aqualung. It was buying your first greatcoat that did it. It simply wasn't possible to find something near to that tatty, chequered monstrosity from which a flute, of all things, issued so precariously, but a greatcoat from the local army surplus was close enough, particularly if you were somewhere out in the provinces. That image of this crazy, probably dangerous individual with unkempt hair, strangely wandering eyes, and an inability to keep both feet on the floor at the same time that we saw on "Top of the Pops" as Jethro Tull and his anonymous backing musicians performed "Witch's Promise" in the winter of 1970, remains to this day one of the most striking I can recall.[1] And, when the greatcoat appeared in all its glory clothing Jethro's *alter ego* on the cover of *Aqualung,* it was clear to us that we were insiders, that we lived in exactly the same crazy world, that we "knew what it was all about," even if we didn't know what it was all about.

With the benefit of thirty years of listening, maybe it was principally about distaste, about the after-effects of the souring of the countercultural dream. But it was also about the control one exerts over one's own destiny, or the lack of it. And it was therefore about the acknowledgment that changing society wasn't quite as easy as the hippies had pretended. That difficulty, a posing of some of the necessary questions, was very much what *Aqualung* was all about, even if it didn't provide any real answers. (And, if it had, what use would it have been? Who ever managed to bring about anything worthwhile by adopting someone else's manifesto?)

Aqualung appeared in the early part of 1971. As Ian Anderson himself would put it later, "[a] comfortable and convenient step or two behind the

---

1 That mimed performance is currently available on the 25th anniversary video (Chrysalis, 1994).

cutting edge of 'progressive rock.'" This sharp end was represented by *In the Court of the Crimson King*, its Gothic splendor and message of doom so heavy that it seemed to belong more to an underworld than to the gray skies of the England into which Aqualung wandered. And Aqualung belonged in 1971, too. Society was not at ease with itself. A first spate of plane hijackings had sent waves of fear through affluent Western society; Jimi Hendrix and Janis Joplin had both stupidly died within the past six months; the first British troops in Ulster were killed as their role became politically highly sensitive; UK unemployment was skyrocketing; Enoch Powell was stoking the fires of racism in speaking out against immigration; Cuba was threatening to erupt again as a battleground between the USA and the USSR; and "Women's libbers" marched on London. And, as if that wasn't enough, pop music was busy galloping off down the course on which it had been set in 1966 by John Lennon's "Tomorrow Never Knows," certainly the boldest attempt within this most ephemeral of activities to make music for the sake of doing so, leaving to others any concern with whether such efforts would come to seem meaningful. And meaningful they did prove to be, in their foundation of a psychedelic otherness that became common mining ground over the next few years. *Aqualung*, though, in the light of Ian Anderson's anachronistic inveighing against the taking of mind-altering substances, suggested that "otherness," being different, beyond society's co-option, was part and parcel of everyday existence, an otherness that was not the pretty thing of the hippies, but was weird, unkempt, and strange.

Aqualung arrived at the right time, then. By 1971, rock was established as a genre to be reckoned with. Post-war hardship was well and truly past, the hysterical brightness and hedonism of Swinging London consigned there also. Rock[2] was enthroned as the medium of rebellion, the embodiment of the newly coined "generation gap"[3]—it was a music that our parents couldn't understand. Although this intentional generational separation through music can be found in the teddy boys' use of rock 'n' roll in the late 1950s, and in the mods and rockers battles on the seafronts of the 1960s, these were mere skirmishes. From the late 1950s onward, the roots of the music of rebellion were being laid far more surreptitiously, in the blues clubs run by Cyril Davies and Alexis Korner, and that finally blossomed in the work of John Mayall, Graham Bond, Davy Graham, Peter

---

2 Descended, as a term, from "rock 'n' roll," Colin MacInnes, in *Absolute Beginners*, had used the term "rock" on its own in 1959, although it was not in common usage to define a genre until around 1967.

3 This term had appeared in the *Boston Globe* in 1967, and was being used in the *Guardian* by 1968.

Green, Eric Clapton, and others in the mid-1960s. It was the British blues boom, and the appropriation of the music of an underclass that established rock as more-than-ephemeral rebellion, and enthroned the electric guitar as the axe with which to cut down the dead music of the past. And, in Aqualung, Cross-Eyed Mary, and the rest of their cast, Jethro Tull set up precursors to the grotesque and marginalized who would become the staple of metal and punk, and so remain to this day. However, these misfits are in part presented to us with what borders on compassion, another legacy of the counterculture: a dominant image here is that of Shirley MacLaine, sad character that she is, at the end of *Sweet Charity*, presented with a flower to mark the resurrection of hope—it is not too difficult to imagine Mary in that role. And so *Aqualung* sits at the crossroads between these two positions—it represents a society rebelling against . . . whatever there is to rebel against, and yet not with the unfocused mindlessness of youth, but with the compassion that potentially recognizes each of us in those who do not have the wherewithal to rebel.

It would be tempting to suggest that these two sides were simply and unambiguously presented on the album. After all, in its original vinyl guise, it was clearly presented as two distinct sides—not only was it physically necessary to turn the thing over half way through (this was not one of those albums where side two was often unheard, at least due to the cunning placing of "Locomotive Breath" toward the end), but each side appeared to be given its own title, that of the cut that began them, namely "Aqualung" and "My God." Some listeners have even constructed narratives in order to make sense of each of these sides. And it is true, side two does focus on Ian Anderson's troubled relationship with established religion, while side one can be seen as consisting of songs observing various aspects of urban experience, but this is to create a division between two clear identities that is not necessarily there. In Anderson's own view: ". . . it was merely that there were some common threads running through some of the songs . . . [t]here are certainly songs that have absolutely nothing to do with any other songs" (not a view I entirely agree with, as will become clear) ". . . the songs were structured into those two sides after it was all done." Even at the time, he was insistent that there was no "concept" involved, no narrative thread: "[I]t doesn't tell a story, doesn't have any profound link between tracks." Indeed, it was only journalists' propensity to finding such links that determined Anderson to give them what they were asking for: *Thick as a Brick*. That listeners do create that identity, do take it as a concept album, irrespective of the original intentions, is important, as we have noted (their freedom to do so also has Anderson's *imprimatur*, of course, and so Anderson perhaps needs to take full blame for the decision). More important here, though, is the presentation. There is a difference between the original vinyl and the subsequent CD packaging. On the CD initially released in 1983, the painting of Aqualung in Steptoe rig (seemingly hiding something under his coat) is backed with the track listing, while the more compassionate painting of Aqualung sitting in the gutter appears on the inside—originally, these two paintings appeared on front and back of the gatefold sleeve, with the track listing on the inside, together with the painting of the band rehearsing in an abandoned church (which was missing entirely from the 1983 CD, but is restored on the 1998 release). The compassionate pose has been downgraded, then, for contemporary audiences, while the Gothic lettering that would subsequently play such a part in early "death metal" (and hence be associated with dangerous grotesqueries and occult fantasies) is highlighted. (In 1987, Tull would unbelievably win the heavy metal Grammy for *Crest of a Knave*, while 1982's *Broadsword and the Beast* was read on the Continent, at least, as tapping into the gothic end of metal.) Even in the spring of 1971 this sleeve appeared portentous, perhaps suggesting that the wake-up call the album issued had deeper targets. And it was easy to confuse this mythical creature, Aqualung, with the one (Ian Anderson) we saw. So much of Jethro Tull's career has been an exercise in identity construction, as stylistically they swerve from early blues, R&B, and hard rock straight through progressive rock (*Passion Play*), folk rock (*Songs from the Wood*), and new wave/synthesizer rock (*A*), on to so-called heavy metal (*Crest of a Knave*), back to quasi-blues (*Catfish Rising*), and on to world music (*Roots to Branches*). Ian Anderson, who was already becoming "Jethro Tull," himself became Aqualung—the straggly hair and coat that identify Aqualung are each well in evidence clothing Anderson on the sleeves of both the earlier albums *This Was* and *Benefit*.

2

Extricating a new album from its sleeve, taking care not to put your sweaty mitts on the vinyl itself, was always something of a ritual—the anticipation to savour it, but the fear of dropping the stupid thing (I never did get to hear Roxy's *Stranded* at the time, for precisely that reason). With the best albums, those first few seconds after the needle had touched down launched you somewhere new, and "Aqualung" was no exception. That opening guitar riff, that short little phrase (for that is all a riff is) was fierce. It just hit you deep in the stomach. A simple little thing, dropping suddenly in pitch and then gradually climbing back up to its first note, but not quite getting there (and dwelling on that failure). And the tone, that fizzy guitar sound of Martin Barre's—full of enormous sonic potential, but keeping it reined in just for the moment, and only for the moment, as later songs show.

I've done the unforgivable—I've jotted down that opening riff, fixing it, draining it of its power so that it can be calmly pondered on the page. Have you ever contemplated the wonder of the butterfly? Before movie photography, butterflies were studied by killing them and pegging them out. In a sense, that's what I've done with this riff—laying it flat on the page so that its details (such as they are) can be studied "out of time." It's not quite as devastating as killing a poor Emperor, of course, since the music can always be set to go again. Indeed, I would argue that paying very close attention to any of this music is only ever worthwhile if the music is "put back together" again afterward. However, on with the demonstration.

Even in jotting down that riff, you can see the alteration I have had to make to that first note (the D) as it returns (as it becomes a D-flat, a flattened version of the original note). It becomes a foreign note, a transgression, a note that does not belong. More than that, it becomes the note on which the music alights as the whole band enters after Anderson's initial phrase. No gentle entry this, the dangerous alteration is present right at the outset. Why dangerous? The opening riff is in G-minor—the switch eleven seconds in ("eyeing little girls")[4] is to D-flat major—farther away, in musical terms, you cannot get. Imagine for a moment that the history of painting consists of canvases that gradually shade from one color into the next—purples shade into blues into turquoises on one, oranges into reds into pinks on another, but the colors are kept well marshalled. Then a painting bursts open in which blues sit next to oranges, greens next to reds. That is the force of the opening to "Aqualung." (The analogy is inexact, of course, for green and red sit well next to each other for physiological reasons—the same is not the case in music—in music, opposites repel.) So, right at the outset, irreconcilable opposites are presented within the very notes of the melody. As I have suggested, these opposites are fundamental to the song, to the album, and to the Jethro Tull worldview.

"Aqualung" plays against the expectations of rock right from the outset. The riff is set apart from the song, through being separated in time. We hear it—we catch our breath—we hear it again—we wait in anticipation as Clive Bunker's drums thunder out a triplet rhythm that has connoted menace ever since it started being used to signal the approach of the Apaches in run-of-the-mill Westerns.[5] We hear it a third time, finally knit into the song under Ian Anderson's opening line. Each of these—the riff, the silence—lasts the same length of time, four beats, i.e., one bar. So far, then, we've had five bars. Then that switch to the new key and the slightly more comforting

---

4 Although it is always better to rely on your own ears when deciphering lyrics (what you think you hear is often more potent for you than what was actually sung), the entire lyrics to the album can be found reproduced in Schramm and Burns, and also on numerous websites—www.cupofwonder.com is as good a starting place as any.

5 A fine contemporaneous example can be found in Spooky Tooth's "Lost in My Dream," *Spooky Two*, 1969.

strummed guitar (but with a menacing, smashed crash cymbal on the off-beat) sitting behind the riff as we hear the rest of the stanza. Note how the tom-toms appear at either extreme of the stereo space (audible from as early as eleven seconds in), making clear right from the outset how "extensive" that space is, how much "room" the band actually has within which to manoeuvre (purely coincidentally, the album was recorded in what had been a church, rather than the small cosy studio commonly used at the time). I shall insist on reading this metaphorically, as representing the intellectual space the album will attempt to cover (and I hope by the end this will not sound so precious as it does at the moment). How long do we get as a result of this switch, before things come to rest? Six bars, actually (but of entirely different music). Now we are beginning to be on familiar ground, because one further hearing of the riff (at twenty-three seconds) is followed again by the six-bar passage. And that same again, and again, now with a richer riff, slightly less bare, doubled in thirds (again, this creates a sense of "size," because there is only one guitar player, but two guitars being played: over-dubbing is, by 1971, becoming a common device for "magnifying" the size, and hence potency, of the music, with the inevitable risk of bombast that makes possible). We are a minute into the song, and its course seems pretty clear. Here is this thoroughly disreputable being, described objectively ("spitting out pieces of his broken luck"—for years I heard it as "lung," which just made it even more disgusting), with distaste (just listen to the way the word "nose" is squeezed out from the side of Anderson's mouth—almost enacting the dripping of Aqualung's snot). He's even addressed at one point, as if in derision—"Hey, Aqualung!" but with no response forthcoming, of course.

Then, at 1:04, the whole scene changes. Well, that in itself is not unusual—songs often divide up into verses and choruses, after all, and they almost invariably did so in the 1960s. But is that—verse and chorus—what we have here? If so, which is which? Verses tend to push the narrative of a song forward while a chorus, in its repetitiveness, provides space to reflect. And, at first, it seems that this is what's happening here in a strange sort of fashion (except that choruses are also often associated with snappy hooks and that certainly isn't the case here). We get a complete change of texture—no riff, acoustic guitar gently strummed in the foreground, and the voice sounding as if at some distance. And, after the irregularity of the opening, the regular four-beat groove that takes over here sounds almost nostalgic, almost wistful. (In pop music, everything tends to proceed in fours—four beats to the bar, four bars to the phrase—well, more correctly, the "hypermetrical group," but let's leave it at "phrase" for now.) It is surely no accident that the point of view of the singer (the "persona") changes at exactly this point also—no longer is he jeering from the other side of the road, he is empathising—"wandering lonely," "leg hurting bad," etc. Gradually the texture grows—after eight bars we repeat, adding bass, and then repeat again, adding kit and piano. Piano? A less forceful, more genteel, instrument than the opening guitar could hardly be imagined at this point, particularly as it coincides with the rather laidback, strongly fore-grounded bass. And then, after four times through (2:14), the pace changes abruptly—the speed doubles, the instruments are attacked with more force, the melodic line shifts from one that predominantly falls, to one that tends to rise and, after four more bars, the voice suddenly appears close to us. This more upbeat music continues while Anderson runs through the lyrics we have already heard in the distance. Some sort of link is being made between the two types of music we have already heard, but how might we understand it?

In a series of essays written to accompany the 25th anniversary box set, novelist Craig Thomas coined two wonderful terms to describe these two types of music: he wrote of "blues-hard rock declamation" and "lyrical-folk introspection." These highlight not only the stylistic differences we can hear in "Aqualung," but also the contrasts of attitude that go hand in hand with them—the declamation shouted from the other side of the road, and the introspection as we get alongside. But Thomas goes further than this, describing these as representing ". . . the clash between the individual and society, between the rural and urban worlds, between happiness (however qualified) and disillusion, [that] is the archetypal tension of so many songs by the band." This is a heady brew—individual/society, rural/urban, happiness/disillusion. If the musicologist Frank Howes was right, "if one seriously examines popular music it is the absence of mind in it, its determined refusal to make any demands on the listener's attention, that makes it popular," then *Aqualung* must be highly unpopular. But it's not (it reached number four in the UK, and number seven in the US, and has sold several million copies since its release), and that means that these pairings deserve a little bit of attention, not least because these "demands on the listener's attention" seem to be what Anderson intended.

These dialogical pairings Thomas proposes—individual/society, rural/urban, happiness/disillusion—are all pretty problematic these days, and they are also strongly political. The relationship between the individual and society was key to hippie ideology—individuals took to themselves the right to be different (marked by clothing, by lifestyle, by attitude) but in so doing, they were supposed to be improving society for the rest of us (and as a minor at the time, I include myself here). The difference between rural and urban existence underpinned the entire Romantic movement—indeed, writers for centuries have bemoaned the loss of the "natural," country way of life. Evan Eisenberg locates this loss even among the ancient Greeks, while Raymond Williams exhaustively traces it in the work of English authors since the eighteenth century. Whether there has ever been a "nature" with which to oppose "culture" remains a controversial point, but it's incontrovertible that some people believe there is. Finally, happiness/disillusion is probably easier to make sense of on a personal level, but in fact none of these three pairings are relevant at just this point. Here, what is at issue is simply the available responses to the tramp in the gutter—the jeer or the empathy. We left the song at the point at which some sort of link was being made between the two. But is this in the nature of a compromise, or is one of these two approaches to prove superior?

At 2:04 into the song, there's a subtle detail, which isn't particularly important for *this* song, but which becomes crucial later in the album—Martin Barre runs through this entire section "hacking" on the guitar, i.e., strumming the strings rhythmically, but by lightly touching them with the left hand, preventing them from vibrating at particular pitches, so that it is only the percussive attack of the plectrum on the strings that is picked up. This technique tends to connote power held in reserve—it becomes manifest as the strings are stopped in the usual way. It is also known as playing "chics," for onomatopoeic reasons. The obligatory guitar solo follows (3:25), but far from the display of virtuosity that the genre had already learnt from Eric Clapton and Jimi Hendrix, this one begins almost as a lament. All rhythmic motion has been lost, with the exception of Clive Bunker's very gentle time-keeping on hi-hat laying the ground for the more full-fledged solo that follows, and all of this over that eight-bar sequence that I originally identified as a possible chorus. It is worth noting that this guitar sits to one side of the stereo spectrum, balanced at the other by the strummed guitar and piano. The guitar is not center-stage, does not take the limelight—it remains part of the communal effort. We have, however, left any suggestion of conventional verse-chorus structure far behind by this point—the song has really followed a path which could be symbolized as: A (hard rock declamation); B (lyrical introspection); C (upbeat compromise between the two). And then, at 4:36, which ought to be pretty close to the end of the song, rather than launching into a final climax, we return to a memory of section B, chords, texture, and all, in which Anderson reminds us of his compassion for the "poor old sod." Finally, at 5:12, we come full circle as section A returns in all its glory, with the doubling guitar this time to the side, knitting the central section into the song. Now of course this movement through the song can be interpreted in a number of ways. Most obvious, perhaps, is to read it as the realization that Aqualung's place is outside society, that the momentary display of compassion doesn't really get us anywhere, that it loses out in the course of the song. For some fans, the outsider is the role Ian Anderson himself has always tended to play, from this early point right up to the present. Alternatively, we might think of it simply as a neat way to wrap up the song: ABCBA has a certain unmusical logic to it, anyway, and were it not for the observation that we so often go out of our way to search for meaning, even where it seems meaning was not intended, I might be satisfied with this. However, I think we need to listen on. This last time, section A finishes with repeats of that opening riff, strangely doubled by a rather forceful piano (which again, I will have to return to later), shifting as had the very opening from the G-minor riff to the D-flat phrase, but the song finishes here. So, even at the very end, although we may be presented with textural certainty, with something that adequately indicates to us that the song has "ended," harmonically things are inconclusive. In order to find out how to respond properly to Aqualung, this ending seems to be saying, we need to listen on.

Opposition and contradiction are key to performing this song, then, not only on this album, but wherever else it has been released. On *Bursting Out*, the audience cheers as we enter the B section, suggesting there is pleasure in recognition of the opposition of styles. What we particularly lose in this rendition is the subtlety of the voice's distance at the beginning of section B—hard to bring off in live performance, certainly at that time. The instrumentation is rethought to fit the live setting (no overdubs possible), although at 5:32, the "[don't worry, it's] only me" carries a rather threatening tone, as if the tramp is about to be beaten up again. In the studio fifteen years later, except for the more prominent piano part, the song retains all its memorable features. (By this time, of course the "Aqualung, my friend" carries extra resonance, as they have been comrades for more than twenty years.)

Opposition and contradiction are key to the whole Jethro Tull project, it seems to me, even on an incidental level. For instance the word "aqualung" itself can be understood in two very different ways. First, it can imply water on the lung, potentially a highly disabling condition, leading to suffocation. Second, it's a device that allows people to breathe in otherwise deadly atmospheres. Indeed, Ian Anderson assumed it was a generic word, rather than a copyrighted name for the device, and narrowly escaped prosecution for copyright infringement. In both cases, the pairing water/air is highlighted, while one reading suggests the impossibility of living in uncongenial atmospheres and the other suggests the possibility of doing so.

There is a deeper historical underpinning to the opposition that appears here between different musical styles. Prior to the mid-1960s, popular musicians appeared either to work unproblematically within a given style (Frank Sinatra, for example, always sang as a latter-day crooner against some modified form of swing backing), or adapted their style to changing tastes (as Elvis Presley gradually moved from rock 'n' roll toward mainstream sentimental pop as the first style appeared to run into the ground in the late 1950s). The term "style" can become confusing here, so it might be best to think of "style" as something many performers share, but adopt a different word—"idiolect"—for the style in which particular singers sing, or musicians play—their personal fingerprints, if you like, by which we identify what they do, and how they differ from others. Both Presley and Chuck Berry were rock 'n' roll singers, for instance, but no rock 'n' roll fan would confuse the two—they each had their own idiolect.

Up until the mid-1960s, individual idiolects always operated within particular styles. What was so revolutionary about this post-hippie music that came to be called "progressive" (originally "progressive pop"—only later "progressive rock") was that musicians acquired the facility to move between styles—the umbilical link between idiolect and style had been broken. Many British musicians became adept at this move between 1966 and 1972—the Nice could wander between flower-power pop ("The Thoughts of Emerlist Davjack," for instance) and reworkings of Slavonic or Latin concert music (such as Leonard Bernstein's "America"), a style mix taken further by Emerson, Lake & Palmer's addition of bawdy ballads ("Jeremy Bender") and love songs ("Still . . . You Turn Me On"). King Crimson shifted between experimental heavy rock ("Lark's Tongues in Aspic Part 2"), free improvisation ("Moonchild"), and classical reworkings ("The Devil's Triangle," based on Gustav Holst's "Mars")—the list could go on and on. What sets Jethro Tull's approach apart, however, is the ability to move between styles *midsong*, to capture the connotations of these styles and put them to use in energizing the emotional possibilities of the song. Ian Anderson claims a far more prosaic origin for this: in answer to Royston Eldridge's question about whether they were seeking stylistic contrast between "very quiet, acoustic things" and "heavy rock things," Anderson answered: "I'm quite aware of doing it, but it's really just fulfilling the desire . . . to be not pigeonholed into a style. In a lot of ways, we'd be . . . a lot more popular as a group if we had a very identifiable style." But, as I said earlier, as human beings we go out of our way to search for meaning, even where meaning was not intended (how else explain our constant failures of communication in interpersonal relationships?), so I think we need to look further than Anderson's prosaic, underplayed comments.

OK Computer

by Dai Griffiths

Chapter Three
OK Computer in the future

[Irving Berlin] created what he had in him to create: the lyrics and tunes that went straight to the hearts of the millions who were like him, except they lacked his talent.

—Wifrid Mellers

(*Begins boiling all over again*) I was watching that South Bank Show thing about fucking Blur—a moment of fucking weakness—and whatsisface, the singer was in one of his schoolrooms playing the piano and he looked around wistfully and went, "(*Solemnly*) I have to leave this room, it's where I failed A-level Music." What?! Why fucking take A-level Music? What do you mean you failed A-level Music? Is there an A-level Music? How d'you do that!? "(*Double-solemnly*) I got my Bach mixed up with my Beethoven." Fucking Bach-hoven. Music's in your fucking bones, man; it's under your fingernails; you play one chord on a guitar and you're a musician—end of fucking story.

—Noel Gallagher

You're better off learning some music theory. You're better off having some feel for music that you don't have to carry in your head, that you can write down.

—Bob Dylan

In the character of the Elegy I rejoice to concur with the common reader; for by the common sense of readers, uncorrupted with literary prejudices, after all the refinements of subtlety and the dogmatism of learning, must be finally decided all claim to poetical honours. The four stanzas beginning "Yet even these bones" are to me original; I have never seen the notions in any other place; yet he that reads them here persuades himself that he has always felt them. Had Gray written often thus, it would have been vain to blame, and useless to praise him.

—Samuel Johnson

Popular songs are the only art form that describes the temper of the times. That's where the people hang out. It's not in books, it's not on the stage, it's not in the galleries.

—Bob Dylan

Forget the centre: the margins are where the signals are coming from. Everything is velocity and disappearance and mutation. [Tricky's] *Maxinquaye* is a work of theory. There is nothing that theory can say that isn't already embedded in this wily, uncanny text.

—Ian Penman

And more: Samuel Johnson wrote in 1750 that "the task of the author is, either to teach what is not known, or to recommend known truths by his manner of adorning them"; Wordsworth wrote (and emphasized) in 1815 that "every author, so far as he is great and at the same time *original*, has had this task of *creating* the taste by which he is to be enjoyed"; T. S. Eliot felt by 1920 that it is "to be expected that the critic and the creative person should frequently be the same person"; and, after he and Kingsley Amis had edited an Oxford poetry anthology each, Philip Larkin wrote in 1974: "we shall have stamped our taste on the age between us in the end."

The idea of the creative-critic, or critical-creator, belongs more assuredly in literature than music, certainly popular music, where expressing contempt for critics is more the done thing. Often smilingly evoked, as clue to its purposelessness and end of story, is the analogy that writing about music is "like dancing about architecture"; whereas *both* dance and architecture lie at interesting aesthetic tangents to music, dance its bodily translation, architecture a complex correspondence to the visualization of form. Such knowing disdain was not always so, and in Schumann, Tovey, Schoenberg, and Robin Holloway, there is a distinguished tradition of composers doubling as critics. Again, this is not so much the case in popular music, half-hearted exceptions like Patti Smith, Morrissey, and Neil Tennant apart (whose criticism was at best a springboard to the proper business of being a professional artist). This is a shame and reflects several possible things: the bureaucratisation of creativity, in Britain at least, with certain kinds of music tied to arts councils and universities; a narrow philistinism in popular music allied to a romantic belief in genius; and the proximity of journalism itself to the needs of the marketing department. In my view, there is room for less professional creativity and for more informed debate over the direction and purpose of new music. Critics are in a very important position, denied creators, of being between text and context, context both as intention (production) and affect (reception): critics can wriggle around between those points and adapt their position tactically. Creators, on the other hand, are, in music rather literally, fixed in a position before the audience, with little room for manoeuvre, and often at the beck and call of the industry (something which tends to undermine their commitment to political views).

Wordsworth's "creating" of taste need not be restricted to influencing popular opinion, but can also attend to quite simple and material things. In the world of *OK Computer* I've inhabited, the websites, interviews, and audience debates were of relatively little concern; what I came to value was, of all things, and quaintly I admit, the "score" of the music produced by the publishers. In the sleeve-notes to the album, Radiohead make a well-deserved and funny joke about reproducing the lyrics "by kind permission even though we wrote them," and it's a pity that, by extension, the name of the person who does all of these transcriptions is seemingly withheld. He or she should, as a first step, be given credit: the transcriptions are useful and dependable. However, they exist only as guitar tablature, and I suggest that some of the band's efforts should go into producing fuller "study scores." Not performance scores, note, though they could end up being similar things. What is needed are the following: bass parts, outline drum parts, piano parts where the piano takes lead (as in "Karma Police"), backing vocals, and other prominent guitar parts and sound effects (though these are often there already). The score would be a variable thing, sometimes with many parts, sometimes few. Piano reduction must be avoided at all cost. I also think that not too much energy should be expended on pitch accuracy. I can tell that the guitar of Bob Dylan's "Bob Dylan's Blues" on *The Freewheelin' Bob Dylan* is out of tune, and I imagine that Dylan or John Hammond were aware of this and preserved the mistuning for effect. But there'd be no reason to make a song and dance about its being anything other than an out-of-tune G chord. Notation became closely associated with "classical" music and being taught to play or sing, as opposed to popular music's more heuristic or improvised ways of learning. Noel Gallagher and Thom Yorke may not be able to read music; be that as it may, in describing a track, some aspects, not all, are best captured through notes and chords, and notation is the easiest way of conveying that information. The very earliest music that survives represents a hard-won human achievement, and it's erroneous to equate the popular of popular music with the avoidance of notation. There's still every need to learn how to read music: not being able to do so is another indication of the lazy, slobby aspect of computer- and TV-centered life, which also plays straight into the hands of scummy, dumbing-down capitalists. Asked if knowledge could inhibit spontaneity, Paul Simon replied that "certainly in popular music and rock and roll, that's not the problem. The problem is people don't know enough." Resist it: learn to read music and speak Welsh! Learn to dance the polka, paint flowers, identify trees in the garden, and speak Finnish!

The way a piece of music remains in the consciousness is a complicated historical process balanced between personal taste and an inherited sense of value. Each person's life maps onto that deal: the records one first hears carry significance partly, I think, because they get played often since there are few competitors in the collection. The attributes "classic," "great," "recommended" must prey on some people more than others: Nick Hornby's splendid novel *High Fidelity* suggests that it may have something to do with gender. Nevertheless, there's every reason to be sceptical of any such claim or description, made up as it is of these partly contingent factors—and even, for critics, an impending deadline! It's worth remembering Chuck Eddy's observation: "the *idea* of genres can be way more interesting than the genres themselves." Rating and actually playing, estimating and actually listening, can be different things. The *memory* of how good Beethoven's Ninth Symphony is, or was, especially when I first heard it, lots of times, suffices. When people declare Shakespeare the greatest author, they're probably not double-checking *Titus Andronicus*, the sonnets, and *Love's Labours Lost* before voicing that view. A lot of pop music estimation is based on that sort of "memory-bank" knowledge: I doubt that those called on to rate records necessarily sit back and experience the thing afresh. Best record ever: click, *Pet Sounds*, click, *Revolver*, click, *OK Computer*. That too is part of the problem of the way pop music is written about, overly contextual, overly sociological, and, increasingly, tied to the demands of marketing and photography: there are in truth few ordinary pieces of writing that make you want to listen to the records again.

If earlier we asked "what is *OK Computer*?" we now ask, "What survives?" Here lies an essential distinction between records and songs: records survive by being played, songs by being sung. When Bruce Springsteen says that "all popular artists get caught between making records and making music," he's capturing this basic distinction. More accurately, *all* people who make records get caught between records and music, technology and technique. In fact, we hardly need the adjective "popular" at all. The key guarantors of a record's survival, to date, have been DJs, either on radio or in clubs. Once the songwriter dies, then the protectors are other singers—the song's ability to be "covered" or "continued by others" becomes an important element. "May your song always be sung," sang Dylan on "Forever Young," giving voice to the songwriter's great hope. "Live forever," as the Gallagher boys say. But consider "Adeste Fideles" or "Stille Nacht," two songs that are unquestionably *doing well*.

Death matters, and death's matters too, since up until that point the songwriter has a stake, financial if nothing else, in insisting that his or her own songs be heard or played. The death of the song, the end of its copyright life, is an important marker. According to Dave Laing's entries for copyright in the *Encyclopedia of Popular Music of the World*, it would seem that the record copyright for *OK Computer* will run out in 2047, when there'll be cheap and cheery copies at your local newsagent. However, the publishing rights will continue to reside with the heirs of the five people listed on the sheet music, until seventy years after the *death* of, presumably, all five of them. Joke about copyright permission they well do ("not waiving but waving" in Christopher Ricks' great pun), but in publishing terms, on the sheet music, Radiohead is a group of five decent chaps in suits called Thomas, Edward, Philip, Jonathan, and—no change—Colin. However, this is all a right mess, with those death-figures (fifty and seventy a lawyer's lucky numbers?) applying only in countries with the requisite degree of concern, and the internet throwing the whole thing into confusion. Copies are now of a quality no longer discernibly inferior to an original. Sheet-music photocopies now have their aural corollary. One of the British retailers, HMV, through the last ten years wrapped its records in tight and annoying tape marked "security protected" to dissuade shop thieves: Thom Yorke, in a splendid joke, drew attention to the irony of this given that so much larceny, of a kind, is now happening flagrantly in the virtual world.

Song or record? As the twentieth century drew to a close, there was useful sleeve-note comment on this situation from two old hands of singing and songwriting. For Bob Dylan, on *World Gone Wrong*, an album of covers released in 1993, "technology to wipe out truth is now available" and "there won't be songs like these anymore, factually there aren't any now." The songs he referred to were old, and he seemed to include one or two of them during most "live" performances on his seemingly never-ending tour. They're old or they're "multiply timed": some of the songs sound old as the hills, emerged from an oral tradition, were recorded in the late 1920s, issued by Harry Smith in the early 1950s, influential on the generation of folk singers of the early 1960s, and rereleased in the 1990s. Dylan seems to understand that the survival of a song is dependent partly on its circulation, a process in danger of being erased by technology, perhaps against the background of a free-market industrial attitude that couldn't care less. This is what fired Dick Gaughan; on *Redwood Cathedral*, issued in 1998, he commented:

> I have watched with alarm the trend of pushing singers into only singing songs they have written themselves. This is simply the record companies trying to maximise profits from song publishing and has two built-in fatal flaws: first, all songs will die with the writer; second, the crafts of song-writer and singer are entirely different and skill in one does not necessarily indicate skill in the other. The whole notion is absurd.

They're good and salutary statements, both, and seem to me to point toward the importance of the cover version and understanding what it is about songs that make them straddle time and place.

The specific question to be asked of a song is, in this sense, how *coverable* it is, or how music moves: moves us and moves across space and time. My guess would be that Radiohead songs are resistant to being continued: they'll always sound like Radiohead. A tribute album called *Anyone Can Play Radiohead* exists already: if anything, the covers are (to my mind) more interesting when the tracks get messed with, usually as a transfer between wings of pop-music's genre prison. "Creep" becomes a dance track, "Fitter Happier" is bunged onto an indie song, "Subterranean Homesick Alien" gets "fucked with" in solidly earnest, industrial music fashion. On the other hand, there's a tendency—Alanis Morissette was the first, so far as I know—for female singers to perform the slower "torch songs" faithfully: "Fake Plastic Trees" from *The Bends* may well end up echoing down the subway platforms of the world. On the tribute album, "No Surprises," "Exit Music," and even "Climbing Up the Walls" from *OK Computer* are all treated this way. Another interesting record is *Strung Out on OK Computer*, a "very Kronos" project (only in LA) by a string quartet called the Section, the first violinist of which, Eric Gorfain, also did the arrangements. They're good and musical: the systems at the start of "Let Down" are performed with admirable precision. The things that cross over very well are—it may seem surprising—the sound effect sections (the slow interlude of "Electioneering," for instance), reinforcing the idea that what you can do with guitar strings isn't so far from what you can do with strings *per se*. This also applies to the motivic work ("Electioneering" again), for something of the same reason. "Airbag" becomes very quartetlike, a reminder that we were hearing motivic material in the bass guitar part. The chords and pieces work well enough, much as they might do arranged for anything: Christopher O'Riley plays Radiohead songs as a classical pianist, often taking the music, tunes, and chords down roads where Chopin and Debussy used to live. The problem is harmonic-formal: why on earth would a piece of music without words repeat a verse section? More interesting is when the arrangement does the equivalent of pop-music's genre change: on the quartet version, "Exit Music," always liable to sink from its pace, gets pepped up by a "character piece" rhythm. Really, to make songs work as instrumental pieces, there'd need to be harmonic or motivic development, in which case better *not* to make the record a tribute (or rendition) and more a reinvention (or appropriation): but then the question, why bother at all? Answer: in order to make something up, using the resources or technology available.

If the *songs* aren't necessarily going to travel, then it's for the *records* to last. That depends on people playing the tracks from *OK Computer* and, if the album is to survive as an album, still playing it as an album. DJs have been to date the great protectors of the legacy, selecting tracks for radio, presenting tracks in clubs. The time of writing is well under a decade from the album's appearance, and so these are extremely early days. The great model to emulate is *Dark Side of the Moon* (1973). I do think that some of the centrality of the sound of that period had something to do with the relation, deep inside British musical culture, of "popular" and "classical" music, and this is something that Radiohead may have recalled. (Then again, Homer Simpson once said that "everybody knows rock attained perfection in 1974—it's a scientific fact.") A more hardboiled version of the future will see *OK Computer* survive not as an album; in this version, all classic albums are idealized nostalgias of unities that were never the case. Radiohead splits up, someone leaves, and the band is invariably reduced to a greatest hits collection. In that scenario, much as I'm the sort of slutty listener for whom *Pablo Honey* was always simply "Creep" with a recklessly generous number of filler tracks, "Creep" gets again to dominate such a compilation, with *OK Computer* reduced to its singles, "Lucky," "Paranoid Android," "Karma Police" (ending again with its noise rather than "Fitter Happier"), and "No Surprises," possibly "Airbag," "Exit Music." The editing is already underway, for all I know, in Radiohead's live shows, in friends' download compilations ("album," again), in the numerical indicators of the record corporation. I don't think it is a matter of five-CD box sets and *availability*: until body technology actually makes us last longer, the desert island principle of selection will still hold sway.

Another argument sure to surface eventually is that *OK Computer* was rated highly, extremely quickly, because everything else around at the time was rubbish. It's not that *OK Computer* was so good, more that everything else was so bad. I don't think this really holds. But to set this assertion in context (and with thanks to rocklist.net for filling out a few gaps), in the appendix [to Dai Griffith's *OK Computer*] you'll find the *New Musical Express* and *Melody Maker* "best of the year" selection for an over-the-top number of years surrounding 1997. You'll see that the diversity of the 1980s and early 1990s eventually disappears as *MM* dies and the *NME* becomes more focussed on rock music, and niche marketing seems to have become the norm. But something else that can be suggested is that a judgment in the present doesn't necessarily survive: *MM*'s choice of *The Young Gods* in 1987 is only the most egregious case of an album that seemed great at the time but seemingly not lasting, Sugar's *Copper Blue* for *NME* in 1992 another. The point is that, at the time, these would have seemed pretty sensible choices. In fact, there was even for a time the sense that many bands were actually influenced by the recordings of Radiohead: the high and expressive voice became a notable sound, in singers like Chris Martin of Coldplay, Matthew Bellamy of Muse, and Martin Grech. The music sociologist may one day wish to consider what this said about masculinity at the close of the twentieth century.

If indeed *OK Computer* is already a classic album then, boy, that's very much a version of the word "classic" glimpsed in passing as the videotape reels fast-forward. The interesting question about the demotic classic, the democratic classic—classic cars, classic kitchenware, classic albums, classic episodes of "The Simpsons"—is how we recognize whether or when any of this stuff is really, no *really*, a classic: when do we take the leap into saying that *Pet Sounds* is up there alongside the Sistine Chapel? Or that *OK Computer* lines up alongside the *Missa Solemnis*? Time, perhaps: the Beatles have lasted for nearly fifty of Beethoven's two hundred (though, unlike Beethoven, they've yet all to die), a mathematical proportion changing by the day. Scale, perhaps: the "dangerous bigness" of the romantic sublime. Here's an important assertion by Edward Macan, in a book essential for anyone keen to emphasize Radiohead's leaning toward progressive rock:

> Effectively tying together twenty or thirty minutes of music on both a musical and conceptual basis is a genuine compositional achievement, and a well-constructed multi-movement suite is able to impart a sense of monumentality and grandeur, to convey the sweep of experience, in a manner that a three- or four-minute song simply cannot.

Scale, length, prolixity: format, again. It's worth emphasizing that albums, long-playing records, aren't the whole story, and we tend to overestimate them, much as one might automatically rate the novel over the short story, the symphony over the short piece. We then project the lack of albums back into a lack on the part of the artist themselves, which is potentially ludicrous: there's no doubt that Chuck Berry could in theory have come up with the "great American novel" of albums, but he tended simply to produce terrific singles. The overvaluation of albums plays, in what was for many years a "structural" or systemic way, against black music and female singers. Even where goddesses like Dusty Springfield or Aretha Franklin produced what can retrospectively be seen as great albums (*Dusty in Memphis* and *Young, Gifted and Black*, say), that's only rather to skew their output as a whole. You can almost smell the sweat of relief on the rock critic's bandana when Stevie Wonder and Marvin Gaye finally get round to classic albums in the 1970s, crisp charmers like "Signed, Sealed, Delivered" and "How Sweet It Is (To Be Loved by You)" mere B-roads pointing to the motorway ahead. This is a deep and complicated point, but it's worth saying: classic albums are white-boy terrain, and behind it lies "art" and some deep memory of what "classic" could mean.

I return once more to the timings. Songs seem to me to have a certain rhythm to them which to an extent determines their content, and record formats don't necessarily define what a *song* should be. Reviewing the rerelease of Randy Newman's first album, Ian MacDonald stuck his neck out and called it a "flawless masterpiece"; I might have saved the approbation for the second album, *Twelve Songs*. The latter is an album more like the collection described earlier in this book by Philip Larkin, with comedy, strange love songs, political comment of a certain kind, and, in "Underneath the Harlem Moon," an amazing cover version transformed through time. But observe these timings: 2:32, 3:03, 2:12, 3:15, 1:55, 2:40, 1:52 (that's the cover), 2:19, 2:40, 2:08, 3:00, 2:15. Twelve tracks, under half an hour (29:52), averaging about two and a half minutes per track. Even on a marvellous recital of his songbook issued in 2003, and now including more extended forms in songs like "The World Isn't Fair" and "The Great Nations of Europe," Newman gets through eighteen tracks in 47:20, still averaging out about just over two and a half minutes. (There are a few really short tracks based on film music, though.) The point I want to suggest is that the range of references, as well as musical styles, in the Newman album are vast. But they're songs first and foremost, working through the material and not staying a moment too long.

Of course, Randy Newman and a piano can't match Radiohead and a lorry-load of technology for sheer, visceral power: it's the three-guitar assault which surely defined the appeal of Radiohead at this point. There was a problem for *Kid A* and *Amnesiac*, the ambitious records that followed *OK Computer*, in that their musical material seemed to imply a different, and possibly more visual, performative context (film, gallery) than the "stadium rock" pattern which was the band's daily bread. But the world of left-field popular music isn't exactly easy to please, open to visitors, or welcoming of the converted. Debates in *The Wire* magazine in 2001 illustrated this perfectly, the charge having been led by Ian Penman in a characteristically terrific and vivifying review of *Amnesiac*. Despite having Yorke on the cover only two years earlier, *The Wire* appeared altogether to ignore *Hail to the Thief*, and the album was nowhere to be found in the copious lists of critical choice for 2003.

In conclusion I'll predict, no less, that *OK Computer* might in time be a focal point for historians of life at the close of the twentieth century. "This is what was really going on." You want to know what 1997 felt like? *OK Computer*: tracks six through eight. Pushed for time?—track seven.

Final Thoughts

These characters are the aesthete, the therapist, and the manager. Both aesthete and therapist are as liable as anyone else to trade in fictions. With the manager it is quite otherwise. For besides rights and utility, among the central moral fictions of the age we have to place the peculiarly managerial fiction embodied in the claim to possess systematic effectiveness in controlling certain aspects of social reality. But what if effectiveness is part of a masquerade of social control rather than a reality?

—Alasdair MacIntyre

By the way, if anyone out there's in marketing or advertising: kill yourself. You are Satan's little helpers: kill yourself, kill yourself. Kill yourself, now. You know what bugs me, though? Everyone here who's in marketing is now thinking the same thing: "Oh, cool. Bill's going for that *anti-marketing* dollar. That's a *huge* market."

—Bill Hicks

Lyrics used by kind permission even though we wrote them.

—Radiohead

Plan X is sharp politics and high-risk politics. It is easily presented as a version of masculinity. Plan X is a mode of assessing odds and of determining a game plan. As such it fits, culturally, with the widespread habits of gambling and its calculations. At its highest levels, Plan X draws on certain kinds of high operative (including scientific and technical) intelligence, and on certain highly specialized game-plan skills. But then much education, and especially higher education, already defines professionalism in terms of competitive advantage. It promotes a deliberately narrowed attention to the skill as such, to be enjoyed in its mere exercise rather than in any full sense of the human purposes it is serving or the social effects it may be having. The now gross flattery of military professionalism, financial professionalism, media professionalism, and advertising professionalism indicates very clearly how far this has gone. Thus, both the social and cultural conditions for the adoption of Plan X, as the only possible strategy for the future, are very powerful indeed.

—Raymond Williams

Top managers were enriched in proportion to the amount of power and security that workers lost: this is the single most important point one needs to know to understand corporate thought in the nineties.

—Thomas Frank

Let It Be

by Colin Meloy

On my insistence, my mother caved in and bought a TV with cable. Our days of borrowing the neighbor's black-and-white television to catch such major network events as *V* and *Shogun* were at an end. Most important, we now had MTV. I braved the nattering of my mother to stay up well past my bedtime to watch "120 Minutes" at 11:00 on Sunday nights. For two hours, the programmers at MTV played videos exclusively by the bands that were dominating the college rock charts: the Cure, Depeche Mode, the Smiths, and XTC. During the week, I would try to catch "Post Modern MTV," the younger sibling of "120 Minutes" at its thirty-minute length, but would often miss it because of its brevity. It wasn't long before it disappeared from the programming schedule, leaving the behemoth "120 Minutes" as the only remaining bastion of College Rock on MTV. I watched the show intently, hoping that each video would be from one of my new favorite bands. I found that even among this, the mainstream representation of the fringe, the Replacements were still on the margin. After seeing the video for "The Ledge," the lead single off of *Pleased to Meet Me*, I understood why: shot in stark, uncompromising black-and-white, the video was comprised of one shot: the various shoed feet of each of the Replacements, while the band members to whom they belonged sat on a couch. For a song that was obviously about teenage suicide, it was a pretty bizarre approach to video-making. In relation to everything else on MTV, it was a complete outcast. By 1988, video budgets were expanding exponentially, and even the more obscure acts, those who peddled their videographies to "120 Minutes," shot big and pushed for flashy production in their videos. "Even though we've signed to a major label," the Replacements' video said, "we still don't give a shit."

On *Let It Be*, the song "Seen Yer Video" lays out the Replacements' approach to mainstream promotion in its one lyric: "Seen yer video / That phony rock and roll / We don't wanna know." I understood then: to make any other sort of video would be nothing short of hypocrisy.

Little did I know, it would be only a year before the Replacements would abandon much of their antiauthoritarianism in favor of a slicker, more industry-friendly image. *Pleased to Meet Me*, itself edging closer to the mainstream accessibility they had eschewed on earlier records, would be followed by the great act-cleaner-upper, *Don't Tell a Soul*. No sooner had this record hit the Sam Goodys of America than Paul Westerberg was being interviewed in *Spin*, talking about how they'd given up drinking, that they wanted to be a decent band, dammit. Whereas the intention was right—a thousand concert promoters across greater North America must have sighed in relief—the essence of the band seemed to dissolve with this concession. I had a poster on my wall—a color printout my uncle had sent me—with a picture of a heavy-lidded Paul Westerberg, staring into the camera. Beside the picture was printed a succinct Westerbergian aphorism: "I've tried to be a punk, a rocker, a drunk. I've finally decided I'm an artist, godammit, an artist."

By the time I got to them, the Replacements' glory days were heavily on the wane. Even though 1990's *All Shook Down*, the band's swansong, received mostly glowing reviews at the time of its release, its shelf-life hasn't measured up to the earlier records, especially *Let It Be*. Bob Stinson, the band's founding lead guitar player, had been out of the band for two years in 1988. The Replacements, while not receiving the attention due to them by the Cure and Depeche Mode-heavy video rotation on "120 Minutes," were taking leaps and bounds in their national visibility; they were, however, only two years away from their dissolution.

* * *

Around midnight, about halfway into the program, the folks at "120 Minutes" would post the upcoming national tour dates for a handful of the bands that had been showcased on the program. I huddled close to the television, the volume turned low so as to not wake my mom, and watched as the list of dates and venues scrolled up the screen. Each band's itinerary would start on one of the coasts and then amble westward or eastward, traversing the great plains and the southern deltas to arrive at the opposite coast. There was one common element in each of the schedules: if a band were heading westward, the itinerary would take a superhuman leap right after a Minneapolis date, landing three days, sometimes a full week, later in Seattle. Heading eastward, the same gap was included: Seattle was followed by a vacuum of dates, on the other side of which the band would re-emerge in such far-flung places as Chicago or Denver or Iowa City. To the booking agents, managers, and MTV programmers, Montana might as well not exist. It seemed to serve only as a stretch of land, a platform on which the great Interstate 90 spreads, a pipeline from one lucrative market to another. I was in a constant state of bereavement. My grandmother got the *New York Times* and I would scan the Sunday section every week to see if there were any concert notices for my favorite bands. On the inside of my locker door at school I had a collection of clipped-out concert advertisements: Echo and the Bunnymen at Radio City Music Hall, Depeche Mode at Madison Square Garden, and an advertisement for a Replacements show at the Beacon Theatre, replete with a picture of the scraggly haired foursome.

The bands that did come to town, the ones that were ambitious enough to launch a tour that included all of the lower forty-eight or had enough commercial radio visibility that would make a Montana appearance practical, were greeted with an enthusiasm that would be unmatched in any other entertainment-laden metropolis. Live performances by rock bands, regardless of their age or popularity, gave every like-minded preteen and teenager in the greater Helena valley area a chance to try out their musty, unused concertgoing personas.

In 1987, just as the Replacements were touring the major cities of America in support of their latest record, the spandexed Canadian acapella troup, the Nylons, paid a visit to Helena, playing a concert at the Civic Center while promoting their latest output, *Happy Together*. The event was quite a sensation around the Middle School, and parents of enthusiastic preteens around the city dutifully shelled out the twenty-odd dollars for tickets. The group had made a pretty solid showing on the *Billboard* charts with their 1984 hit "Na Na Hey Hey Kiss Him Goodbye" and were riding on the coattails of their second chart hit, an acapella rendition of the Turtles' "Happy Together." My mother had their latest record and I had heard their recent hit on the radio, but I was driven to go to the show more out of desperation to see live music. The show was packed; when the Nylons eventually took the stage, all unitards and mustaches, the entire population of the Helena Middle School rushed the stage, myself included, caught up in the excitement of a live performance. I stayed up front with my schoolmates, cheering during the song breaks, singing along to the songs I recognized. It wasn't until halfway through the concert, during a particularly steamy breakdown in which one of the members of the group walked downstage and, mugging for the audience, stuck his hand down his pants, grabbed his crotch, pulled his hand out and licked it, that I had a moment of epiphanic clarity. I glanced to my right and saw a classmate, a girl named Sarah, scream shrilly at this Nylon's sexually charged gesture, and reach out for him, her eyes rolled back in her head in erotic desperation.

I had spoken with Sarah in the foyer of the Civic Center earlier that evening. She, like myself, was at the show largely on the insistence of her parents. She was only vaguely familiar with the Nylons through what little she had heard on the top-forty radio stations in town. But here she was, screaming and weeping like this was 1964 and the four obviously flaming Nylons were nothing other than John, Paul, George, and Ringo.

And yet there I was too, already a self-described music snob who had long thrown away his Boston and Robert Palmer tapes, cheering along with her. I was deeply ashamed. After the concert, I stood out in the empty parking lot as I waited for my father to pick me up and felt flushed with despair, thankful that there were none of the skater set at the concert—they, naturally, would not be caught dead at a Nylons concert.

* * *

Belmont was a ski hill about half an hour outside of Helena. It was relatively cheap and the snow was decent most of the year. My dad, in an effort to increase my number of group-related sports activities, talked me into joining the Belmont Junior Ski Team. "It'll help you learn to work with people," he said. I was already bemoaning my seemingly needless participation on the Middle School's seventh grade basketball team—I spent the vast percentage of game time on the bench—so my dad figured this would be good alternative.

Practices were on Saturdays and a bus would pick up the team at the Colonial Inn at eight AM, delivering us to the bottom of the ski hill. It was a thirty-minute bus ride, during which I would have to listen to the hotshots on the team issue jocky challenges to each other and recklessly boast about their sexual escapades. I always brought my walkman along and stayed silent in the front of the bus, hoping to avoid any crossfire from the slung insults and challenges. I brought *Let It Be* on these Saturdays, because it was ideal music to ski to, but there was an ulterior motive in that most of the record was loud enough to drown out my fellow bus riders.

On the third Saturday of the season, the bus deposited us at the ski hill and we all marched up to the lodge where we prodded and shoved our overstuffed ski bags into lockers and under benches. Then we were off to the top of the hill where the instructor was ready to give us our morning drills. We practiced kick turns and pole planting and then did some practice runs. I was sore, uncomfortable, and quiet. Where my teammates absorbed our coach's instructions and improved with each run, I faltered as my movements came under increasing scrutiny. By the afternoon, when the rest of the team gathered together at the bottom of the course and trash-talked each other's runs, I stood apart on my own, afraid to join in and secretly thankful that no one was inviting me. The hours of practice inched along at glacial speed until the coach took me aside.

"How ya doin', Colin?" he asked. He was smiling, but his brow was creased with concern.

"I'm fine," I said.

"Maybe you want to hit free-ski a little early today?" he asked.

"Sure," I said.

"All right. See you next Saturday," he said, patting my back. Just as I was turning to ski off, he shouted, "Hey! Great job today! Keep working on those turns."

As I glanced to nod at him, I noticed the entire rest of the team, standing in a group, watching me ski away. One leaned over and whispered in another's ear. I shuddered with embarrassment. Back down at the chair-lift line, I put my headphones on and blasted *Let It Be*. "Wanna be something / Wanna be anything!" shouted Paul Westerberg and I spent the rest of the day tuning out the world.

* * *

When the spring hit and the snow had melted away and our seventh grade year was drawing to a close, Mark and I started spending time in the hills behind his house. Our camping and hiking acumen had grown considerably and we now packed for our overnighters in the meadow with a practical economy. We built a lean-to in a stand of trees overlooking the meadow and cobbled together a circle of rocks where we built massive bonfires; we whittled birch branches for roasting sticks and had hot dogs and s'mores on warm summer evenings. We bowed out of normal junior high weekend activities in favor of these short camping trips. I couldn't stand the basketball and football games that would take place on Friday evenings and Saturday afternoons. I was anxious and uncomfortable at the school dances, and I was rarely invited to classmates' parties. If Mark suffered under the same social inadequacies, he never let on. He stayed active in sports and even had a few brief trysts with girls. However, watching Monty Python movies at my mom's house or hanging out in his basement playing Dungeons and Dragons always seemed to trump whatever other plans Mark had going on during the weekend. I broached the subject one evening while we were sitting in our lean-to, poking at the dying fire. I had been quizzing him on the more popular kids in our class; he hung out with them every once and a while and knew of all their comings and goings.

"John just dumped April," he said, pushing a piece of wood closer to the fire. "She's pretty bummed out. They were at a party last weekend and she totally freaked out."

"Do you think I'm popular?" I asked.

He paused, thinking. "People know who you are," he conceded.

I was secretly thrilled.

"Do you think people like me?" I ventured.

"Yeah," he said. "I think so. I mean, they don't *not* like you."

"Cool," I said, and then: "You're kinda popular."

"I guess, maybe," he said.

"Do you ever think you might be less popular for hanging out with me?" I asked.

"I don't know," he said. "But I don't really care."

* * *

Eighth grade came on and with it, a host of new hurdles and heightened pressures. The obligation to go to school dances increased. The year before, I had been one of many kids who were too nervous or grossed out to attend these dances, but now with the collective maturation of my entire class, I could no longer hide behind these excuses. As a consequence, my absence at dances was noted. Mark tried to talk me into going to the first dance of the school year.

"It's cool," he said as we walked down the hall after school. "All that happens is the music plays and all the guys stand at one end of the gym and all the girls sit in the bleachers. Every once in a while a slow song will come on and a few of the girls will come down and slow dance with some of the guys but mostly everybody just stands there looking at each other."

"Sounds stupid," I said. "What kind of music is it?"

Mark rolled his eyes. "They don't play punk rock, if that's what you're getting at. They play . . . I don't know . . . dance music."

"Bleagh," I muttered, sticking out my tongue. "I'd go if they played decent music."

"Yeah, right," said Mark.

After school, I wandered over to the gymnasium and stood by the door, watching the members of the Pep Club string brightly colored ribbon and streamers through the rafters. Two older looking kids were setting up the DJ station. One was standing out in the middle of the floor while the other tested the speakers, some bland Richard Marx hit blasting intermittently from the cones. Kids were starting to line up at the window of the school store to pick up their tickets and I wandered over and got in line, fishing my school ID out of my backpack. The events of the evening slowly unfolded to me while I waited my turn: I imagined my father dropping me off in front of the school that night; I imagined walking into the dark gymnasium, dressed in my finest Gotcha clothing and the stone-washed jeans that sat unused in my dresser-drawer because I was too shy to wear them; I imagined standing among the other boys, the popular boys, on one side of the gym, watching the swarm of girls in the bleachers, picking out the one I would ask to dance. Mark's statement of earlier that summer rang in my ears: "I mean, they don't *not* like you."

I turned and walked out, pocketing my school ID.

* * *

Through elementary school, I had always been tall for my age. Because of this, I was often recruited to play on the basketball team. My dad had enjoyed a bit of fame in his junior high and high school days as a basketball player and he enthusiastically supported me when I went out for try-outs. Even though my raw ability on the court left a little to be desired—I was slow and clumsy and could not take my eyes off the ball when I was dribbling—I was always a shoe-in because of my height. By eighth grade, however, most of the kids who regularly went out for the basketball team had caught up or surpassed me in height. I was relegated to positions other than center in the try-outs—positions that required more skilled strategies than my "stand-under-the-basket-and-get-the-rebound" approach to being a center.

Mark and I went to try-outs on the same day. We were immediately separated in the first round when Mark was selected to vie for a position on the first-string team; I was sent to the other side of the gym. Over here, there were two types of contenders: kids like myself who were there more out of parental obligation or as a matter of habit than for any real love of the game; and aspiring jocks who had been rejected in the first round for the main team. This convergence was a terrible thing: the former group were beginning to realize they were not cut out for the sporting life, and the latter were overcome with bitterness and resentment and were likely to take it out on their inferior teammates.

During our first practice, I was on the receiving end of this resentment. We had just split the team into skins and shirts for a scrimmage—as luck would have it, I had been selected for the skins team and reluctantly peeled my shirt from my skinny, pale chest. I had been worried about this, as I was very sensitive about the state of my physique at the time. Also, I had a common abnormality in my ribcage—a protruding zyphoid, a pea-sized piece of bone jutting from my sternum. I was placed as a forward and my opposing team member was a red-haired kid named Nick. Because all of his friends had made the first-string team, Nick was a red-haired, fat-headed ball of holier-than-thou attitude and had spent the entire practice thus far showing off his dribbling skill and taking needless three-point shots during earlier scrimmages.

As soon as play started and I was guarding him, Nick started making fun of my protruding zyphoid. "What's that?" he asked. "Your third nipple?"

I desperately tried to come up with an adequate comeback and scanned his body for some sort of physical deficiency I could poke fun at, but either he had none, or I was too on-the-spot to find one. I froze and tried to ignore him. He grinned at me. There were beads of sweat balling up on his upper lip and I thought to myself, "What's that? Did you spit on yourself?" but refrained from saying it aloud, all too aware of how lame a retort it would be.

After practice, I caught up with Mark, whose team had been practicing on the other side of the gym.

"How'd you like it?" he asked as we stuffed our gym clothes into our lockers.

"I didn't," I said.

That night in my room, I laid on my belly and stared at the whirring capstans inside my Sony Sports boombox, the now well worn cassette of *Let It Be* within, while "Unsatisfied" blared through the speakers. I fought back the tears.

* * *

All through eighth grade, my uncle continued to send me tapes of the music he was discovering while living in Eugene. He sent me Robyn Hitchcock's *Globe of Frogs* backed with Camper Van Beethoven's *Our Beloved Revolutionary Sweetheart* on a single TDK SA-90 and I ate the stuff up voraciously. Paul rarely sent mixes; mostly it was two albums linked on a single cassette, with a few songs thrown on the end to make up for dead tape. Sometimes the combination of the two bands would clash stylistically (Cowboy Junkies' *Trinity Session* backed with Donner Party's eponymous second record) but within the context of the TDK, it made perfect sense. Mostly Paul would send me the tapes unprompted; sometimes he would ask me for requests; one time, he sent a tape wholly on accident—expecting to receive a collection of early Robyn Hitchcock songs, I tore open a package from Paul and discovered an unlabeled cassette. Assuming it to be empty, I threw the tape on my boombox and was surprised to find the tape was filled. The music was obviously dated—the vocal delivery, the drums and guitars all sounded like they were lifted from the mid-seventies—a music that was completely unlike my collection at the time. And yet the fact that it had a place in my uncle's record collection kept me with it. The third song, a gorgeous acoustic number, stuck out to me. It began with the line "Won't you let me walk you home from school / Won't you let me meet you at the pool . . . "

I talked to my uncle later that week. "Oh," he said when I brought up the unlabeled cassette, "I didn't mean to send you that, sorry. You can send it back if you want."

"I kind of like it." I said, "Who is it?"

"You like it?" he said. "That's Big Star. The Replacements sing about them, you know. That song 'Alex Chilton' is about them." He sang the bridge to me over the phone: "I never travel far / Without a little Big Star."

In the absence of song titles, I had made up my own and written them on the cassette's insert. On the other end of the line, he read the names of the songs of the record jacket and I read him what I had invented.

"September Gurls," he said. "That's 'gurls' with a 'u.'"

"I have 'December Boys Got It Bad.'" I responded.

He laughed through the receiver.

Fittingly, the song that I had loved so much on first listen was called "Thirteen": "Maybe Friday I can / Get tickets for the dance . . ." Though I had yet to attend a dance, much less ask a girl to one, the line still gave me the melancholy shivers. I began to wonder if I would ever ask a girl to a dance.

* * *

At home, I was listening to music like it was medicine. As soon as I got home from school, I would head upstairs to my room and press play on my Sony Sports cassette player. The room would fill with music and I would lie on my bed, staring at the constellations of glow-in-the-dark green spots that covered my ceiling in an inexact replica of the cosmos. My mother and I had spent an afternoon covering my ceiling with the spots while listening to *The Queen Is Dead* on repeat on my stereo. My mother said all the songs sounded the same. And again, she wondered if they were gay.

"No, mother," I said—though this time, I was less convinced myself.

I listened to *Let It Be* endlessly. The record seemed to encapsulate perfectly all of the feelings that were churning inside me. The leap from seventh to eighth grade had felt like a quantum shift and my head was reeling from the changes. My eccentricities were becoming more and more pronounced against the status quo of my schoolmates. I was fitting in less and less. I'd been told by older classmates that middle school girls were easy, but I could barely bring myself to speak with them, let alone try to get in their pants.

Your age is the hardest age
Everything drags and drags
Think it's funny? You ain't laughin' are you
Sixteen blue
Sixteen blue

Paul Westerberg's weary voice sounded from my boombox and I trembled to think that here I was, thirteen, and the "hardest age" was still three years in the making. I felt like yelling at the stereo, "Well, thirteen ain't so easy either!"

My guitar lessons were one saving grace. I arrived at the door of Al Estrada's apartment every Monday night to be taught new chord structures and scales on my black hollow-body guitar. One day I showed up and Al told me that he'd decided I was ready to move on.

"Move on?" I asked.

"You know, take the next step," he responded. "I have a brother who's an amazing guitar player. I mean, really amazing. He goes on tour with rock bands all the time. He gets hired by other guitar players to teach them songs. I mean, he's really good."

"Okay," I said, though I honestly didn't feel like I'd taken any steps at all. I was still struggling with some of the more rudimentary guitar techniques.

Al's brother lived in the Stuart Homes and when my dad dropped me off in his cul-de-sac the next week, I half expected to see lovely Lynette come walking out from one of the carsick-green houses. I marched up to the door of the apartment and knocked. Al's brother answered. He was tall and gangly and he had long, stringy black hair that hung over his shoulders. He was wearing a tank top and a thin gold chain around his neck and he invited me in.

"Hi, dude," he said.

"Hi," I said. I hadn't ever been called "dude" before.

On the phone earlier that week, he had told me that the way he preferred to teach guitar was by having his students bring in music they'd like to be taught. He said they absorbed the lessons better. He brought out his guitar—a bright purple thing with jagged edges—and said, "So, what do you got for me?"

Reaching into my backpack, I pulled out three tapes: *Louder Than Bombs*, *Never Mind the Bollocks*, and *Let It Be*. He shuffled through them wordlessly as I took my guitar out of its case.

"I never heard of any of this stuff," he said. "But whatever."

We started with the Replacements. I wanted to learn "Sixteen Blue." He listened quietly, tugging at strands of his hair and toying with his gold chain. He played a few chords on his guitar and said, "I think I got it" and he showed me the chords. We played the chords together for a moment. I could hear the melody beginning to surface from beneath what I was playing and I was ecstatic. I nodded in appreciation to Al's brother and he smiled, though it was obvious that he found the simplicity of the song's arrangement tedious. He showed me the chords to the chorus and then said, "And then it sounds like the dude solos . . ." he paused for a moment, listening to Bob Stinson's heavenly, understated solo, "But that's kind of a pansy solo. Try this on for size—here, play along." He then began playing frantic, lightning-fast arpeggios up and down the neck while I played the two chords of the verse.

by Erik Davis

IV
In the Middle of the Air

In the Light You Will Find the Road

"Stairway to Heaven" isn't the greatest rock song of the 1970s; it is the greatest spell of the 1970s. Think about it: we are all very sick of the thing, but in some primordial way *it is still number one*. Everyone knows it, everyone—from Dolly Parton to Frank Zappa to Pat Boone to Jimmy Castor—has covered it, and everyone with a guitar knows how to play those notorious opening bars. As far as rock radio goes, "Stairway" is generally considered to be the most-requested and most-played song of all time, despite the fact that it runs eight minutes and was never released as a single. In 1991, *Esquire* magazine did some back-of-the-envelope calculations and figured that the total time that "Stairway" had been on the air was about forty-four years—and that was over a decade ago. Somewhere a Clear Channel robot is probably broadcasting it as you read these words. And no wonder: when classic rock stations roll out their Top 500 surveys, which they still do with disarming frequency, odds are overwhelming that this warhorse will take the victory lap. Even our dislike and mockery is ritualistic. The dumb parodies; the *Wayne's World*-inspired folklore about guitar shops demanding customers not play it; even Robert Plant's public disavowal of the song—all these just prove the rule. "Stairway to Heaven" is not just number one. It is *the One*, the quintessence, the closest AOR will ever get you to the absolute.

If any Zeppelin song deserves to be dubbed a "myth," it is this one. But what does that mean, to call a song a myth? So far I have been too lazy to define the word, trusting, like the man said about porn, that you will know it when you see it. You could define myth in the romantic terms that probably informed Page and Plant: myths are Big Stories that tell poetic truths about humanity and its role in the cosmos. The "hero's journey," the monomyth popularized by Joseph Campbell, is such a poetic archetype, and certainly informs my own view of Percy and his ramblings through the landscape of   ♒︎⚜︎🜍︎① ("Percy" being the character we follow through the album, as well as Plant's nickname). After walking the "road of trials" and encountering the Goddess, the hero achieves the apotheosis of the "ultimate boon"—what Percy will glimpse at the heights of heaven's stairway. Campbell emphasizes that this peak comes halfway through the diagram of the hero's journey; after this he must return to ordinary reality and reintegrate, as "master of the two worlds." This is the developmental process that Percy does not follow: he wants further highs and juicier goddesses. And he will rue the day.

Mythology is more than an abstract story or a universal code, however. Mythology is also deeply embedded in human practice. Traditionally, myths are acted out; even their verbal transmission is a highly charged performance. Even more important is the relationship between myth and ritual. Rituals, like taking communion or dancing around a maypole, perform and sustain the transforming fictions of mythology just as much as mythology explains or demands ritual. So if "Stairway to Heaven" is a successful myth, then what rituals support it? What practice sustains the song that Lester Bangs memorably described as being "lush as a kleenex forest"? The song itself hints at the answer when Percy suggests that great things will happen if we "listen very hard" and all "call the tune." The central rite of "Stairway to Heaven" was and continues to be this: *hearing the damn thing over and over again.* Whether you call up a file on your iPod, or call your radio station to vote, or call your spouse a goofball for playing the song just one more time, "Stairway" makes its peculiar magic known through the brute force of all ritual: repetition. Even those of us who have no desire to sustain the mystery, who can't wait for this number to be swept into the dustbin of history, continue to feel its presence in sonic memory. On the surface this presence goes against Walter Benjamin's famous argument that mechanical reproduction—which churns out all those copies of ♒︎⚜︎🜍︎① in the first place—saps the "aura" from works of art. Though Benjamin was talking principally about visual art, his argument works for music as well: the special magic of live performance is leached away when you record and reproduce the event with modern technology. But in the case of "Stairway," the very banality that results from the staggering number of times this track has been played over the last thirty-odd years only underscores the awful majesty of the song, its weird air of *necessity.*

The "magic" of "Stairway to Heaven" lies with a power at once more mechanical and more spellbinding than the commodity fetishism discussed earlier: the power to literally become a part of our minds. Here's what I mean: close your eyes, shuffle through your mental jukebox for "Stairway to Heaven," and then drop the virtual stylus or laser beam or whatever you want to call it onto the song in your brain. If you are like millions of other people now living, you can probably reproduce a decent mock-up of this track from memory. If you sit with it for a while, you might even score some personal associations out of the deal—tasty madeleines like the pungent reek of Thai-stick, or the Christmas morning promise of a teenage grope.

All this is all very ordinary of course. All of us have used commercial recordings to sound our souls; all of us know songs that resonate, songs that stick. But we rarely turn the situation around and consider the possibility that, as the nineteenth-century Belgian physiologist Joseph Delboeuf wrote, "The soul is a notebook of phonographic recordings." Delboeuf's quotation popped out at me from an essay by Friedrich Kittler, the contemporary German media theorist I cited earlier. In his text, Kittler suggests that the analogy between the brain and the record player is, as the geeks like to say, nontrivial. Like the sounds on a record album, physiological memory is a product of something like *inscription*, as associative neural pathways are laid down, deepened, and reinforced through repetition and reward. Kittler suggests that our experience of listening to a phonograph also models the crucial transition between physiology and consciousness: a stylus tracing a groove reproduces nothing more than physical vibrations in the air, but in our minds these vibrations transform, as if by magic, into the meaningful presence of voice and song. With the phonograph, as with our brains, we move continuously between spark and sense. Kittler takes the analogy even further, and asks: What if the song of our own soul, of our internal psychic life, is simply the result of our peculiar ability to "listen" to the continual playback of recordings etched into myriad neural grooves? This is what Kittler means when he describes the brain as a "conscious phonograph."

Obviously, the activity of self-awareness and recall is significantly more plastic and creative than this analogy implies. Nonetheless, our ability to rather faithfully "read" Led Zeppelin tracks directly from our internal memory banks proves that, if our brains are exposed to enough repetitions, they can act more or less like a phonograph or a tape recorder. This is evident enough in our recall of the voices of friends and family, but becomes even more obvious when we are mentally "recording" actual recordings like "Stairway to Heaven." This juncture, where sound technology and self-awareness coincide, is also where things start to get strange. Listening to familiar recordings, Kittler notes, "[It is] as if the music were originating in the brain itself, rather than emanating from stereo speakers or head phones." The membrane between self and recorded other breaks down, "as if there were no distance between recorded voice and listening ears." When the tune comes to you at last, it comes from within; but this "within" is no longer your own. "You" are pre-recorded; your head is humming.

Of course, sonic viruses—aka, songs—try to worm their way into our heads every day. And even successful infections do not make magic. A thousand years of heavy rotation would not suffice to enchant "The Piña Colada Song" or "Ice Ice Baby," to say nothing of that excruciating woman who instructs you on the art of leaving voice mail messages. The forces that transform "Stairway" into ritual lie inside the song, in its charismatic deployment of words and music. However you feel about it personally—and I'll be fine if I don't hear it again until I'm old—"Stairway to Heaven" is the quintessence of Led Zeppelin's commercial sorcery. I choose the term *quintessence* quite consciously: the *quinta essentia*, the fifth element. Plato believed the quintessence to be an invisible ether that pervades all space, including the distant stars; in alchemy it came to be seen as the animating spirit of all things, a living spark that could be purified and extracted from baser elements but that infused them all. "Stairway to Heaven" is the culmination of an alchemical drama, the fourth song on the fourth album by a quartet consciously invoking the four elements. It lasts about two-times-four minutes long and begins, as more than one writer has described, "squarely": with four famous phrases, each four measures long, that unfold with a stately charm free of syncopation.

Having set up all these quaternities, Zeppelin squeezes something *quintessential* from them over the course of the tune. As Susan Fast demonstrates, the melodic and rhythmic "squareness" that opens the song also conceals "a harmonic and formal openness and irregularity" that runs throughout the piece, and that breaks the initial static formality. This motive essence carries Percy, and us, through the different stages of the song, the best description of which belongs to Chuck Eddy:

> [The song is] constructed *as* a stairway, with four steps; on every subsequent one, the music gets louder, and you can either turn the volume higher or turn the radio off. If you vote "yeah," to reach the top step, the altar, you will do anything.

My only beef with Eddy here is the number of steps; as you might expect, I count *five*. But no matter. The quintessence of the piece lies in this *yeah!*, the assent to the ascent, the embrace of Percy's apotheosis in the final verse, when he finally groks the unity of all things. Here the volume and tempo produce a culminating sense of *arrival*, but even more important is the fact that, following Page's heavenly Telecaster solo, the instruments all play in unison for the first time in the piece. The polyphony and counterpoint that characterize the song's opening—which interlaced distinct melodies and separate instrumental lines—have finally given way to a single riff, to fusion. This unity mirrors Percy's glimpse into the nondual nature of reality. But it also reflects the alchemy that characterizes great rock combos: a sense of togetherness, like fair D'Artagnan and the three musketeers. All for one and one for all.

The journey of "Stairway to Heaven" also progresses from acoustic to electric, a classic Zeppelin move that here suggests the passage from an enchanted pastoral world into a contemporary zone of power and aggression. Robert Walser claims that the song thus "combines contradictory sensibilities without reconciling them," and is therefore "postmodern." I'm not sure what Walser is talking about here. For all its prettiness, "Stairway to Heaven" is a volatile song; it is not balanced but *spills forward* toward the final refrain. But by the standards of rock and roll, the tune's musical development is quite organic, which is hardly a typical postmodern value. The transition between the song's steps recalls a description of musical composition that Page gave a reporter in 1970: "the whole thing just grows like an acorn or something." As Walser would say, such organicism is certainly an "ideology"—in the same interview, Page admits that he's "a romantic" with a soft spot for pre-Raphaelite ideals. The point, though, is that Page is a *realized* romantic, that "Stairway to Heaven" embodies the pre-Raphaelite combination of medieval romance and modern rule breaking. "Stairway to Heaven" resonates, not because it mashes up contradictions, but because it *integrates* the traditionalism of the acoustic into the propulsive domain of electric pop. During the final riff, for example, Page supplies rhythm guitar with a clean Fender XII twelve-string; instead of the crunchy Les Paul one might expect at the climax, we hear a chiming, essentially acoustic timbre. The dramatic fanfare that announces the transition to the electric finale (at 5:35) is also probably the most traditional element of the piece; in the West, such three-note flourishes have been used for centuries to indicate auspicious events. Playing this passage live, Page would underscore its ceremonial function by pointing his double-necked guitar—itself looking more like a weird Renaissance lute than a postwar electric instrument—directly toward the heavens, as hieratic a gesture as we have in rock.

That said, I agree with Fast that the shift from acoustic to electric in "Stairway" suggests a movement away from mythological time and into present circumstances. That's what happens to Percy anyway, when you look at the placement of "Stairway to Heaven" in the album's song sequence. When Percy first steps onto the stairs, he leaves the wisdom of Evermore's ancestral vale behind; when he jumps off at the end, he finds himself in the urban park of "Misty Mountain Hop," surrounded by potheads and cops. On the original LP, of course, Percy also had to pass through silence to get from the end of "Stairway" to the next song: the silence that stretched, sometimes interminably, between the end of side one and the beginning of side two. This rupture, imposed by the vertical ascent of the stylus, marks "Stairway to Heaven" as the discontinuous peak of Percy's journey, and not just another stage of his horizontal wandering across the plain. When Percy reaches the top of the stairway, the gods, their noses as yet unpunched, satisfy his spiritual wanderlust by showing him clips of a visionary drama before granting him, finally, a transcendent flash of gnosis.

We could spend all day with the lyrics. You'd get tired, and I'd get sued, and we still wouldn't be any closer to unpacking all the hints and allusions buried in Percy's frothy shaman chant. It's a zoo in there. Walser makes the excellent point that the song's various images, characters, and philosophical concerns are fundamentally fragmentary: they suggest myth without telling us one. For him, again, this becomes a postmodern gesture: "Stairway" is a "very open text" that "invite[s] endless interpretation." Robert Plant said as much himself when he noted, "The only thing that gives ['Stairway to Heaven'] any staying power at all is its ambiguity." And the lyrics themselves tell you that words have more than one meaning, that you can always change whatever (interpretive) path you are on. But none of this explains why Zeppelin's fractured fairy tale *resonates* while so many pomo pastiches provide little more than the tinny clash of ironic referentiality.

One hint lies in a story that Plant has told about the composition of the lyrics. Page brought the elements of the tune more or less finished to Headley Grange, and one night, sitting before the fire and in a somewhat sour mood, Plant set pen to paper and the words flowed out of him with unnatural ease. "There was something pushing it saying, 'You guys are OK, but if you want to do something timeless, here's a wedding present for you.'" Why Plant mentions a wedding is unclear. Who is marrying whom? In any case, Plant lays the lyrics at the feet of an external agent, a creative daemon. Thomas Friend will tell you that this daemon is a demon, of course, while others might invoke Moroccan hashish or the singer's uncanny knack for self-mythologizing. No matter. What Plant's tale articulates is the "mythic" sense that, behind the lyric fragments, behind the scenes, *something mysterious is calling us forward*. These lyric fragments are aligned so that, like the constellations of the night sky, they suggest patterns that draw us, and Percy, deeper into the gloom. That's why Percy almost disappears as a character in the song. We feel his familiar wanderlust when he looks toward the west and feels a gnostic longing for "leaving." But now his longing has made him an empty vessel for larger forces, for a visionary capacity beyond his usual ken.

I agree with Friend that the Lady we meet at the beginning of the song is not the light-shining goddess at the end, although the latter may be the transfiguration of the former. Instead, this first lady is a sort of Everysoul, the spark in us all. In this, she recalls the gnostic figure of Sophia, the exiled female power who must climb her way back to heaven and whose name means knowledge, just as this lady is associated with "knowing." Her stairway is clearly a bridge between worlds, a symbol that the comparative religionist Mircea Eliade connected with ideas of sanctification, death, and deliverance. The journey suggested in the first two verses, then, is a gnostic journey through the afterlife. I know I am out on a limb here, but it's the only way I can explain the curious word substitution that Robert Plant makes in many live performances of the song, including those featured on *The Song Remains the Same* and the 2003 DVD. During the second verse, Plant rather clearly says "if the *stars* are all closed." Bootleg listeners know that Plant sometimes changed lyrics live, throwing in alternate words and warping his diction. But I hear something deeper in the claim that, if the "stars" are closed, then "a word" can still win the Lady her goal.

The roots of the gnostic-hermetic tradition, including the Order of the Golden Dawn and Crowley's Thelema, lie in Egypt. And the root of Egyptian religion lies in death and magic. Around 2300 BC, at the end of the fifth dynasty, hieroglyphic writings began to appear for the first time on the walls inside the pyramids built to house the dead kings in the great necropolis of Saqqara. These collections of spells and prayers, appropriately known as the Pyramid Texts, are devoted to providing the dead pharaoh with the spells and instructions he will need on his harrowing journey through the afterworld. The pharaoh's goal was the heaven of the "imperishable stars," where he would partake in the eternal life of the sun god Re, though the joint was eventually taken over by Osiris, the dying and resurrected consort of Isis, the Queen of Light. Pharaoh had many paths to go by on his journey, but one sure route described in the texts was a stairway or ladder—perhaps the first stairway to heaven in world religion, if you don't count the pyramids themselves. Once the pharaoh made his ascent, he would face various barriers and malevolent threshold dwellers. This is where magic came in, because only the proper words and spells would allow him to pass.

Two millennia later, the symbol of the stairway to heaven reappeared in some mystery cults and gnostic sects of Late Antiquity. One of the central symbols of the Mithraic mystery cult—a powerful rival to Christianity in the last centuries of pagan Rome—was a ladder with eight rungs. The first seven rungs, as well as the seven different metals that composed them, were associated with the seven planets, or "wandering stars." At that time the cosmos was widely considered to be a sort of onion, with earth at the center and each higher layer ruled by one of the planets. Beyond these seven heavens lay the empyrean, the eighth "rung" of the fixed stars. This model was interpreted in different ways, but for many gnostics, the planetary rulers were essentially demonic: they imprisoned the soul through the machinery of fate, an oppressive system of astral control that trickles down to us today in the gentler lore of astrology. Like the Egyptian pharaoh, the gnostic prepared for death by learning the proper spells that would allow him to circumvent the various boss characters and portals that this cosmic computer game placed between him and the highest heaven. If the gateways of these star-worlds are closed, in other words, a word will open them up. In "Stairway to Heaven," once the Lady utters her magic word, the scene shifts and we enter the "Celtic" landscape of forests and pipers and hedgerows that will dominate the tune until the finale. With this passage, the Lady's word becomes song.

The mystic in me likes this gnostic reading of the Lady's stairway. But it doesn't account for the most notable aspect of Plant's slippage between "stars" and "stores": that the Lady's astral journey is a commercial undertaking. This may be the strangest juxtaposition of the entire record: bathed in an acoustic mood that radiates pastoral nostalgia, Percy sings about shopping. The lady doesn't even barter for the stairway; she *buys* it. Tom Friend insists that she pays for it with her immortal soul, of course, but that satanic fantasy misses the true "evil" of her heretical purchase, which is its utter banality. Our modern commercial culture has disenchanted the world by reducing every possible value—"all that glitters"—to a single gold standard (which isn't even gold anymore). Everything has its price: Celtic magic, bardo maps, mystic rapture. Everything is part of the market. So the Lady buys her stairway, says the word, and gets a songbird that sings, just like a record that plays. Could it really be this simple? Is the stairway to heaven that the Lady buys just . . . a copy of "Stairway to Heaven"?

Such self-referentiality would help explain a crucial feature of the song's lyrics: the persistence of images involving music, voices, listening, and sound. We hear a songbird and a babbling brook, while Percy somehow "sees" voices; then we hear whispers about some tune we might call; then we meet a piper who, it seems, will preside over a giggling forest. As the verses progress, Percy also shifts his focus from "I" to "we" and finally to "you," to the "dear Lady." He tells her that the humming in her head will not go away because the piper continues to call "you." In many live performances, however, a different story emerges. In the Earls Court appearance captured on the DVD, for example, Plant directly addresses the listeners of the song: "Dear *people*," he sing-says, "can you hear the wind blow?" His eyes smolder like a feral cherub, and he splays the fingers of his right hand open as he lets us in on the secret: "*our* stairway lies on the whispering wind." Then we realize that the wind he's talking about is blowing off the Marshall stacks, that the stairway is made of the song and sound all around us, carrying us up and forward. And that's exactly when Jimmy's resplendent fanfare erupts.

Now unless we snuck into the show or ripped the DVD, we *bought* this stairway. The point is obvious but crucial: rock's head-humming ecstasies and mythic leaps toward authenticity are embedded in the commercial and technological matrix of media culture. Tucked within Percy's medieval image of the piper lies an idiom of the modern market: those who pay the piper call the tune. The piper is not calling all the shots; we exercise control because *we give Led Zeppelin our money.* If we stop, they stop. But this service economy does not prevent gnosis, at least within the song's virtual world. That is what the fanfare and the song's finale are all about. As Walser rightly notes, heavy metal guitar solos often signify transcendence over and against the oppression created by the drums, which "rigidly organize and control time." Page's Telecaster jingle signifies such transcendence here, without necessarily delivering it. But the real apotheosis lies in the final riff, where "we" join Percy as he winds down the phonograph road, toward that perfect moment when all is one and one is all. This flash is the goal of all mystic yearning: the awareness of nonduality, the total grok, the secret sauce on the Big Enchilada.

Such nondualism is pretty stock stuff for hippie mystics, however. Far more curious is the gnostic weirdness that may lie in the next line: "to be a rock and not to roll." At first, this verse seems like more of Plant's cutesy wordplay. But, again, the very banality should alert us that we are near something important, and what we are near, at least if a contemporary mystic named Michael Hoffman is to be believed, is a rather bracing insight into the nature of reality. Influenced by esoteric Christianity and Neil Peart's lyrics for Rush, Hoffman offers, on his immense and compelling Ego Death website, a spiritual vision of absolute determinism. Hoffman believes that the cosmos is an unchanging mass of spacetime, a totally fixed continuum that he calls the "block universe." We live absolutely predetermined lives, like styluses following the groove of an LP. What the gnostic glimpse provides is a direct experience of this block universe, and the recognition that our ordinary sense of agency and control is a cybernetic illusion. Hoffman does believe in a rabbit hole out of this matrix, though it is very narrow: redemption lies in totally accepting the divine will that infuses the block universe, an experience of transcendental freedom that Hoffman finds mirrored in gnostic Christianity, heroic doses of psychedelics, and some rock lyrics—including "Stairway to Heaven." This is the goal: to die to our egos and their false sense of moving through a world of choice—to be a rock, in other words, and not to roll.

Needless to say, Hoffman's vision is not the dominant Christian interpretation of "Stairway to Heaven." That such interpretations persist, even to this day, is another sign of this song's theological import. In their relatively recent covers of the tune, for example, both Pat Boone and Dolly Parton replaced the final lines with more conventional Godtalk, Boone going so far as to offer this Trinitarian retort: "when three in one is all in all." But for more extreme Christian readings, we must turn again to Thomas Friend, the most articulate and studied of Led Zeppelin's inquisitors. In *Fallen Angel*, Friend reasonably argues that if Zeppelin are indeed Satanic proselytizers, then their Satanism is going to show itself here, in their most popular song. Friend begins his exegesis with the vaguely ominous character of the piper. He cites Ezekiel 28, where the prophet rails against the prince of Tyre, conventionally interpreted as a figure for Lucifer. Ezekiel enumerates all the honors God bestowed upon the angel before he rebelled, including the incredible "workmanship of thy tabrets and of thy pipes." Tabrets are tambourines, like the one Plant often shook live during "Stairway to Heaven," or the one favored by Tracy on "The Partridge Family." Friend then connects Ezekiel's piper to an astral being that Aleister Crowley describes in *The Vision and the Voice*, the Master Therion's experimental record of scrying his way through John Dee's Enochian calls. After voicing the 22nd Aethyr, LIN, Crowley encounters a rapturous audio-visual being:

> This Angel has all the colours mingled in his dress; his head is proud and beautiful; his headdress is of silver and red and blue and gold and black, like cascades of water, and in his left hand he has a pan-pipe of the seven holy metals, upon which he plays. I cannot tell you how wonderful the music is, but it is so wonderful that one only lives in one's ears; one cannot see anything any more.

Notice these seven metals: not only do they suggest the seven planetary metals of the Mithraic ladder of initiation, but they are here laid out in the stepwise shape of the pan-pipe, itself a kind of stairway. Pan, of course, is the horniest of the Greek deities, a nature god of woods and mountains who hooted tunes when he wasn't mounting nymphs or partying with Dionysus. With his horns, goat-hooves, and lascivious leer, Pan helped shape the later Christian image of the devil, and Friend is surprising no one when he claims that Crowley's Enochian friend is actually Lucifer. However, even readers familiar with the febrile ways of anti-rock crusaders may be surprised to learn from Friend that this being's wonderful music, which Crowley heard in 1909, is actually "Stairway to Heaven."

Of course, if Aleister Crowley had encountered Lucifer in the astral realms, he would be the first to tell you about it. What Crowley's vision is really about is music's daemonic power, its capacity to transport, transmute, and entrance the self. That's what the piper represents, whether he is the pied piper of Hamlin or the satyr Pan or the Piper at the Gates of Dawn, the unnamed forest god who enchants Rat and Mole in Kenneth Grahame's deeply Satanic *The Wind in the Willows*. The piper seduces through music, an erotic mystery that binds us in its very wildness. For rural romantics like Grahame, this wildness is associated with nature, with the elemental charm of an earth still capable of absorbing rootless moderns into her sublime flesh. The piper's appearance in "Stairway to Heaven" not only indicates Zeppelin's romantic belief in such pagan power, but their attempt—successful, one would have to say—to both unleash the spell and reflect on the musical process of enchantment itself.

Friend's satanic vision of the piper, then, represents more than the iconographic drift of Pan. To see the piper as Satan is also to refuse the rapture of music, a refusal that derives in part from that paranoid sense of control and agency that Hoffman suggests blocks our access to transcendental freedom—a freedom that sometimes comes when we simply submit to the beat. The divine has nothing to do with it: such rapture is our *natural* right. Passionate music fans all know such transport, those moments when "one only lives in one's ears." I pity those who experience such fusions of pleasure and transcendence as threats and not reasons to live. Nonetheless, Friend is not totally off base: there is an edge of darkness to such rapture, as with all genuine dissolutions of self. We are right to invoke the large metaphors of the supernatural. When William Burroughs saw Zeppelin live, the concert reminded him of the goat-god trance music he had witnessed in the mountains of Morocco, and he warned that such performances "must tap the sources of magical energy, and this can be dangerous." But he also compared "Stairway to Heaven" to a high school Christmas play. So much for fear of music.

The darkest supernatural myth about Zeppelin's most mythic song is that if you play the recording backward, you will hear Satanic messages encoded in Plant's vocals. The idea that some rock records contain "backmasked" messages goes back to the Beatles' "Revolution 9," which was rumored to contain the reversed announcement that "Paul's a dead man." As far as I can tell, Christian anti-rock crusaders got into the act in 1981, when a Michigan minister named Michael Mills hit Christian radio with the news that phrases like "master Satan," "serve me," and "there's no escaping it" were hidden in the grooves of the Zeppelin hit. Noting wryly that words "certainly do have two meanings," Mills argued on one program that the "subconscious mind" could hear these phrases, which is why sinful rock musicians put them there in the first place. Soon backmasking became the Satanic panic *du jour*, giving paranoid Christians technological proof that rock bands like Queen, Kiss, and Styx (!) did indeed play the devil's music. While most people, Christian or otherwise, found all this rather silly, these fears did reflect more pervasive fears that the media had become a subliminal master of puppets—fears that would themselves come to inspire some 1980s metal.

In retrospect, what stands out most in the backmasking controversy is the marvelous image of all these preachers screwing around with turntables. Though one doubts that Minister Mills was chillin' with Grandmaster Flash or DJ Kool Herc, rap musicians and Christian evangelicals both recognized that popular music is a material inscription, one that can be physically manipulated in order to open up new vectors of sense and expression. For both evangelicals and rap DJs, the vinyl LP was not a transparent vehicle of an originally live performance, but a source of musical meaning itself, a material site of potential codes, messages, and deformations of time. Alongside the more kinetic and rhythmic innovations introduced by scratch artists like DJ Grand Wizard Theodore, we must also speak of a "Christian turntablism": slow, profoundly unfunky, obsessed with linguistic "messages." Some evangelical TV broadcasts from the early 80s even include top-down shots of the minister's DJ decks so that viewers can admire the technique of squeezing sense from sound. However, while rap and all the sampled music that follows it treats the vinyl LP as an open form capable of multiple meanings and uses, Christian turntablists remained *literalists*, convinced that they were revealing a single "fundamental" message intentionally implanted in the grooves by a diabolical author. Unfortunately, when it came to "Stairway to Heaven," these DJs for Jesus could not agree on the exact wording of Led Zeppelin's insidious messages. Once again, ambiguity trumps.

At the time, Led Zeppelin's Swan Song label responded to the brouhaha with the statement, "Our turntables only play in one direction." Occultists following the controversy also chimed in, pointing out that the first fellow to intentionally play records backward may have been none other than Aleister Crowley. In an early issue of *The Equinox*, Crowley argues that an aspiring magician should "train himself to think backwards by external means." He offers some suggestions: learn to walk backward, speak backward, and "listen to records reversed." All these reversals recall the original fantasy lurking behind the satanic backmasking scare: the backward recitation of the Lord's Prayer, a key element of the Black Mass that Renaissance Inquisitors almost surely invented from the screams of their torture victims. But Crowley is actually being far more methodical here. In seeking to prepare the aspirant for the terrifying act of "crossing the Abyss," Crowley wants the magician to break the hold of habitual thinking and to understand, in a dispassionate fashion influenced by Theravadan Buddhist meditation, the causal chains that give rise to the self. In any case, Crowley believed that ordinary consciousness could be subverted and expanded through the technological manipulation of phonographs and film, and he wrote about it in *1912*. No wonder Page described Crowley as the only Edwardian to embrace the twentieth century: he was a media hacker from the very beginning.

So what happens when we take Crowley's advice and start playing Led Zeppelin records backward? If you get your hands on a Technics deck or decent sound software and reverse the central verses of "Stairway to Heaven," you will probably hear the slurring, sucking sonic taffy that you'd expect. But if the appropriate passages are properly isolated, and you are prompted beforehand, then you are likely to hear things like "Here's to my sweet Satan" or "There's no escaping it." I certainly did, although the actual phrases sounded more like "Yish tomai swee Zaydn" and "Hair-airs no esgaybin id." Weird, yes, but probably nothing more than what the British musician and writer Joe Banks calls "Rorschach Audio." Banks developed the term to explain Electromagnetic Voice Phenomena, an occult exploration of audio technology that began in earnest in the 1950s. EVP investigators believe that if you tape empty radio frequencies or the silent passages on prerecorded media, and then listen to these recordings intently, you will eventually stumble across disincarnate voices traditionally ascribed to the dead. Some EVP recordings do indeed sound pretty creepy. But Banks argues that our brains excel at projecting patterns onto ambiguous data, particularly when "experts" prep us by stating beforehand what "messages" we are about to hear—a consistent element of both EVP and backward-masking presentations. It's the lesson of Colby's gatefold all over again: the voices, the messages, are in your head.

Some individual words in the purported messages tucked inside of "Stairway" do seem to pop out at you more or less objectively, but this can be explained by the phenomenon of phonetic reversal. Phonemes are the basic chunks of words, like "lay" and "dee," and when you reverse them, you create widely different combinations of sounds. Inevitably, some of these new combinations will fit together and seem to make sense without any additional tampering. This effect was convincingly demonstrated by the Zephead behind the Achilles Last Stand fansite, who took perhaps the most convincing reversible line in the original recording—the verse about changing the road you're on—and sampled the same verse from twelve live recordings, nearly all of them bootlegs. He then reversed the samples, *et voilà*! Twelve more-or-less creepy toasts to "mai sweet Zaydn." No subliminal engineering is necessary—only an uncanny coincidence of phonemes. But we should not mock the uncanny, here as anywhere. That fact is that, within only two minutes worth of singing, "Stairway to Heaven" contains at least seven reversed phrases of a suggestively devilish nature, including four mentions of Satan, or Seitan, or Sadie, or something like that. Moreover, these sonic simulacra are buried in a tune about pipers and whispers and listening really hard, a tune that, for a spell, ruled the world. I'm not saying that supernatural forces are afoot. I'm just saying it makes you wonder.

Exile on Main St.

by Bill Janovitz

If *Exile on Main St.* set the bar for what rock and roll should sound like, the album packaging established a standard of what it might look like: raw, enigmatic, spooky, black-and-white images of the band in various settings. Here is a prime example of the tragic downsizing of artwork that became inevitable as CDs edged out twelve-inch vinyl albums. Much of the concept and the photography itself comes from Robert Frank, a Swissborn émigré to the United States whose groundbreaking collection *The Americans* got right at the broken heart of America and its people—in urban and rural settings both.

Look a little closer: the "collage" on the front of *Exile* is actually a single shot, apparently from the wall of a New York tattoo parlor, a picture taken by Frank. The photos—some of which are featured in the *Exile on Main St.* layout—were taken on a cross-country drive in 1955 and '56 in a used car, funded in part by a Guggenheim Fellowship. The resulting book was highly influential in both form and content. If not the first, *The Americans* was one of the earliest examples of a photography book that dedicated a whole page to each photograph, with blank pages alternating opposite. The pictures are ostensibly taken in a verité style, but the results are as subjective as the most affecting works of art, particularly poetry. Frank has said, "When people look at my pictures, I want them to feel the way they do when they want to reread a line of a poem." As Jack Kerouac wrote in his introduction to the published collection, "Robert Frank, Swiss, unobtrusive, nice, with that little camera he raises and snaps with one hand he sucked a sad poem right out of America onto film, taking rank among the tragic poets of the world."

Kerouac also writes in his introduction, that the pictures remind him of "that crazy feeling in America when the sun is hot on the streets and the music comes out of a jukebox or a funeral," which dovetails nicely with *Exile on Main St.* Frank met Kerouac at a party in New York soon after the French publication of *The Americans* (an American publisher could not be secured until a year after the French publication). In photographs such as "Rooming House—Bunker Hill, Los Angeles," Frank was providing a photographic parallel to the works not just of the Beats, but echoing back to Beat predecessors like author John Fante (*Wait Until Spring, Bandini*).

It is perfect that the highly impressionistic author and poet Kerouac was chosen to pen the introduction to Frank's groundbreaking work, just as it seems so fitting that the Stones chose Frank to provide the album's artwork. Frank's is a visual—and the Stones' an aural and musical—travelogue across America and another "sad little poem right out of America." Frank's photos are deeply moving, searing their image onto the mind's retina of the viewer, particularly for an introspective suburban adolescent seeing them for the first time, freshly exposed to that "other" America that it sometimes takes an outsider's eye to see. Later, books by Diane Arbus and works by Frank's mentor Walker Evans would find their way into my hands, but I was a decidedly unworldly Long Island teenager hungry to discover what Greil Marcus later called "that old, weird America" in his book *Invisible Republic: Bob Dylan's Basement Tapes.*

Frank, another obvious exile, became known for his ability to virtually disappear, to blend in with his surroundings, capturing with his small camera the faces, the tiny dramas, and the surface Americana that he observed. Small things taken for granted in America fascinated him: signs, cars, clothes, attitudes. Of one incident with a sheriff who runs him out of town, he says, "We think that only happens in films."

The pictures in *The Americans* tend to concentrate on small spaces. A shot of an empty bar in Las Vegas where a boy in a loud printed shirt stares into the glow of a jukebox—which the Stones used in the *Exile* artwork—looks claustrophobic, as the daylight tries to seep in through the porthole windows of the doors while the bar seems always nocturnal by nature, fighting against the outside world. Almost everything is dimly lit, and everything is in black and white. Even the exterior shots, the facades of brick buildings, have that Edward Hopper-like melancholy light. There is an insular feeling to the book as whole, a hemmed-in quality that flies in the face of the romantic vision of an America "from sea to shining sea," with windswept plains of "amber waves of grain." Instead we find these small places, a Gothic America of funerals, crosses, stormy moorlike hills; with characters reminiscent of Eleanor Rigby grasping at fleeting moments of simple happiness and human interaction, as the clock of the human condition ticks on; "lives of quiet desperation," with only photographs offering some measure of immortality to these anonymous souls. As Kerouac notes in his introduction, "you end up finally not knowing any more whether a jukebox is sadder than a coffin."

In Domique Tarlé's indispensable book *Exile*—another collection of stunning photographs, taken by Tarlé while present at the *Exile on Main St.* sessions—Rolling Stones Records honcho Marshall Chess, son of Chess Records founder Leonard Chess, recalls: "Over the years with the Stones we'd allow in writers and photographers—the right ones, those who would fit in with our scene. People like Robert Frank, who Mick turned me on to after seeing his book *The Americans*. Robert became known as the father of realism because he'd become so invisible that people would do anything in front of him. We chose him to do the *Exile* cover, which he shot in Super 8."

John Van Hamersveld was gracious in sharing with me some of the logistics in putting the *Exile on Main St.* package together. John had been a graphic artist within the rock and roll counterculture that blossomed in Los Angeles in the mid-1960s. After designing concert posters for Pinnacle Promoters and movie posters such as his classic for the surf film *Endless Summer*, he moved into album cover art, designing the *Magical Mystery Tour* LP for the Beatles. In 1970 he created the Johnny Deco (aka "Johnny Face") poster, with a comic book–like smiling guy with prominent lips, which he feels influenced the famous Stones' "tongue-and-lip" logo, designed by John Pasche and Jagger, which debuted in the artwork for *Sticky Fingers* (Jagger had been photographed wearing a "Johnny Face" T-shirt earlier).

In 1971, beginning to focus more on building on his success in designing album covers, Van Hamersveld met with photographer and art director for United Artists Records, Norman Seeff, a "beatnik-like artist from Johannesburg, South Africa." Seeff had a deal with the Stones for putting together a songbook. The two got the call to come and meet with Jagger and Richards at the Bel Air villa where the Stones were staying in Los Angeles while they put the finishing touches on *Exile* at Sunset Sound. As Van Hamersveld wrote in his "Imaging the Stones" postscript to Tarlé's book:

> As I was there sitting next to Jagger, Robert Frank walks into the room with a small super eight millimeter Canon camera. I knew of him from a meeting in New York from 1968. After I left he takes Jagger to downtown Los Angeles to film him on the real seedy parts of Main Street.

Most fans know that the Rolling Stones romanticized 1950s America, much in the same way people like me respond to the Stones heyday of the 60s and 70s, and *Exile* in particular. Van Hamersveld told me that the band saw themselves as carrying the torch of not just the blues artists they emulated, but of all sorts of artists, including those associated with the Beats:

You must understand now, Robert Frank was 50 years old in 1972, there standing in the living room of a Bel Air, Mediterranean villa, lush, and old world, they, the Stones image, of wealth, success, as pop culture post dandies, post hippies, now bluesmen looking back into the '50s, (Marshall) Chess and his connections. Frank the photographer, holding the 8mm camera, under his arm, is there now an old hipster from the '50s, as an artist from NYC. At the villa were Keith and Mick, as they outwardly, loved Frank for his connections to the beat attitude, and smoking pot then with Ginsberg. They were the Beat! We seated there on the couches, we were in our thirties, the new hip, he as a father figure . . .

Jagger knew how to sell it all. He has always been a student of American pop culture in general, with a keen awareness of cutting-edge artists. As with Elvis Presley before them, the Stones had already shown a well-developed ability to co-opt and make marketable the underground and raw street culture. Unlike Presley, however, who was down in the trenches, born poor in the South, Jagger was an effete upper-middle-class kid from the London suburbs, who had spent his adolescence listening to blues, soul, country, and rock and roll records. Somehow, with his earthier guitar-slinging foil, Richards, as a catalyst, he has been able to capture the essence of American roots musical forms, so much so that he transitioned quickly from a fan mimicking his idols to a genuinely adroit and influential soul singer himself. Forget the "blue-eyed" qualifier; Jagger is a great soul and blues singer in his own right. Take, for example, his performances on "Let It Loose" as a gospel-informed soul ballad, or "All Down the Line" as a flip side, a rave-up where Jagger's all-out performance might compete with similar up-tempo numbers from Otis Redding, Don Covay, or any of his Southern soul influences.

Presley, an early hero of Jagger's, was able to pull off similar feats a decade or so prior, integrating and owning his influences and thus producing something new. Yet while Presley grew up surrounded by African-American culture, Jagger had to make due with hard-to-find, secondhand sources. But like Presley, James Brown, and others, Jagger convincingly concocted a beguiling mix of simmering macho bluesman sexuality cut with a dose of androgyny—a heavier dose for Jagger than Elvis, but perhaps not as much as, say, Little Richard, another key influence on the Rolling Stones.

Is it any wonder, then, that Jagger not only understood how to sell the band musically but visually as well? He had taken the baton from ex-manager Andrew Loog Oldham, who had helped craft the Stones' early image as the Beatles' dark-horse cousins. Keith recalls being attracted to Oldham in part because, working under Brian Epstein, "he got together those very moody pictures of (the Beatles) that sold them in the first place." In taking up the reins from Oldham, Jagger was able to finesse the one-trick-pony, bad-boy image into a somewhat more mature and multilayered "bad young jet-setting men" image—decadent rock and roll aristocrats. You know, the kind of thing he sang about on their later return to roots, "Some Girls":

Well now we're respected in society
We don't worry about the things that we used to be
We're talking heroin with the President
Yes there's a problem, sir, but it can't be bent

"Royalty's having a baby" was a refrain often heard from a sneering Keith Richards down in Nellcôte, while Mick was off with Bianca during her pregnancy, concurrent with the recording of *Exile on Main St.*

The Stones could still transmit the dirty feel of the underground outsider, even as they were becoming the biggest band in the world. They weren't Iggy and the Stooges or Lou and the Velvets; they had just outlasted the Beatles and had to prove that they were not overstaying their welcome. But the punters were dying for someone to carry it all on, to offer even a shred of meaning to all the death and darkness that accompanied the end of the 1960s and the cynical blankness that was staring down at them from the barrel of the 1970s. Van Hamersveld recalled Jagger's reaction to their layout for the cover for the record when he brought it by Sunset Sound to show to the band:

"They'll love it!" I clearly understand what he means: "They'll" is a clear understanding of what the artist knows about his audience. This is pop visual language, the assumption, and the reflection of the sideshow of the inner business environment. The Crazy Business on display!

Frank took the Super 8 film of the band slumming down on Main Street in seedy downtown Los Angeles, the city's version of Manhattan's Bowery. Jagger told Robert Greenfield of *Rolling Stone* while they were still out in LA, Main Street is "real inner city," where "you can see pimps, knives flashing." As Frank might have done decades prior, Jagger took Frank and his movie camera and went out seeking a certain side of America: the dangerous authentic street down on Main St. Remember: Jagger told Marhall Chess that Frank was "the father of realism." The Stones were after something: an early 1970s zeitgeist.

So there, on the back cover and inner sleeves, is the band in various shots: walking down the street, under porn arcade awnings, laughing. Accompanying these shots are scrawled bits of lyrics, lines that don't even necessarily correspond with the recorded versions, and more band shots, in the repetition of the Super 8 film frames, adding an even more surreal tint, a druggy trail. Central to the back cover is a shot of Jagger, yawning. Is it weariness? Ennui? It enhances the hangover-sleepy languor of the record. But we also see "buddies" Jagger and Richards practically arm-in-arm at the microphone in the studio, warm light shining from underneath, a bottle of Old Grand Dad whiskey clutched in Jagger's hands, a can of beer in Keith's.

If there is one photograph that was singularly responsible for my rock fantasies, that made me know from an early age what I wanted to do and be, eventually leading to my tenure in a band, it was that one. Just as in all the live shots of the two of them in the classic pose, both singing at the same microphone, there seems to be a relaxed camaraderie between the two musicians. They look to be having a great time singing together. I wanted nothing more than such simple pleasure. It seems many rock and rollers feel the same. At times it seems like Aerosmith has modeled their whole image on such photos of Jagger and Richards. And in my conversation with the producer Paul Q. Kolderie, he brought the photo up as well, pointing out that the way they *looked* distinguished the Stones from their rootsy rock and roll peers, particularly from American bands. "The Stones seemed to be cooking up their own English brew with it all and it had to do more with the way they looked: the shaggy hair," explained Kolderie, recalling his perspective as an impressionable fourteen-year-old. "And that picture on *Exile* with Mick and Keith singing backup vocals—which is a picture taken in L.A., right?—with the Old Grand Dad, and you think, *okay, this is the life for me, pal.* That and *Fear and Loathing in Las Vegas* ruined my life because they made it seem like the coolest thing you could do was just get as wasted as possible."

While the Stones were subscribing to a certain tradition, a variation on that trekked by Frank and Kerouac and the like, the band was also promoting their own rock and roll myth: a band of young friends in their prime, living in a big mansion on the beach in France, recording all night in the basement, chicks, drugs, and booze flowing, having a blast every night. Well, perhaps the only part mythological was the last bit. We all know about the love/hate relationship between the Glimmer Twins. When you're an adolescent, though—as I was when I was having these dreams of *Exile* rock grandeur—all you want to do is spend time with your friends. How could spending every night with them jamming be anything *but* a blast?

Well, all it took for me, when I finally got to taste a little bit of the rock and roll fantasy, was maybe one year recording and touring before that romantic notion of "a good time, all the time," as character Viv Savage so eloquently put it in *This Is Spinal Tap*, was thoroughly debunked. Six or twelve weeks together, and your buddies and musical soulmates become your annoying brothers, or your college dorm roommate and his girlfriend in for the weekend: you just can't seem to escape them. And according to all accounts of the making of *Exile on Main St.*, that huge villa did start to feel awfully claustrophobic and dysfunctional at times, particularly near the end of the sessions.

And no one, *no one*, can look as "elegantly wasted" as Keith Richards, captured by the right photographer. The cheesy snapshot photos that exist from my time on the road show mostly bloated guys with eyes red not just from booze, but also bad camera flashes, sitting in front of slimy deli trays and German phallic graffiti in closets-*cum*-dressing rooms; not how I had imagined it.

Frank clipped up frames from his Super 8 film, Van Hamersveld was in charge of putting all the pieces together. As he told me, "It seemed as if I had become the artisan arranger, a design mystic that had dropped by to give my blessing. This was the making, in a classic printmaking style of an artful image for graphic history, as myth. All the parts and pieces made sense." The postcards that came in the original album and subsequent CD rereleases were from an ill-fated photo session with Seeff (Keith was late and stumbled in the shots) that was considered for the album cover. "Make postcards" is what an unapologetic Richards told Van Hamersveld and Seeff, making an accordion-like movement with his hands. Some pens were rounded up from the Flax art store and Jagger scrawled out the incomplete credits—mistakes, oversights, and all.

The record changed from its previous working title of *Tropical Disease* to its now famous name. "We were exiles and there was a certain spirit on that album—you can throw us out but you can't get rid of us," recalled Keith Richards in a 2002 interview for *Mojo* magazine. "Who would understand if we called it *Exile on the Rue Des Bosches*! And since 1964 or '5 we'd been spending nine months of every year in America, and a lot of the songs, the things that come out, are things you've thought about on the road. It's all American music basically—or if you want to take it all the way, it's all African." Perhaps it is obvious to point out, but Frank himself was essentially an exile on Main St., USA, during his cross-country trip. The Stones clearly identified with this, though they could never be flies on the wall, not with all their fame. We can see this on display in the documentary film that Frank made of the subsequent American tour in support of *Exile*. The musicians stick out like exotic gypsies or extraterrestrials in hotel lobbies, Southern juke joints, and the like.

Looking at *Exile*, we are supposed to believe that these Riviera tax refugees spend their free time on seedy streets hanging with pimps in front of porn theaters rather than on Mediterranean beaches. And, in fact, we do buy it. We want to suspend our disbelief. And we can do so easily because the music alone is so convincing. But it is a combination of memory, fantasy, imagination, and the band's reality at the time that informs the record. As Bill Wyman details in his book *Stone Alone*, the Stones had lived and played in squalor in the early days. And Keith must still have been frequenting some shady places from time to time in the quest to feed his habit. In a *Rolling Stone* article documenting the Stones' "farewell tour" of England in 1971, Robert Greenfield describes the same sort of sleazy dressing rooms "filled with parasites" that Jagger sings about on "Torn and Frayed."

More than a decade later, when Van Hamersveld met with John (Johnny Rotten) Lydon to discuss providing the design for Public Image Limited's 1984 record *This Is What You Want*, Lydon admitted that the design of *Exile* was influential to the rough, black-and-white, cut-up graphic look of 1970s punk rock. It seems this influence was deeper than the mere look of the surface (scrawled writing, newspaper headlines, etc.). As Van Hamersveld recalled, Lydon also made the point that the *Exile* artwork taught the nascent punk rocker that the look of the cover art informs the overall band image and prepares the listener for what he or she is about to hear. So while the music certainly influences the decisions about how the record should look, it actually works the other way as well; the artwork informs the listener how to feel about the music it contains.

"*Exile* doesn't try anything new on the surface, but the substance is new," Van Hamersveld points out. And punk rock, especially early punk rock, was nothing really new at the base of it; it was all the same three chords and rock and roll vocals, albeit exaggerated in delivery and perhaps a bit more raw in form than most mainstream rock of the era. Lydon, and especially the Sex Pistols' manager, Malcom McClaren, had learned that it was all about packaging and marketing. John Hamersveld had learned that lesson years before as a commercial artist and through working with rock artists like the Stones. The latter were selling, or at least defining, a lifestyle for him and his peers. He recalls taking stock of the "cultural landscape" as 1970 rolled around:

> Sex, drugs, and rock n' roll has made its way into the pop language. Pop Art's look of self-conscious innocence in the early sixties has changed by the end of the decade to a slick, crafted image as a marketing tool for the record companies. [Regarding] Keith: A lot of what I'd learned at art school came home to roost. About selling a look, an attitude, an image— like what kind of hair you wanted. By the seventies the Rolling Stones Tongue-and-Lip design is the most sexual image in the media culture. Jagger's mouth and words have become a symbol and registered trademark image to be merchandised by 1971.

Anyone familiar with Keith Richards' interviews over the years, but particularly and pointedly around the time of Mick Jagger's first solo record, will be aware of how important the concept of the band is to Keith. On *Exile on Main St.*, the individual musical ego is sublimated for the good of the whole. The sum of the parts is greater. Whenever he was pitched the idea of doing a solo record, Andy Johns said Keith would brush it off. In *Keith Richards, Life as a Rolling Stone*, by Barabra Cherone, Johns recalled that he continued to pressure Keith with the idea, after all the sing-alongs at Villa Nellcôte and then more urgently after recording *"Happy"*:

> Keith started singing these cowboy songs and his voice was incredible. So I said "Goddamn, Keith, when are you gonna make an album of your songs, 'cause it's so good." And Keith sorta went, "no, man." But I kept on at him and I usually get my own way.
>
> For a month I kept on without pressuring him too much, and in the end he said, "Listen, if I made a fuckin' album of my own I'd only get all the boys to play on it anyway. So it would be a fuckin' Rolling Stones album wouldn't it? Why don't we get on with the Rolling Stones album we're doing now?" That sort of stunned me.

If there was a gang mentality, an attitude of "we're all in this together" *before* their self-imposed "exile" in France, the relationship as a group was apparently cemented during the recording of *Exile on Main St.* Which is not to say they all became one big happy family—but they were a family, albeit a slightly dysfunctional one. After the heat of all the drug busts, the death of Brian Jones, and now the tightening of the financial screws that came with being in the top tax bracket, the band felt forced from their own country, run out by the authorities. They had been at the butt-end of breathtakingly poor business decisions and exploitative contracts—the most recent, with Allen Klein, was the bad deal to end bad deals. Now they needed the help of one of Jagger's society friends, Prince Rupert Loewenstein, to figure out the pros and cons of becoming tax exiles. He recommended two years in France.

"In a way it was a great thing for the band," Richards told *Mojo* magazine. "Everybody had to look each other in the eye and say, 'All right, we'll do it in exile, in France' . . . in a way I think it was when the Stones decided, we're in this for a longer haul than anybody thought. Even ourselves."

The band members actually ended up quite dispersed, with Charlie Watts near Avignon and the newlyweds Mick and Bianca Jagger in St. Tropez—which apparently suited Bianca, who wished to keep herself distanced from the project. Bill Wyman's longtime partner during these years, Astrid Lundström, has said that up until the recording of *Exile*, the Stones and their families rarely socialized outside of the band and related activities. "The Stones only got together to work," she recalled. "But here, we were suddenly all thrown together in a foreign country, having to see more of each other." Wyman himself notes that when they first got down there, the band did indeed socialize often and by choice. "On Saturday Keith would arrive [at Wyman's place] with Anita and the kids, and there would be a few hangers-on like Ahmet Ertegun who came over from America. And then Mick would come by on his motorbike, and it was all very social, people jumping in the pool with their clothes on, things like that."

Keith, his wife Anita Pallenberg, and their son Marlon ended up in the grand 1899 *Belle Epoque* mansion, Villa Nellcôte, in Villefranche-sur-Mer, down near Nice and Cannes. It was a tired old mansion, its glamour long ago faded, but there was a stunning view of Villefranche Harbor from its wide-tiered terrace. Long owned by the Bordes shipping family, it had been used during World War II by the occupying German forces. Remnants of this time were still evident: there were swastika grates over the vents and suicide-morphine vials in the cellar (which were disposed of before Keith could find them). The driveway led up to the house through a thick and lush "jungle," which served well for the needed privacy. There was plenty of space to spread out—sixteen rooms and a private beach. "It was one of those places where you could go, 'Yeah, I could live here!'" said Keith. But important to our story are the three levels of cellar that would eventually be juryrigged into a recording studio.

Keith, long-time "sixth Stone" Ian Stewart, Bill Wyman, and others made various excursions to scout out possible venues where they could record, with the Rolling Stones Mobile Studio truck parked outside. The truck, with its state-of-the-art studio control room built in, had been used already by the Stones for some of *Sticky Fingers*.

Dominique Tarlé was a young French photographer who had befriended the Stones on previous occasions, and he ingratiated himself into the Stones scene full-time for the *Exile on Main St.* sessions, resulting in the masterpiece book *Exile*, which captures not only his jawdropping photos, but also a priceless oral history from various people on the scene at Nellcôte during that summer. "Keith told me that he was looking for a place where he could store all the sound equipment and possibly somewhere they could use it as well. So they started to look for a kind of theatre," Tarlé recalled. "He decided it was time to record an album and realized that maybe he was sitting on the studio, as there were three storeys of cellar underneath his house. So the Rolling Stones Mobile Unit was summoned down to Nellcôte."

Jo Bergman, who ran the band's office and acted as a liaison, says one of the reasons they ended up at Keith's house is that they feared they would never get him to some of the remote places they had been scouting. "At least we can get him down in the basement," she recalled was the dominant sentiment at the time. In his book *Rolling with the Stones*, Bill

Wyman recalls, regarding the studio at Nellcôte, "we could guarantee Keith would be there."

Fans of the Stones should be thankful for Tarlé's pictures, which capture the decadence of the house, the lifestyle, if not the grand scope of the place. Like Robert Frank's photos, Tarlé's tend toward the shadowy, the insular, the intimate. He, too, is a fly on the wall in the dimly lit rooms, bottles and bongs lined up on sound baffles as players lounge and play—music and otherwise. In his foreword to the book *Exile*, Keith Richards wrote, "I realize, looking at these moments he captured, that he was part of the family, the band, in fact. He was also an exile in his own country. The quality of blending into the furniture and the fittings, I was rarely aware that he was working (WHICH *IS* RARE!)." Anita Pallenberg has claimed that the book is "like our family album."

Many of the photos have shown up before in various publications and, along with Robert Frank's photography and the overall album packaging, they add to the listener's image of the record and aid us in envisioning the time and place so central to this legendary recording. We can see the decrepit basement, the damp on the walls. The summer heat is palpable in the shots of shirtless and barefoot musicians as they collaborate, guitars in hand, sitting at a piano, lying down on the floor with headphones on, listening to other musicians record parts right in front of them. We are with them sitting at the dining room table littered with the remnants of a meal, ashtrays full, Campari and wine bottles empty, strumming cover songs with guests like Graham Parsons and John Lennon. We see dogs, rabbits, kids, records, motorcycles, boats, chandeliers, and guitars, lots of guitars.

How could a kid not get wrapped up in these images? I am thirty-eight at the time of this writing, most of my "professional career" as a musician is behind me, and this record and these accompanying photos still make me want to pick up a guitar, call up some friends, bust open a bottle, and sing all night in the basement or at the kitchen table. This is the essence of playing music: joy, the sort of unbridled fun that makes up most of childhood and so precious little of adulthood. It is also an unfortunately small percentage of playing (and especially touring) in a professional band. As Paul Kolderie said to me, such pictures ruined our lives; on some level, we succumbed to the fantasy. Sure, there are moments of glory even for a club-and-theater-level band like mine—we may not have always been playing to huge audiences, but man, we were touring around the world! Drinking, singing, laughing, making new friends, we went from basements and pizza to limos and *digestifs* at the Odeon (and back to basements and pizza). Believe me, we never bought into it, realizing it was all a fleeting farce, as we consciously tallied up the expenses that would be coming out of our recoupable balance at the label. But there was a part of me that always just wanted to relax and go with it, enjoy it, live like rock stars and have fun.

Countless bands have been willing accomplices to ridiculously one-sided contracts for shots at this fantasy. It's how the record industry has survived for so long: the rock star myth.

Such photographs are clearly inspired snapshots taken over a long period of time—time that was doubtless also filled with tedium, frustration, fatigue, downtime, boredom, bitterness, insecurities, jealousy, and other adult-sized emotions that come with a bunch of artists and hangers-on living and working right on top of each other for months on end, with no clear schedule and dysfunctional or nonexistent communication. Even the pictures that show the downtime, by the very virtue of being photos, inject a sense of import, or at least worthiness, by drawing attention to the subject. They fail to capture the outright depression and malevolence that can settle in on a homesick and hungover band stranded, for example, at a truck stop buffet on an interstate somewhere in the middle of Iowa. I mean, look at what I just wrote: even those words make it seem way more romantic than it is!

All accounts of *Exile* are heavy on the dark side, not just the relatively minor inconveniences that came with the recording. In a 1995 interview, Jagger looked back, not too fondly:

> (We were) just winging it. Staying up all night. . . Stoned on something; one thing or another. So I don't think it was particularly pleasant. I didn't have a very good time. It was this communal thing where you don't know whether you're recording or living or having dinner; you don't know when you're gonna play, when you're gonna sing—very difficult. Too many hangers-on. I went with the flow, and the album got made. These things have a certain energy, and there's a certain flow to it, and it got impossible. Everyone was so out of it. And the engineers, the producers—all the people that were supposed to be organized—were more disorganized than anybody.

And Bill Wyman explained:

> . . . We worked every night, from 8pm to 3am, until the end of June [1971], although not everyone turned up each night. This was, for me, one of the major frustrations of this whole period. For our previous two albums we had worked well, been pretty disciplined and listened to producer Jimmy Miller. At Nellcôte things were different and it took me a while to understand why.

Wyman recounts that further distractions came when "recording in Keith's basement had not turned out to be a guarantee of his presence. Sometimes he wouldn't come downstairs at all." And he didn't enjoy the "dull and boring" jam sessions that constituted most of the initial nights of recording. Keith and Anita's lifestyle "was becoming increasingly chaotic" and drugs were taking their toll on Keith and subsequently on the recording process. Possibly in retaliation, Mick would often not show up; perhaps being a newlywed was a further distraction, his and Bianca's wedding having just taken place on May 12. Then there was their announcement, a month later, that Bianca was expecting a baby. The two lovebirds were often jetting off for holidays in the middle of the time period set aside for recording. The tit-for-tat kept on escalating.

And even when the recording was going well, it was disorganized. Bill Wyman recalled, negatively, that Andy Johns would often be trying to record overdubs in the basement kitchen while people, dogs, and children ate and made noise in the same room: "I remember Gram Parsons sitting in the kitchen in France one day, while we were overdubbing vocals or something. It was crazy. Someone is sitting in the kitchen overdubbing guitar and people are sitting at the table, talking, knives, forks, plates clanking. . . . It was like one of those 1960s party records in which everyone felt they should be involved."

But the main negative that he points to in the making of *Exile* was the increasing reliance on hard drugs. "Whatever people tell you about the creative relationship between hard drugs and making of rock & roll records, forget it," he writes. "They are much more a hindrance than a help." Wyman notes that Mick was very concerned about Keith and that the hard drugs were dividing the *Exile* personnel into camps—those who abused, and those who enjoyed in relative moderation or abstained altogether. The latter were often not included in the recording process and were made to feel alienated. Wyman showed up on one occasion to discover two of his bass parts rerecorded by Keith. And the new parts, Bill felt, were inferior to those he'd recorded.

But for all the problems and obstacles, the Stones could ultimately sell the rock and roll myth because they lived it. The lived all of it, the positives and the negatives. They even succeed at transforming the awful side of the lifestyle into a myth of decadent glamour. Not that Keith set out to, but is it any wonder his image influenced so many musicians to spike up their hair, take up smack, and cultivate their skin-and-bones physiques? I never even tried to pull it off, but always secretly wished I could. Others looked lame and ultimately died trying, including Johnny Thunders, never mind third- and fourth-generation wannabes like Guns N' Roses or the Black Crowes. That's why Elvis Costello's rise was such a pivotal moment for dweebs like me. (To paraphrase the quote attributed to David Lee Roth: most critics love Elvis Costello because most critics *look like* Elvis Costello.) But I still had a poster of Jagger and Richards up on my wall, at which my father would shake his head and mumble out of the corner of his mouth, "Your heroes, eh?" The Glimmer Twins knew the attraction of the down and dirty street, the drugged and dangerous. "I gave you the diamonds / you gave me disease," Jagger scrawled in the album jacket. Coinciding with a famous *Rolling Stone* cover shot and interview with Keith Richards, the whole of *Exile on Main St.* offers up the sleazy glamour referred to now as junkie chic. The Stones were cementing their image and in turn, defining the prototypical image of a 1970s rock and roll band.

And much of that impression hinged around Keith's increasing prominence in the band's public image, a trend that had started gradually back around Brian Jones' death in 1969. In many ways, *Exile* is considered Keith's record: recorded at his house, more or less on his schedule, vocals down in the mix, guitars up. All accounts talk about long leisurely dinners set for double-digit guests, lasting until roughly midnight, when a vampiric Keith would beckon the musicians and crew to work. He would often disappear again for hours while, according to him, he put son Marlon to bed. Finally, he would reemerge in the wee hours ready to work again, by which point the others had usually drifted off or disappeared. But the sessions would usually last until dawn, players emerging out of the dank, dark, hot cellar into the morning daylight of the Riviera. "The days just ran into days and we didn't get any sleep," remembered Mick Taylor in *Mojo*. "I remember staggering out of the basement at six in the morning and the sunlight hitting my eyes and driving home." They were ghoulish outsiders, nocturnal vampires, exiles from the daylight.

* * *

All the different rooms and stalls in the Nellcôte house and its huge cellar were potential recording spots, resulting in a good amount of natural ambience, the kinds of sounds that lend a recording "warmth." It also led to ad-hoc experimentation. "You'd sort of jam an acoustic guitar into the corner of one of these cubicles and just start playing and you'd hear it back you'd think, 'that doesn't sound anything like what I was playing, but it sounds great,'" noted Keith. "So you started to play around with the basement itself, aiming your amplifier up at the ceiling instead of like normal." Wyman notes that his amp would be on one floor of the basement, while he would be on a different level, and that often the musicians were not in the same room together, though when they were "it was even more hot and sticky."

"I think it was a bunch of stoned musicians cooped up in a basement, trying to make a record," explained Mick Taylor. "Definitely the situation contributed to the music on a technical level—the fact that it was in a dingy basement, badly equipped. We wouldn't dream of making an album like that these days."

The band had recorded in unconventional nonstudio environments before, such as Mick's home, Stargroves in Newbury, England, also using the Mobile Unit. So this was not a new idea for them. But there are many considerations in recording outside of a studio, amenities taken for granted, like means of communication between the control room and the live room. Andy Johns had to run back and forth between the truck and basement to relay messages. "We would be hollering down, 'Are you ready?'" recalled Bill Wyman. Mick McKenna, the engineer in charge of the truck, said, "there was . . . a little CB microphone designed for the producer, but you could also record harmonica with it. There was also a black and white camera, but obviously these things weren't working too well then."

The Stones have always been known to record in an old-school manner, with the band all in one room, even Mick singing in a hand-held mic, to record the basic tracks (drums, bass, rhythm guitar, scratch or "guide" vocal). This can be seen in such films as Jean-Luc Godard's *One Plus One*, also known as *Sympathy for the Devil*, which documents the making (not just the recording) of the song of the same name. The band often writes and collaborates on arrangements in the studio, and pity the engineer who does not have the tape machine running at all times, lest a magical take, or even a reference point, fails to get captured.

After the mid-1960s, as recording techniques became more sophisticated, the idea of singing in the same room with the other instruments and amplifiers became increasingly discouraged by most engineers, as it inevitably results in the bleeding of one instrument's sound into the microphones set up to capture the sound of other instruments. Thus, the engineers lose the level of control they seek to maintain over the sound for the rest of the work, especially the mixing, of the track. To avoid such a scenario, modern-day recording technique has engineers trying to isolate each sound into isolation booths, with the drums in a "live room." The players can all be in the same room, but the amplifiers and vocalist are usually in isolation booths, with glass to peer through. The ideal for many engineers is to push up a fader on a mixing console and hear only that intended instrument. But on the majority of Stones tracks, in addition to hearing Mick Jagger's intended main lead vocal (recorded once the final take is chosen from among a variety of recordings of the same song) you can also almost always hear "ghost" tracks of his guide vocal underneath the mix. On some tracks, it sounds almost as prominent as an actual vocal "take," difficult to distinguish from the backing vocals.

In an interview with *Tape Op* magazine's Philip Stevenson, Andy Johns spoke about his goal in recording rock and roll bands:

Stevenson: Your work has a very natural sound. It wears well. A lot of modern recordings don't. They are too fatiguing to listen to over and over.

Did you set out with a specific sound in your head that you always tried to get, or is your style more an evolved product of the way you were taught to do things?

Johns: . . . As far as the thing sounding natural I suppose it's because I've always liked rock and roll bands, so my idea, even if I've done a lot of overdubs and put a lot of things on the tracks, is really to integrate them so it sounds like you're at the best rehearsal the band ever did. Just like one big lovely noise.

Stevenson: Instruments sound like instruments and it sounds like people are playing them—

Johns: Yes! People playing as opposed to some fucking sample repeating itself over and over.

Stevenson: It's sad that some people will grow up never having heard that "people playing" sound.

Johns: Yeah, it's good for me though. It means the competition's thinning out! [*laughs*]

"*Exile* changed the way I thought about things," explained Johns further. "Up until that point I was extremely fast—that was one of the qualities people admired. If they could do a run through with 5 or 6 or 8 pieces and you had your sound by the end of their run through, because you never know—'they-may-never-get-it-the-same-again-and-they're-artists, and all that'—so, I was very quick, BUT *Exile* . . . actually took a year. I grew up as a person and was less intimidated by the musicians and all that, and I started taking my own sweet time a bit more after *Exile*."

* * *

Almost everything on *Exile* absolutely swings, due in large part to producer Jimmy Miller, a drummer/percussionist by training, who is widely credited with helping the Stones find their famous grooves. By the time he started work with the Stones, Miller already had some very groovy productions to his credit, like "Gimme Some Lovin'" and "I'm a Man," by the Spencer Davis Group, and a whole string of classic Traffic albums. He came on board after *Their Satanic Majesty's Request*, the first record the Stones produced themselves (after Andrew Loog Oldham had been jettisoned). Miller's first production was the muscular "Jumping Jack Flash" single in 1968, which was heavy on sixteenth-note shaker percussion and unique, hard-to-identify textures wheezing in the background. This bold track heralded in a new sound for the Stones, the basis of the sound for which they are most famous: the "Stonesy" sound, with a prominent Keith Richards riff and crunchy electric guitars that almost always blend together with a percussive acoustic guitar track at varying levels of prominence. Piano tracks usually add yet another percussive element in addition to extra melodic support, and organs add at least some steady padding (filling out the empty spaces at the "bottom" of a recording)—if not outright and glorious hooks, as in the coda of "You Cant Always Get What You Want" or "I Got the Blues."

Perhaps as important as the guitars in a Miller production, shakers and tambourines add movement and groove to the relatively straightforward crisp backbeats played by Charlie Watts. In turn, with the steady beat and underlying groove being driven by the percussion, Watts is free to play inventive fills. There is a Motown influence, clearly. And there is looseness, a human element that makes the sound funky. This production template clearly influenced other groups—both those who hired Miller and those not necessarily employing him, like the Kinks' 1970 single "Lola," or the Faces on any number of tracks.

Glyn Johns, who had been an early supporter of the Stones, and their main English recording engineer since day one, recalled:

> Jagger came to me after *Satanic Majesties* and said, "We're going to get a new producer," so I said, "OK, fine." He said, "We're going to get an American." I thought, "Oh my God, that's all I need. I don't think my ego can stand having some bloody Yankee coming in here and start telling me what sort of sound to get with the Rolling Stones." So I said, "I know somebody! I know there's one in England already and he's fantastic, and he's just done the Traffic album: Jimmy Miller." And it was a remarkably good record he made, the first record he made with Traffic. I said, "He's a really nice guy." I'd met him, he'd been in the next studio room and I said, "I'm sure he'd be fantastic." Anything but some strange, lunatic, drug addict from Los Angeles. So, Jagger actually took the bait and off he went, met Jimmy Miller and gave him the job.

Bill Wyman explained it, "I think that everybody knew that we had to get back to our roots, you know, and start over. That's why we got Jimmy Miller as a producer and came out with *Beggar's Banquet* and those kinds of albums after, which was reverting back and getting more guts—which is what the Stones are all about."

This was a time that found many rock and rollers giving up the excesses of mid-to-late-1960s psychedelia and finding inspiration in the roots of rock and roll and beyond. In 1967, Bob Dylan and the group which soon became known as the Band, had retreated to the Woodstock, New York, area to spend days on end recording in the basement of the Big Pink house, resulting in the much-bootlegged and eventually released *Basement Tapes*. These tracks were murky home recordings, primitive but authentic-feeling soulful takes on amalgams of public domain folk, gospel, country tunes, and archaic musical forms—coupled with lyrics influenced by old myths and folklore. This was mixed with the sound that the Band became famous for, both with and without Dylan: two keyboards, an organ and an upright piano, a guitar or two (electric and acoustic), a solid, funky, Muscle Shoals-like rhythm section, and raw layered harmonies, rarely tight, often loose. Such a sound had more to do with what the Rolling Stones had been playing earlier in their career than with what they were doing immediately before hooking up with Jimmy Miller.

The Band's leader, Robbie Robertson, articulated the formulation of the Band's sound in the liner notes to the reissue of *Music from Big Pink*:

> [With the Band] the song is becoming the thing, the mood is becoming the thing . . . there's a vibe to certain records, whether it's a Motown thing or a Sun Records thing or a Phil Spector thing. I wanted to discover the sound of The Band. So I thought, "I'm not gonna play a guitar solo on the whole record. I'm only going to play riffs." I wanted the drums to have their own character. I wanted the piano not to sound like a big Yamaha grand. I wanted it to sound like an upright piano . . . I didn't want screaming vocals. I wanted sensitive vocals where you can hear the breathing and the voices coming in . . . I like the voices coming in one at a time like the Staple Singers did . . . All these ideas came to the surface and what becomes the clear picture is that this isn't just clever. This is emotional and this is story telling. You can see this mythology.

From 1968 on, many groups and artists followed these paths back to the folk, blues, soul, and country roots of rock and roll: the Grateful Dead, the Beatles, the Byrds, Creedence Clearwater Revival, Eric Clapton, Van Morrison, and the Flying Burrito Brothers, with Gram Parsons and Chris Hillman, who melded southern soul, country, and rock into what Parsons described as "cosmic American music."

By the release of *Exile*, the Stones had long been established as a blues- and roots-based group, but Jagger—perhaps viewing the glam rock of Bowie and T. Rex (whose leader, Marc Bolan, stopped by the final sessions for *Exile* in Los Angeles), and underground sounds of the Velvets et al., as more exciting and artistically relevant—was distancing himself from the record even as the Stones were finishing up *Exile on Main St.* "This new album is fucking mad," he recalled in 1971.

There's so many different tracks. It's very rock & roll, you know. I didn't want it to be like that. I'm the more experimental person in the group, you see I like to experiment. Not go over the same thing over and over. Since I've left England, I've had this thing I've wanted to do. I'm not against rock & roll, but I really want to experiment . . . The new album's very rock & roll and it's good. I think rock & roll is getting a bit . . . I mean, I'm very bored with rock & roll. The revival. Everyone knows what their roots are, but you've got to explore everywhere. You've got to explore the sky too.

Anita Pallenberg says, "It was also the period where Mick thought, 'God what are we going to do next and how long is it going to last?' All of that was still going on."

Nevertheless, at least under the sway of Keith Richards, the Stones saw themselves as part of these traditions, getting back to their blues roots (mostly country-blues and folk) on the raw-sounding *Beggar's Banquet* in 1968. Is it any wonder then that trad-blues purist Mick Taylor was installed as a replacement for the Elmore James-inspired Brian Jones?

The Stones recorded "Country Honk" in a Jimmie Rodgers style for the 1969 LP *Let it Bleed*. Their next record, *Sticky Fingers*, contained the country song "Dead Flowers," the traditional Mississippi Fred McDowell country blues "You Gotta Move," and the churchy gospel-soul of "I Got the Blues." This was the direction of the band. Country and soul melded with blues and the heavy rock and roll riffing the Stones were known for— all intensified by Jagger's self-conscious experimental leanings—leading up to *Exile on Main St.*, perhaps the finest realization of what Gram Parsons was getting at when he coined the term "cosmic American Music." And when they got to France, it seems the band was able to process such influences more consciously. Keith explained, "But by being in Europe and having had time to think about it, all of us had been picked up by working in the south of America and the people we'd met and musicians. After all, Gram Parsons was down there with us and there were loads of other musicians popping in and out."

Richards and the Stones met and hung out with Parsons and the Byrds in Los Angeles beginning in the late 1960s, while mixing *Beggar's Banquet*, and then later again when the Americans stopped in London. "Gram Parsons blew into town with the Byrds, who were playing Blasés," recalled Richards. Parsons was present for much of the summer at Nellcôte. It appears he was mainly there for inspiration and for the hang, as it seems that no one is able to place him directly on any track on *Exile*. "The reason Gram and I were together more than other musicians is because I really wanted to learn what Gram had to offer," Keith told an interviewer. "Gram was really intrigued by me and the band. Although we came from

England, Gram and I shared this instinctive affinity for the real South." Parsons ended up traveling along with the Stones during their 1971 "farewell tour" of the United Kingdom and stayed at Nellcôte for most of the *Exile* sessions.

Hiring the American Jimmy Miller, then, was consistent with the Stones wanting to get back, to find the real heart of American roots music, "the real South." Miller was at the helm during what many regard as the Stones at their untouchable peak, and Keith Richards has said that Jimmy Miller was "at the height of his talents" during *Exile on Main St.* "Nobody has really stated how important Jimmy Miller's contributions to *Exile* were," Mick Taylor told *Mojo*. ". . . A good drummer, a talented producer and our guide." Taylor pointed out how the band would often hit creative roadblocks, with songs just not coming together, and Miller often offered the solution. "I remember he actually got behind the drum kit to show Charlie how to play a particular beat." Indeed, Miller did the same on "You Can't Always Get What You Want," from *Let It Bleed*. That is Miller playing the song's shuffling beat, which Charlie never latched on to. It's a beat I don't believe Watts has ever played on subsequent live versions. And that is Jimmy Miller on the drums on *Exile's* "Happy."

"The Rolling Stones were never great musicians," continued Taylor. "When I first joined them I couldn't believe how bad they were. I thought, 'How do they make such great records?' When I met Jimmy it all fell into place. It is not about being great musicians but about a certain kind of chemistry the band has." Andy Johns has said on many occasions that when the Stones were not clicking, they were dreadful, "they could sound like the worst band on the planet. Just awful, like antimusic. But when it finally came together, it was like magic."

Pet Sounds

by Jim Fusilli

Chapter Six
"I Keep Looking for a Place to Fit In . . ."

Despite the instrumentals and "Sloop John B," *Pet Sounds* is defined by its highly personal look at love and its place in a young man's life. To a great degree, it's Brian Wilson's worldview based on what he's observed and experienced, and what he expects; only Tony Asher seems to have had input on the thematic concept and often he was interpreting Brian's feelings and notions.

Pet Sounds conveys wide-eyed Brian's sense of discomfort in a world where he lacks the control that he has in the recording studio. What's so striking about many of the songs is how openly they reveal the level of Brian's self-knowledge. Clearly, he explored his own insecurities and knew them painfully well. He knew his shortcomings, real and perceived, and demanded more of himself. He articulated what he discovered about himself, the world he inhabited and the one he wished for, and he did so largely without guile, without pretense. His words and music are startlingly frank.

Such is the case with "I Just Wasn't Made for These Times." This is the song that told me I was not alone. If you are an ardent fan of *Pet Sounds*, I suspect it is the same for you. What a remarkable thing it is to know that there's someone out there who understands how you feel and feels the same way—and who not only feels as you do, but can articulate your feelings better than you can.

I love Dylan, Joni Mitchell, and Leonard Cohen, all of whom have written lyrics that gave me insight into myself and the world around me at least as well as any other works of art I've explored. But to this day I am astonished at the power and precision of the lyrics Brian and Asher wrote for "I Just Wasn't Made for These Times."

I keep looking for a place to fit in where I can speak my mind.
And I've been trying hard to find the people that I won't leave behind.
They say I got brains but they ain't doing me no good.
I wish they could.
Each time things start to happen again,
I think I got something good going for myself,
But what goes wrong?
Sometimes I feel very sad.
I guess I just wasn't made for these times.

Isn't that the purest expression of a child's insecurity that you've ever read? My goodness, that's *The Catcher in the Rye* in one verse and one chorus.

And Brian at this point was twenty-three; he was married to a lovely, dedicated young woman; he was the leader of the most popular American musical group; he could ask virtually any musician in LA to record his music and they would willingly do so, which meant he was respected for his achievements and his potential. People loved him: Audree, Carl, Dennis, Marilyn. Marilyn's family. Mike and Al, too. Murry, in his own perverse way. He had friends and caring associates like Blaine, Carol Kaye, and Chuck Britz. Brian even had two dogs, Banana and Louie.

But he didn't see it. He was lost in turmoil.

"Each time things start to happen again, I think I got something good going for myself. But what goes wrong?"

Asher warned against considering the lyrics of *Pet Sounds* Brian's autobiography. But Brian said the sentiments in "I Just Wasn't Made for These Times" are his. "[The song is] about a guy who was crying out because he thought he was too advanced and that he'd eventually have to leave people behind," Brian said. "All my friends thought I was crazy to do *Pet Sounds*."

Asher said, "It takes a lot of courage for an artist to expose himself in such a personal way . . . I thought maybe Brian would not want to make such a raw, emotional statement. But he did, and it took a lot of guts."

Brian certainly was aware of the dedication of the group's fans. He knew we were listening. We were present in his mind. In the liner notes to *All Summer Long* and *Summer Days (and Summer Nights!!)*, for example, he speaks directly to us. "Thank you for giving me the incentive to create our records," he writes in the former. But it's not really possible to say for sure whether he intended "I Just Wasn't Made for These Times" to serve as a lifeline to others. When an artist is working at his level, with that type of intensity, the energy typically is focused inward, and the world exists only in the complexity of one's own thoughts.

In 1996, he said of *Pet Sounds*, "When I listen to it today, I feel like somebody really took the time to create some honest music. Somebody like me." This, I think, is a telling comment. It's as if Brian the man is acknowledging the work of Brian the musician.

Not one of us could be like Brian the musician. Well, very, very few of us. But many of us had much in common with Brian the man.

He added, "Be aware of the love in those songs that is able to give the listener the feeling of being loved."

* * *

"I Just Wasn't Made for These Times" recalls a Spector production with its flashes of harsh, almost military drumming, layers of effusive guitars, and surround-sound keyboards and saxophones. And yet it's Brian, too; Brian with an expanding arsenal. The tremolo electric bass under the vocal is joined by the clip-clop temple blocks, the Theremin, and instruments that can't be heard individually but contribute to the overall impression when blended with other sounds—the tack piano, for example, and a banjo. There's a harmonica in there somewhere, echoing the Theremin.

And there are increasingly familiar time changes, the inventive use of dynamics, jazz inflections on the chords, the avoidance of the root notes by Pohlman on bass. With sections in G minor, E-flat major, C minor and B-flat major, the structure is eminently logical and fluid, but Brian mixes them up in the arrangement and uses instrumental interludes to make it all fresh and engaging. Add to that the layered vocal harmonies—in the "sometimes I feel very sad" section, there are at least four separate vocal parts that cause a moment of disorientation. The result is a sense of discomfort amid tranquility, just as Blaine's drumming and the chilling sound of the Theremin are echoes of danger amid the potential for serenity. Those wonderful juxtapositions are as much an accurate reflection of Brian's perspective on his life as are the song's lyrics.

In October 1965, months after "Sloop John B" was finished, the group recorded "The Little Girl I Once Knew," a bouquet for Marilyn in which Brian expresses his desire for a girl he ignored before she blossomed. She belongs to another—at this point, could it be a Brian Wilson song if there weren't extenuating circumstances?—but he'll "be moving in one day."

"The Little Girl I Once Knew," which was initially released as a single, is firmly in the musical style of *Pet Sounds*, particularly the richness of its arrangement, but it also alludes to previous Beach Boys hits. Thus, it's another bridge between the past and the forthcoming watershed album. Mike gives the song plenty of "pow-pow-pows," a "look out, babe," and a "split, man," and there's an organ solo and a cheery, unfettered twelvestring guitar. The chorus modulates from B major to D major, thus allowing for a characteristic escalating Beach Boys vocal statement.

The inventive "la-doo-day" part in E major that sets up the return to the D major allows Brian to unleash his falsetto above the harmonies, thus creating a statement of pure joy and confidence. Since this is a song about what has already happened, there's no doubt from Brian's point of view: he knows he will win her. As a songwriter, Brian, in "The Little Girl I Once Knew," demonstrates that he has refined the technique of seeming to wander far from the logic of his composition only to return triumphantly to confirm the emotional intent of the work. The technique is employed time and again in *Pet Sounds*, though never to evoke a sense of unbridled joy.

As for the four seconds of dead air that occur twice in the song: though they must have driven disc jockeys crazy when the song was released as a single, "The Little Girl I Once Knew" somehow needs them. As the song is constructed, you simply cannot move from the verse to the chorus without them. I mean, you can, but you'd destroy the flow and eliminate the tension that precedes the joyous chorus. Of course, Brian knew four-second tacets in the middle of a pop single were unacceptable. But as a composer and arranger, he was going where he wanted to, convention be damned.

* * *

In November 1965, the Beach Boys appeared on a Jack Benny TV special. Though Brian had stopped touring, he did TV appearances with the group. On this occasion, he helped lip-synch "California Girls," and then appeared in a skit with Benny and Bob Hope in which the two comedians play, shall we say, seasoned surfers. They drive up in a hot rod as the Beach Boys gather round and invite Benny and Hope to hang with them. There's a pretty funny gag about how having a flat head helps when you want to carry a surfboard.

"Maybe you guys would like to join our club," Brian says, his eyes never straying from the cue cards. "We really turn on, man." A career in acting was not an option.

Later, done up again in their J. C. Penney candy-striped shirts and chinos, the group does a live version of "Barbara Ann" with Brian on bass. During Carl's guitar solo, Brian attempts a run in the midsection and loses his place. He stops playing, looks at Mike, and says, "Whoops." It's not a great moment in rock history, not exactly the Beatles on Sullivan.

The big skit in the special features the tightfisted Benny dropping in on Walt Disney and asking for 110 free tickets to Disneyland, so he can take the cast and crew out for a treat. Maybe he invited the note-dropping, cue-card-reading Brian. Maybe not.

By the way, in exchange for the tickets, Benny agreed to perform a tribute to Disney in the style of the Italian movies of the era—which a dubious Mr. Disney deemed "earthy." What follows is "Maria Poppins," complete with a song whose chorus is "mozzarella, provolone, parmigiano, pasta." Benny wears a mustache and pronounces every other word with a mock Italian accent: "I'm-a not-a gonna forget-a you!" It's not great, either.

* * *

The Beatles' new album arrived in December 1965. *Rubber Soul* presented its creators as growing in musical sophistication and daring, much as *The Beach Boys Today!* and *Summer Days (and Summer Nights!!)* represented a step ahead for the California group.

As it was with the Beach Boys, it's hard to pinpoint precisely when the Beatles took their forward step. For example, "Yesterday" and "You've Got to Hide Your Love Away," songs that appear on *Help!*, the predecessor to *Rubber Soul*, are as accomplished as any track on the latter. But *Rubber Soul* was a cohesive artistic statement that spanned an entire album. In large part, albums by pop groups at the time were a gathering point for a few new hits, some of which had previously been released as singles, surrounded by filler. To state it simply, the Beatles destroyed this model by making their "filler" at least as good as their potential hits: if, for example, "Drive My Car," "Norwegian Wood," and "Michelle" were considered marketable as hit singles, "I'm Looking Through You," "Nowhere Man," and "In My Life" are at least as strong in form and performance.

Incidentally, we're talking about the UK versions of the Beatles' albums here; we can assume that the hometown *Rubber Soul* is the statement the Beatles wanted to make. The UK edition track listing is "Drive My Car," "Norwegian Wood," "You Won't See Me," "Nowhere Man," "Think For Yourself," "The Word," "Michelle," "What Goes On," "Girl," "I'm Looking through You," "In My Life," "Wait," "If I Needed Someone," and "Run for Your Life." The US edition replaces "Drive My Car" with "I've Just Seen a Face" and "What Goes On" with "It's Only Love." "Nowhere Man" and "If I Needed Someone" are conspicuously absent from the US version, which fails to present the group accurately in its maturing form. I mean, contrast "Drive My Car" with "I've Just Seen a Face": the former is a tale dripping with cynicism, the latter the story of a happy boy.

(Incidentally, Brian heard the US version. You'd think Capital would have thrown him a complimentary copy of the original, but apparently not.)

Love is the unifying lyrical theme of *Rubber Soul*, and it's viewed from varying perspectives. The lyrics show the Beatles growing up. Though they use the word "girl" as a synonym for "woman," they aren't talking about puppy love. They've experienced life a bit by now, and understand its nuances. The female characters present in the lyrics are varied and vivid. For example, no one would mistake the woman in "Norwegian Wood" for

Paul's Michelle; the woman in George's "If I Needed Someone" is treated far less reverentially than the subject of John's "In My Life," and so on.

Rubber Soul shows musical unity as well—not as easy a trick as it seems since the group was in an experimental mood and featured four lead vocalists on the album. Many of the songs are built on the foundation of an acoustic guitar and Ringo's tambourine, though there is bouzouki, harmonium, and sitar as well as all sorts of distortion of guitar, bass, and keyboards. Thus, the music is simultaneously consistent and adventurous.

Brian loved *Rubber Soul*. Though he considered the Beatles competition, he admired them and didn't hesitate to say so. He also understood how the music of the two groups differed. The Beatles, he said, "will simplify to its skeletal form an arrangement, where I would be impelled to make it more complex."

"Like 'Norwegian Wood' with one voice and a sitar," he said. "I would've orchestrated it, put in background voices, done a thousand things. But the fact that the Beatles can do things with such simplicity is what makes them so good."

With friends, he gushed over *Rubber Soul*. "This album blows my mind because it's a whole album with all good stuff!" he said. "I'm gonna try that . . . *Rubber Soul* is a complete statement, damn it, and I want to make a complete statement."

He decided to implement his new vision immediately, though "Sloop John B" and the instrumental then known as "Run James Run" were already in the can. McCartney and Lennon drew from their lives for inspiration for the lyrics on *Rubber Soul*—Paul was having trouble with girlfriend Jane Asher, and John was openly complaining about Cynthia, who might have considered a temporary restraining order upon hearing "Run for Your Life"—and Brian decided to do so as well. After hearing *Rubber Soul*, he decided there would be no songs with puff themes like "Be True to Your School," "Amusement Parks U.S.A.," or even "California Girls." What he'd done on the second side of *The Beach Boys Today!* and at times on *Summer Days (and Summer Nights!!)*, he would now do for an entire album, as the Beatles had done.

He brought in Tony Asher and work began. Brian told his new songwriting partner, "We're not going to do typical Beach Boys songs, so forget anything that comes to mind when you think of one . . . If I wanted that kind of song, there are plenty of other people who could do them." The two worked at Brian's home on Laurel Way throughout January and February 1966.

Chapter Seven
"But Sometimes I Fail Myself . . ."

Marilyn understood that Brian was digging deep into himself for *Pet Sounds*. "I think Brian's songs on that album came from a tortured person," she told David Leaf. "From the moment I met Brian, he was always in self-turmoil, unhappy about his life and his feelings, and he was just never happy with himself."

After hearing Brian's lyrics on "Don't Hurt My Little Sister," "She Knows Me Too Well," and "The Little Girl I Once Knew," Marilyn had to understand that at least some part of *Pet Sounds* was going to discuss their relationship. She knew "You Still Believe in Me" was about her.

"He knew that he was not a good husband and that I was lonely, and really didn't get much back from him, and he made me cry all the time," she said, when asked about that song. "It was like there wasn't much of a relationship. The only way we related was musically. I could always sing the parts he needed me to . . . I understood, and I could hear, and I could sing." Brian believed Marilyn would always forgive him, that her faith in him was boundless. To his mind, that was the definition of love. At least, it was the love he wanted coming his way.

With Asher, he took the basic theme of "You're So Good to Me" and re-examined it for "You Still Believe in Me." Liberated, at least in his mind, from the constraints of writing a pandering pop hit, and having lived through more than a year of marriage, the theme now bore the weight of his sense of artistic freedom, of budding maturity, and of new experiences, as Lennon and McCartney's new songs did on *Rubber Soul*.

In the words and the emotion of his singing, Brian seems to confirm Marilyn's perspective—that he had failed her. "After all I've done to you, how can it be you still believe in me?" he asks in the song. He offers an explanation for his misbehavior, and it's much more than a rationalization. "I can't help how I act when you're not here with me. I try hard to be strong but sometimes I fail myself."

But he knows ultimately he's at fault. He remembers he had given her his word. "And after all I've promised you, so faithfully, you still believe in me." Ashamed, he adds, "I want to cry."

The dichotomy of music and lyrical theme that appears in "Wouldn't It Be Nice" is far more pronounced in "You Still Believe in Me," the second song on the album. The backing track begins with shimmering, metallic single notes on the piano—one of the musicians reached inside the piano to pluck its strings to achieve the effect. The single notes give way to guitars and keyboards that, though vibrant, lack the optimistic brightness of those in the intro to "Wouldn't It Be Nice," its immediate predecessor. To reinforce the confused, poignant mood, Brian employs bicycle bells, a bicycle horn, finger cymbals, and for additional contrast and tension, a bass harmonica and bass clarinet. The electric bass plays a joyless figure. The overall feel is akin to an image of a boy and his bike lost in a dark cavern or on a lonely stretch of road. The statement all but renounces "Wouldn't It Be Nice," sending a signal that *Pet Sounds* will not be a collection of standard Beach Boys fare.

Though the song seems to dart in different musical directions, it's relatively static, fortifying the eerie undercurrent. The song begins in B major, a key rarely used in pop, and remains in B major. The G-sharp major chord below the first, and only, time the word "love" is invoked in the song is particularly striking; on the second pass, the G-sharp major chord hits below the word "fail." In a rare example of the bassist emphasizing the root in a Brian Wilson arrangement, Carol Kaye hits the G-sharp in both instances. It's as if Brian wanted there to be no confusion for the listener: in his mind, at least in this song, love equals failure.

The vocals on "You Still Believe in Me" are nothing short of remarkable. After opening with a unison statement in which the group issues a gloomy hum, Brian enters with a subdued lead that builds steadily to the top of his falsetto. The group re-enters to sing the title, and Brian repeats the melody of the first verse.

Brian sings "I want to cry" by himself, his voice soaring then coming down, note by extended note. Mike and Al restate in the baritone range what Brian sang, and then all the voices, with Brian on top, join in to dart around and under Brian's original line, repeatedly referring to the B note that begins the phrase.

Yet another tempo change and kettledrums reinforce the majesty of the moment. The finger cymbals tap on the two. And to confuse us even further, the bicycle horn bleats on every other four into the fade.

* * *

Brian dropped acid for the first time before the summer of 1965, and later told Marilyn it had been a spiritual confrontation with God. As Timothy White reported, "He seemed exhilarated. He seemed distraught. He never seemed the same again." He didn't mean that Brian got better, more secure, or happy. Marilyn hated the drugs, and she moved out.

My observations tell me that drugs are the last thing people who are troubled need. I had lunch with Fleetwood Mac's Peter Green, perhaps the best rock guitarist in an era when Clapton and Hendrix thrived, and he couldn't even manage the menu. Some thirty years earlier, Green's schizophrenia, exacerbated by psychedelic drugs, sent him into a horrific downward spiral from which he had only recently begun to emerge when we met.

Jaco Pastorius's manic depression was aggravated by drugs and drink, and the bassist lost his ability to perform up to his high, high standards. I was in a rehearsal hall in midtown Manhattan and one of the techs who worked there came up to me and said, "Hey, your buddy Jaco is here." He really didn't mean "buddy," since I'd never met Pastorius. He meant "idol." He pointed to the corner and there was a filthy, piss-stained homeless man leaning against a doorframe, head bobbing, jaw slack, and he was all but ready to drop to the carpet.

"Very funny," I said to the tech.

He stared at me. "I'm not kidding, man."

I went to the corner. It was Jaco.

Shortly thereafter, he was killed by a bouncer outside a Florida nightclub. A policeman showed me a photo of Pastorius on his deathbed, his head swollen and dented, his face a gruesome smear of yellows and purples.

Perhaps drugs exacerbated Brian's fall, which accelerated following the release of *Pet Sounds*. It's hard to believe that his mental health—which, we now know, is deeply affected by schizophrenia and depression—profited from the experimentation.

As *Pet Sounds* began to take shape, drugs were just becoming an increasingly important part of Brian's life. I look at it this way: he already had *Pet Sounds* in his head. Maybe the drugs created a temporary giddiness that masked the anxiety of freedom and encouraged him to take risks, particularly with his arrangements. Maybe they helped him forget for a while his perceived inadequacies, his woes with Marilyn, the demons his father had instilled his brain.

Apparently, he was clear-headed when he came to work. Carol Kaye said, "I never saw any drugs with Brian in the studio at all."

* * *

In 1965, Capitol wanted to issue a Beach Boys greatest hits album for Christmas. It wasn't the world's worst idea. Considering *Pet Sounds* was coming, maybe it would have been smart, at least from a musical perspective, to signal that Phase One of the group's career was at its end. But Capitol was thinking not from a musical perspective, but from a marketing one, and the group didn't want to do it.

Instead, they went to Western with some acoustic guitars and sang whatever came to mind. The Beach Boys Unplugged. This album, *Beach Boys Party!* really blows. Again with the exclamation point! They sing three Beatles songs and one by Dylan. (There's no evidence that either the Beatles or Dylan recorded a Beach Boys song in return.)

They mock "I Get Around" and "Little Deuce Coupe." Imagine doing that—mocking your own work, music some people cherish.

Brian and Mike do a decent job on the Everly Brothers' "Devoted to You." Marilyn is singing in the background. Dean Torrence of Jan & Dean dropped in and suggested they sing a song made popular by the Regents. This thing was already fucked, so why not? Brian sang lead with Torrence, Hal Blaine played tambourine, Carl was on guitar, someone worked the bass. Everybody sang along, and the voices sounded pretty good.

And when 1966 began, the year of *Pet Sounds*, the Beach Boys had a monster hit with their ragtag version of "Barbara Ann." It became the group's first number one hit in the UK. Those fun-loving Beach Boys!

The world of rock and pop was exploding with Dylan, the Beatles, and the Byrds, while the Beach Boys were covering the Regents. They also did "Alley Oop" on *Beach Boys Party!* It had previously been recorded by such luminaries as the Dyna Sores, Dante & the Evergreens, and the Hollywood Argyles.

"Barbara Ann" killed "The Little Girl I Once Knew." Who's going to listen to that innovative track when anybody can sing along to "ba-ba-ba Ba-Barbara Ann"?

"Barbara Ann" had production values only marginally better than Edison reciting "Mary Had a Little Lamb." It's said that the Beach Boys resented the success "Barbara Ann" achieved. But Mike and Al weren't as eager as Brian, Dennis, and Carl to move in a new direction. A number-one hit is a number-one hit. You've got to give the people what they want, right?

Brian was home now, writing new, challenging music and cutting tracks with the studio musicians Blaine had dubbed the Wrecking Crew.

Mike, Al, Dennis, Carl, and newcomer Bruce were out there, and they knew what the fans wanted. They wanted "Barbara Ann."

In 1996, when the album was reissued, Brian expressed enthusiasm for *Beach Boys Party!* He said, "We were cookin' . . . Our mood was up and we were on our way." As for "Barbara Ann," Brian said, "Our good friend Dean Torrence came by just in time to sing the lead with me . . . He and I were screeching those high notes. Dean always did have a handsome face." Huh?

Brian now includes "Barbara Ann" in his live set.

Chapter Eight
"I Know There's an Answer . . ."

Two of Brian's songs on *Pet Sounds* contain lyrics written by collaborators other than Tony Asher: "I Know There's an Answer," which was co-authored by Terry Sachen, soon to become the group's road manager; and "I'm Waiting for the Day," which was cowritten with Mike Love back in 1964.

"I Know There's an Answer" was originally entitled "Hang on to Your Ego," until Mike objected to its references to LSD. He edited the lyrics, replaced a few words. "[It] was too much of a doper song for me," Mike said. "So I came up with the alternative lyric, which reflected finding yourself." He added, "Brian didn't balk. Maybe he cared, maybe he didn't. He didn't say anything to me directly."

Most of the lyrics remain the same despite Love's contribution. Brian's literal admission of culpability—"How can I come on when I know I'm guilty"—becomes the more *Pet Sounds*-like "I know now but I had to find it by myself."

With lines like "they isolate their heads and stay in their safety zones" and "they come on like they're peaceful but inside they're so uptight," the lyrics seem an oddity when compared with the elegance and empathy of the rest of the recording.

"I'm Waiting for the Day," on the other hand, fits beautifully on the album. It's a tale from the naïve perspective that pervades *Pet Sounds*. Here, a man proclaims his willingness to come to the emotional rescue of a young girl who's been cast aside. He's given her strength, helped her carry on, but she's not ready to return his affection. So, he tells her he's "waiting for the day when you can love again."

A surprisingly biting bit of youthful machismo rears up in the outro: "You didn't think that I could sit around and let him work. You didn't think that I could sit around and let him take you . . . You didn't think that I could sit back and let you go."

On "I Know There's an Answer," Mike and Al sing the fourteen-bar verses and Brian the chorus. The group sound is all but missing from the track: just a little bit of low-key harmony under the second part of the verse and the chorus. Mimicking what Brian sang on his "Ego" demo, Mike adds a kind of a modest "doo-be-doo-be-doo" that fills an emerging silence that didn't need to be filled.

Brian takes the lead on "I'm Waiting for the Day" and goes at it with unassuming and restrained exuberance. The group members enter almost gratuitously, with little effect, and are hardly missed when they drop out. They return for the triumphant closing.

In both cases, the musical arrangement and performance are superior to the lyrics and vocals.

Aside from the chiming guitar, reprised once again here, and Pohlman's electric bass, the arrangement of "I Know There's an Answer" is dominated by timpani, tambourine, and bass harmonica—Brian gave Tommy Morgan plenty of room for his harmonica solo; "Wail on that baby," Brian told him—and the unusual instrumental mix that unfolds as the song progresses. A banjo enters well into the song—at the 1:45 mark, in fact—following flutes that had turned up a second or so earlier only to drop out and return for the fade. Three saxophones and a reedy organ control the midsection, giving the performance its somber underpinning.

"I'm Waiting for the Day" is another example of the dichotomy of *Pet Sounds*. Booming timpani and sharp, intentionally sloppy drums introduce the song, followed by flutes and an organ, suggesting something big and almost celebratory. Suddenly, there's silence save for an E major chord played four-beats-to-the-bar on the organ, Brian's boyish voice, and an oboe echoing the melody. At the bridge, flutes and a gently strummed guitar float under Brian's vocal, though not before what sounds like plucked piano strings make a very brief but alluring statement. Later, after the third pass at the bridge, a melancholy string section plays an interlude that quotes, though not directly, the chorus and bridge. A snappy figure on bass and the timpani accompany the energetic coda.

In interviews, Brian never gushed over either of the songs, and Bruce Johnston didn't much care for "I Know There's an Answer"—"Not one of my favorite songs," he said. "It just never, ever felt right to me." But Bruce loved "I'm Waiting for the Day."

"Great Brian . . . beautiful, dumb background parts," he told Leaf. "It's like having all the scruffy characters that are in *Oliver* show up at the Royal Albert Hall. They don't belong, but it fits."

Carl loved the dynamics of "I'm Waiting for the Day." He said, "The intro is very big, then it gets quite small with the vocal in the verse with just a little instrumentation and then, in the chorus, it gets very big again, with background harmonies against the lead. It is perhaps one of the most dynamic moments of the album."

* * *

In early 1966, while the Beach Boys were on a tour that included a stint in Japan, Brian was in Los Angeles mixing some of the instrumental tracks for *Pet Sounds*, arranging and recording other backing tracks he'd written. Brian had Asher come to his house almost every day to polish lyrics for songs, in some cases that he had yet to finish.

Though he would sometimes fritter away the morning while Asher waited, Brian was working at a frantic pace, managing the whole thing in his head, this album that would go beyond what the Beatles had done with *Rubber Soul*. It was just a matter of getting it out in a way that other people could understand and, in turn, play and sing. Then everybody could hear it. Brian didn't have an "overarching concept," Asher said. But he wanted to speak from his heart.

Brian played him a few completed tracks or sketched out the harmonic structure on piano. They'd talk for a while, sometimes for a long while, before getting down to work. They'd talk about nothing in particular or about what they knew about women and romance. They were developing a working relationship, getting along fine. But they were both aware that they had to produce something memorable.

"You realize as long as you're schmoozing with each other and talking about other stuff, nobody's under any pressure to create greatness," Asher said. "But when you sit down and begin to work—Brian would begin to play and I would grab a pencil and a pad of paper—there's a certain self-imposed pressure."

Brian had already told Marilyn he was going to make the greatest rock album ever. That's a pretty good example of self-imposed pressure.

There was a sense among the Beach Boys that Brian was going to create his best work. Carl thought he was growing at an incredible pace. Al saw a glimmer of his vast potential in "Let Him Run Wild." Dennis thought he could do anything. Bruce said, "While we were [in Japan], Brian sent us an acetate of 'Sloop John B' for our listening pleasure. Notice I didn't say approval." Not that Bruce minded. He loved what he heard. "It was the final mix where the track drops out and there are only voices. It was fabulous!"

The studio pros also knew Brian was onto something special. Many of them had watched him blossom, and they saw he was ready to make a significant leap in his craft. "Brian was amazing us with the different kinds of arranging and orchestrating, placing different sounds with different musical instruments," said Carol Kaye. "You knew he was becoming one of music's greatest talents." She called him "a one-man operation."

"He never had an outside arranger come in," she said. "He engineered, wrote, arranged and orchestrated the music, showed us on the piano how it went for feel. Plus he sang most, if not all, of the parts. He was totally in charge of everything."

Many of the musicians said he worked with a heightened sense of urgency during the *Pet Sounds* sessions. "During *Pet Sounds*, Brian would not be funny or laughing at things," said guitarist Jerry Cole. "He would walk in and he wouldn't smile. He had a definite plan in his head. Sometimes we'd work seven at night until seven in the morning." After the musicians left, Brian would stay in the studio. Cole said he'd stay there twenty hours at a time.

Though under pressure, Brian was unfailingly courteous. He had a deep regard for the musicians. They worked hard for him and they didn't treat his sessions like just another gig. They were the best in LA and they wanted to play his music. Maybe it wouldn't have mattered if he was a good guy or not—most of them had done excellent work for Phil Spector, after all—but they appreciated Brian, and knew he appreciated them.

"His generosity was overwhelming," Cole said. "If we were going late, he would have food catered for all the guys. The only guy who did that constantly was Frank Sinatra."

When the group returned from Japan, Brian called them in to learn their vocal parts for the bulk of *Pet Sounds*. "We didn't have a clue what was going on until we got there," said Al Jardine. "The way a vocal session would work is that Brian would invite you into the booth to hear the track, then we would work on the parts. We would just go to the piano and start working from there. Get a sense of where the parts were, share ideas, throw parts back and forth."

Sometimes, Carl and Dennis would get a preview at Brian's house. Al wasn't invited, he said, because he wouldn't smoke pot with them.

Carl called the vocal sessions "fun and easy," saying his training from Brian when they were kids permitted him to catch on quick. "The vocal parts on *Pet Sounds* were fascinating, so beautiful and maybe mixed more subtly than on some of our earlier records," he said. "The one song that sticks out in my mind the most is 'Wouldn't It Be Nice.' Brilliant parts. It was hard to sing without getting tears in your eyes."

Brian was developing his spiritual streak, a deeper interest in a supreme being. He'd always considered his music divinely inspired, but he was trying to get his mind and soul to a higher plane.

The 1964 incident on the airplane wasn't the only time he snapped but, according to Timothy White, shortly thereafter he'd begun to pray. It soothed his mind. During the *Pet Sounds* session, Brian held little prayer meetings. Carl joined him. "Brian would actually write down prayers on paper," Carl recalled. "We'd pray for guidance, to make the most healing sounds."

"You see," he said, "by that time recording had become a church to us. We were really in awe of the fact that you could record something, and it would have a healing effect and soothe the soul."

Looking back, Brian said, "God was with us the whole time we were doing this record. God was right there with me . . . I could feel that feeling in my head. In my brain."

* * *

Brian always had a keen sense of what the marketplace wanted in a pop song by the Beach Boys. Surfing, the beach, cars, girls; an idealized image of California where fit young men surfed, drove fast cars, and hung out with Hawaii island dolls in French bikinis by a palm tree in the sand.

But now he was going to record a pop song with the word "God" in the title . . .

Ramones

by Nicholas Rombes

Ramones in Their Time

What distinguishes rock-crit punk writing from the mid-1970s from most subsequent rock criticism is that a good deal of it was written by the musicians themselves, including Patti Smith, Richard Hell, Andy (Adny) Shernoff, Peter Laughner, and others. If there is any such thing as a punk canon that includes not only bands but also other writers and artists, then its initial formulation can be traced to the underground press and fanzines of the era, where the contours of the punk sensibility were articulated not only by professional rock critics, but by the musicians themselves. In a 1976 essay for *Trouser Press*, for instance, Dictators' guitarist Scott "Top Ten" Kempner paid homage to critic Richard Meltzer, providing a sort of bibliographic account of his writings:

> A few years later, a second book appeared, entitled *Gulcher* [1972] (gulcher . . . gulture . . . culture, get it?). Like the first book, one can start at any point and read, in any direction. *Gulcher* is subtitled, *Post-Rock Cultural Pluralism in America (1649–1980)* and is the official document of the under-the-counter culture. Recognizing that rock itself is no longer the true focal point of the culture, Meltzer covers everything from wrestling and booze to television and bottlecaps.

Like Kempner and so many others, Richard Hell not only wrote about punk, but did so in such a way that performed punk's anarchy on the page. In a 1976 article about the Ramones in *Hit Parader*, Hell wrote that the "music the Ramones create from these feelings [of frustration] is incredibly exciting. It gives you the same sort of feeling you might derive from savagely kicking in your smoothly running tv set and then finding real thousand dollar bills inside." If Hermann Goering popularized the line "whenever I hear the word culture, I reach for my pistol," then punk popularized the gesture of reaching for a guitar or a pen in the face of culture, not to destroy it, but to transform it.

And yet, many of the rock-crit writers did help to make safe a sort of narcissistic confessionalism that marks much of the criticism of our era. The first-person reportage of writers like Bangs and Marcus and Meltzer, in the Jack Keruoac tradition, opened the door in rock criticism for the wholesale elevation of the personal to the public, a diary-entry journalism, which is great if you happen to be a good writer, but nothing short of horrible if you don't. When everything is permitted, it's hard not to be seduced by your own reflection in the mirror, and for these writers the mirror that punk held up was hard to look away from. Today, almost all rock criticism takes the form of personal anecdote and memoir; as in the movie *High Fidelity*, we want to see the story *and* the story about the story. We want writers to show their faces, to confess a secret, to show us that they are no better than us. Writers like Meltzer and Bangs and Tosches were blogging before there were blogs, and made it safe to talk about rock by talking about yourself.

Although it helped to create the confessionalist critic, punk itself was resistant to such openness. If anything, punk depersonalized itself, rejecting the needy, confessional introspection of progressive rock. The Ramones were perhaps the purest and most brilliant of depersonalized punk bands, appearing in an unchanging uniform, sharing the same last name, and making music that re-articulated over and over again a single idea. Even their "I Wanna" and "I Don't Wanna" first-person songs were less about people than characters, concepts, ideas, ways of behaving. In fact, it is this unchanging purity that accounts, more than anything else, for the failure of the Ramones to fully enter the mainstream of American popular music. For rock is built on the myth of change, a fact that serves record companies well, as they promote the evolution of bands to keep pace with the changing tastes of the marketplace. Early Beatles, late Beatles. Early Stones, late Stones. Early R.E.M, late R.E.M. Early Elvis, late Elvis, Vegas Elvis.

But punk stood against evolution and technical growth because this implied a growing expertise and mastery of music that ran counter to punk's studied amateurism, and because it suggested a future that, especially in punk's British strain, should not exist. Besides, why change a good thing? If you've found your music, your sound, your stance, why push it into something else? This is why for so many punk and new wave bands, the marker of selling out was not signing to a major label, but rather adapting your sound to suit market tastes. So many punk bands—ranging from the Sex Pistols to the Dead Boys—self-destructed rather than buy into the myth of evolution, of change, of progress. The Ramones' uniformity can be seen on a recording of a remarkable early television studio perform-ance, among the first visual recordings of the band, preceding Amos Poe's 1976 documentary on CBGB, *Blank Generation*, and the 1977 documentary *Punking Out*. There is no audience, just the band in a white television stu-dio with a home-made "Ramones" banner draped on the wall behind them. Without any ceremony they break into "Loudmouth" and continue for twenty minutes, pausing only long enough midway through for John-ny and Dee Dee to take off their leather jackets.

Documenting the influence of the Ramones, and punk in general, on post-1970s music is perilous. In retrospect, the Ramones' sound—fast, loud, simple—served as a blueprint for scores of bands and movements in the 1980s, 90s, and today. As much as the Ramones looked backward for inspiration—to early Beatles, surf rock, Iggy Pop—at the time they offered an alienated future rock, concocting a sound that, while echoing the past, was really disconnected from tradition. The very fact that we can look back to the Ramones with nostalgia attests to their triumph in mass culture: "Hey, ho, let's go" is played as a rallying cry not only during New York Yankees games, but in many other baseball parks across the country, right along with "classic" rock snippets from bands ranging from Queen to Van Halen.

This is where distinctions between 1970s-era punk and its incarnations in the 1980s and 1990s become clear, as we'll see later on. Even a slight familiarity with bands such as Black Flag or the Minutemen, or with punk magazines like *Punk Planet*, reveals a level of progressive politics and seri-ousness that distinguishes it from its 1970s roots. If there was a political dimension to the Ramones, the Dead Boys, the Sex Pistols, the Adverts, and other bands, it was ambiguous and contradictory, a mix of anarchist sentiments, fascist symbols (such as the Swastika), and anti-liberal human-ist sentiments. Indeed, early issues of *Punk* are a testament to the self-dep-recating humor that informed Ramones-era punk, and if anything punks—especially in the United States—mocked the political seriousness and message music of the hippies.

Looked at from one angle, punk provided the corrective to what, by the 1970s, had become the absorption of uncritical liberalism into mass cultural forms. If Johnny Ramone was punk's most famous conservative (his line at the Rock and Roll Hall of Fame induction ceremony—"God bless President Bush, and God bless America"—was widely reported in his obituaries in September 2004), he was certainly not its only one. If the free and easy sixties were, on one level, a reaction to the uptight fifties, then punk was a return to order premised on disorder, rendered all the more contradictory when considered in light of the excesses of the scene as depicted in books like *Please Kill Me*. In this context, it's not surprising that one of the outgrowths of punk was the straight edge scene in the early 1980s, where sobriety itself became a form of rebellion in the context of punk excess.

Sure the Ramones were associated with New York City, but were they city kids? It seems a sort of dumb question, but it had resonance in 1975 and 1976 and went to the heart of perceptions about punk's authenticity. The Ramones had all met in Forest Hills, New York, described by Monte Melnick as "a middle-class, mostly Jewish suburb in the borough of Queens." Part of the energy of the CBGB scene—and the underground scene in general—was this ambiguity about the social class and status of its performers. Were the Ramones suburban kids? What about the preppy-looking Talking Heads? While Clinton Heylin might be right that "the Ramones . . . were no teenage delinquents," you wouldn't know that from reading Dee Dee's book *Lobotomy* or stories about them in *Please Kill Me*. In an early issue of *New York Rocker*, Suzanne Schwedoch devoted an entire column to musing on the relationship between suburban kids and the emerging underground New York City scene. "This report from the lowest echelons of rock by an un-authority on the local scene is a desperate plea for NY rockers to try their stuff out in suburbia where aimlessness just may be converted into new fans and generate some sparx of enthusiasm from the hoards of boreds who listen to dying d.j.s on the FM dials."

David Thomas, who along with Peter Laughner founded Cleveland's Rocket from the Tombs, puts the allure poetically:

> We were into this Urban Pioneer thing, which was a bunch of kids born in the suburbs to middle-class families, moving back into the city, because they thought the city should live. The city I loved everybody else hated: it was totally deserted, people fled when the sun went down. It was run down, but we thought it was beautiful at the time of youth when you're prone to romanticism.
>
> I wondered at what point a civilization hits its peak and then begins to decline. All those deserted cities, the jungle overgrows them: at what point does the city die? At what point do the people who live there no longer understand the vision of the builders?

As noted earlier, the "deserted city," whether by planners' design, economic blight, or racial tension, gives rise in this case to inspiration. An inspiration not to those left in it, but to those raised outside it: suburban kids who saw it as a beautiful, romantic thing.

Crisis and disintegration often lead to rejuvenated cultural forms, and this is certainly true of early and mid-1970s popular culture. The punk movement—and the Ramones in particular—drew upon and made their own an eccentric mix of pop culture references ranging from *Mad* magazine to Roger Corman. Indeed, *Punk* magazine editor John Holstrom had studied with Harvey Kurtzman, founder of *Mad*. Legs McNeil, who was also involved in the publication and who in fact gave it its name, became the resident punk: "So it was decided I would be a living cartoon character, like Alfred E. Neuman was to *Mad* magazine."

Unlike the serious prog-rock and concept albums of the era that distanced themselves from the mundane triviality of popular culture, *Ramones* is laced with references to movies, news events, history, and the ordinary happenings of everyday life. As Donna Gaines has noted, "the Ramones' songwriting reflects their obsession with popular culture and Americana. Johnny and Dee Dee were war-movie fiends, and the whole band loved television, surf culture, comic books, and cartoons." The filmic world evoked on Ramones is one of B-movies, cult movies, and horror films. *The Texas Chainsaw Massacre* was released in 1974, the year many of the album's songs were written. Film scholar Robin Wood has written that "central to the film—and centered on its monstrous family—is the sense of grotesque comedy, which in no way diminishes but rather intensifies its nightmare horror. . . . The film's sense of fundamental horror is closely allied to a sense of the fundamentally absurd." This sense of comic-horror infuses the album's fifth track, "Chainsaw," a sort of homage to the film. This was also the era of the vigilante film, most forcefully expressed in *Straw Dogs* (1971) and *Death Wish* (1974), in which Charles Bronson plays a tolerant New York City architect who turns to vigilantism after his wife is murdered. Mixed with the album's humor is a deeper menace and sense of pervasive violence running through songs like "Beat on the Brat" and "Loudmouth" ("I'm gonna beat you up") that is reminiscent of films like *Death Wish* and that in fact constitutes a wholesale rejection of the feel good, peace-love-and-understanding ethos that informed the rhetoric of the counterculture. For if in 1969 audiences were expected to see the violence of *Easy Rider* as tragedy visited upon well-meaning (if not innocent) drifters, by 1974 films like *Death Wish* pretty much had audiences rooting for those committing the violence.

Like the emerging punk scene itself, films in the mid-1970s were a heady mix of high and low, art and trash, domestic and foreign. Ads from an August 1975 issue of the *Village Voice* (during a time when the Ramones were playing at CBGB) offer a glimpse of the variety of films playing in New York City. At the Bleeker Street Cinema, you could see Bergman's *The Seventh Seal* and *Wild Strawberries*, Fellini's *Roma*, Hitchcock's *The 39 Steps*, and Satyajit Ray's *Two Daughters*. *The Eiger Sanction* was playing (for only $1.00) at St. Mark's Cinema, while a theater on Broadway at 49th showed *The Texas Chainsaw Massacre*. The Elgin, meanwhile, offered Mick Jagger in *Performance*, Jonathan Demme's *Caged Heat*, as well as *Don't Look Now*, *El Topo*, and *The Harder They Come*. Or you could catch Russ Meyer's *Super-Vixens*, rated X (in the mid-1970s, X-rated movies were advertised alongside "family" movies in both underground and mainstream newspapers in New York City, including the *New York Times*). The blurb for *SuperVixens* might just as well have come out of the punk imagination:

> an all out assault on today's sexual mores, and more, a frontal attack against women's lib . . . blasting through the male "machismo" syndrome, kicking the hell out of convention, hang-ups, convictions, obsessions! The whole bag . . . cops, robbers, sexually aggressive females, rednecks, sick men-of-war, unfaithful wives, impotence, athletic prowess, the 32-second satisfaction, cuckolding, breast fixation vs. hat jobs, egotism and other fun 'n games, racing cars, selfabuse . . . and even death and reincarnation!

And of course PG-rated *Jaws* ("8th Record Week!") was playing just about everywhere, with its own image of a huge shark about to munch a practically nude female swimmer.

The most punk moment in any movie from that era has nothing at all to do with punk rock or punk style. About midway through Martin Scorsese's *Taxi Driver*—which opened in 1976, just months before *Ramones* was released, and which was shot in the summer of 1975—Travis Bickle (Robert DeNiro) sits in his New York apartment watching "American Bandstand" on his crappy TV. Scorsese cuts between kids slow dancing to Jackson Browne's "Late for the Sky" and Travis watching in a kind of resigned numbness ("sitting here with nuthin' to do") as if the "normal" world being depicted on TV were utterly and forever out of reach for him. He has a gun in his hand, which he occasionally aims at the screen. Later, in a startling shot, we see a transformed Travis standing outside at the edge of a crowd listening to a hackneyed speech by a politician. Travis has changed: he is sporting a Mohawk (punk?) haircut that signals his radical rejection of the "normal" world depicted on "American Bandstand." While the film escalates into increasing and frenzied violence at this point, I think it is the few quiet moments where we see Travis watching the TV with a sort of deep and menacing sadness that best captures the spirit of loneliness that punk emerges from and addresses.

In *Midnight Movies*, J. Hoberman wrote that seen "strictly as a youth movement, punk was a kind of perverse, high-speed replay of the counterculture—complete with its own music, press, entrepreneurs, fellow travelers (including more than a few ex-hippies), and, ultimately, movies." Punk films from this era include John Waters's *Pink Flamingos* (1973) and *Female Trouble* (1975), Derek Jarman's *Jubilee* (1977), and Amos Poe's *Blank Generation* (1976) and *The Foreigner* (1977). However, while these and other films are no doubt central to the articulation of a punk sensibility, it is another film, David Lynch's *Eraserhead* (1977), which, like *Taxi Driver*, captures the sense of outsiderness that informs punk. In *Eraserhead*, Henry

(Jack Nance) is the ultimate outsider, existing in a world so degraded that it's simply beautiful. He is practically inarticulate, defining himself though his actions, not his words. And that electroshock hair is as alarming as anything worn by Richard Hell or Sid Vicious. Above all, *Eraserhead* offers the illusion of a complete and separate world; like punk, its influences can (and have been) traced and demystified in dry studies of influence, and yet there is something about *Eraserhead*, and about punk, that manages to escape the most determined efforts to explain away its mystery.

And although it is beyond the scope of this book, it is also worth noting that from the very beginning, do-it-yourself "punk" cinema was an important part of the emerging punk music scene. Filmmakers like Amos Poe, who was also a writer for the *New York Rocker*, helped define the punk aesthetic in film and often wrote for or were featured in the music newspapers and fanzines that emerged in New York City in the mid-1970s. In a 1976 profile on Poe in *New York Rocker*, Matthew Fleury, in his discussion of Poe's films *Night Lunch* (1975) and *Blank Generation* (1976), called Poe's work "presence filmmaking" and noted that Poe considered the Zapruder film of the Kennedy assassination "the greatest single footage ever shot" because it captured, unintentionally, history.

Earlier I wrote that *Ramones* was either the last great modern record or the first great postmodern one. The more you listen to it, the more you realize: of course it's the first great postmodern one, and that's largely because it tunes in on the sound and the hum of our era. It gives shape and form to the low, almost imperceptible "oceanic sound" that Don DeLillo writes about in his novel *White Noise* (1985). The message the album conveys is, finally, noise. If the album can be said to be "about" anything, then it is about noise. That's why standard rock-crit discussions of the lyrics or the personalities of the band members are ultimately dead ends. Of course it would seem that all rock albums are about noise, but many are not, not in the least because they regard noise as a given. But, like a Jean-Luc Godard film from the 1960s, *Ramones* incessantly interrogates the formulation of its own sound. When Simon Frith wrote that "punk queried the 'naturalness' of musical language," I think this is what he was getting at: punk is as much a theory of music as it is music.

It has become commonplace to suggest that punk music was authentic and pure and somehow directly opposed to the tainted sellout status that widespread acceptance brings. In his excellent book *Subculture*, Dick Hebdige, writing about punk, notes, "as soon as the original innovations which signify 'subculture' are translated into commodities and made generally available, they become 'frozen.' Once removed from their private contexts by the small entrepreneurs and big fashion interests who produce them on a mass scale, they become codified, made comprehensible, rendered at once public property and profitable merchandise." More recently,

Stacy Thompson has suggested that one of punk's fundamental desires is "the desire to resist the commercial realm, and especially commercial music." Yet what does it really mean to claim this about punk, especially in its mid-1970s incarnation? The Ramones were not rebelling against popular music, but rather against how popular music had come to be defined and experienced. If today we tend to think in terms of selling out versus not selling out, we need to be careful not to project these concerns backward to the 1970s. For there was less worry about "selling out" to the mainstream than there was desire to replace mainstream music with something better, something more alive, something unexpected. The Ramones, in particular, desired a hit; after all, they believed in and were passionate about their music, and they wanted to share it with others beyond the cramped space of CBGB. As Seymour Stein, the cofounder of Sire records who signed the Ramones to Sire in 1975, has said, "their melodies were very catchy and stayed with me, dancing around in my head, and it was absolutely clear that for better or worse, underneath it all was a pop-band mentality." Others, such as Craig Leon, who produced *Ramones*, share this view: "Quite honestly, we thought we were creating a hit pop record. The Bay City Rollers, Herman's Hermits, and the Beatles were our competition in our minds. But do bear in mind we were laughing all the way through it."

Casting the Ramones and other bands as anti-corporate and antimainstream means that you have to ignore the tremendous amount of care and energy that went into promoting themselves. The Ramones, in particular, were very much aware of the press and publicity they were generating, and were active participants in shaping their image and generating further press interest, as this 1977 interview from the *New York Rocker* suggests:

> *What was the turning point?*
> **Dee Dee**: That festival [the 1975 summer Rock Festival at CBGB].
> **Tommy**: The turning point was . . . when Lisa Robinson came down . . . actually we got some nice writeups from some people and we sent them out to the people in the trades, with a little picture of us.
> **Johnny**: I think we had a list of 100 people and we hit everybody.
> *Did you lick the envelopes yourselves?*
> **Tommy**: Yeah, addressed them and everything.

This form of do-it-yourself publicity, while much different in scale than the massive promotional engines that sustained supergroups like Led Zeppelin and the Eagles, was nonetheless driven by a desire to reach a broad audience. Rather than look at their success as something to be ashamed of, or as some sort of sellout, the Ramones remained keenly aware that, as one of the earliest punk bands to sign to a label, they were in many ways responsible for the potential success and viability of the emerging punk scene. "We were the first CBGB-punk-type group to get signed," Tommy noted, "and that was important because I think we opened up the doors."

While punk in the 80s and 90s very much cast itself in opposition to mainstream, corporate interests, and while recent writing on punk (often by academics) casts punk as a sort of Marxist music for the people and by the people, it's instructive to remember that in its early days, many punk bands desired and actively courted mainstream success.

And yet, despite the melodic, pop-oriented sensibility that character-ized early punk and the Ramones' first album in particular, there is some-thing—other than the obviously raw sound—that assured punk's margin-ality.

* * *

Please, dear reader, don't cast down this book when I remind you of the ironic dimension to the Ramones. Irony is a notoriously slippery word, often used as shorthand for insincerity, or intellectual aloofness, or post-modern cynicism. Rest assured, I use it in none of these senses. Instead, I'm using irony in a broader sense to suggest that one of the defining fea-tures of punk was its awareness of itself as punk. This does not mean it was insincere, any more than I would suggest you were insincere for dress-ing a little nicer than usual to meet someone you liked. Now, the Ramones have been called ironic before, but often in a dismissive way, as when Greil Marcus writes that "much has been made of punk's antecedents in . . . the arty, ironic New York scene that emerged in 1974—especially as exempli-fied by the Ramones. 'Beat on the brat / with a baseball bat'—what could be more punk than that?"

I think Marcus gives the band too much credit, and not enough. Cer-tainly the Ramones did emerge from the New York scene that included Andy Warhol, Lou Reed, Patti Smith, and others whose work could be characterized as highly self-conscious. As Craig Leon notes, "the Ramones were much more part of the NY underground 'art' scene of The Velvets and Warhol & Co. They had much more in common with bands like Tele-vision and Patti Smith's group than the Sex Pistols and other so-called punk bands." And yet the immediacy and rawness in their performance and recorded music discredits the claim that they were more self-con-sciously artistic. Watching an early video of the band tearing, with deter-mined fury, through a twenty-minute set in a television studio with no audience, it's hard to see the irony anywhere. And yet . . . can punk—and its glam-rock predecessors—be completely separated from the sort of camp sensibility that Susan Sontag described as "camp"? "Camp is the consistently aesthetic experience of the world. It incarnates a victory of 'style' over 'content,' 'aesthetics' over 'morality,' of irony over tragedy." Camp combats "the threat of boredom. The relation between boredom and Camp taste cannot be overestimated. Camp taste is by its nature possible only in affluent societies, in societies or circles capable of experiencing the psychopathology of affluence." In a discussion with Sontag in 1978, Richard Hell told her, "the generation I belong to has more in common among its members than any other generation that ever existed because of television and public school systems." An album like *Ramones* is both an acknowledgment and a fierce rejection of this sentiment: saturated in pop culture, the album nonetheless rejects again and again easy connections to its influences and sources, which remain locked tightly in its self-contained songs.

Questions about whether or not punk was ironic are not merely academic questions put to punk thirty years later, but in fact constituted the tension and contradictions typical of the scene. Early accounts of the Ramones and other underground or punk bands raised the same questions. A 1976 issue of *New York Rocker* noted that the "Ramones hit hard, but when all the smoke and fury have subsided, one may recognize that despite the overwhelming amplification, the group is operating through the most basic devices of irony and understatement." In that same issue, in the essay "The Clothes Nose: Sniffing Out NY Rock Dress Sense," Robert Swift says this of the Ramones: "Pretty calculated, but they'll probably say they have no money. Rounded haircuts—Beatles/Standells/kid's cereal commercials, and a singer with a kink in neck. Clothes are worn out levis, tee shirts, scuffed shoes or sneakers, sneers, and shades. A sort of Momma's boy punk. All in all done to perfection, and ultimately it looks unforced." If not ironic, this hyper-awareness of style, as both legitimate and as camp, is one of the major differences between punk and progressive rock, for whom style was, even at its most theatrically excessive, unreflective. In this sense, punk's indebtedness to glam rock is crucial, for while the Ramones are remembered as being almost antistyle in their unchanging uniform, they were heavily influenced by glam rock. According to Dee Dee Ramone:

> Joey had a band called Sniper [prior to the Ramones]. He was trying to break into the New York "glam" circuit that was happening around then. . . . The glitter took a lot of upkeep and the gear was expensive. We would get custom-made snakeskin boots sent from England via Granny Takes a Trip in New York. Johnny Thunders and Tommy Ramone both went to London to get the right stuff to be the top flashmen about town. Johnny Ramone had an exact replica of the James Williamson outfit with the leopard collar that James wore in the Stooges' *Raw Power* stage. John also had silver lame pants from Granny Takes a Trip that he wore for the first few Ramones gigs.

If the Ramones rejected the continual reinvention of style in their own formulation of style (just as their music rejected updating and modification), then this was not out of an ignorance or rejection of style, but rather out of an understanding that minimalism (no makeup, no costume changes, no glitter, etc.) could quite possibly form the basis of a new style. The album does make you wonder, though, how seriously you should be taking this. The punk generation grew up not only with TV, but with cable, and with all the repetition ("reruns"), irony, and camp that the medium engendered. As Robert Ray has noted, the "new self-consciousness also flourished on television, where 'Rowan and Martin's Laugh-In' (1968–73), 'The Carol Burnett Show' (1967–1978), and NBC's 'Saturday Night Live' (1975-) all featured irreverent media parodies, particularly of movies and TV news. Other regular series could not be taken straight: 'All in the Family' (1971–79), 'The Rockford Files' (1974–1979), 'Happy Days' (1974–1984), 'Mary Hartman, Mary Hartman' (1976), and 'Soap' (1977–1981) all traded on obviously ironic uses of standard television formulas." The beautifully complicating thing here is not that *Ramones* offered itself as an ironic rock album, but that it might be received that way by an audience raised in a TV culture that always questioned the codes of sincerity. Or, looked at another way, punk irony was gradually evolving into the new norm, replacing the macho sincerity and you-better-take-this-concept-album-seriously of progressive rock, which would help explain punk's delayed acceptance into the mainstream and its late-blossoming stature: it came at the very beginning of a decades-long process of incorporating irony into the mainstream, in which a show like "Late Night with David Letterman" was key. In 1976, *Ramones* sounded both very wrong and very right. Today it just sounds very right, not because the music on the album has changed but because the conditions into which that music enters have. Listeners coming to *Ramones* for the first time today are conditioned to accept it because they have heard it before—perhaps without knowing it—in the very music that the Ramones helped to create. In this sense, the Ramones' career is about creating the conditions under which their music would be retrospectively accepted. As Jon Savage has suggested in his study of British punk: "In the mid-1960s, pop had been modernistic: reveling in an everlasting present, without reflection or theory. In the late 1960s, pop became 'progressive,' an idea implying some forward, unitary motion. Early seventies stars like David Bowie and Roxy Music broke up this linear motion with a plethora of references taken from high art, literature and Hollywood kitsch. As the new generation, the Sex Pistols were a finely tuned mixture of the authentic and the constructed."

Besides, isn't all performance, whether writing, acting, singing, dancing, or whatever, self-conscious by its very nature? Perhaps, but punk was predicated on a deliberate assault on the elaborate, overproduced, self-serious music of the era, and it is this reactionary nature that imbued punk with a complicated ironic stance. In short, unlike the music of its day, which sought to extend a tradition (i.e., Led Zeppelin or Eric Clapton "extending" the blues), punk sought to reject tradition. For even though it's true the music of the Ramones points back to an earlier time, as Craig Leon and others have noted, this earlier music is referenced not so much for its sound or style, but rather for its energy. While it's pretty easy to hear the blues in Zeppelin's "Dazed and Confused," it's not so easy to hear Herman's Hermits in "Loudmouth." It's harder to think of another rock album that, upon is initial appearance, sounded so little like anything that had come before it.

Is it surprising that a movement like punk—with its rejection of the musical indulgence and decadence of progressive rock—would embrace the iconography of fascism, which also rejected "decadence"? I suppose now is as good a time as any to say that I think people who have written about punk have by and large tended to go to great lengths to dismiss, underplay, minimize, and even ignore the fascist iconography in the punk scene. Dick Hebdige has argued that the use of the swastika, for instance, cannot be read as a political sign, and that, indeed, most punks "were not generally sympathetic to the parties of the extreme right." He goes on to say, "the swastika was worn because it was guaranteed to shock." Stacy Thompson, meanwhile, argues Nazi codes, as used by punks, drew attention to unequal economic relations under the capitalist system.

Mary Harron comes closest to best explaining the use of fascist imagery in punk and by the Ramones in particular. "Joey Ramone was a nice guy, he was no savage right-winger," she has said. "The Ramones were problematic. It was hard to work out what their politics were. It had this difficult edge, but the most important thing was needling the older generation." If liberal humanist rock critics and scholars today are wary of dwelling on the conservative, sometimes reactionary political dimensions of punk (Johnny Ramone was a longtime conservative), while at the same time devoting page after page to delineating the socially engaged political subtleties of Bob Dylan or Bruce Springsteen or Ani DeFranco, then it's at the risk of minimizing one of the many complexities of punk. Joe Harrington has suggested that these flirtations with fascist sentiments and iconography were the result of the "politics of boredom," noting that "we'd reached the stage where young people who could afford the luxury of playing Rock 'n' Roll strictly for the amusement of it had grown so blasé that they literally wanted to see the world disintegrate for their own amusement. Far from being anti-war like the hippies, the new kids welcomed carnage of any kind as a kind of liberation from their dull shopping mall surroundings."

Dear reader, please permit me one anecdote here. The first Ramones song I remember hearing was "The KKK Took My Baby Away," from 1981's *Pleasant Dreams*. I had found the album in my girlfriend's record collection (was she my girlfriend or was I just hanging around with her one summer?) and I thought it was a funny and scary song at the same time, and of all the post-1977 Ramones music, that's the song that still reminds me the most of their earlier records. I borrowed the album, played it a lot, and wondered: How could they get away with using the KKK like that in a song? Why wasn't there a controversy or something? It wasn't that the lyrics of the song were racist; in fact, the narrator was obviously dating an African American girl, and I assumed he was white, and therefore not racist. But it wasn't that, it was those letters: KKK. Not that I was Mr. Sensitive, or anything, but those letters—like the symbol of the swastika— they just weren't things you casually used in pop songs.

The sense of disequilibrium and unease that's generated by moments like this is perhaps something that we ought to preserve, rather than justify or explain away, which is why arguments that punk (or the Ramones) used Nazi imagery or references for mere shock value, or to draw attention to their outsider status, seem lame. On their first album, the Nazi references (and other references to violence) might be ironic, or they might not be. Their power resides in precisely this ambiguity. In this regard, the Ramones were part of a larger movement in the United States that was producing what film critic Robin Wood refers to as "incoherent texts." Wood doesn't use the word incoherent to indicate a disparagement, but rather to refer to movies, primarily from the 1970s, that reflect the social, moral, and political instability of the era. As Woods says: "I am concerned with films that don't wish to be . . . incoherent but are so nonetheless, works in which the drive toward the ordering of experience has been visibly defeated." For Wood, films like *Taxi Driver* and *Looking for Mr. Goodbar* cannot provide easy endings or clear-cut heroes and antiheroes, not because they are bad or poorly made films, but rather because they are products and commentators on the crisis of confidence that characterized mid-1970s America. The unresolved contradictions that make the Ramones' first album so dizzying—Are the songs sincere or ironic? Are the fascist references political or naïve expressions of defiance? If the Ramones hate hippies, why do they look like hippies with their long hair?—speak to a moment in American history when such ambiguity was part of the larger fabric of cultural life.

I Ain't Marching Anymore

by Dan Connelly

Phil Ochs Taught Me How to Love Again

The Christers, radicals, reactionaries, teetotalers, janissaries, communists, and the straight-edgers and I have all found a high in common. We are juiced on indignation. We have an agenda, a movement, a plan (maybe just an angle) for a major paradigm shift. We have wet dreams about marches and protests and strikes and living through Sergei Eisenstein's *October* but we do nothing. We read pamphlets and books and listen to folk music and punk rock and we fantasize and do nothing. We become "political" to get our indignation fix. Our pretensions of "political consciousness" amount to so much masturbation.

That being said, Phil Ochs is my favorite way to masturbate. When I was in high school, I was angry (obviously). I would wear flannel at inappropriate times of year and lather and soak my oversized *Army of Darkness* T-shirt until a fold of sweat formed where my tits sagged and the curve of my gelatinous paunch began. I was a soft little communist piglet. For a period of time, I kept a slim Noam Chomsky book or a pamphlet of the Communist Manifesto in the front pocket of one of my flannel shirts. During student assemblies I would heft the book several inches in front of my spectacles and silently read as obnoxiously as I could. Take that, adolescent social hierarchy. Take that, whorish displays of Orchesis. Take that, student body president. Take that, Z-list ex-comedian motivational speaker. Take *that*, ex-prom queen horrifically disabled by drunk driving accident.

There was something large, brutal and simple in my affectations of political consciousness and meaningless, mean-spirited displays of defiance. I did not want to listen to a technically proficient musician. I wanted someone who agreed with me violently and overtly, who preferred unflinching directness to a message blunted by metaphor or abstract language. I wanted to listen to the songs of a journalist.

Phil Ochs had the qualities I desired. He had a unique directness in his music, a coherent political immediacy and relevancy. Ochs combined his vocal conscience with sometimes anthemic, sometimes theatrically maudlin music. The album *I Ain't Marching Any More* contains all the fiercely subversive hymns that I loved immediately, like "Draft Dodger Rag," "That's What I Want to Hear," "Links on the Chain," and a few of the gentler songs that I learned to tolerate. I just wanted to listen to something that I could pump my fist to, something that allowed me vicariously to experience active radicalism. I could get that feeling without having to pontificate endlessly about social problems I had never personally experienced in white suburbia.

I did not have to be a philosophy major in waiting to feel self-important.

The feeling of political involvement that Ochs' music generates has nothing to do with a 60s folk nostalgia kick. I got the same feeling from certain punk rock songs. The Clash, Reagan Youth, Stiff Little Fingers, and Dillinger Four had a similar influence on me. Punk rock, however, generally tried to squeeze its political messages through the tepid filter of personal experience. Every time I hear someone say "the personal is political" I want to slap their emo-glasses off their pimply faces. The people who say that are the people who try to make the political personal. They want to invoke private drama in the face of public events. Or they go the nose-in-the-air, Gang of Four, art-punk route and make fun of the clueless bourgeois.

Contemporary leftist political music, regardless of genre, seizes onto abstractions and screams until they sound fiery—almost as though it is shameful to protest something openly. Phil Ochs sang about the news of the day and did not mince words about his radicalism. He felt free to express his political beliefs in specific terms and impress his listeners with a particular vision. He did not blanch at creating music that was dependent on a knowledge of contemporary affairs, a knowledge base that would grow more and more arcane as time passed. In that way, Ochs overshadowed many of his peers and predecessors. He produced work with more scope and acid than Pete Seeger and Woody Guthrie and he did not "move on" from his folk roots to mass market apolitical, stoner music like Bob Dylan. Phil Ochs is overlooked because of his unrelenting critiques of the times. He is overlooked because he chose to sing about how the USS *Thresher* deserved to be destroyed. About how Billie Sol betrayed Texas. About the redemption of Paul Crump. About race rioting and about how Mississippi has "torn out of the heart of" America with its backwardness and villainy.

Ochs sang about dodging the draft, rallying working people into a union, combating racism and mourning the martyrs of the civil rights movement, and the complacency of the mainstream liberal movement.